ARCHITECTURAL DETAILING
FOR
COMMERCIAL CONSTRUCTION

ARCHITECTURAL DETAILING
FOR
COMMERCIAL CONSTRUCTION

Gene Farmer

McGRAW-HILL, INC.

New York St. Louis San Francisco Auckland Bogotá
Caracas Hamburg Lisbon London Madrid
Mexico Milan Montreal New Delhi Paris
San Juan São Paulo Singapore
Sydney Tokyo Toronto

Library of Congress Cataloging-in-Publication Data

Farmer, Gene (Eugene Davis)
  Architectural detailing for commercial construction / Gene Davis.

       p.   cm.
  1. Architectural drawing—Detailing.   2. Commercial buildings—
Designs and plans.   I. Title.
NA2718.F37   1991   725′.21′028—dc20   91-14147
ISBN 0-07-019983-3   CIP

1 2 3 4 5 6 7 8 9 0   DOC/DOC   9 7 6 5 4 3 2 1

ISBN 0-07-019983-3

*The sponsoring editor for this book was Joel E. Stein, the editing supervisor
was Caroline Levine, the designer was Sue Maksuta, and the production
supervisor was Pamela A. Pelton. It was set in Helvetica by Techna Type,
Inc.*

Printed and bound by R. R. Donnelley & Sons Company.

This book is dedicated to my wife Audrey, my son Christopher, and my daughter Alexis, whose support and encouragement made it a reality.

I also want to thank Hugo Araque, who worked on the development of some of the detail drawings, and give a special thanks to my friend Dale Jennings for his untiring efforts. His dedication and countless hours of work were instrumental in making this book possible.

Contents Listing
of Details

SECTION 7: RC–G 7

Standard masonry construction with sloped reinforced concrete tie beam.
Prefabricated wood truss and plywood roof deck with no insulation.

RCG 1	Intermediate condition: End	RCG 1
RCG 2	End condition	RCG 2
RCG 3	End condition with lower beam	RCG 3
RCG 4	End condition with window	RCG 4
RCG 5	End condition with storefront	RCG 5
RCG 6	End condition with door	RCG 6
RCG 7	Side condition	RCG 7
RCG 8	Side condition with lower beam	RCG 8
RCG 9	Side condition with window	RCG 9
RCG 10	Side condition with storefront	RCG 10
RCG 11	Side condition with door	RCG 11

SECTION 8: RC–H 8

Standard masonry construction with level reinforced concrete tie beam.
Wood truss and plywood roof deck with sloped insulation.

RCH 1	Intermediate condition: End	RCH 1
RCH 2	End condition	RCH 2
RCH 3	End condition with lower beam	RCH 3
RCH 4	End condition with window	RCH 4
RCH 5	End condition with storefront	RCH 5
RCH 6	End condition with door	RCH 6
RCH 7	Side condition	RCH 7
RCH 8	Side condition with lower beam	RCH 8
RCH 9	Side condition with window	RCH 9
RCH 10	Side condition with storefront	RCH 10
RCH 11	Side condition with door	RCH 11

REINFORCED MASONRY CONSTRUCTION

SECTION 9: RM–A 9

Reinforced masonry construction with sloped beam.
Hollow core concrete roof deck with no insulation.

RMA 1	Intermediate condition: End	RMA 1
RMA 2	Intermediate condition: Side	RMA 2
RMA 3	End condition	RMA 3
RMA 4	End condition with lower beam	RMA 4
RMA 5	End condition with window	RMA 5
RMA 6	End condition with storefront	RMA 6
RMA 7	End condition with door	RMA 7
RMA 8	Side condition	RMA 8
RMA 9	Side condition with lower beam	RMA 9
RMA 10	Side condition with window	RMA 10
RMA 11	Side condition with storefront	RMA 11
RMA 12	Side condition with door	RMA 12

SECTION 10: RM–B 10

Reinforced masonry construction with level beam.
Hollow core concrete roof deck with sloped insulation.

RMB 1	Intermediate condition: End	RMB 1
RMB 2	Intermediate condition: Side	RMB 2
RMB 3	End condition	RMB 3
RMB 4	End condition with lower beam	RMB 4

SECTION 11: RM–C   **11**
Reinforced masonry construction with sloped beam.
Prestressed concrete twin tee roof deck with no insulation.

SECTION 12: RM–D   **12**
Reinforced masonry construction with level beam.
Prestressed concrete twin tee roof deck with sloped insulation.

SECTION 13: RM–E   **13**
Reinforced masonry construction with level beam.
Steel joist and metal roof deck with no insulation.

SECTION 14: RM–F 14
Reinforced masonry construction with level beam.
Steel joist and metal roof deck with insulation board.

SECTION 15: RM–G 15
Reinforced masonry construction with sloped beam.
Prefabricated wood truss and plywood roof deck with no insulation.

SECTION 16: RM–H 16
Reinforced masonry construction with level beam.
Wood truss and plywood roof deck with sloped insulation.

GENERAL CONSTRUCTION

SECTION 17: FOOTINGS 17

SECTION 22: DOORS, WINDOWS, AND INTERIORS — 22

SECTION 23: MISCELLANEOUS — 23

SECTION 26: MASTERS

Introduction

This book is the result of a system of detailing employed in my own practice. After years of working drawing production, I came to the realization that the detailing phase of our work seemed to be very repetitious. An investigation of several recently completed projects confirmed my suspicions, revealing many very similar details. It was at that moment that I realized that I had to do something about this repetition. Further analysis revealed that repetition seemed to be an inherent part of the detailing process. Unable to change the detail requirements, I wondered what I could do to take advantage of the repetition.

I quickly found that most wall section details consist of two or three distinct and separate parts. The first part is the lower or foundation, the second is the intermediate, which could consist of one or more levels, and the third part is the upper or roof beam.

Consistent in all of our projects there seemed to be a finite number of detail options at each of these three levels. The first option was the vertical load-bearing structural system employed. I have identified two load-bearing structural systems: concrete masonry with reinforced concrete beams and reinforced masonry. The second option is the horizontal structural system. Of these there are four: pre-stressed hollow-core concrete slabs, prestressed concrete twin tees, steel joist with a metal deck, and prefabricated wood trusses. The third option is the configuration of the bearing wall: Is it solid block or does it have a window or a door, either swinging or overhead?

After identifying the various options, I went on to develop and note a generic standard detail drawing of each option. Each option's scale and size is carefully coordinated so that the various options can be easily combined. Noting has been located such that it will align from option to option as the details are used in conjunction with one another. With this library of standard details, we have the capability of detailing much more thoroughly and quickly than ever before. The drafter can now concentrate on the unique aspects of the project, such as specified connections or finishes, without having the tedious task of reproducing over and over the standard structural elements.

Detail elements required for a particular project can be selected from the book, copied onto an adhesive-backed vellum such as Raven, Appli-K, or other similar products, trimmed, and directly applied to the drawing sheet. Because all lines and lettering presented herein are crisply drawn with black ink on drafting vellum, the xerox vellum image should appear equally crisp. The final completed tracing can be blueprinted at a slightly slower speed to avoid ghosting, without any appreciable loss of clarity.

The standard details are designed to be used as is; however, modifications as required can be easily made. Minor modifications, such as beam and reinforcing sizes, finishes, or additional noting, can be made directly on the adhesive-backed mylar. Images on the mylar can be easily erased with a white pencil eraser in an electric eraser. Major modifications can be made by blanking out portions of the standard detail and copying onto an 8½″ × 11″ sheet of tracing vellum. The modifications can then be inked onto the vellum, with the modified detail being copied onto an adhesive-backed mylar for direct application to the drawing.

In addition to the generic details which are combinable with one another, this book also contains many individual details which are intended to be used alone, and a variety of blank schedules, legends, and notes, which can be filled in by the user. Also included is a detailed explanation of sheet organization and detail layout.

Using the Details

The standard details are designed to be used as is. To use, simply place the detail in any photocopy machine capable of accepting single sheet paper. First, make a normal copy on bond paper to check copy contrast, quality, and detail alignment. If satisfied, feed one sheet of self adhesive mylar into the machine and start the copy process. The self adhesive mylar is manufactured by several companies including Rayven and Kroy. Make sure the mylar has a matte surface capable of receiving ink and is compatible for use with your photocopy machine. Once the copy is made, trim the excess vellum away from the copied detail, using standard scissors or an Xacto knife. (See Fig. A.)

To position the detail on the drawing sheet, I suggest that you use light vertical and horizontal layout lines drawn with a nonprint pencil. Once the final position has been set by the layout lines, peel the adhesive mylar from its backing, align, and press into place. (See Fig. B.) Some vellums are more adhesive than others and can be more easily repositioned. I recommend that you test a piece of adhesive vellum on your tracing medias before working on the actual drawing.

Starting at the top and working down, smooth out and remove all bubbles with a scale, triangle, or the edge of your hand. Take care during this process not to create wrinkles. If something goes wrong and wrinkles appear or the mylar is damaged, it can be removed and another copied and applied in its place.

Modifying the Detail

As previously mentioned, the standard details are designed to be used as is; however, modifications both minor and major can be easily made. Minor additions such as beam or reinforcing sizes, finishes, or additional noting can be made directly

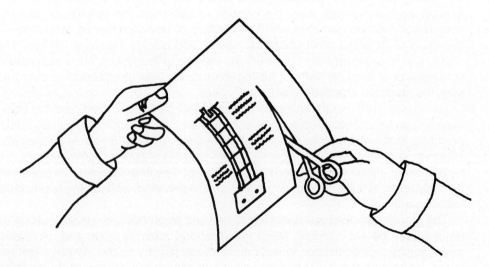

FIG. A

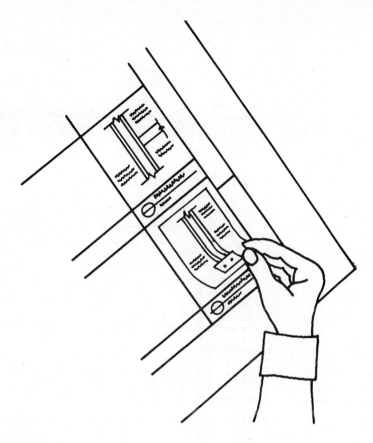

FIG. B

on the photocopied adhesive backed mylar. Again, to accomplish this make sure you are using a matte-surfaced mylar. All lettering in the book was done with a 0.70 mm size drafting pen, using Higgins Black Magic Ink. A sheet of lettering guidelines has been included for use in keeping lettering heights consistent with that on the details. (See MAS 1 in Sec. 26.) We use this sheet behind the drafting sheet after application of the mylar detail for even and consistent lettering.

Minor deletions such as the deletion of reinforcing, or a note, can again be made directly on the adhesive-backed mylar. The photocopied image can be easily removed through the careful use of a "white pencil" eraser (not white vinyl) in an electric eraser. I have found that the Faber Castel White #73 eraser works quite well on photocopied mylar.

Major deletions or modifications can also be quite easily made. To make larger deletions, a sheet of plain white paper can be cut and precisely positioned over the original detail to mask out unwanted areas or noting. (See Fig. C.) A little rubber cement can be used to help hold the mask in place during the copying process. Once the original has been properly masked, follow the normal photocopy process onto the adhesive-backed mylar. If preferred, an intermediate photocopy can be made onto 8½" × 11" tracing vellum. The required revisions can then be made on this intermediate which then becomes a revised new original detail. (See Fig. D.) Photocopying onto the mylar would then be the same as for any other standard detail. The end result is either a modified mylar or a new standard detail. The obvious advantage to the use of an intermediate is the ability to reuse the newly created detail. Modifications made directly on the adhesive-backed mylar are for one time use only.

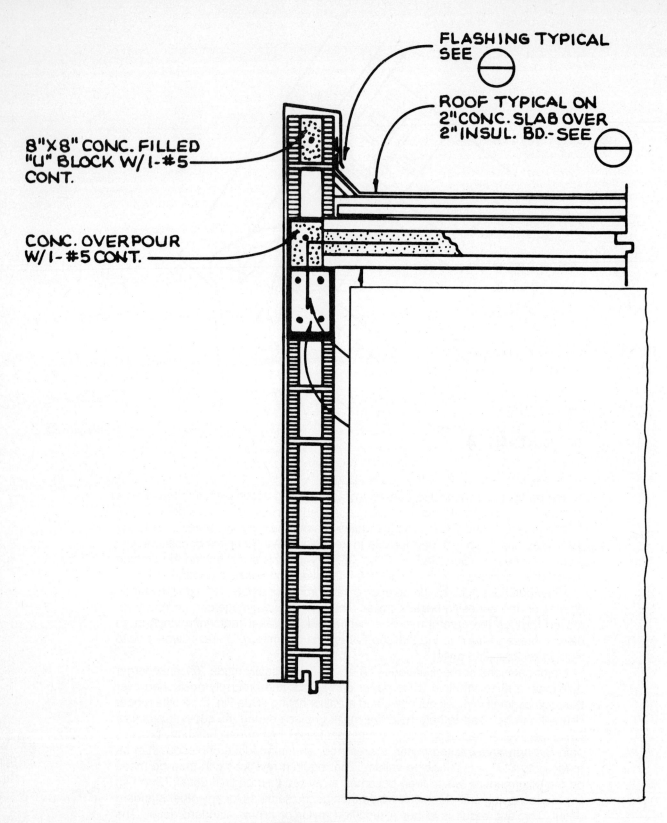

8"X8" CONC. FILLED "U" BLOCK W/1-#5 CONT.

CONC. OVERPOUR W/1-#5 CONT.

FLASHING TYPICAL SEE ⊖

ROOF TYPICAL ON 2"CONC. SLAB OVER 2"INSUL. BD.-SEE ⊖

FIG. C

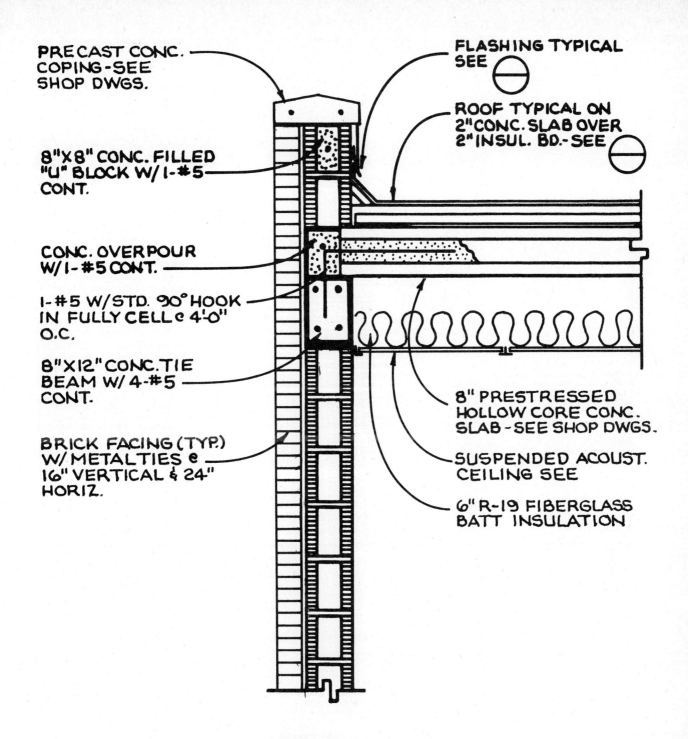

PRECAST CONC. COPING-SEE SHOP DWGS.

FLASHING TYPICAL SEE ⊖

8"X8" CONC. FILLED "U" BLOCK W/1-#5 CONT.

ROOF TYPICAL ON 2"CONC. SLAB OVER 2"INSUL. BD.-SEE ⊖

CONC. OVERPOUR W/1-#5 CONT.

1-#5 W/STD. 90°HOOK IN FULLY CELL @ 4'-0" O.C.

8"X12"CONC.TIE BEAM W/4-#5 CONT.

8" PRESTRESSED HOLLOW CORE CONC. SLAB-SEE SHOP DWGS.

BRICK FACING (TYP.) W/METAL TIES @ 16" VERTICAL & 24" HORIZ.

SUSPENDED ACOUST. CEILING SEE

6" R-19 FIBERGLASS BATT INSULATION

FIG. D

Creating New Standard Details

Because of the space limitations on the length of this book, intermediate wall section conditions have not been included. However the system has been designed to allow for the easy modifications of roof condition details into intermediate condition details. To do this the user must first copy onto a clean blank piece of bond paper the length of generic concrete block wall shown in MAS 2 (Sec. 26). After deciding on the exact length of block you will require above the intermediate bearing con-

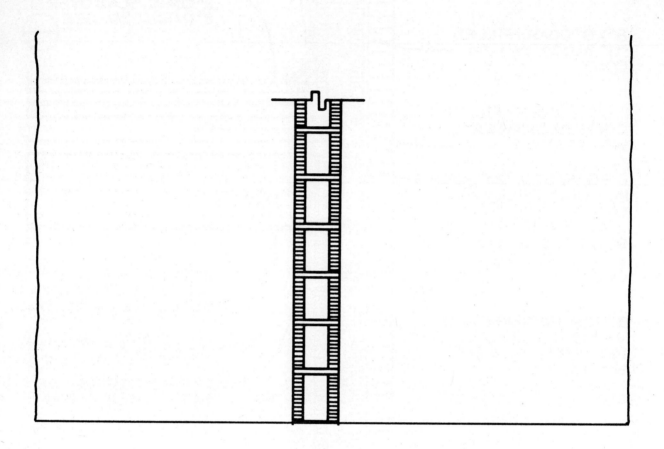

FIG. E

dition, cut horizontally across the sheet with an Xacto knife. (See Fig. E.) Now select the proper intermediate condition, e.g., Prestressed Hollow Core Concrete Slab, Prestressed Concrete Twin Tees, etc. (See Fig. F.) The final step before copying is to carefully position the bond copy with the concrete block over the original detail. Make sure the upper and lower block walls align and that the bond copy adequately masks out all unwanted parts of the original detail. The final step is to copy the entire composite onto a new 8½″ × 11″ sheet of vellum. Using the previously discussed electric eraser, remove any unwanted lines or marks; you now have a new standard intermediate condition detail. (See Fig. G.) Using this and a minimum amount of effort you should be able to almost double the number of details in your personal detail file.

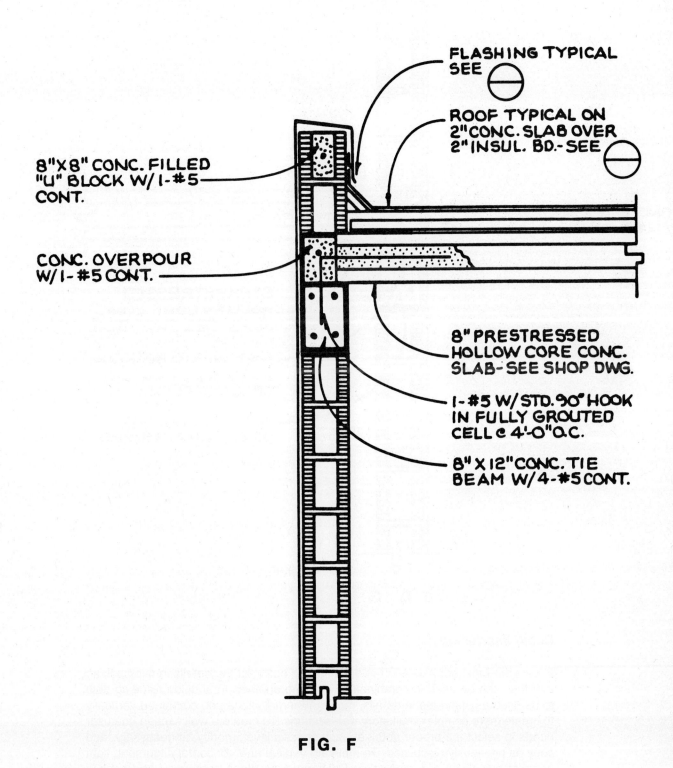

FLASHING TYPICAL
SEE ⊖

ROOF TYPICAL ON
2" CONC. SLAB OVER
2" INSUL. BD.- SEE ⊖

8"X8" CONC. FILLED
"U" BLOCK W/1-#5
CONT.

CONC. OVERPOUR
W/1-#5 CONT.

8" PRESTRESSED
HOLLOW CORE CONC.
SLAB- SEE SHOP DWG.

1-#5 W/STD. 90° HOOK
IN FULLY GROUTED
CELL @ 4'-0" O.C.

8"X 12"CONC. TIE
BEAM W/4-#5 CONT.

FIG. F

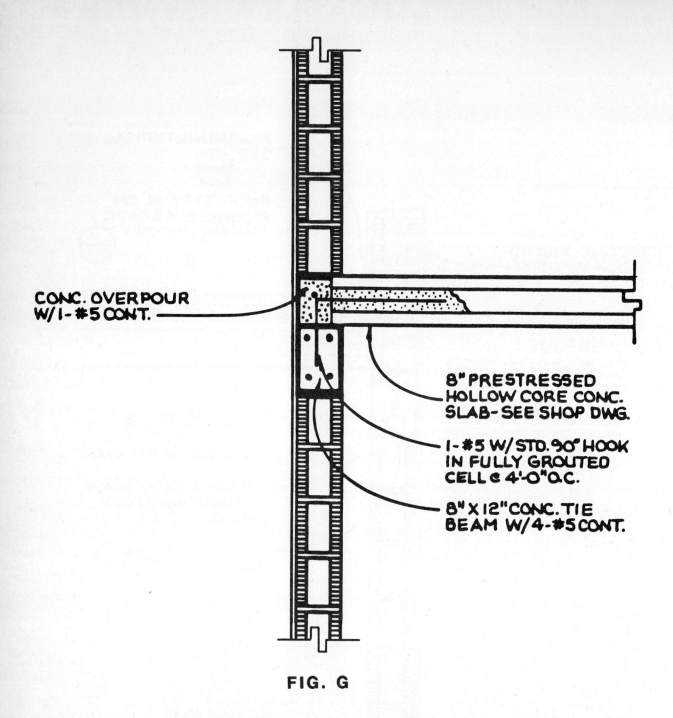

CONC. OVERPOUR
W/ 1-#5 CONT.

8" PRESTRESSED
HOLLOW CORE CONC.
SLAB - SEE SHOP DWG.

1-#5 W/STD. 90° HOOK
IN FULLY GROUTED
CELL @ 4'-0" O.C.

8" X 12" CONC. TIE
BEAM W/4-#5 CONT.

FIG. G

Detail Interfacing

Great care has been taken in the drawing and noting of the details in this book so that they can be used in combination with one another. In addition to being able to be used as stand-alone details, many of the details can be combined vertically to create more complex multistory wall sections. To create a wall section, the user needs to select the proper detail at each specific level, modify as necessary, and copy as previously discussed. To maintain vertical and horizontal alignment, light nonprint guidelines are imperative. Each separate detail is trimmed and applied on the sheet creating the final section. (See Figs. H, I, and J.) Using the detail notations presented in this section, i.e., RB1, RB6, etc., a supervisor can direct a detail drafter through a kind of "detail shorthand" in the drawing of a wall section, i.e., bottom to top RB4 - RB5 - RB9.

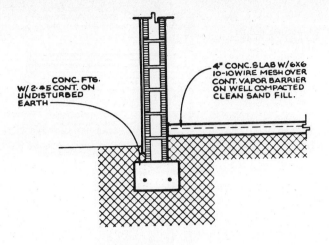

CONC. FTG.
W/ 2-#5 CONT. ON
UNDISTURBED
EARTH

4" CONC. SLAB W/ 6X6
10-10 WIRE MESH OVER
CONT. VAPOR BARRIER
ON WELL COMPACTED
CLEAN SAND FILL.

FIG. H

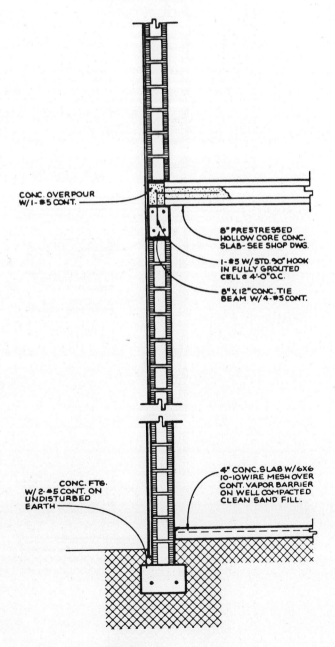

CONC. OVERPOUR
W/ 1-#5 CONT.

8" PRESTRESSED
HOLLOW CORE CONC.
SLAB- SEE SHOP DWG.

1-#5 W/ STD. 90° HOOK
IN FULLY GROUTED
CELL @ 4'-0" O.C.

8" X 12" CONC. TIE
BEAM W/ 4-#5 CONT.

CONC. FTG.
W/ 2-#5 CONT. ON
UNDISTURBED
EARTH

4" CONC. SLAB W/ 6X6
10-10 WIRE MESH OVER
CONT. VAPOR BARRIER
ON WELL COMPACTED
CLEAN SAND FILL.

FIG. I

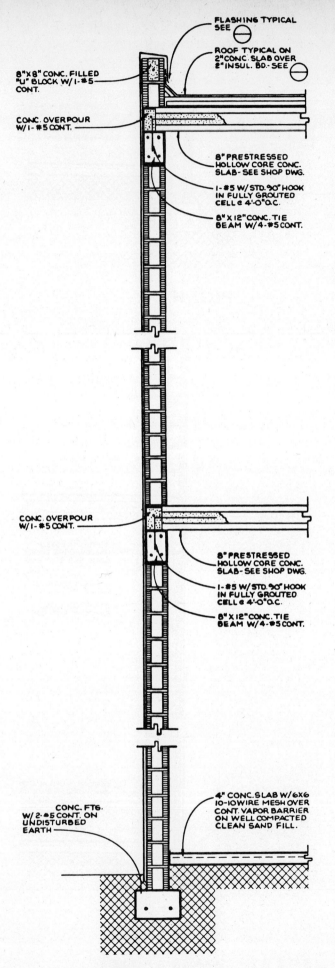

FLASHING TYPICAL
SEE ⊖

ROOF TYPICAL ON
2" CONC. SLAB OVER
2" INSUL. BD.- SEE ⊖

8"X8" CONC. FILLED
"U" BLOCK W/ 1-#5
CONT.

CONC. OVERPOUR
W/ 1-#5 CONT.

8" PRESTRESSED
HOLLOW CORE CONC.
SLAB- SEE SHOP DWG.

1-#5 W/ STD. 90° HOOK
IN FULLY GROUTED
CELL @ 4'-0"O.C.

8"X12"CONC. TIE
BEAM W/4-#5 CONT.

CONC. OVERPOUR
W/ 1-#5 CONT.

8" PRESTRESSED
HOLLOW CORE CONC.
SLAB- SEE SHOP DWG.

1-#5 W/ STD. 90° HOOK
IN FULLY GROUTED
CELL @ 4'-0"O.C.

8"X12"CONC. TIE
BEAM W/4-#5 CONT.

CONC. FTG.
W/ 2-#5 CONT. ON
UNDISTURBED
EARTH

4" CONC. SLAB W/ 6X6
10-10 WIRE MESH OVER
CONT. VAPOR BARRIER
ON WELL COMPACTED
CLEAN SAND FILL.

FIG. J

Detail Layout

Traditionally, one of the most difficult problems in the detailing process was the actual layout of the detail sheet. Without a planned method of organizing the sheet, details tended to overlap one another reducing the clarity not only of the entire sheet but sometimes of individual details.

To avoid the clarity problems mentioned above, my system of detailing has established as its base a grid to be superimposed onto the detail sheet, i.e., tracing vellum. This grid, which can be used on any standard or custom-bordered sheet, consists of three evenly spaced vertical and two evenly spaced horizontal lines. (See Fig. K.) These lines form twelve equal rectangles. Spaced at a distance of 1¼ inches from the bottom of each box, another horizontal line is drawn. This line serves to define the title areas of each detail. (See Fig. L.)

While the thickness of these grid lines can vary, a good rule of thumb is to draw these lines at the same thickness as the sheet borders.

Most of the details presented in this book have been drawn at a size to fit easily within one detail box. As details are combined vertically or horizontally multiple boxes can be used. In this instance intermediate box and title lines are omitted. Figure M illustrates a completed detail sheet; notice single, double, and triple box detail configurations.

Summary

There you have it. With this book, a typical photocopy machine, and several pieces of standard equipment, i.e., scissors, eraser, pens, etc., you are ready to begin. Remember, the details in this book are presented as a starting point; the potential of their use and growth is limited only by the imagination of the user. Good luck!

Gene Farmer

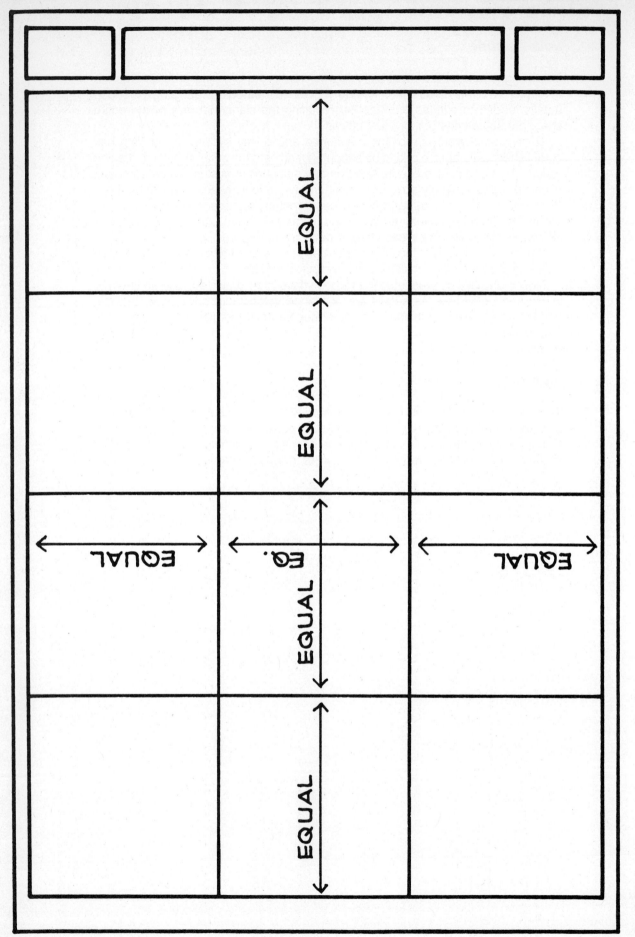

FIG. K

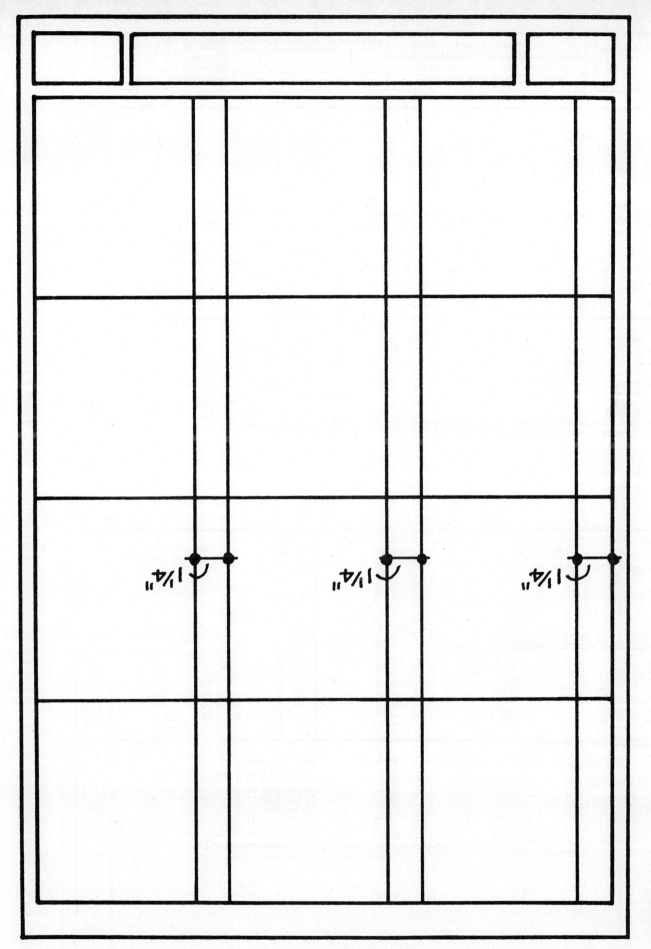

FIG. L

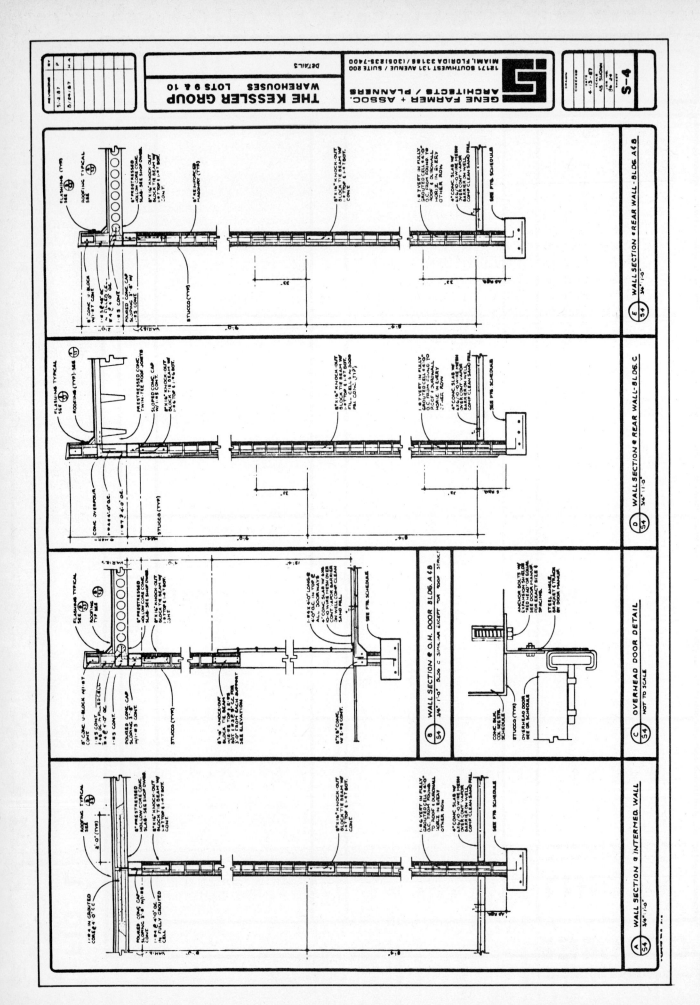

FIG. M

SECTION 1: RC–A

Standard masonry construction with sloped reinforced concrete tie beam.
Hollow core concrete roof deck with no insulation.

ARCHITECTURAL DETAILING
FOR
COMMERCIAL CONSTRUCTION

1

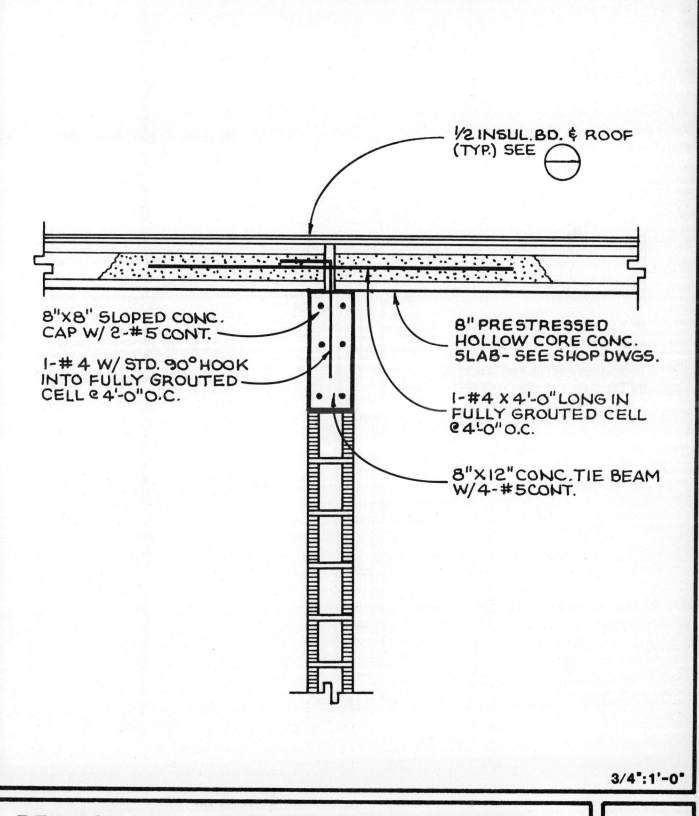

½ INSUL. BD. & ROOF (TYP.) SEE ⊘

8"x8" SLOPED CONC. CAP W/ 2-#5 CONT.

1-#4 W/ STD. 90° HOOK INTO FULLY GROUTED CELL @ 4'-0" O.C.

8" PRESTRESSED HOLLOW CORE CONC. SLAB- SEE SHOP DWGS.

1-#4 X 4'-0" LONG IN FULLY GROUTED CELL @ 4'-0" O.C.

8"X12" CONC. TIE BEAM W/ 4-#5 CONT.

3/4":1'-0"

REINFORCED CONCRETE BEAM: SLOPED HOLLOW CORE ROOF DECK: NO INSULATION

INTERMEDIATE CONDITION: END

RCA 1

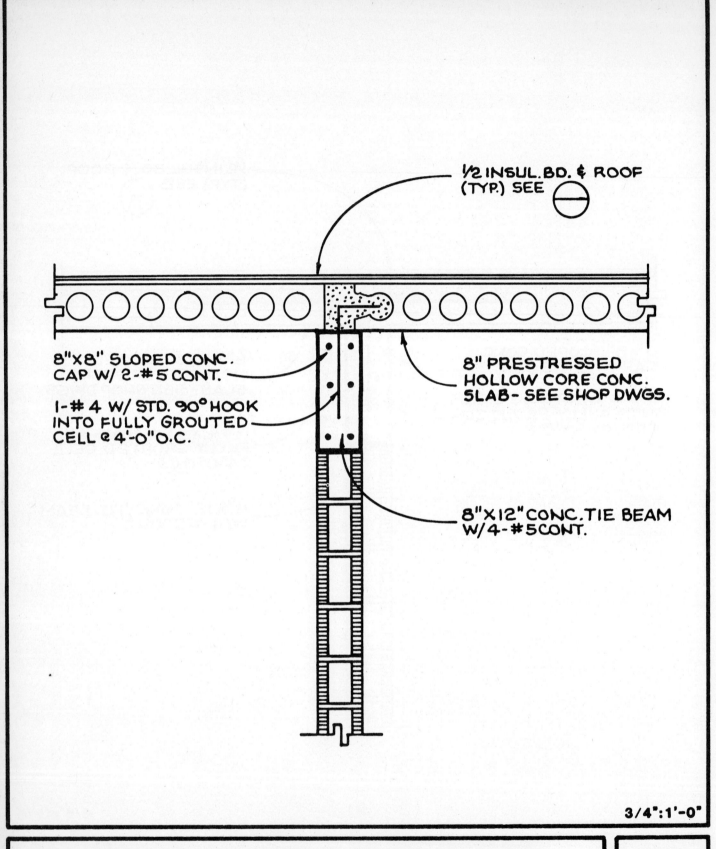

½ INSUL. BD. & ROOF (TYP.) SEE ⊖

8"x8" SLOPED CONC. CAP W/ 2-#5 CONT.

1-#4 W/ STD. 90° HOOK INTO FULLY GROUTED CELL @ 4'-0" O.C.

8" PRESTRESSED HOLLOW CORE CONC. SLAB- SEE SHOP DWGS.

8"x12" CONC. TIE BEAM W/4-#5 CONT.

3/4":1'-0"

REINFORCED CONCRETE BEAM: SLOPED HOLLOW CORE ROOF DECK: NO INSULATION INTERMEDIATE CONDITION: SIDE

RCA 2

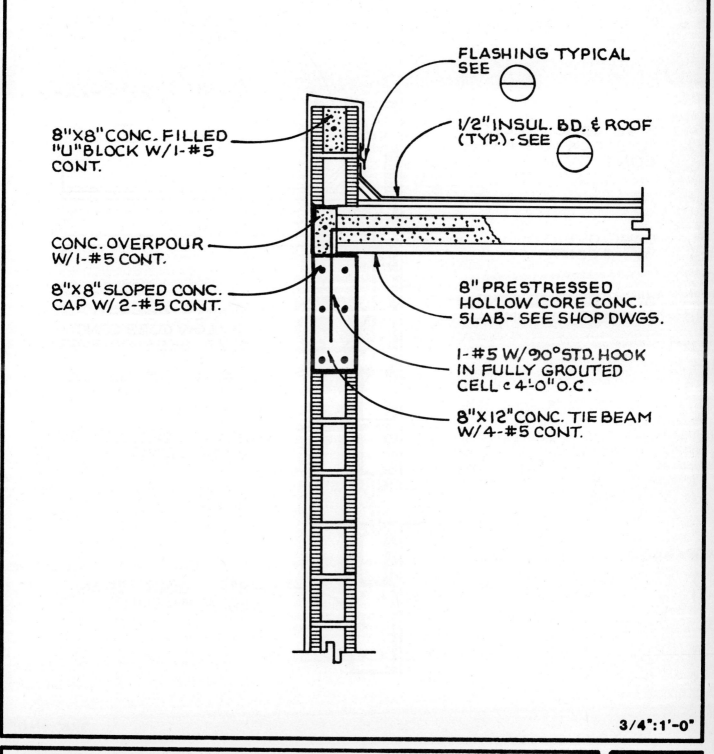

FLASHING TYPICAL
SEE ⊖

1/2" INSUL. BD. & ROOF
(TYP.) - SEE ⊖

8"X8" CONC. FILLED
"U" BLOCK W/1-#5
CONT.

CONC. OVERPOUR
W/1-#5 CONT.

8"X8" SLOPED CONC.
CAP W/ 2-#5 CONT.

8" PRESTRESSED
HOLLOW CORE CONC.
SLAB- SEE SHOP DWGS.

1-#5 W/90° STD. HOOK
IN FULLY GROUTED
CELL ¢ 4'-0" O.C.

8"X12" CONC. TIE BEAM
W/4-#5 CONT.

3/4":1'-0"

**REINFORCED CONCRETE BEAM: SLOPED
HOLLOW CORE ROOF DECK: NO INSULATION
END CONDITION**

**RCA
3**

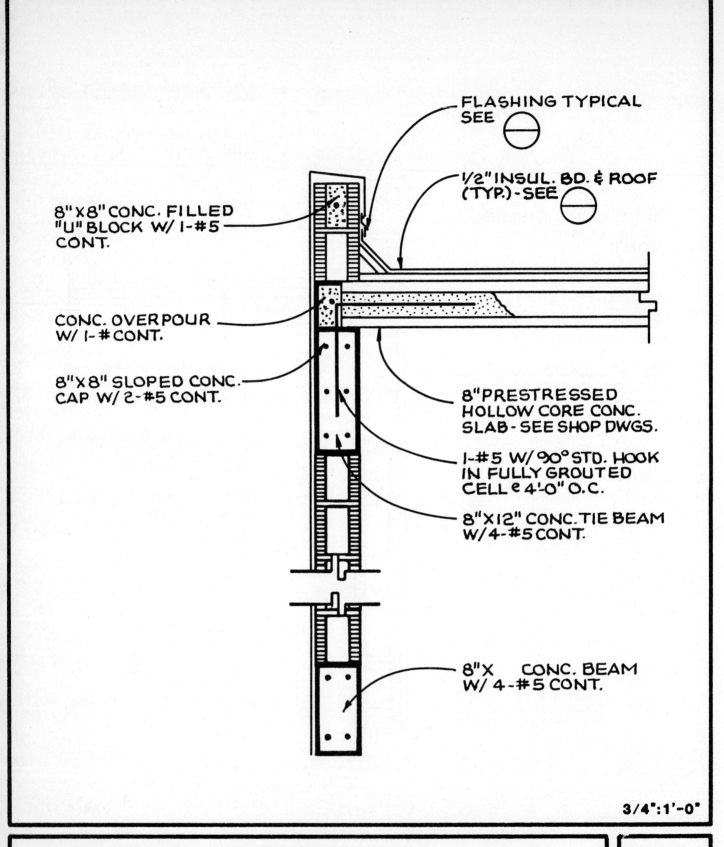

FLASHING TYPICAL
SEE ◯

½" INSUL. BD. & ROOF
(TYP.) - SEE ◯

8"x8" CONC. FILLED
"U" BLOCK W/ 1-#5
CONT.

CONC. OVERPOUR
W/ 1-# CONT.

8"x8" SLOPED CONC.
CAP W/ 2-#5 CONT.

8" PRESTRESSED
HOLLOW CORE CONC.
SLAB - SEE SHOP DWGS.

1-#5 W/ 90° STD. HOOK
IN FULLY GROUTED
CELL @ 4'-0" O.C.

8"x12" CONC. TIE BEAM
W/ 4-#5 CONT.

8"X   CONC. BEAM
W/ 4-#5 CONT.

3/4":1'-0"

REINFORCED CONCRETE BEAM: SLOPED
HOLLOW CORE ROOF DECK: NO INSULATION
END CONDITION: LOWER BEAM

RCA
4

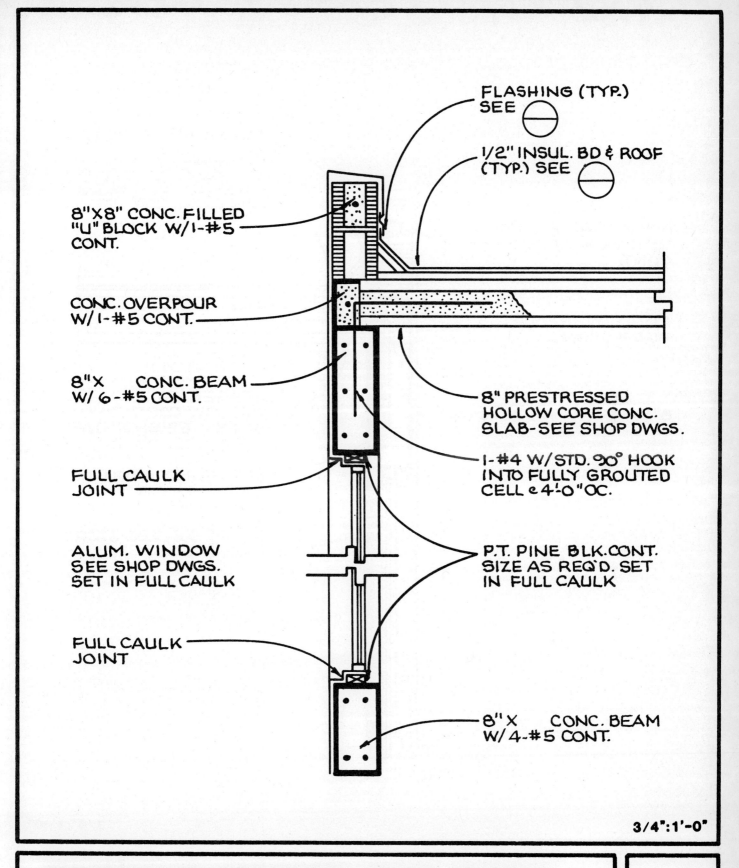

FLASHING (TYP.)
SEE ⊖

1/2" INSUL. BD & ROOF
(TYP.) SEE ⊖

8"X8" CONC. FILLED
"U" BLOCK W/ 1-#5
CONT.

CONC. OVERPOUR
W/ 1-#5 CONT.

8"X   CONC. BEAM
W/ 6-#5 CONT.

FULL CAULK
JOINT

ALUM. WINDOW
SEE SHOP DWGS.
SET IN FULL CAULK

FULL CAULK
JOINT

8" PRESTRESSED
HOLLOW CORE CONC.
SLAB-SEE SHOP DWGS.

1-#4 W/STD. 90° HOOK
INTO FULLY GROUTED
CELL e 4'-0"OC.

P.T. PINE BLK.CONT.
SIZE AS REQ'D. SET
IN FULL CAULK

8"X   CONC. BEAM
W/ 4-#5 CONT.

3/4":1'-0"

REINFORCED CONCRETE BEAM: SLOPED HOLLOW CORE ROOF DECK: NO INSULATION
END CONDITION: WINDOW

RCA
5

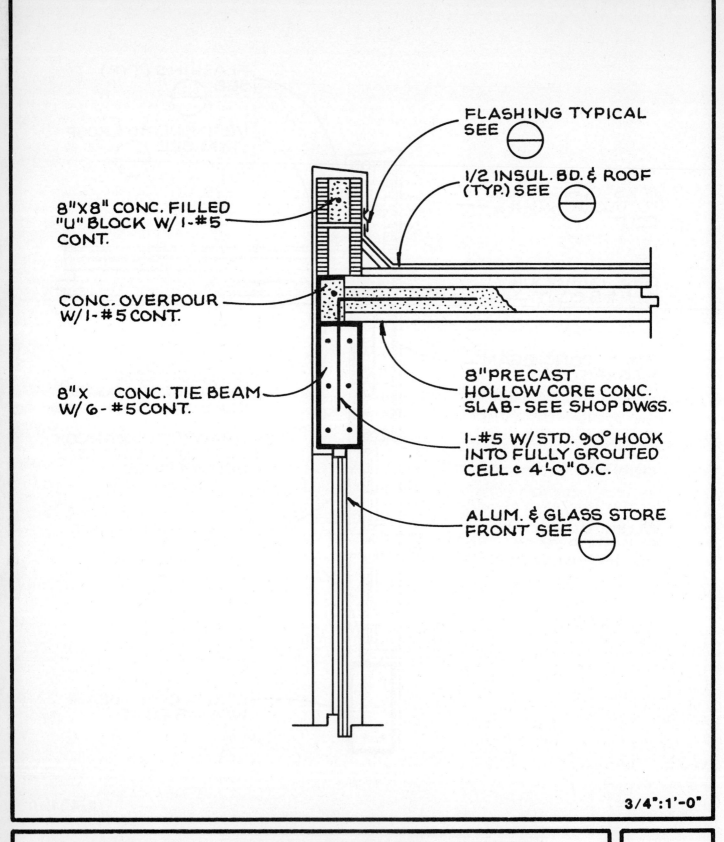

FLASHING TYPICAL SEE ⊘

1/2 INSUL. BD. & ROOF (TYP.) SEE ⊘

8"X8" CONC. FILLED "U" BLOCK W/ 1-#5 CONT.

CONC. OVERPOUR W/ 1-#5 CONT.

8"X CONC. TIE BEAM W/ 6-#5 CONT.

8"PRECAST HOLLOW CORE CONC. SLAB - SEE SHOP DWGS.

1-#5 W/ STD. 90° HOOK INTO FULLY GROUTED CELL @ 4'-0" O.C.

ALUM. & GLASS STORE FRONT SEE ⊘

3/4":1'-0"

REINFORCED CONCRETE BEAM: SLOPED HOLLOW CORE ROOF DECK: NO INSULATION

END CONDITION: STOREFRONT

RCA 6

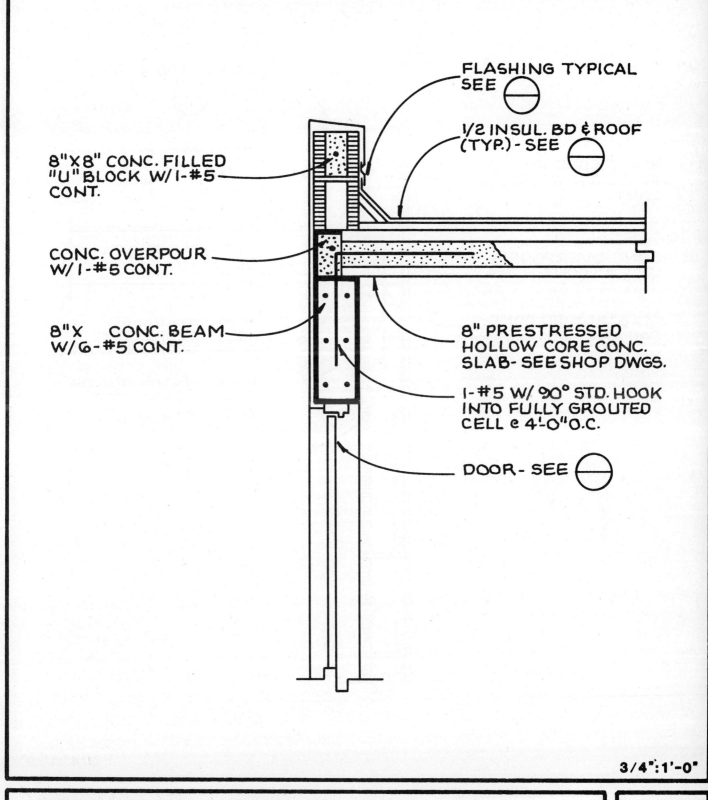

FLASHING TYPICAL
SEE ⊘

½ INSUL. BD & ROOF
(TYP.) - SEE ⊘

8"X8" CONC. FILLED
"U" BLOCK W/1-#5
CONT.

CONC. OVERPOUR
W/1-#5 CONT.

8"X   CONC. BEAM
W/6-#5 CONT.

8" PRESTRESSED
HOLLOW CORE CONC.
SLAB- SEE SHOP DWGS.

1-#5 W/90° STD. HOOK
INTO FULLY GROUTED
CELL e 4'-0"O.C.

DOOR- SEE ⊘

3/4":1'-0"

**REINFORCED CONCRETE BEAM: SLOPED
HOLLOW CORE ROOF DECK: NO INSULATION
END CONDITION: DOOR**

**RCA
7**

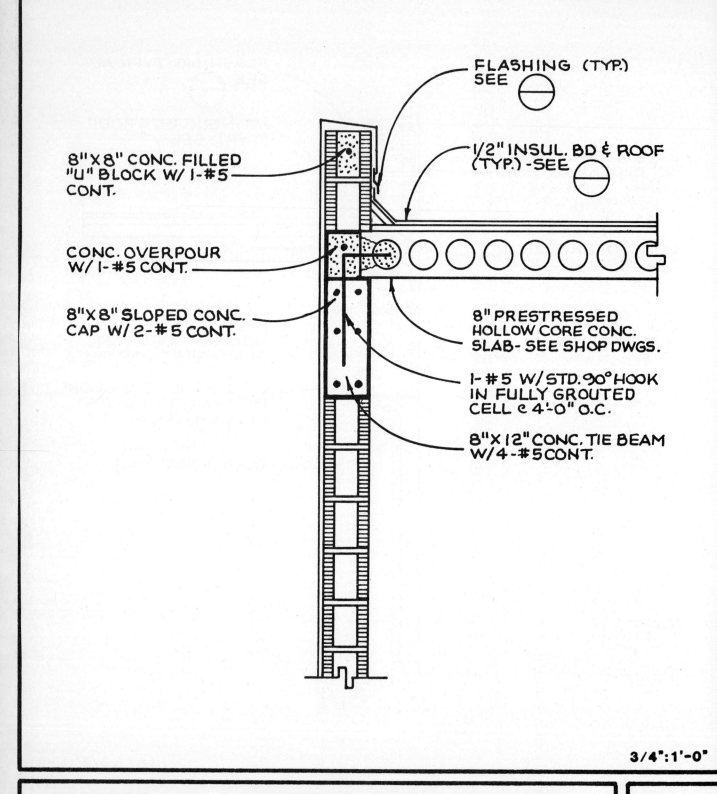

FLASHING (TYP.) SEE ⊖

1/2" INSUL. BD & ROOF (TYP.) - SEE ⊖

8"X8" CONC. FILLED "U" BLOCK W/ 1-#5 CONT.

CONC. OVERPOUR W/ 1-#5 CONT.

8"X8" SLOPED CONC. CAP W/ 2-#5 CONT.

8" PRESTRESSED HOLLOW CORE CONC. SLAB- SEE SHOP DWGS.

1-#5 W/ STD. 90° HOOK IN FULLY GROUTED CELL @ 4'-0" O.C.

8"X12" CONC. TIE BEAM W/ 4-#5 CONT.

3/4":1'-0"

REINFORCED CONCRETE BEAM: SLOPED HOLLOW CORE ROOF DECK: NO INSULATION SIDE CONDITION

RCA 8

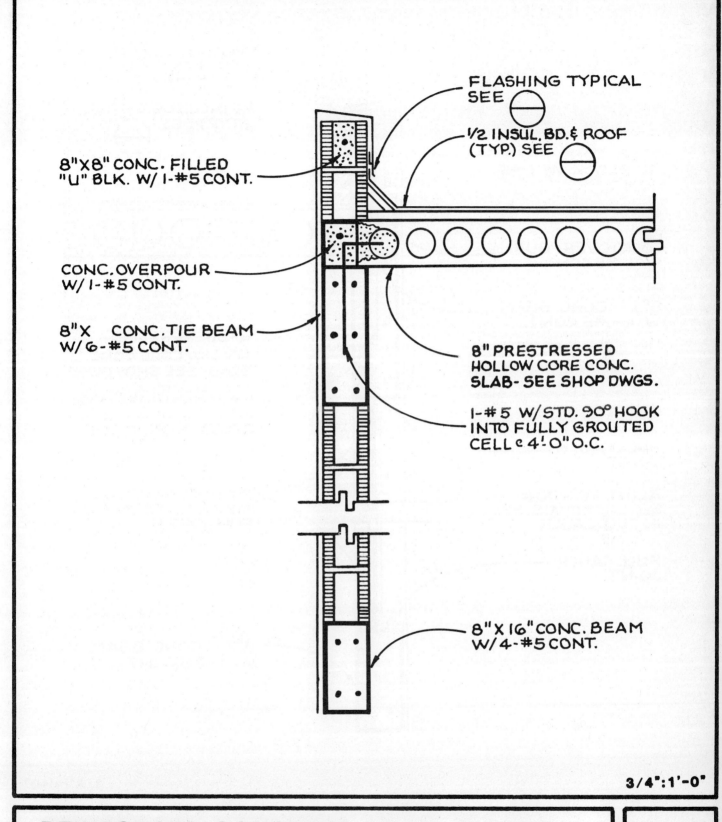

FLASHING TYPICAL
SEE ⊖

½ INSUL. BD. & ROOF
(TYP.) SEE ⊖

8"X8" CONC. FILLED
"U" BLK. W/ 1-#5 CONT.

CONC. OVERPOUR
W/ 1-#5 CONT.

8"X   CONC. TIE BEAM
W/ 6-#5 CONT.

8" PRESTRESSED
HOLLOW CORE CONC.
SLAB- SEE SHOP DWGS.

1-#5 W/ STD. 90° HOOK
INTO FULLY GROUTED
CELL @ 4'-0" O.C.

8"X16" CONC. BEAM
W/ 4-#5 CONT.

3/4":1'-0"

**REINFORCED CONCRETE BEAM: SLOPED
HOLLOW CORE ROOF DECK: NO INSULATION
SIDE CONDITION: LOWER BEAM**

**RCA
9**

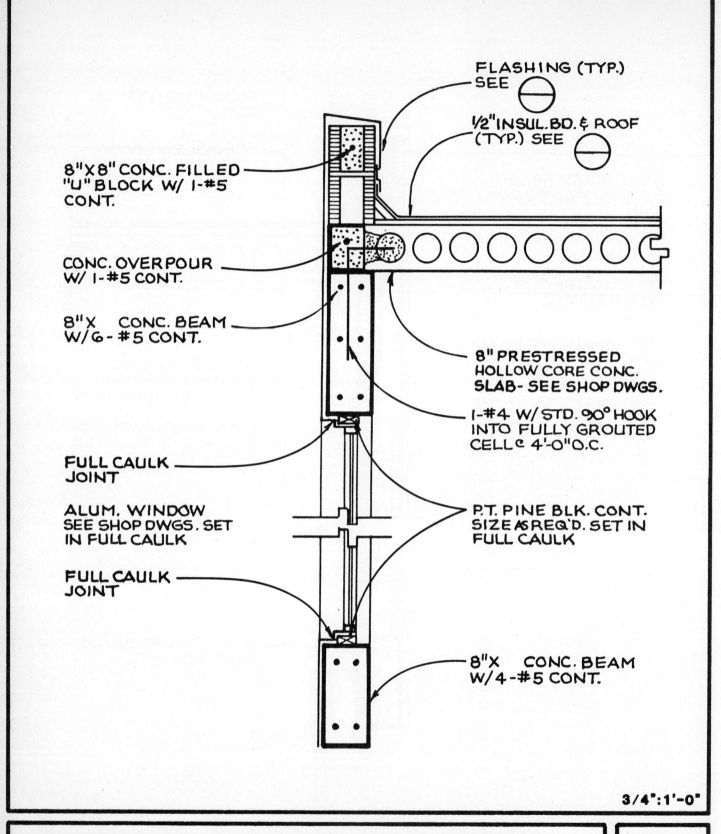

FLASHING (TYP.) SEE ⊖

½" INSUL. BD. & ROOF (TYP.) SEE ⊖

8"X8" CONC. FILLED "U" BLOCK W/ 1-#5 CONT.

CONC. OVERPOUR W/ 1-#5 CONT.

8"X CONC. BEAM W/ 6-#5 CONT.

8" PRESTRESSED HOLLOW CORE CONC. SLAB- SEE SHOP DWGS.

1-#4 W/STD. 90° HOOK INTO FULLY GROUTED CELL @ 4'-0" O.C.

FULL CAULK JOINT

ALUM. WINDOW SEE SHOP DWGS. SET IN FULL CAULK

P.T. PINE BLK. CONT. SIZE AS REQ'D. SET IN FULL CAULK

FULL CAULK JOINT

8"X CONC. BEAM W/ 4-#5 CONT.

3/4":1'-0"

REINFORCED CONCRETE BEAM: SLOPED HOLLOW CORE ROOF DECK: NO INSULATION

SIDE CONDITION: WINDOW

RCA 10

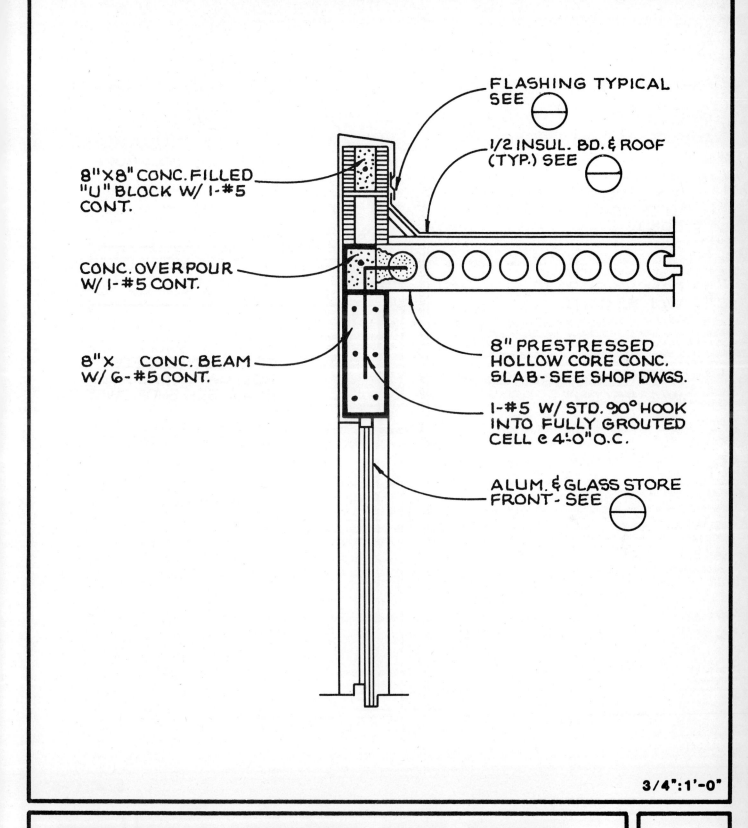

FLASHING TYPICAL
SEE ⊖

1/2 INSUL. BD. & ROOF
(TYP.) SEE ⊖

8"X8" CONC. FILLED
"U" BLOCK W/ 1-#5
CONT.

CONC. OVERPOUR
W/ 1-#5 CONT.

8" PRESTRESSED
HOLLOW CORE CONC.
SLAB- SEE SHOP DWGS.

8"X   CONC. BEAM
W/ 6-#5 CONT.

1-#5 W/ STD. 90° HOOK
INTO FULLY GROUTED
CELL @ 4'-0" O.C.

ALUM. & GLASS STORE
FRONT- SEE ⊖

3/4":1'-0"

**REINFORCED CONCRETE BEAM: SLOPED
HOLLOW CORE ROOF DECK: NO INSULATION
SIDE CONDITION: STOREFRONT**

**RCA
11**

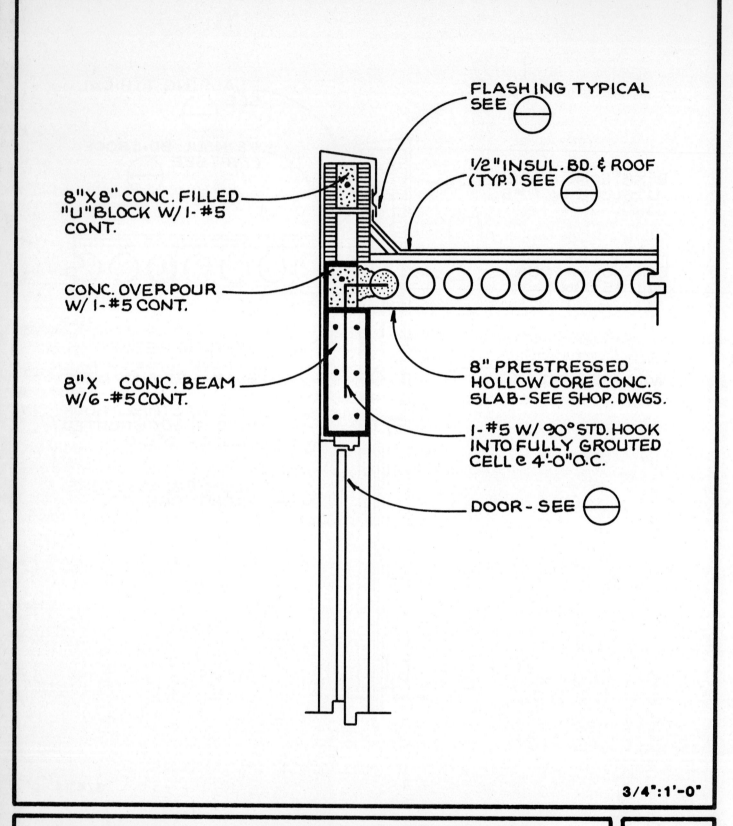

FLASHING TYPICAL
SEE ⊖

½" INSUL. BD. & ROOF
(TYP.) SEE ⊖

8"X8" CONC. FILLED
"U" BLOCK W/1-#5
CONT.

CONC. OVERPOUR
W/1-#5 CONT.

8"X CONC. BEAM
W/6-#5 CONT.

8" PRESTRESSED
HOLLOW CORE CONC.
SLAB-SEE SHOP. DWGS.

1-#5 W/90° STD. HOOK
INTO FULLY GROUTED
CELL @ 4'-0" O.C.

DOOR - SEE ⊖

3/4":1'-0"

REINFORCED CONCRETE BEAM: SLOPED
HOLLOW CORE ROOF DECK: NO INSULATION
SIDE CONDITION: DOOR

RCA
12

SECTION 2: RC–B

Standard masonry construction with level reinforced
concrete tie beam.
Hollow core concrete roof deck with sloped insulation.

ARCHITECTURAL DETAILING
FOR
COMMERCIAL CONSTRUCTION

2

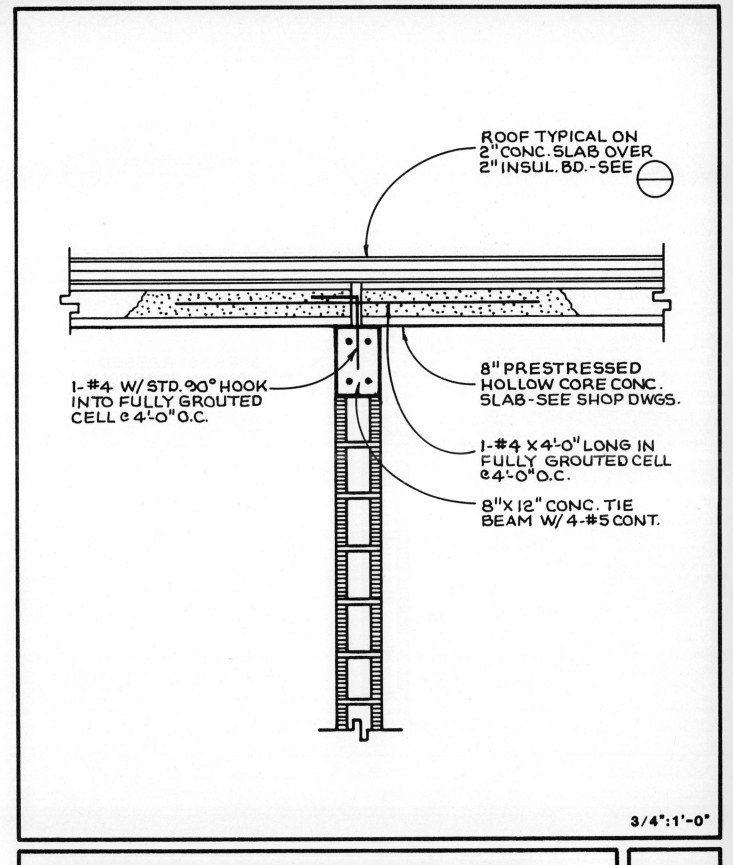

ROOF TYPICAL ON
2" CONC. SLAB OVER
2" INSUL. BD.-SEE ⊖

1-#4 W/ STD. 90° HOOK
INTO FULLY GROUTED
CELL @ 4'-0" O.C.

8" PRESTRESSED
HOLLOW CORE CONC.
SLAB - SEE SHOP DWGS.

1-#4 X 4'-0" LONG IN
FULLY GROUTED CELL
@ 4'-0" O.C.

8"X 12" CONC. TIE
BEAM W/ 4-#5 CONT.

3/4":1'-0"

**REINFORCED CONCRETE BEAM: LEVEL
HOLLOW CORE ROOF DECK: SLOPED INSUL.**

INTERMEDIATE CONDITION: END

**RCB
1**

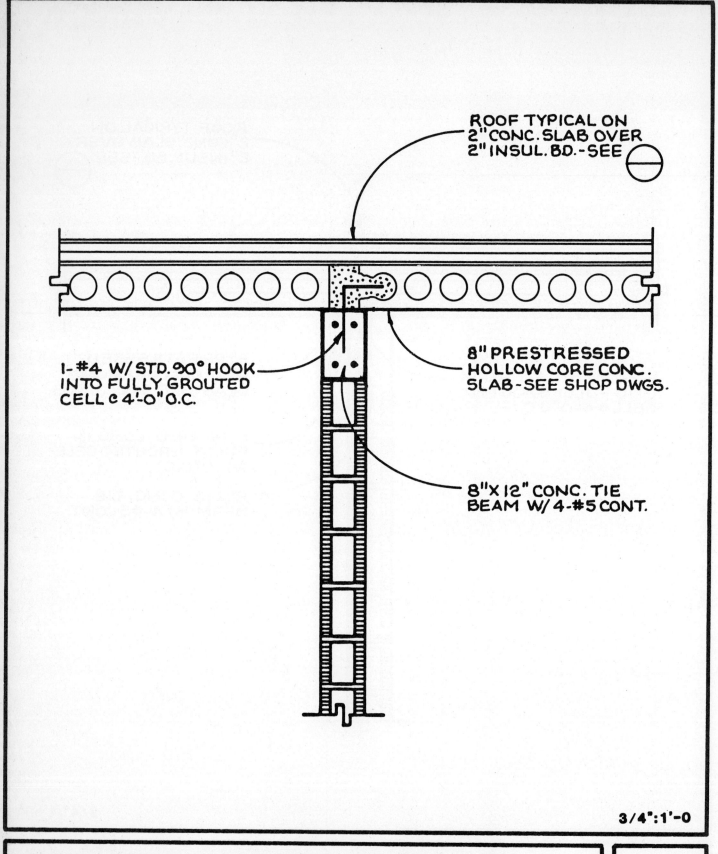

ROOF TYPICAL ON
2" CONC. SLAB OVER
2" INSUL. BD.- SEE

1-#4 W/STD. 90° HOOK
INTO FULLY GROUTED
CELL ℄ 4'-0" O.C.

8" PRESTRESSED
HOLLOW CORE CONC.
SLAB - SEE SHOP DWGS.

8" X 12" CONC. TIE
BEAM W/ 4-#5 CONT.

3/4":1'-0

**REINFORCED CONCRETE BEAM: LEVEL
HOLLOW CORE ROOF DECK: SLOPED INSUL.**

INTERMEDIATE CONDITION: SIDE

**RCB
2**

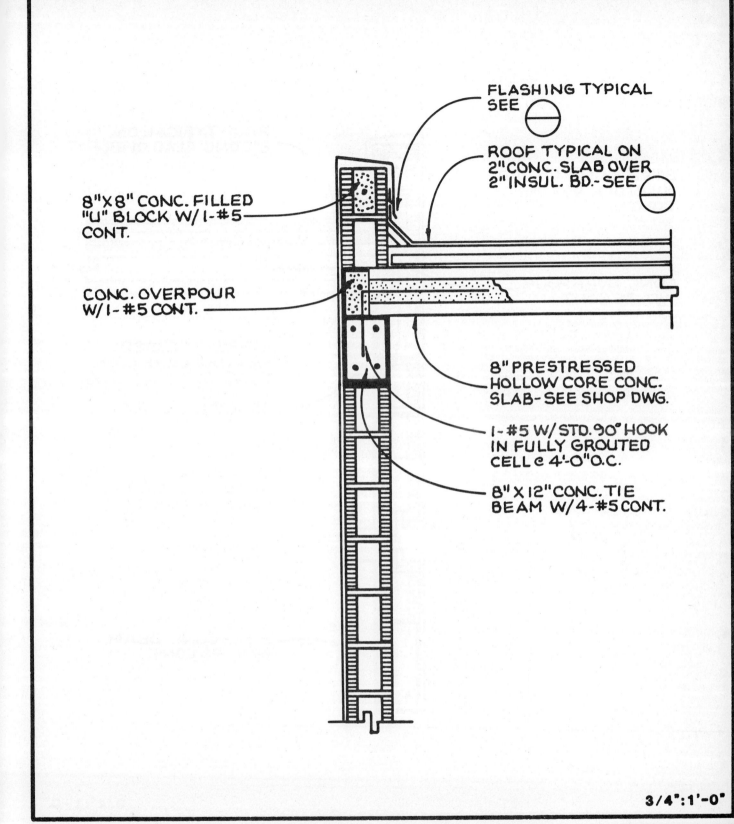

FLASHING TYPICAL
SEE ⊖

ROOF TYPICAL ON
2" CONC. SLAB OVER
2" INSUL. BD.- SEE ⊖

8" X 8" CONC. FILLED
"U" BLOCK W/ 1-#5
CONT.

CONC. OVERPOUR
W/ 1-#5 CONT.

8" PRESTRESSED
HOLLOW CORE CONC.
SLAB- SEE SHOP DWG.

1-#5 W/ STD. 90° HOOK
IN FULLY GROUTED
CELL @ 4'-0" O.C.

8" X 12" CONC. TIE
BEAM W/ 4-#5 CONT.

3/4":1'-0"

**REINFORCED CONCRETE BEAM: LEVEL
HOLLOW CORE ROOF DECK: SLOPED INSUL.**

END CONDITION

**RCB
3**

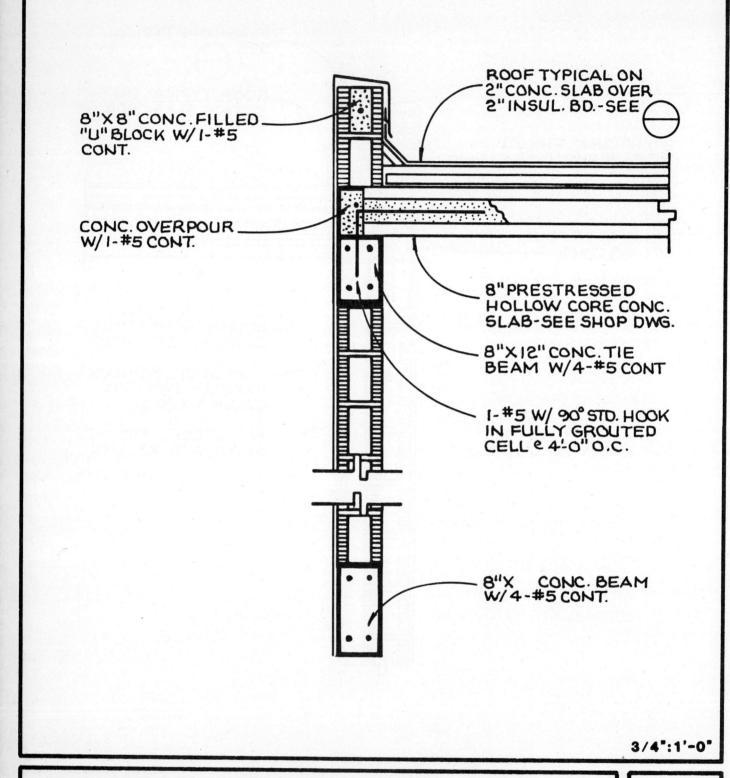

8"X8" CONC. FILLED "U" BLOCK W/ 1-#5 CONT.

CONC. OVERPOUR W/ 1-#5 CONT.

ROOF TYPICAL ON 2" CONC. SLAB OVER 2" INSUL. BD.-SEE ⊖

8" PRESTRESSED HOLLOW CORE CONC. SLAB-SEE SHOP DWG.

8"X12" CONC. TIE BEAM W/ 4-#5 CONT

1-#5 W/ 90° STD. HOOK IN FULLY GROUTED CELL e 4'-0" O.C.

8"X   CONC. BEAM W/ 4-#5 CONT.

3/4":1'-0"

REINFORCED CONCRETE BEAM: LEVEL HOLLOW CORE ROOF DECK: SLOPED INSUL.

END CONDITION: LOWER BEAM

RCB 4

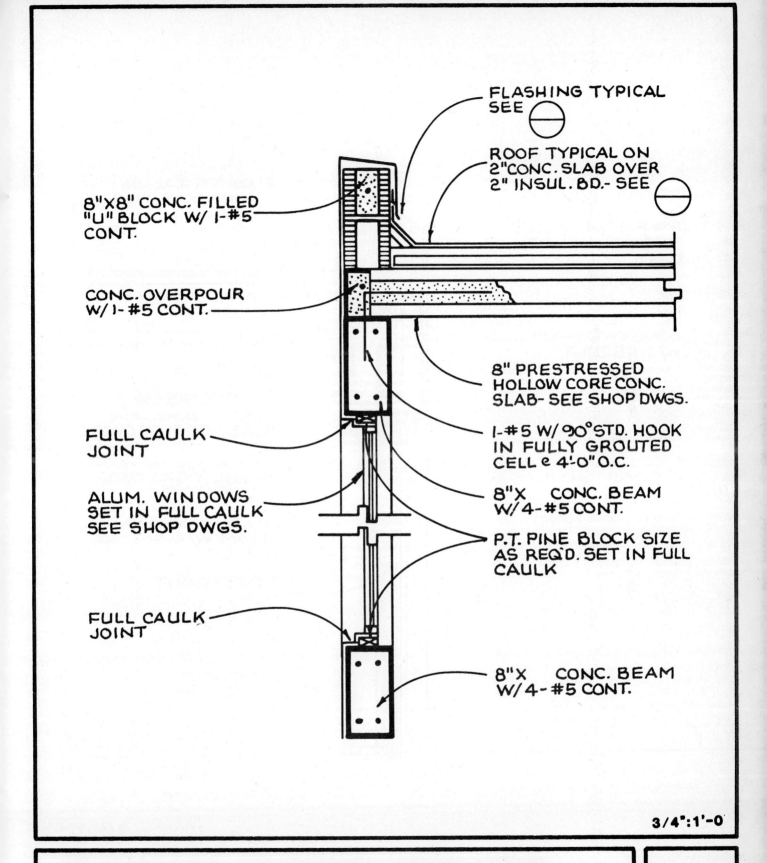

FLASHING TYPICAL SEE ⊖

ROOF TYPICAL ON 2"CONC. SLAB OVER 2" INSUL. BD.- SEE ⊖

8"X8" CONC. FILLED "U" BLOCK W/ 1-#5 CONT.

CONC. OVERPOUR W/ 1-#5 CONT.

8" PRESTRESSED HOLLOW CORE CONC. SLAB- SEE SHOP DWGS.

FULL CAULK JOINT

1-#5 W/ 90° STD. HOOK IN FULLY GROUTED CELL @ 4'-0" O.C.

ALUM. WINDOWS SET IN FULL CAULK SEE SHOP DWGS.

8"X CONC. BEAM W/4-#5 CONT.

P.T. PINE BLOCK SIZE AS REQ'D. SET IN FULL CAULK

FULL CAULK JOINT

8"X CONC. BEAM W/4-#5 CONT.

3/4":1'-0

REINFORCED CONCRETE BEAM: LEVEL HOLLOW CORE ROOF DECK: SLOPED INSUL.
END CONDITION: WINDOW

RCB 5

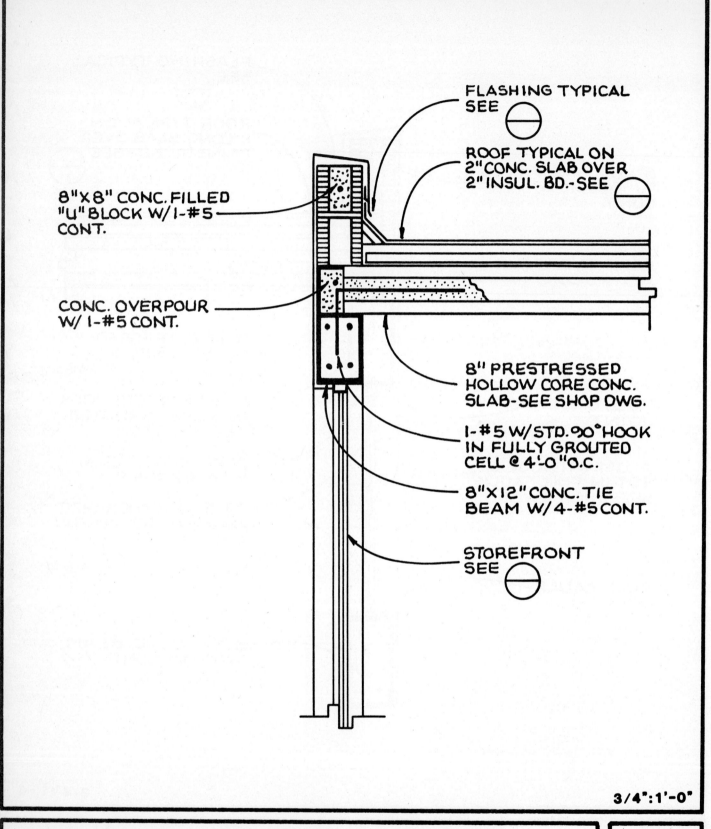

FLASHING TYPICAL SEE ⊘

ROOF TYPICAL ON 2" CONC. SLAB OVER 2" INSUL. BD.-SEE ⊘

8"X8" CONC. FILLED "U" BLOCK W/1-#5 CONT.

CONC. OVERPOUR W/ 1-#5 CONT.

8" PRESTRESSED HOLLOW CORE CONC. SLAB-SEE SHOP DWG.

1-#5 W/STD. 90° HOOK IN FULLY GROUTED CELL @ 4'-0" O.C.

8"X12" CONC. TIE BEAM W/4-#5 CONT.

STOREFRONT SEE ⊘

3/4":1'-0"

REINFORCED CONCRETE BEAM: LEVEL HOLLOW CORE ROOF DECK: SLOPED INSUL.

END CONDITION: STOREFRONT

RCB 6

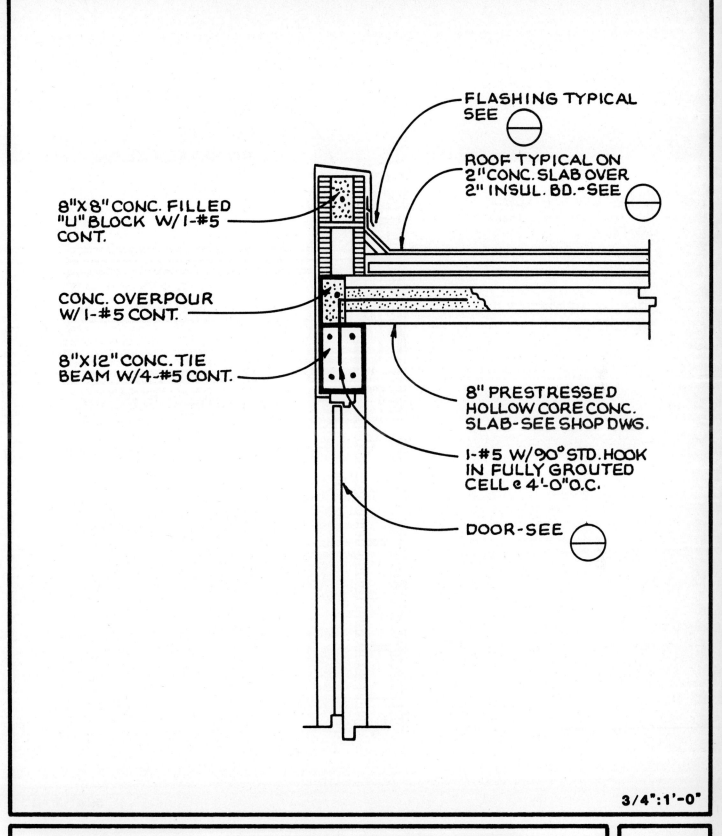

FLASHING TYPICAL
SEE ⊖

ROOF TYPICAL ON
2" CONC. SLAB OVER
2" INSUL. BD.-SEE ⊖

8"X 8" CONC. FILLED
"U" BLOCK W/I-#5
CONT.

CONC. OVERPOUR
W/I-#5 CONT.

8"X12" CONC. TIE
BEAM W/4-#5 CONT.

8" PRESTRESSED
HOLLOW CORE CONC.
SLAB- SEE SHOP DWG.

1-#5 W/90° STD. HOOK
IN FULLY GROUTED
CELL @ 4'-0" O.C.

DOOR-SEE ⊖

3/4":1'-0"

**REINFORCED CONCRETE BEAM: LEVEL
HOLLOW CORE ROOF DECK: SLOPED INSUL.**

END CONDITION: DOOR

**RCB
7**

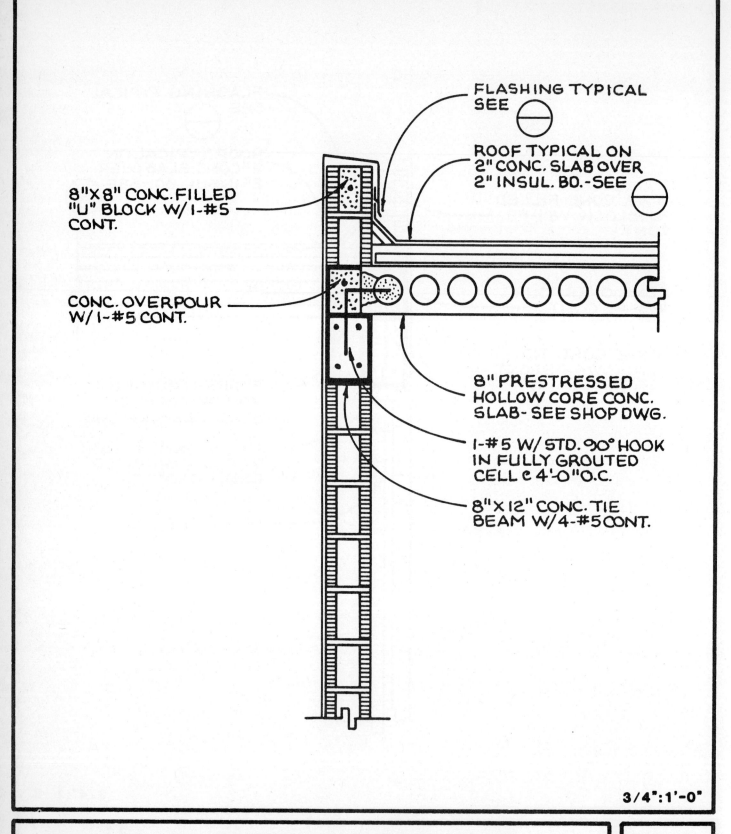

FLASHING TYPICAL
SEE ⊘

ROOF TYPICAL ON
2" CONC. SLAB OVER
2" INSUL. BD.-SEE ⊘

8"X 8" CONC. FILLED
"U" BLOCK W/ 1-#5
CONT.

CONC. OVERPOUR
W/ 1-#5 CONT.

8" PRESTRESSED
HOLLOW CORE CONC.
SLAB- SEE SHOP DWG.

1-#5 W/ STD. 90° HOOK
IN FULLY GROUTED
CELL @ 4'-0"O.C.

8"X 12" CONC. TIE
BEAM W/ 4-#5 CONT.

3/4":1'-0"

**REINFORCED CONCRETE BEAM: LEVEL
HOLLOW CORE ROOF DECK: SLOPED INSUL.**

SIDE CONDITION

RCB
8

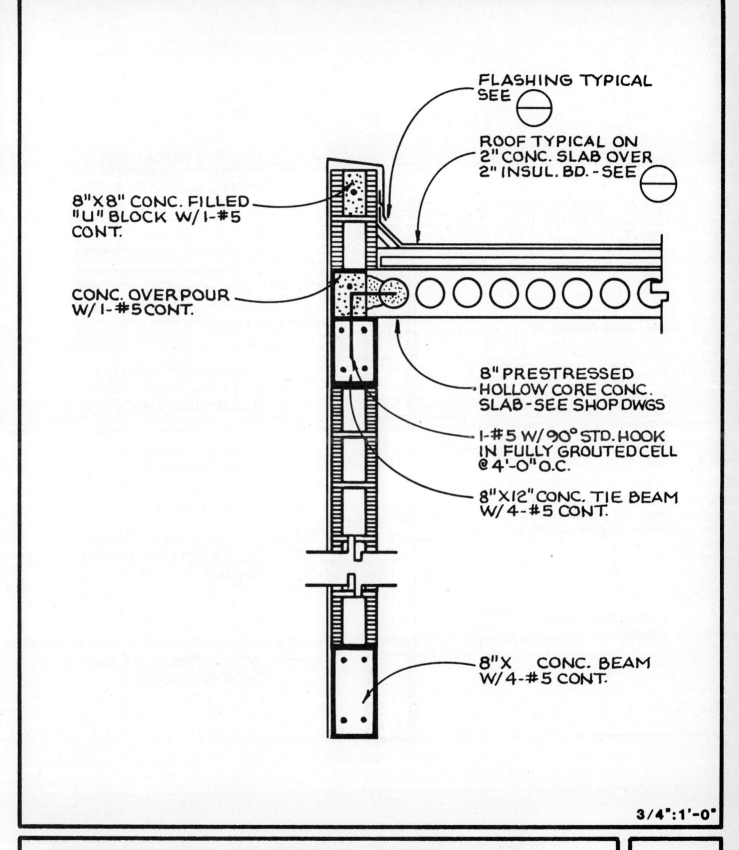

FLASHING TYPICAL
SEE ⊖

ROOF TYPICAL ON
2" CONC. SLAB OVER
2" INSUL. BD. - SEE ⊖

8"X8" CONC. FILLED
"U" BLOCK W/ I-#5
CONT.

CONC. OVERPOUR
W/ I-#5 CONT.

8" PRESTRESSED
HOLLOW CORE CONC.
SLAB - SEE SHOP DWGS

I-#5 W/ 90° STD. HOOK
IN FULLY GROUTED CELL
@ 4'-0" O.C.

8"X12" CONC. TIE BEAM
W/ 4-#5 CONT.

8"X   CONC. BEAM
W/ 4-#5 CONT.

3/4":1'-0"

REINFORCED CONCRETE BEAM: LEVEL HOLLOW CORE ROOF DECK: SLOPED INSUL.

SIDE CONDITION: LOWER BEAM

RCB 9

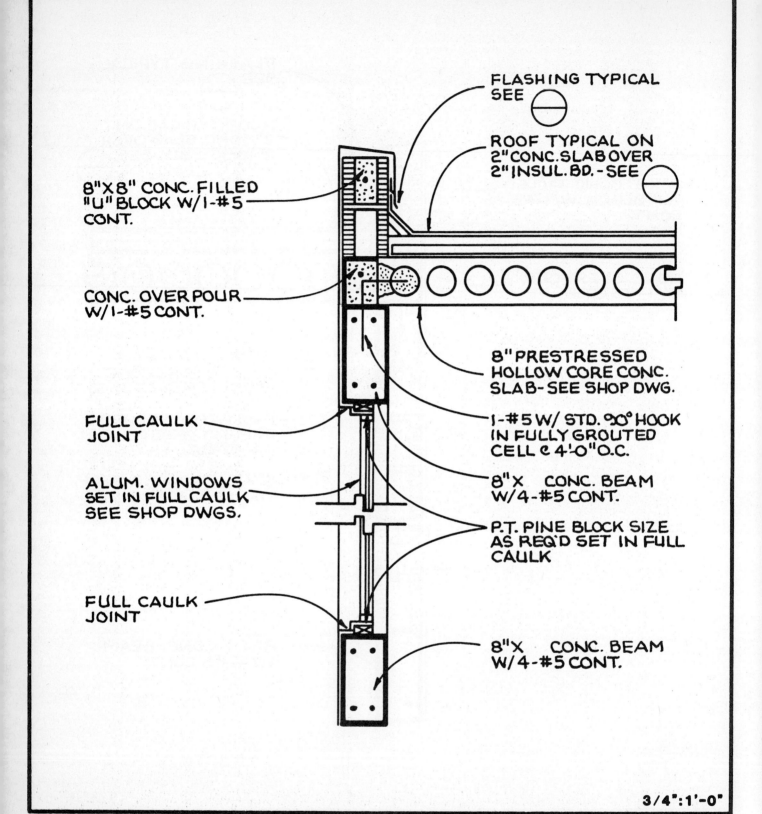

FLASHING TYPICAL SEE ⊖

ROOF TYPICAL ON 2" CONC. SLAB OVER 2" INSUL. BD. - SEE ⊖

8"X8" CONC. FILLED "U" BLOCK W/ 1-#5 CONT.

CONC. OVER POUR W/ 1-#5 CONT.

FULL CAULK JOINT

ALUM. WINDOWS SET IN FULL CAULK SEE SHOP DWGS.

FULL CAULK JOINT

8" PRESTRESSED HOLLOW CORE CONC. SLAB - SEE SHOP DWG.

1-#5 W/ STD. 90° HOOK IN FULLY GROUTED CELL @ 4'-0" O.C.

8"X CONC. BEAM W/ 4-#5 CONT.

P.T. PINE BLOCK SIZE AS REQ'D SET IN FULL CAULK

8"X CONC. BEAM W/ 4-#5 CONT.

3/4":1'-0"

REINFORCED CONCRETE BEAM: LEVEL HOLLOW CORE ROOF DECK: SLOPED INSUL.

SIDE CONDITION: WINDOW

RCB 10

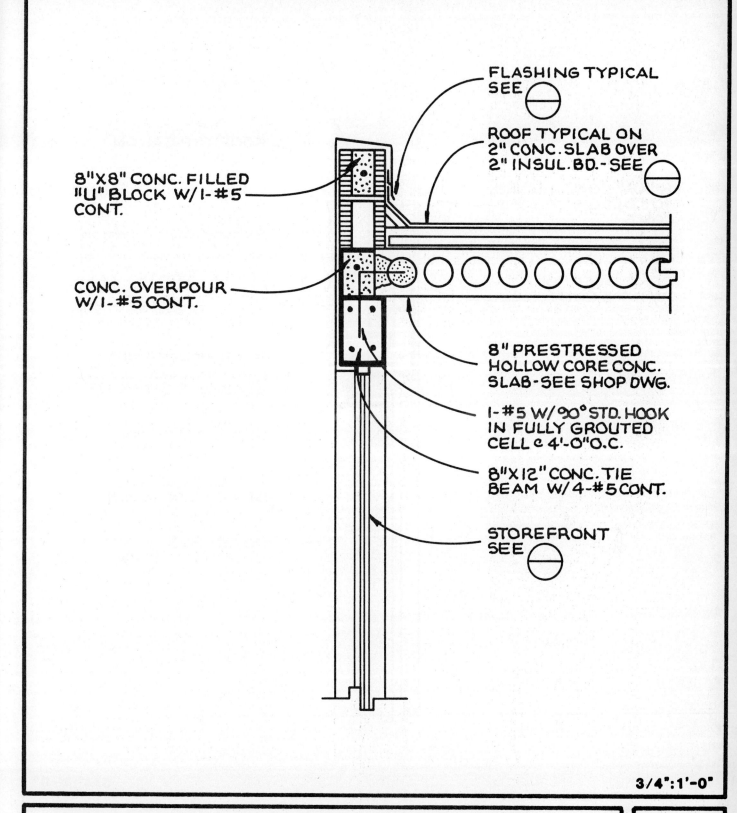

FLASHING TYPICAL
SEE ⊖

ROOF TYPICAL ON
2" CONC. SLAB OVER
2" INSUL. BD.- SEE ⊖

8"X8" CONC. FILLED
"U" BLOCK W/I-#5
CONT.

CONC. OVERPOUR
W/I-#5 CONT.

8" PRESTRESSED
HOLLOW CORE CONC.
SLAB-SEE SHOP DWG.

I-#5 W/90° STD. HOOK
IN FULLY GROUTED
CELL ℮ 4'-0"O.C.

8"X12" CONC. TIE
BEAM W/4-#5 CONT.

STOREFRONT
SEE ⊖

3/4":1'-0"

**REINFORCED CONCRETE BEAM: LEVEL
HOLLOW CORE ROOF DECK: SLOPED INSUL.**

SIDE CONDITION: STOREFRONT

**RCB
11**

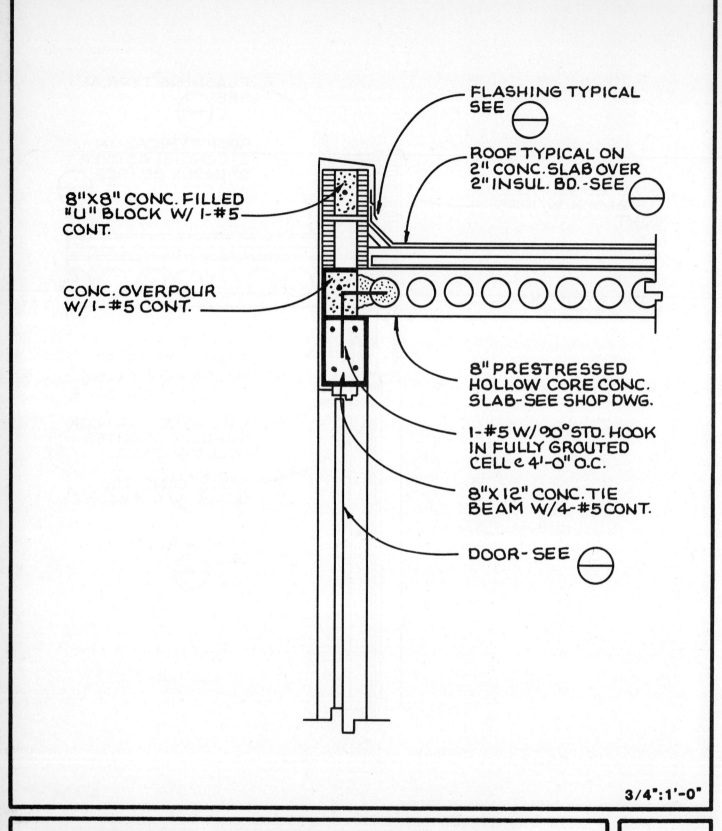

FLASHING TYPICAL SEE ⊖

ROOF TYPICAL ON 2" CONC. SLAB OVER 2" INSUL. BD. - SEE ⊖

8"X8" CONC. FILLED "U" BLOCK W/ 1-#5 CONT.

CONC. OVERPOUR W/ 1-#5 CONT.

8" PRESTRESSED HOLLOW CORE CONC. SLAB-SEE SHOP DWG.

1-#5 W/90° STD. HOOK IN FULLY GROUTED CELL @ 4'-0" O.C.

8"X12" CONC. TIE BEAM W/4-#5 CONT.

DOOR-SEE ⊖

3/4":1'-0"

REINFORCED CONCRETE BEAM: LEVEL HOLLOW CORE ROOF DECK: SLOPED INSUL.

SIDE CONDITION: DOOR

RCB 12

Standard masonry construction with sloped reinforced concrete tie beam.
Prestressed concrete twin tee roof deck with no insulation.

ARCHITECTURAL DETAILING
FOR
COMMERCIAL CONSTRUCTION

3

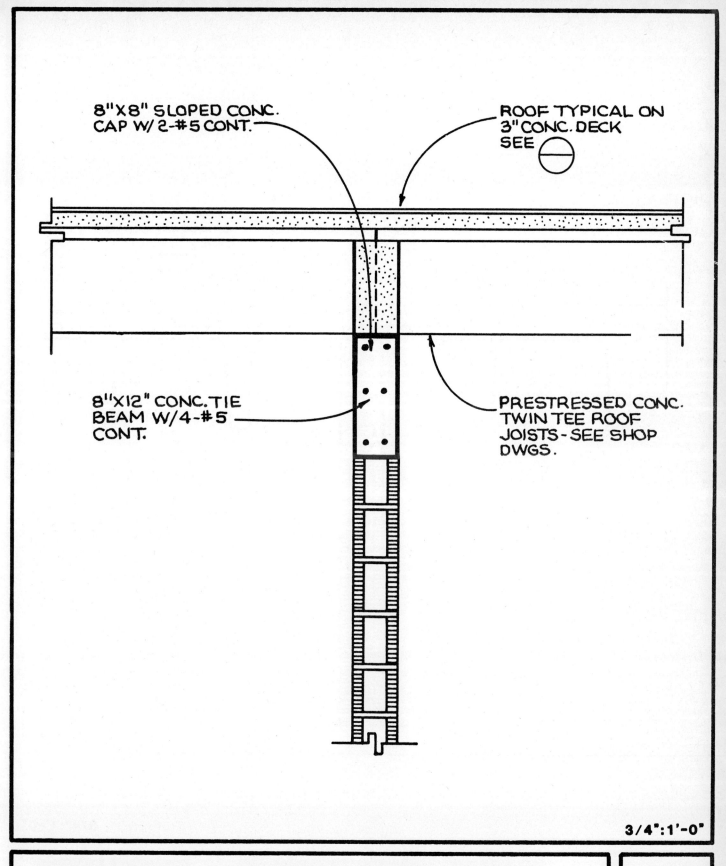

8"X8" SLOPED CONC.
CAP W/ 2-#5 CONT.

ROOF TYPICAL ON
3"CONC. DECK
SEE ⊖

8"X12" CONC. TIE
BEAM W/4-#5
CONT.

PRESTRESSED CONC.
TWIN TEE ROOF
JOISTS-SEE SHOP
DWGS.

3/4":1'-0"

**REINFORCED CONCRETE BEAM: SLOPED
TWIN TEE ROOF DECK: NO INSULATION**

INTERMEDIATE CONDITION: END

**RCC
1**

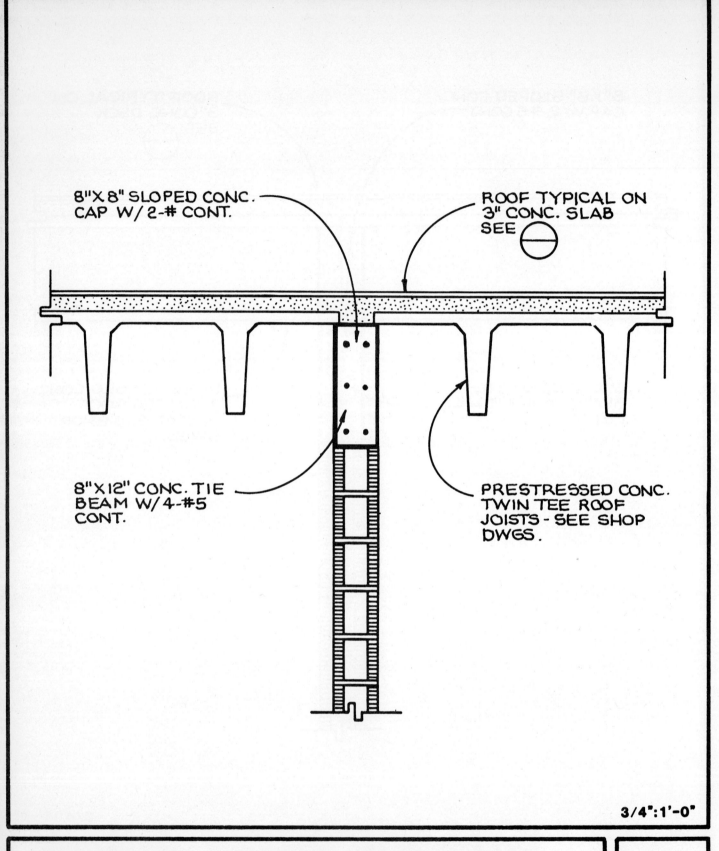

8"X 8" SLOPED CONC. CAP W/ 2-# CONT.

ROOF TYPICAL ON 3" CONC. SLAB SEE ⊖

8"X12" CONC. TIE BEAM W/ 4-#5 CONT.

PRESTRESSED CONC. TWIN TEE ROOF JOISTS - SEE SHOP DWGS.

3/4":1'-0"

REINFORCED CONCRETE BEAM: SLOPED TWIN TEE ROOF DECK: NO INSULATION

INTERMEDIATE CONDITION: SIDE

RCC 2

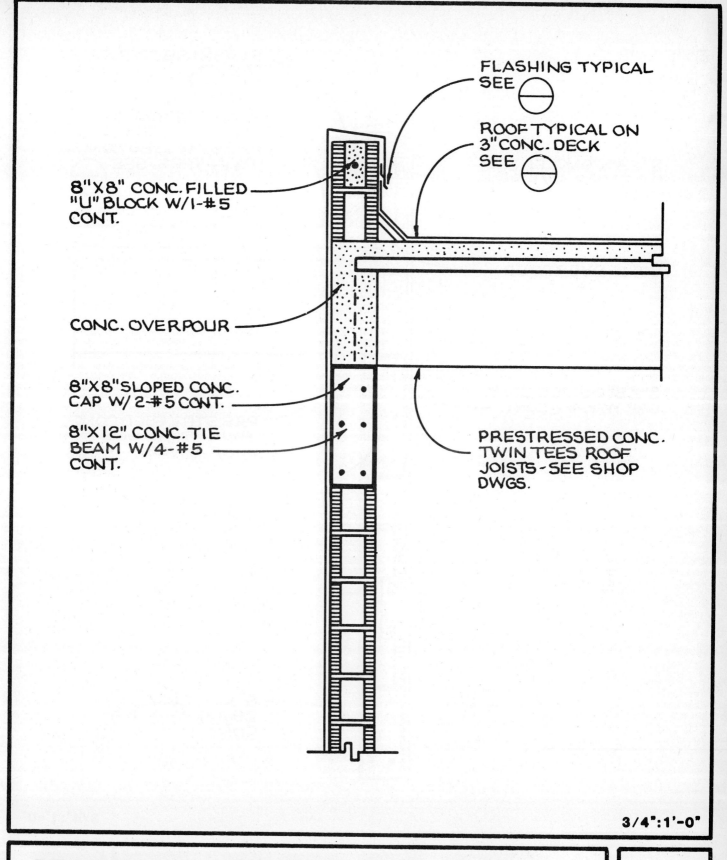

FLASHING TYPICAL SEE ⊖

ROOF TYPICAL ON 3" CONC. DECK SEE ⊖

8"X8" CONC. FILLED "U" BLOCK W/1-#5 CONT.

CONC. OVERPOUR

8"X8" SLOPED CONC. CAP W/2-#5 CONT.

8"X12" CONC. TIE BEAM W/4-#5 CONT.

PRESTRESSED CONC. TWIN TEES ROOF JOISTS - SEE SHOP DWGS.

3/4":1'-0"

REINFORCED CONCRETE BEAM: SLOPED TWIN TEE ROOF DECK: NO INSULATION

END CONDITION

RCC 3

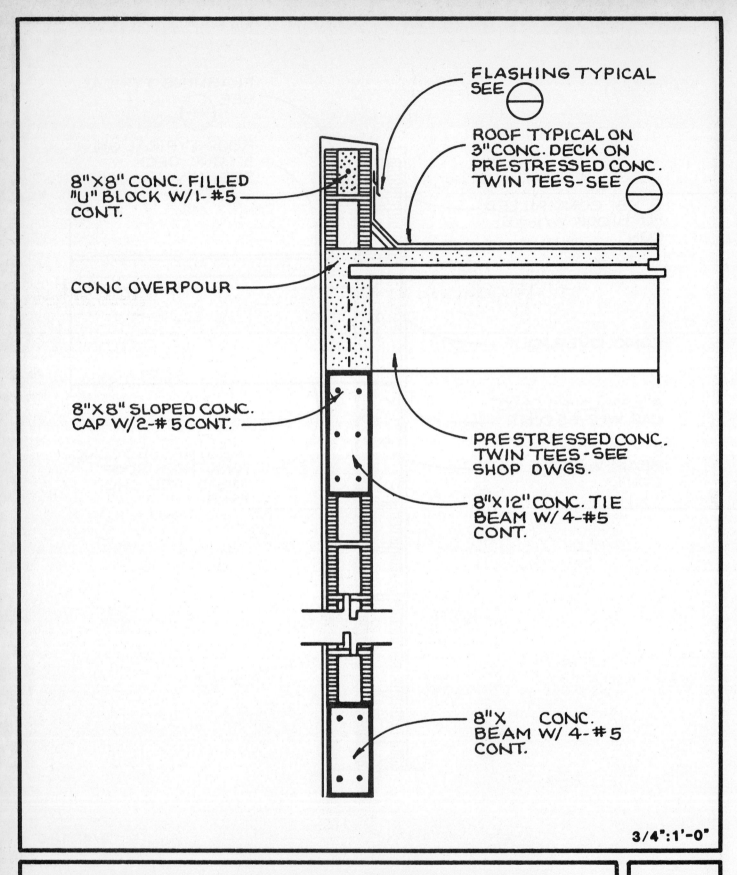

FLASHING TYPICAL SEE ⊘

ROOF TYPICAL ON 3" CONC. DECK ON PRESTRESSED CONC. TWIN TEES-SEE ⊘

8"X8" CONC. FILLED "U" BLOCK W/1-#5 CONT.

CONC OVERPOUR

8"X8" SLOPED CONC. CAP W/2-#5 CONT.

PRESTRESSED CONC. TWIN TEES-SEE SHOP DWGS.

8"X12" CONC. TIE BEAM W/ 4-#5 CONT.

8"X   CONC. BEAM W/ 4-#5 CONT.

3/4":1'-0"

REINFORCED CONCRETE BEAM: SLOPED TWIN TEE ROOF DECK: NO INSULATION

END CONDITION: LOWER BEAM

RCC 4

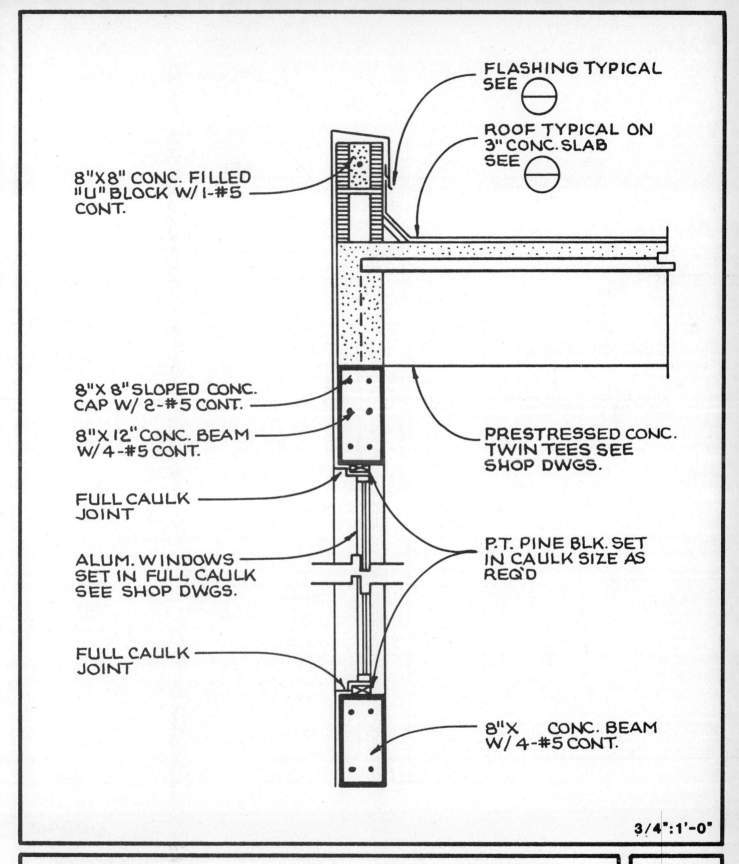

FLASHING TYPICAL
SEE ⊖

ROOF TYPICAL ON
3" CONC. SLAB
SEE ⊖

8"X8" CONC. FILLED
"U" BLOCK W/ 1-#5
CONT.

8"X 8" SLOPED CONC.
CAP W/ 2-#5 CONT.

8"X 12" CONC. BEAM
W/ 4-#5 CONT.

FULL CAULK
JOINT

ALUM. WINDOWS
SET IN FULL CAULK
SEE SHOP DWGS.

FULL CAULK
JOINT

PRESTRESSED CONC.
TWIN TEES SEE
SHOP DWGS.

P.T. PINE BLK. SET
IN CAULK SIZE AS
REQ'D

8"X   CONC. BEAM
W/ 4-#5 CONT.

3/4":1'-0"

REINFORCED CONCRETE BEAM: SLOPED
TWIN TEE ROOF DECK: NO INSULATION
END CONDITION: WINDOW

RCC
5

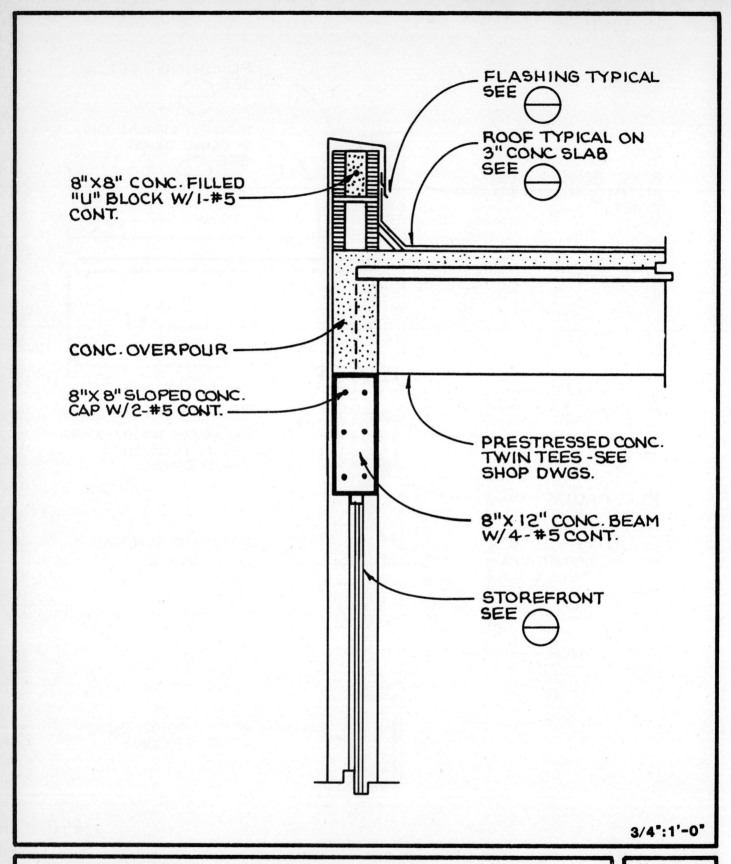

FLASHING TYPICAL SEE ⊖

ROOF TYPICAL ON 3" CONC SLAB SEE ⊖

8"X8" CONC. FILLED "U" BLOCK W/1-#5 CONT.

CONC. OVERPOUR

8"X 8" SLOPED CONC. CAP W/2-#5 CONT.

PRESTRESSED CONC. TWIN TEES -SEE SHOP DWGS.

8"X 12" CONC. BEAM W/4-#5 CONT.

STOREFRONT SEE ⊖

3/4":1'-0"

REINFORCED CONCRETE BEAM: SLOPED TWIN TEE ROOF DECK: NO INSULATION

END CONDITION: STOREFRONT

RCC 6

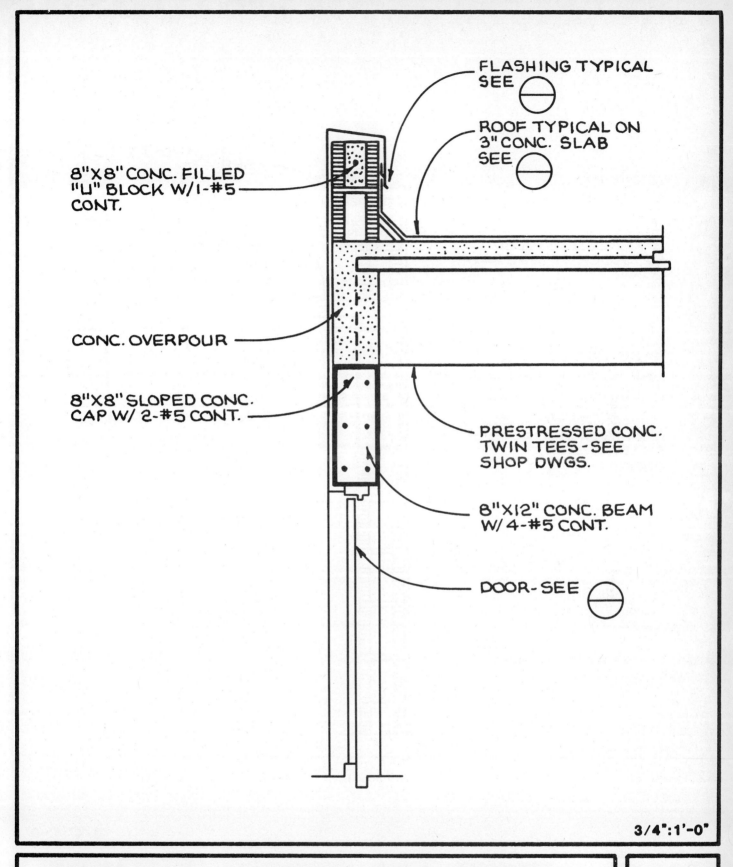

FLASHING TYPICAL
SEE ⊝

ROOF TYPICAL ON
3" CONC. SLAB
SEE ⊝

8"X8" CONC. FILLED
"U" BLOCK W/1-#5
CONT.

CONC. OVERPOUR

8"X8" SLOPED CONC.
CAP W/ 2-#5 CONT.

PRESTRESSED CONC.
TWIN TEES-SEE
SHOP DWGS.

8"X12" CONC. BEAM
W/4-#5 CONT.

DOOR-SEE ⊝

3/4":1'-0"

**REINFORCED CONCRETE BEAM: SLOPED
TWIN TEE ROOF DECK: NO INSULATION
END CONDITION: DOOR**

**RCC
7**

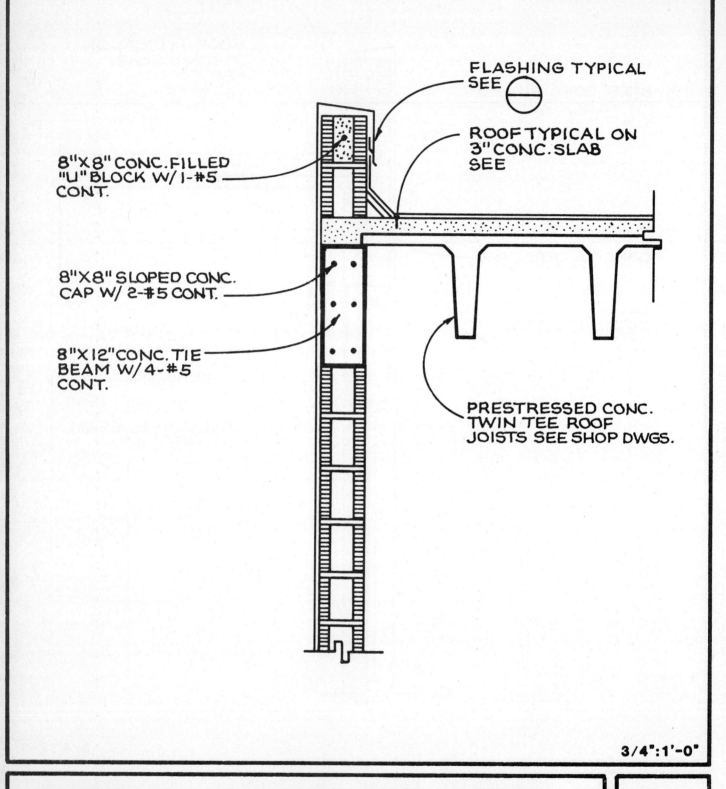

FLASHING TYPICAL
SEE ⊖

ROOF TYPICAL ON
3" CONC. SLAB
SEE

8"X 8" CONC. FILLED
"U" BLOCK W/ 1-#5
CONT.

8"X 8" SLOPED CONC.
CAP W/ 2-#5 CONT.

8"X 12" CONC. TIE
BEAM W/ 4-#5
CONT.

PRESTRESSED CONC.
TWIN TEE ROOF
JOISTS SEE SHOP DWGS.

3/4":1'-0"

REINFORCED CONCRETE BEAM: SLOPED
TWIN TEE ROOF DECK: NO INSULATION
SIDE CONDITION

RCC
8

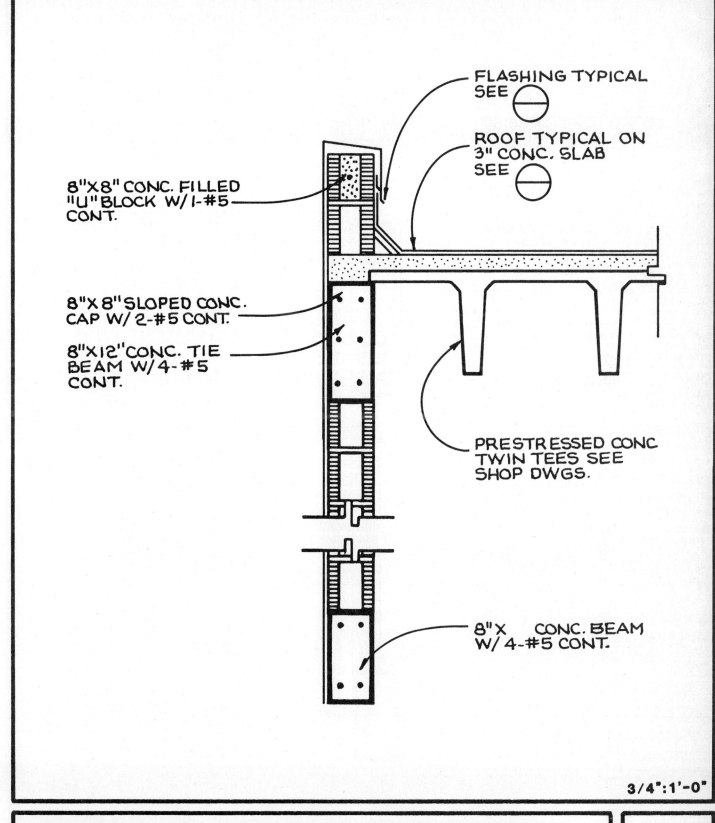

FLASHING TYPICAL
SEE ⊘

ROOF TYPICAL ON
3" CONC. SLAB
SEE ⊘

8"X8" CONC. FILLED
"U" BLOCK W/ I-#5
CONT.

8"X8" SLOPED CONC.
CAP W/ 2-#5 CONT.

8"X12" CONC. TIE
BEAM W/ 4-#5
CONT.

PRESTRESSED CONC
TWIN TEES SEE
SHOP DWGS.

8"X CONC. BEAM
W/ 4-#5 CONT.

3/4":1'-0"

**REINFORCED CONCRETE BEAM: SLOPED
TWIN TEE ROOF DECK: NO INSULATION
SIDE CONDITION: LOWER BEAM**

**RCC
9**

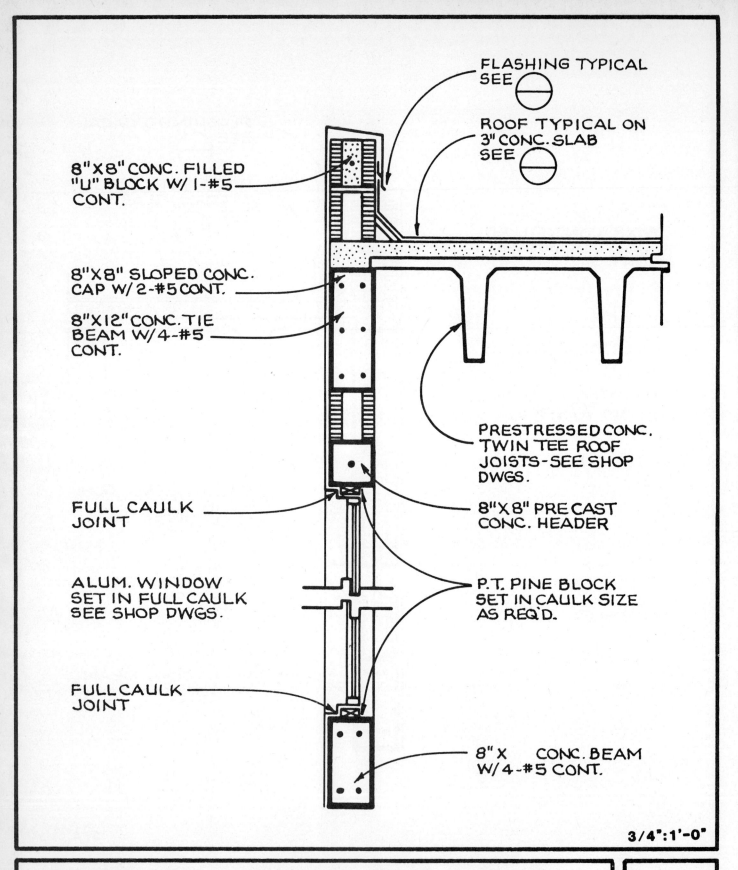

FLASHING TYPICAL
SEE ◯

ROOF TYPICAL ON
3" CONC. SLAB
SEE ◯

8"X8" CONC. FILLED
"U" BLOCK W/ 1-#5
CONT.

8"X8" SLOPED CONC.
CAP W/ 2-#5 CONT.

8"X12" CONC. TIE
BEAM W/4-#5
CONT.

PRESTRESSED CONC.
TWIN TEE ROOF
JOISTS-SEE SHOP
DWGS.

FULL CAULK
JOINT

8"X8" PRECAST
CONC. HEADER

ALUM. WINDOW
SET IN FULL CAULK
SEE SHOP DWGS.

P.T. PINE BLOCK
SET IN CAULK SIZE
AS REQ'D.

FULL CAULK
JOINT

8"X   CONC. BEAM
W/ 4-#5 CONT.

3/4":1'-0"

**REINFORCED CONCRETE BEAM: SLOPED
TWIN TEE ROOF DECK: NO INSULATION
SIDE CONDITION: WINDOW**

**RCC
10**

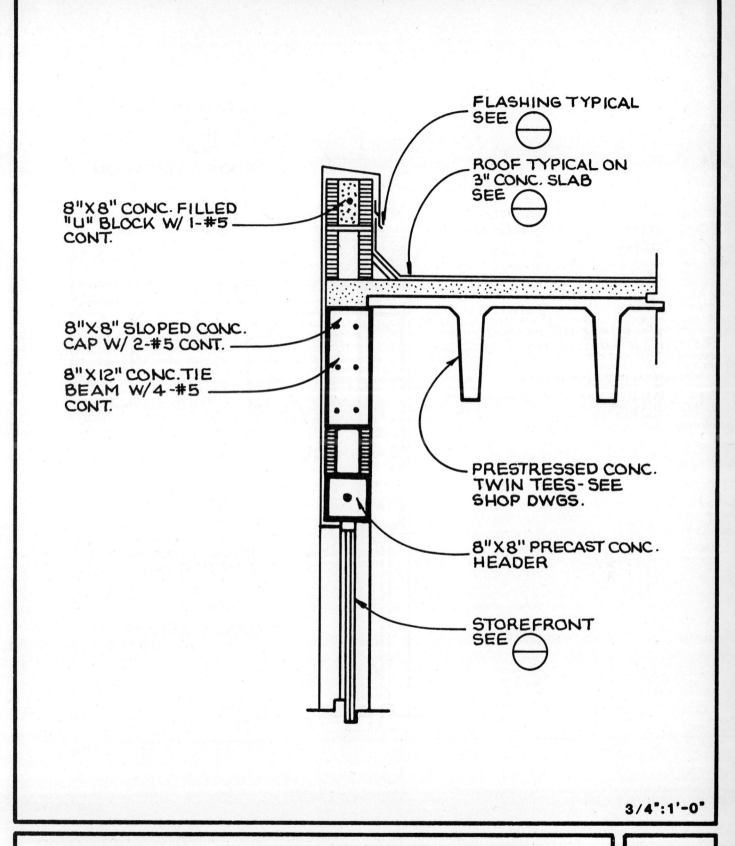

FLASHING TYPICAL
SEE ⊖

ROOF TYPICAL ON
3" CONC. SLAB
SEE ⊖

8"X8" CONC. FILLED
"U" BLOCK W/ 1-#5
CONT.

8"X8" SLOPED CONC.
CAP W/ 2-#5 CONT.

8"X12" CONC.TIE
BEAM W/4-#5
CONT.

PRESTRESSED CONC.
TWIN TEES- SEE
SHOP DWGS.

8"X8" PRECAST CONC.
HEADER

STOREFRONT
SEE ⊖

3/4":1'-0"

**REINFORCED CONCRETE BEAM: SLOPED
TWIN TEE ROOF DECK: NO INSULATION**

SIDE CONDITION: STOREFRONT

**RCC
11**

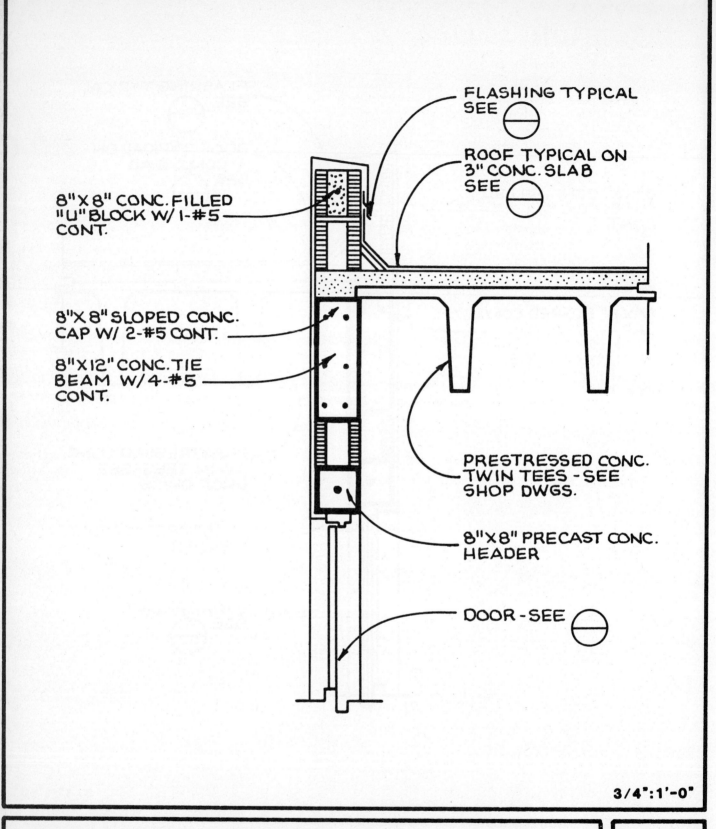

FLASHING TYPICAL
SEE ⊖

ROOF TYPICAL ON
3" CONC. SLAB
SEE ⊖

8"X 8" CONC. FILLED
"U" BLOCK W/ 1-#5
CONT.

8"X 8" SLOPED CONC.
CAP W/ 2-#5 CONT.

8"X12" CONC. TIE
BEAM W/ 4-#5
CONT.

PRESTRESSED CONC.
TWIN TEES - SEE
SHOP DWGS.

8"X 8" PRECAST CONC.
HEADER

DOOR - SEE ⊖

3/4":1'-0"

REINFORCED CONCRETE BEAM: SLOPED
TWIN TEE ROOF DECK: NO INSULATION
SIDE CONDITION: DOOR

RCC
12

SECTION 4: RC-D

Standard masonry construction with level reinforced
concrete tie beam.
Prestressed concrete twin tee roof deck with sloped insulation.

SECTION 4: RC-D

ARCHITECTURAL DETAILING
FOR
COMMERCIAL CONSTRUCTION

4

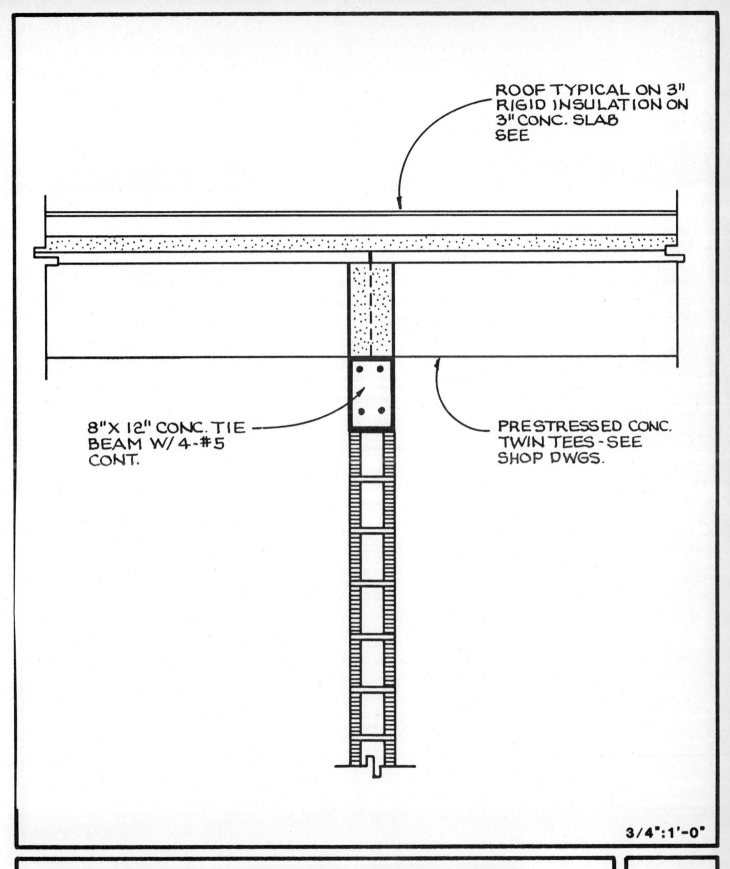

ROOF TYPICAL ON 3"
RIGID INSULATION ON
3" CONC. SLAB
SEE

8"X 12" CONC. TIE
BEAM W/ 4 -#5
CONT.

PRESTRESSED CONC.
TWIN TEES - SEE
SHOP DWGS.

3/4":1'-0"

REINFORCED CONCRETE BEAM: LEVEL
TWIN TEE ROOF DECK: SLOPED INSUL.

INTERMEDIATE CONDITION: END

RCD
1

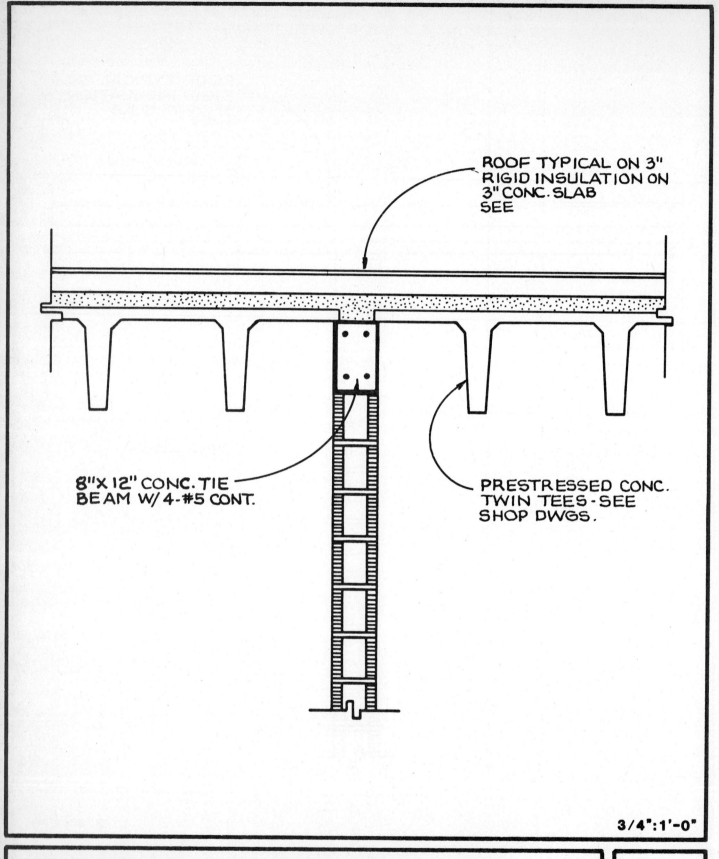

ROOF TYPICAL ON 3"
RIGID INSULATION ON
3" CONC. SLAB
SEE

8"X 12" CONC. TIE
BEAM W/ 4-#5 CONT.

PRESTRESSED CONC.
TWIN TEES - SEE
SHOP DWGS.

3/4":1'-0"

**REINFORCED CONCRETE BEAM: LEVEL
TWIN TEE ROOF DECK: SLOPED INSUL.**

INTERMEDIATE CONDITION: SIDE

**RCD
2**

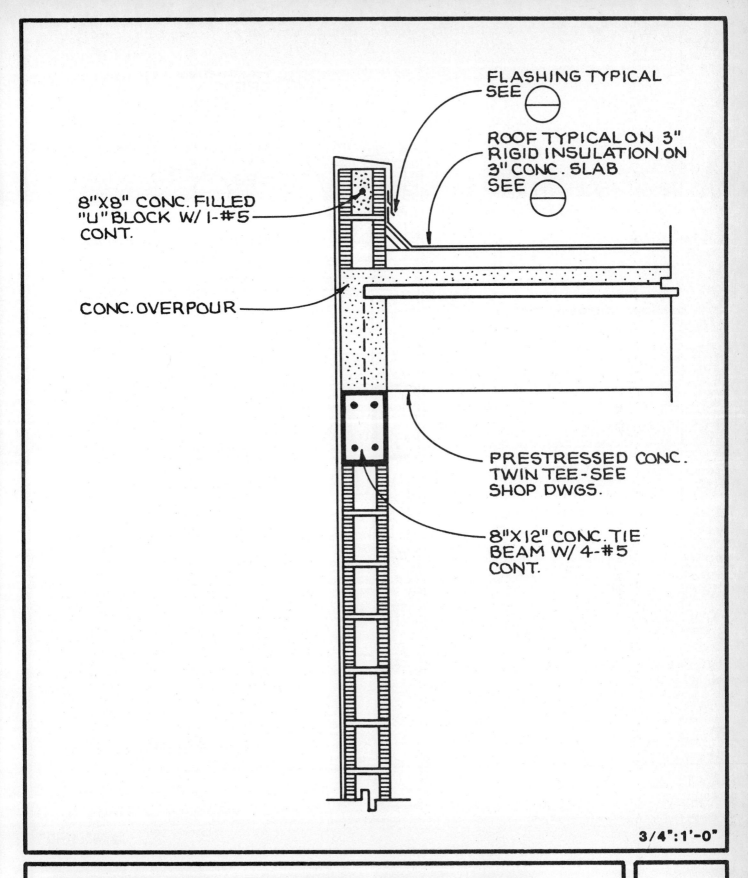

FLASHING TYPICAL
SEE ⊖

ROOF TYPICAL ON 3"
RIGID INSULATION ON
3" CONC. SLAB
SEE ⊖

8"X8" CONC. FILLED
"U" BLOCK W/ 1-#5
CONT.

CONC. OVERPOUR

PRESTRESSED CONC.
TWIN TEE - SEE
SHOP DWGS.

8"X12" CONC. TIE
BEAM W/ 4-#5
CONT.

3/4":1'-0"

REINFORCED CONCRETE BEAM: LEVEL
TWIN TEE ROOF DECK: SLOPED INSUL.

END CONDITION

**RCD
3**

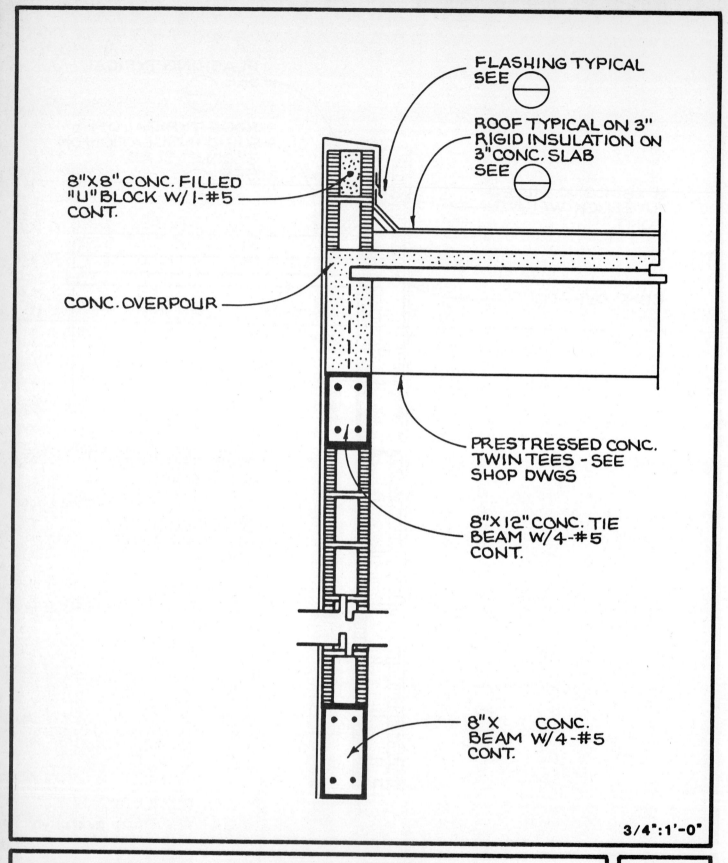

FLASHING TYPICAL
SEE ◯

ROOF TYPICAL ON 3"
RIGID INSULATION ON
3" CONC. SLAB
SEE ◯

8"X8" CONC. FILLED
"U" BLOCK W/1-#5
CONT.

CONC. OVERPOUR

PRESTRESSED CONC.
TWIN TEES - SEE
SHOP DWGS

8"X12" CONC. TIE
BEAM W/4-#5
CONT.

8"X   CONC.
BEAM W/4-#5
CONT.

3/4":1'-0"

**REINFORCED CONCRETE BEAM: LEVEL
TWIN TEE ROOF DECK: SLOPED INSUL.**

END CONDITION: LOWER BEAM

**RCD
4**

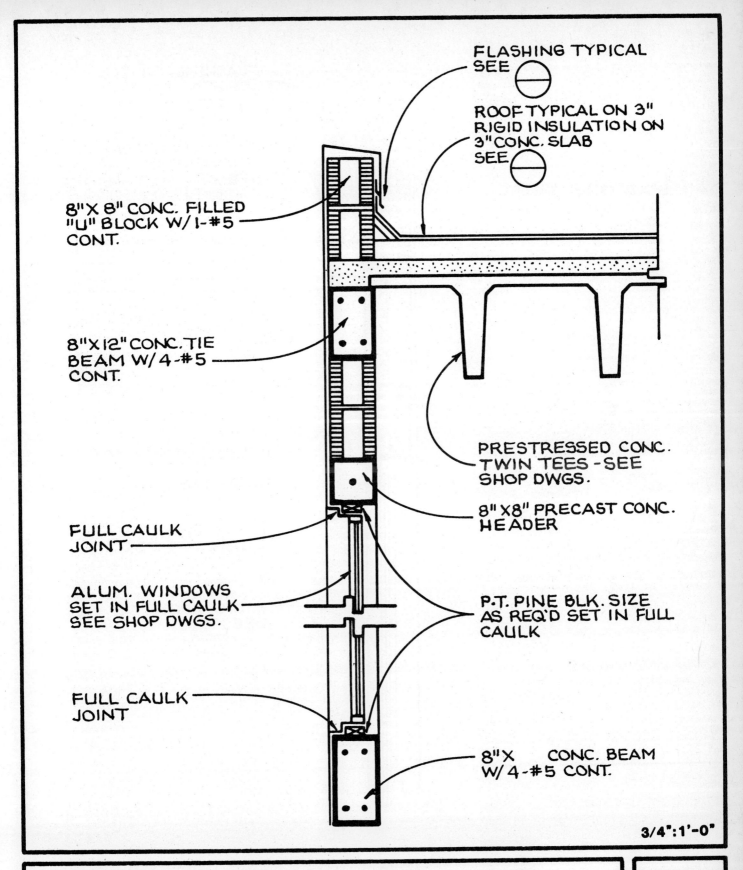

FLASHING TYPICAL SEE ⊘

ROOF TYPICAL ON 3" RIGID INSULATION ON 3" CONC. SLAB SEE ⊘

8"X 8" CONC. FILLED "U" BLOCK W/ 1-#5 CONT.

8"X12" CONC. TIE BEAM W/4-#5 CONT.

PRESTRESSED CONC. TWIN TEES - SEE SHOP DWGS.

FULL CAULK JOINT

8" X8" PRECAST CONC. HEADER

ALUM. WINDOWS SET IN FULL CAULK SEE SHOP DWGS.

P.T. PINE BLK. SIZE AS REQ'D SET IN FULL CAULK

FULL CAULK JOINT

8"X   CONC. BEAM W/ 4-#5 CONT.

3/4":1'-0"

REINFORCED CONCRETE BEAM: LEVEL TWIN TEE ROOF DECK: SLOPED INSUL.

END CONDITION: WINDOW

RCD 5

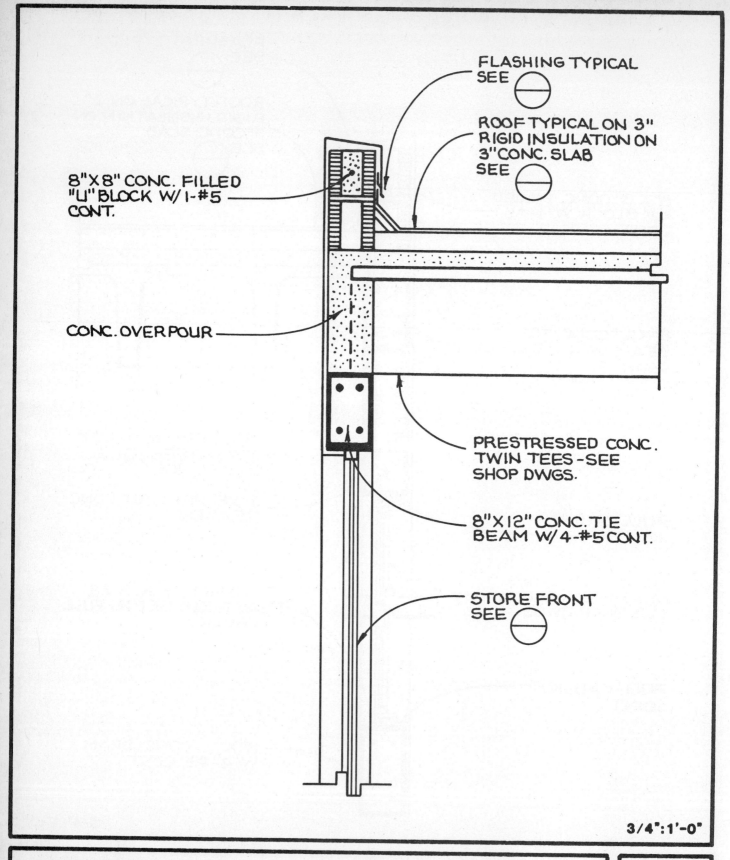

FLASHING TYPICAL
SEE ◯

ROOF TYPICAL ON 3"
RIGID INSULATION ON
3" CONC. SLAB
SEE ◯

8"X8" CONC. FILLED
"U" BLOCK W/ I - #5
CONT.

CONC. OVERPOUR

PRESTRESSED CONC.
TWIN TEES - SEE
SHOP DWGS.

8"X12" CONC. TIE
BEAM W/ 4 - #5 CONT.

STORE FRONT
SEE ◯

3/4":1'-0"

REINFORCED CONCRETE BEAM: LEVEL
TWIN TEE ROOF DECK: SLOPED INSUL.

END CONDITION: STOREFRONT

RCD
6

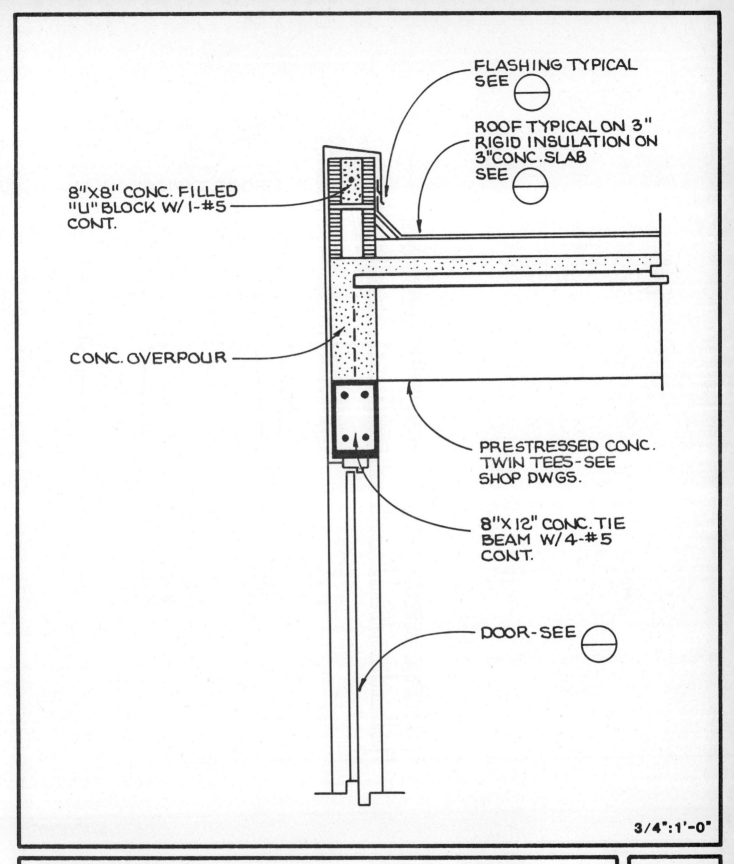

FLASHING TYPICAL
SEE ⊖

ROOF TYPICAL ON 3"
RIGID INSULATION ON
3"CONC.SLAB
SEE ⊖

8"X8" CONC. FILLED
"U" BLOCK W/ 1-#5
CONT.

CONC. OVERPOUR

PRESTRESSED CONC.
TWIN TEES-SEE
SHOP DWGS.

8"X12" CONC. TIE
BEAM W/ 4-#5
CONT.

DOOR-SEE ⊖

3/4":1'-0"

**REINFORCED CONCRETE BEAM: LEVEL
TWIN TEE ROOF DECK: SLOPED INSUL.
END CONDITION: DOOR**

**RCD
7**

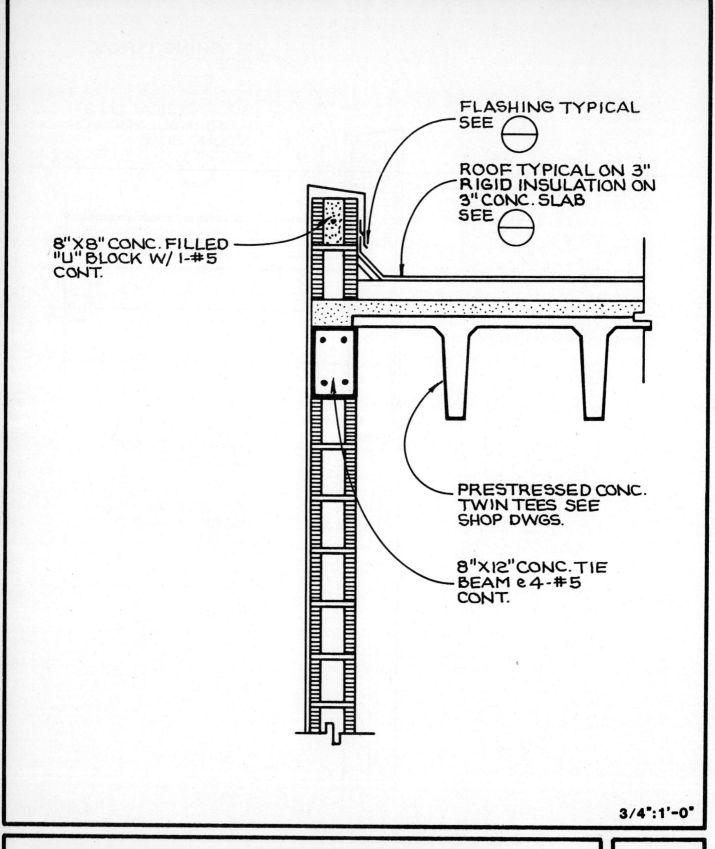

FLASHING TYPICAL
SEE ⊖

ROOF TYPICAL ON 3"
RIGID INSULATION ON
3" CONC. SLAB
SEE ⊖

8"X8" CONC. FILLED
"U" BLOCK W/ 1-#5
CONT.

PRESTRESSED CONC.
TWIN TEES SEE
SHOP DWGS.

8"X12" CONC. TIE
BEAM e 4-#5
CONT.

3/4":1'-0"

**REINFORCED CONCRETE BEAM: LEVEL
TWIN TEE ROOF DECK: SLOPED INSUL.**

SIDE CONDITION

**RCD
8**

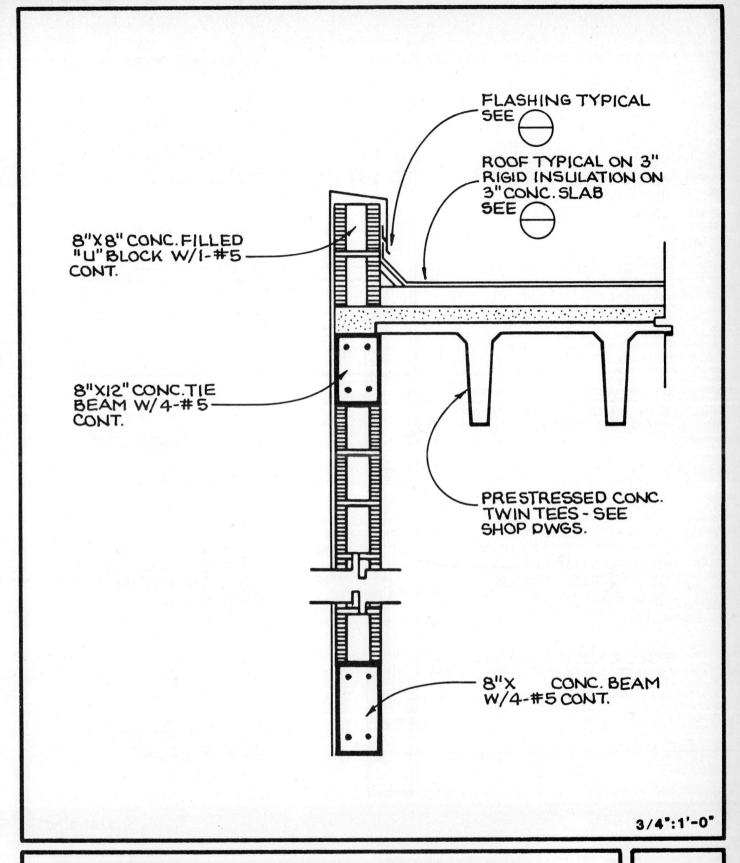

FLASHING TYPICAL
SEE ⊖

ROOF TYPICAL ON 3"
RIGID INSULATION ON
3" CONC. SLAB
SEE ⊖

8"X8" CONC.FILLED
"U" BLOCK W/1-#5
CONT.

8"X12" CONC.TIE
BEAM W/4-#5
CONT.

PRESTRESSED CONC.
TWIN TEES - SEE
SHOP DWGS.

8"X   CONC. BEAM
W/4-#5 CONT.

3/4":1'-0"

**REINFORCED CONCRETE BEAM: LEVEL
TWIN TEE ROOF DECK: SLOPED INSUL.**

SIDE CONDITION: LOWER BEAM

**RCD
9**

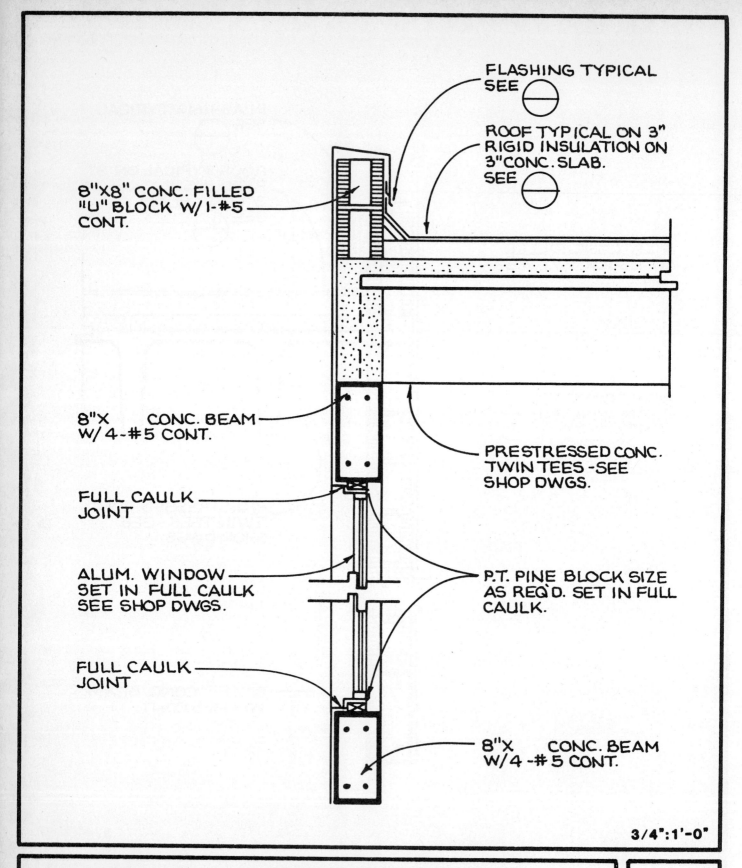

FLASHING TYPICAL
SEE ⊖

ROOF TYPICAL ON 3"
RIGID INSULATION ON
3" CONC. SLAB.
SEE ⊖

8"X8" CONC. FILLED
"U" BLOCK W/ 1-#5
CONT.

8"X   CONC. BEAM
W/ 4-#5 CONT.

FULL CAULK
JOINT

ALUM. WINDOW
SET IN FULL CAULK
SEE SHOP DWGS.

FULL CAULK
JOINT

PRESTRESSED CONC.
TWIN TEES -SEE
SHOP DWGS.

P.T. PINE BLOCK SIZE
AS REQ'D. SET IN FULL
CAULK.

8"X   CONC. BEAM
W/ 4-#5 CONT.

3/4":1'-0"

| REINFORCED CONCRETE BEAM: LEVEL TWIN TEE ROOF DECK: SLOPED INSUL. SIDE CONDITION: WINDOW | RCD 10 |

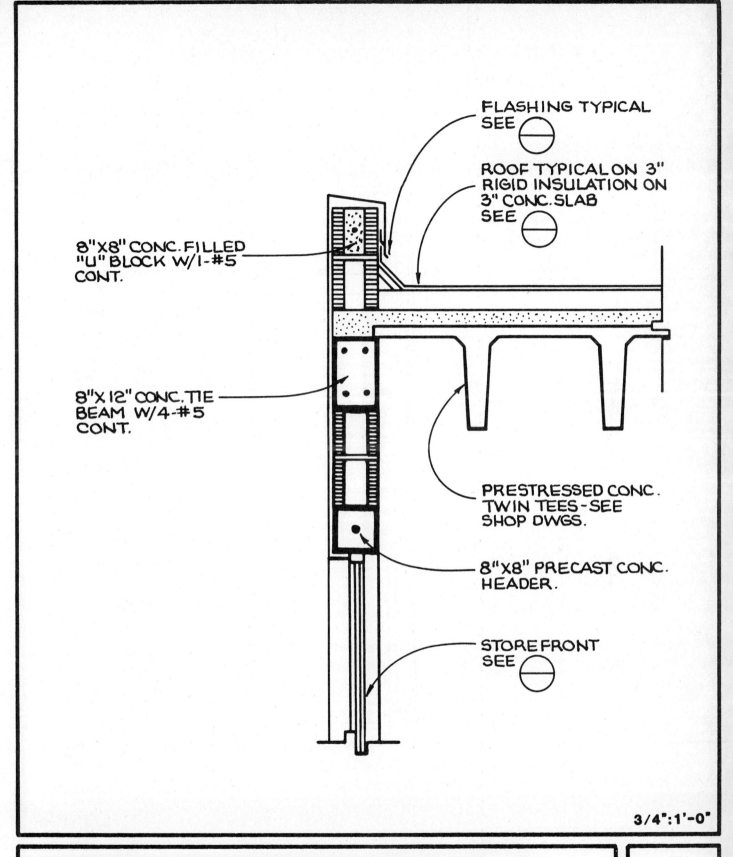

FLASHING TYPICAL
SEE ⊖

ROOF TYPICAL ON 3"
RIGID INSULATION ON
3" CONC. SLAB
SEE ⊖

8"X8" CONC. FILLED
"U" BLOCK W/1-#5
CONT.

8"X 12" CONC. TIE
BEAM W/4-#5
CONT.

PRESTRESSED CONC.
TWIN TEES - SEE
SHOP DWGS.

8"X8" PRECAST CONC.
HEADER.

STOREFRONT
SEE ⊖

3/4":1'-0"

**REINFORCED CONCRETE BEAM: LEVEL
TWIN TEE ROOF DECK: SLOPED INSUL.**

SIDE CONDITION: STOREFRONT

**RCD
11**

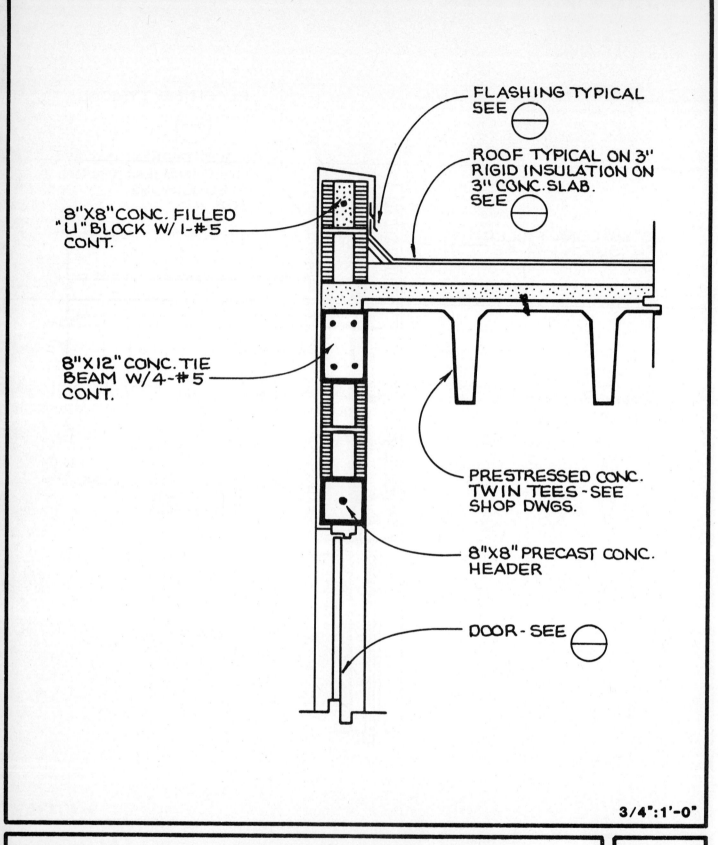

FLASHING TYPICAL
SEE ⊖

ROOF TYPICAL ON 3"
RIGID INSULATION ON
3" CONC. SLAB.
SEE ⊖

8"X8" CONC. FILLED
"U" BLOCK W/ 1-#5
CONT.

8"X12" CONC. TIE
BEAM W/4-#5
CONT.

PRESTRESSED CONC.
TWIN TEES - SEE
SHOP DWGS.

8"X8" PRECAST CONC.
HEADER

DOOR - SEE ⊖

3/4":1'-0"

**REINFORCED CONCRETE BEAM: LEVEL
TWIN TEE ROOF DECK: SLOPED INSUL.**

SIDE CONDITION: DOOR

**RCD
12**

SECTION 5: RC—E

Standard masonry construction with level reinforced
concrete tie beam.
Steel joist and metal roof deck with no insulation.

RCE 1   Intermediate condition: End
RCE 2   End condition
RCE 3   End condition with lower beam
RCE 4   End condition with window
RCE 5   End condition with storefront
RCE 6   End condition with door
RCE 7   Side condition
RCE 8   Side condition with lower beam
RCE 9   Side condition with window
RCE 10 Side condition with storefront
RCE 11 Side condition with door

ARCHITECTURAL DETAILING
FOR
COMMERCIAL CONSTRUCTION

5

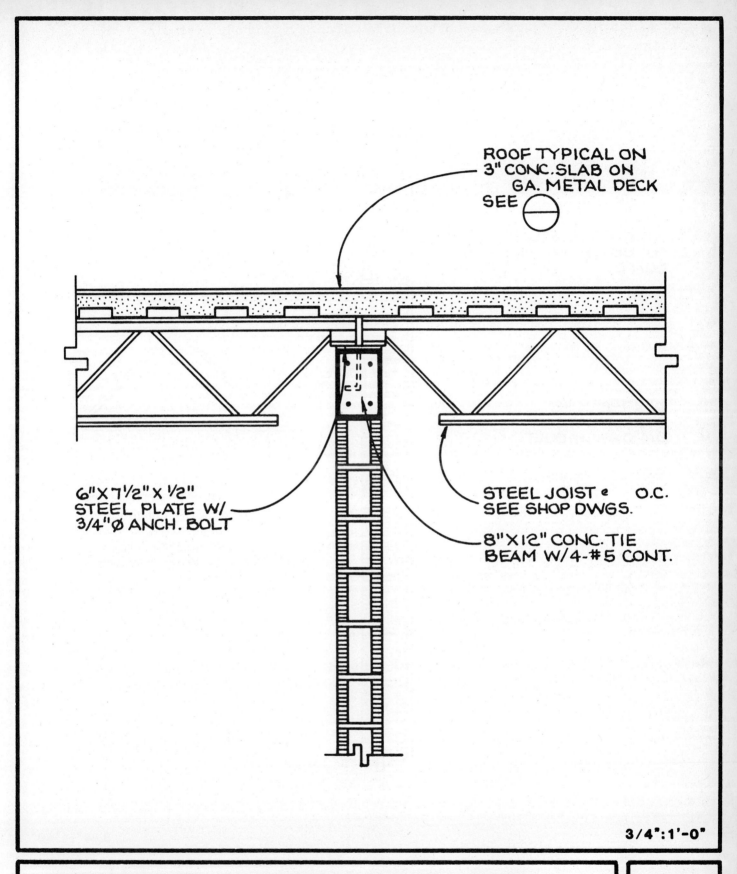

ROOF TYPICAL ON
3" CONC. SLAB ON
GA. METAL DECK
SEE ⊖

6"X 7½"X ½"
STEEL PLATE W/
3/4"Ø ANCH. BOLT

STEEL JOIST e   O.C.
SEE SHOP DWGS.

8"X 12" CONC. TIE
BEAM W/4-#5 CONT.

3/4":1'-0"

**REINFORCED CONCRETE BEAM: LEVEL
STL JOIST & MET ROOF DECK: NO INSULATION

INTERMEDIATE CONDITION: END**

**RCE
1**

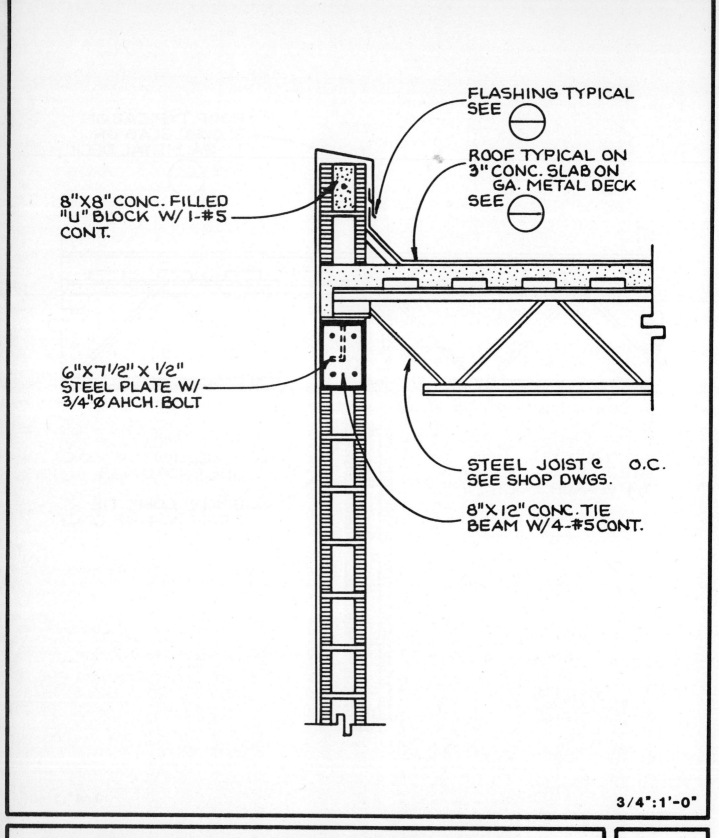

FLASHING TYPICAL
SEE ⊖

ROOF TYPICAL ON
3" CONC. SLAB ON
GA. METAL DECK
SEE ⊖

8"X8" CONC. FILLED
"U" BLOCK W/ 1-#5
CONT.

6"X7½" X ½"
STEEL PLATE W/
¾"Ø AHCH. BOLT

STEEL JOIST @   O.C.
SEE SHOP DWGS.

8"X12" CONC. TIE
BEAM W/ 4-#5 CONT.

3/4":1'-0"

**REINFORCED CONCRETE BEAM: LEVEL
STL JOIST & MET ROOF DECK: NO INSULATION.
END CONDITION**

**RCE
2**

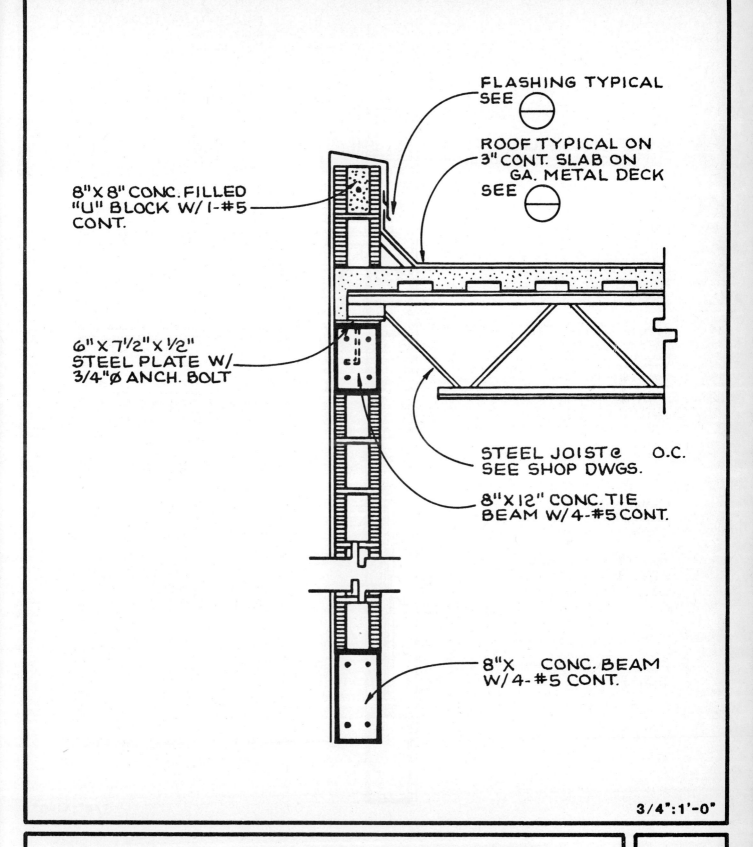

FLASHING TYPICAL
SEE ⊖

ROOF TYPICAL ON
3" CONT. SLAB ON
GA. METAL DECK
SEE ⊖

8" X 8" CONC. FILLED
"U" BLOCK W/ 1-#5
CONT.

6" X 7½" X ½"
STEEL PLATE W/
¾" ∅ ANCH. BOLT

STEEL JOIST @   O.C.
SEE SHOP DWGS.

8" X 12" CONC. TIE
BEAM W/ 4-#5 CONT.

8" X   CONC. BEAM
W/ 4-#5 CONT.

3/4":1'-0"

REINFORCED CONCRETE BEAM: LEVEL
STL JOIST & MET ROOF DECK: NO INSULATION
END CONDITION: LOWER BEAM

**RCE
3**

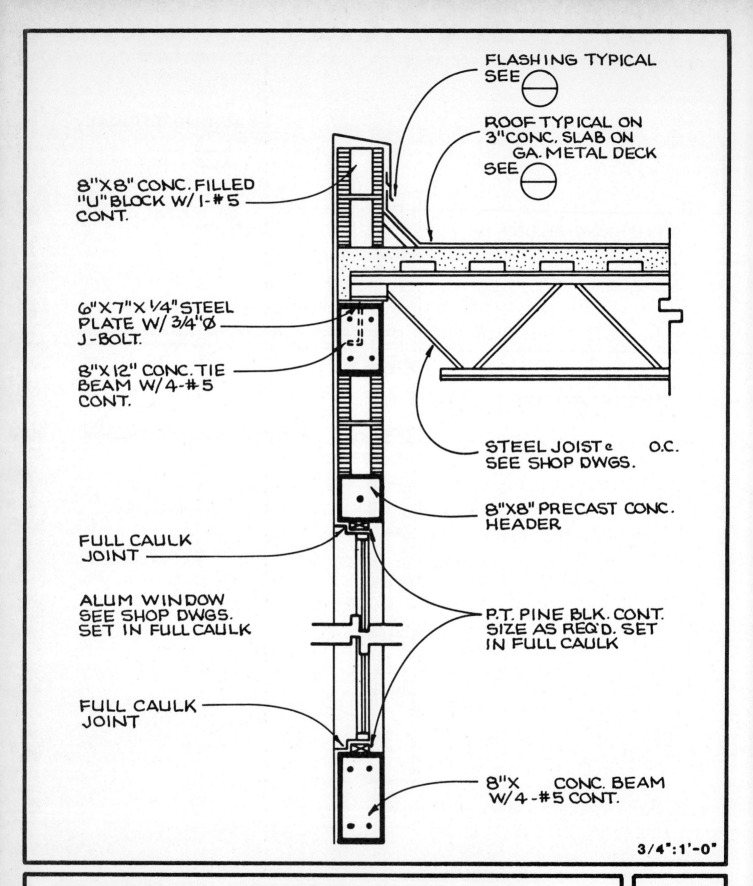

FLASHING TYPICAL
SEE ⊖

ROOF TYPICAL ON
3" CONC. SLAB ON
GA. METAL DECK
SEE ⊖

8"X8" CONC. FILLED
"U" BLOCK W/ 1-#5
CONT.

6"X7"X ¼" STEEL
PLATE W/ ¾"⌀
J-BOLT.

8"X 12" CONC. TIE
BEAM W/ 4-#5
CONT.

STEEL JOIST ℮   O.C.
SEE SHOP DWGS.

8"X8" PRECAST CONC.
HEADER

FULL CAULK
JOINT

ALUM WINDOW
SEE SHOP DWGS.
SET IN FULL CAULK

P.T. PINE BLK. CONT.
SIZE AS REQ'D. SET
IN FULL CAULK

FULL CAULK
JOINT

8"X   CONC. BEAM
W/ 4 -#5 CONT.

3/4":1'-0"

REINFORCED CONCRETE BEAM: LEVEL
STL JOIST & MET ROOF DECK: NO INSULATION
END CONDITION: WINDOW

RCE 4

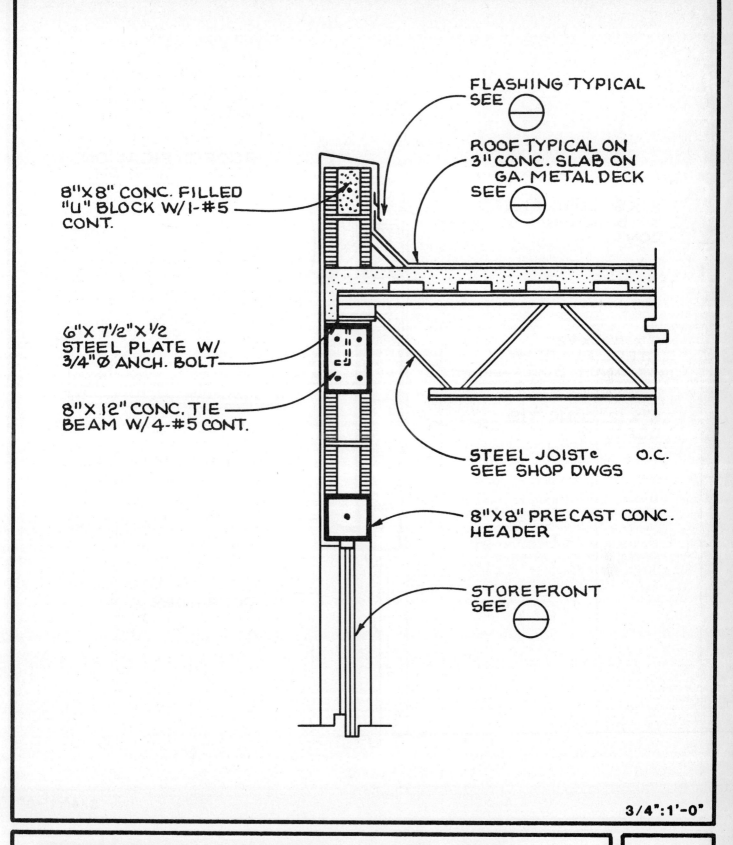

FLASHING TYPICAL
SEE ⊖

ROOF TYPICAL ON
3" CONC. SLAB ON
GA. METAL DECK
SEE ⊖

8"X8" CONC. FILLED
"U" BLOCK W/1-#5
CONT.

6"X 7½"X ½
STEEL PLATE W/
3/4"Ø ANCH. BOLT

8"X12" CONC. TIE
BEAM W/4-#5 CONT.

STEEL JOISTᵉ   O.C.
SEE SHOP DWGS

8"X8" PRECAST CONC.
HEADER

STOREFRONT
SEE ⊖

3/4":1'-0"

REINFORCED CONCRETE BEAM: LEVEL
STL JOIST & MET ROOF DECK: NO INSULATION
END CONDITION: STOREFRONT

RCE
5

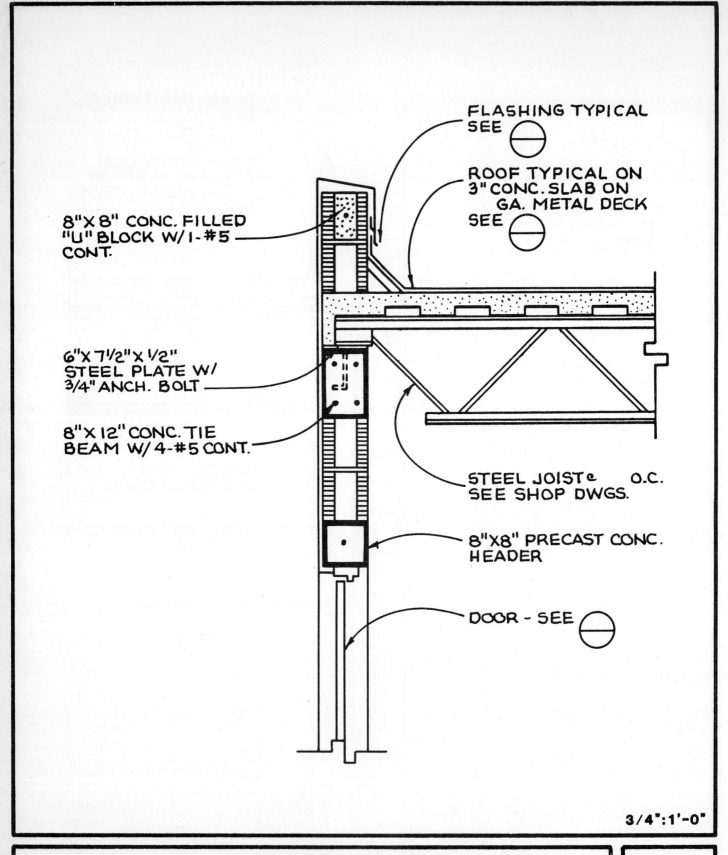

FLASHING TYPICAL
SEE ⊖

ROOF TYPICAL ON
3" CONC. SLAB ON
GA. METAL DECK
SEE ⊖

8"X 8" CONC. FILLED
"U" BLOCK W/ 1-#5
CONT.

6"X 7½"X ½"
STEEL PLATE W/
¾"ANCH. BOLT

8"X 12" CONC. TIE
BEAM W/ 4-#5 CONT.

STEEL JOIST @   O.C.
SEE SHOP DWGS.

8"X 8" PRECAST CONC.
HEADER

DOOR - SEE ⊖

3/4":1'-0"

**REINFORCED CONCRETE BEAM: LEVEL
STL JOIST & MET ROOF DECK: NO INSULATION
END CONDITION: DOOR**

**RCE
6**

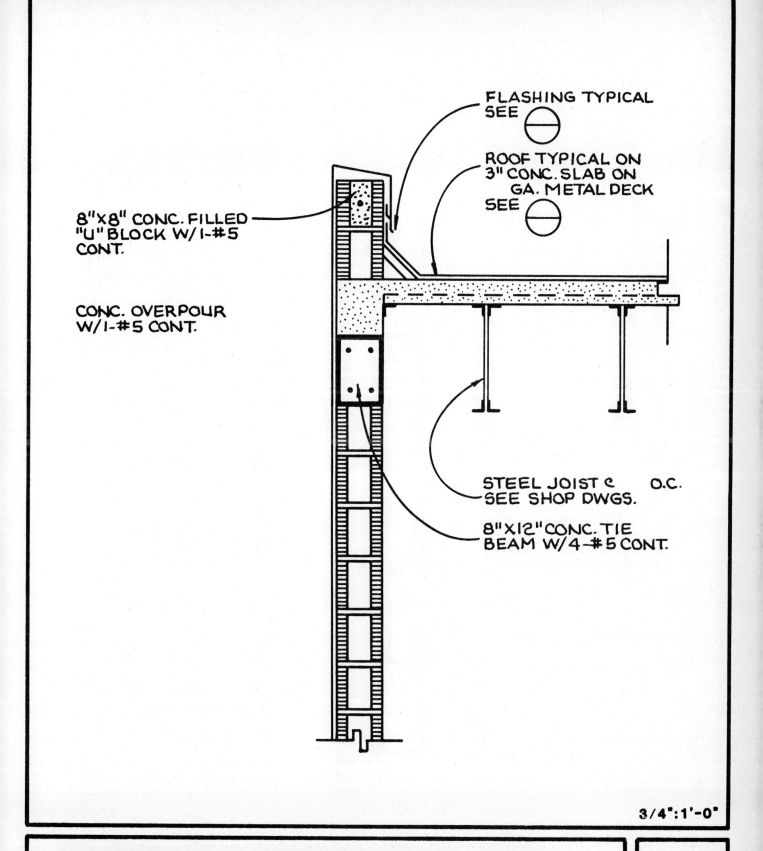

FLASHING TYPICAL
SEE ⊘

ROOF TYPICAL ON
3" CONC. SLAB ON
GA. METAL DECK
SEE ⊘

8"X8" CONC. FILLED
"U" BLOCK W/I-#5
CONT.

CONC. OVERPOUR
W/I-#5 CONT.

STEEL JOIST ℄   O.C.
SEE SHOP DWGS.

8"X12" CONC. TIE
BEAM W/4-#5 CONT.

3/4":1'-0"

REINFORCED CONCRETE BEAM: LEVEL
STL JOIST & MET ROOF DECK: NO INSULATION.
SIDE CONDITION

RCE
7

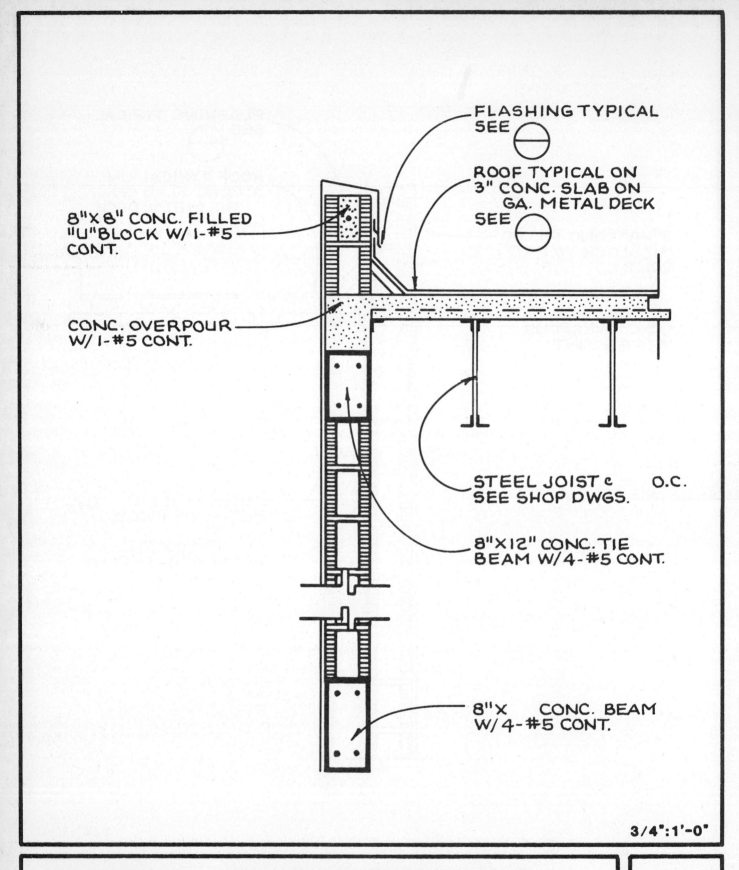

FLASHING TYPICAL
SEE ⊖

ROOF TYPICAL ON
3" CONC. SLAB ON
GA. METAL DECK
SEE ⊖

8"X 8" CONC. FILLED
"U"BLOCK W/ 1-#5
CONT.

CONC. OVERPOUR
W/ I-#5 CONT.

STEEL JOIST ¢   O.C.
SEE SHOP DWGS.

8"X 12" CONC. TIE
BEAM W/ 4-#5 CONT.

8"X   CONC. BEAM
W/ 4-#5 CONT.

3/4":1'-0"

**REINFORCED CONCRETE BEAM: LEVEL
STL JOIST & MET ROOF DECK: NO INSULATION
SIDE CONDITION: LOWER BEAM**

**RCE
8**

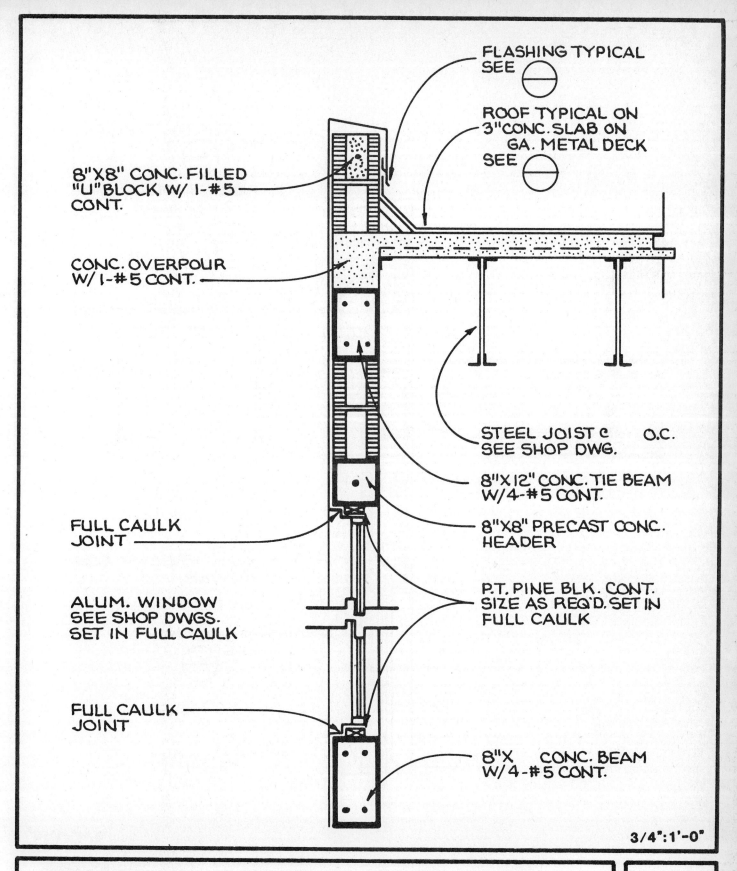

FLASHING TYPICAL
SEE ⊖

ROOF TYPICAL ON
3"CONC.SLAB ON
GA. METAL DECK
SEE ⊖

8"X8" CONC. FILLED
"U"BLOCK W/ 1-#5
CONT.

CONC. OVERPOUR
W/ 1-#5 CONT.

FULL CAULK
JOINT

ALUM. WINDOW
SEE SHOP DWGS.
SET IN FULL CAULK

FULL CAULK
JOINT

STEEL JOIST ¢   O.C.
SEE SHOP DWG.

8"X12" CONC.TIE BEAM
W/4-#5 CONT.

8"X8" PRECAST CONC.
HEADER

P.T. PINE BLK. CONT.
SIZE AS REQ'D. SET IN
FULL CAULK

8"X   CONC. BEAM
W/4-#5 CONT.

3/4":1'-0"

REINFORCED CONCRETE BEAM: LEVEL
STL JOIST & MET ROOF DECK: NO INSULATION
SIDE CONDITION: WINDOW

RCE
9

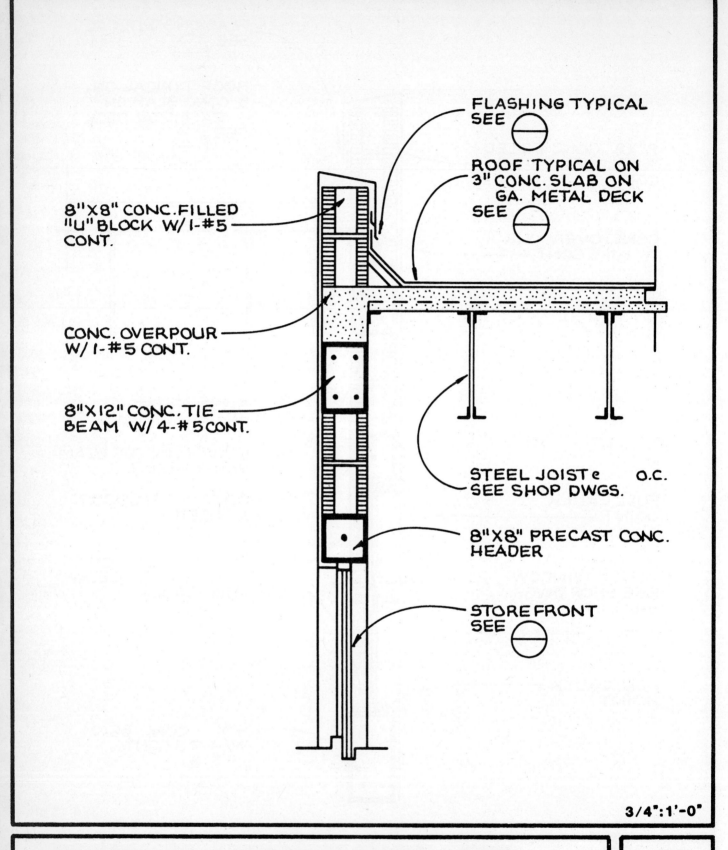

FLASHING TYPICAL
SEE ⊖

ROOF TYPICAL ON
3" CONC. SLAB ON
GA. METAL DECK
SEE ⊖

8"X8" CONC. FILLED
"U" BLOCK W/ 1-#5
CONT.

CONC. OVERPOUR
W/ 1-#5 CONT.

8"X12" CONC. TIE
BEAM W/ 4-#5 CONT.

STEEL JOIST e   O.C.
SEE SHOP DWGS.

8"X8" PRECAST CONC.
HEADER

STOREFRONT
SEE ⊖

3/4":1'-0"

**REINFORCED CONCRETE BEAM: LEVEL
STL JOIST & MET ROOF DECK: NO INSULATION.**

SIDE CONDITION: STOREFRONT

**RCE
10**

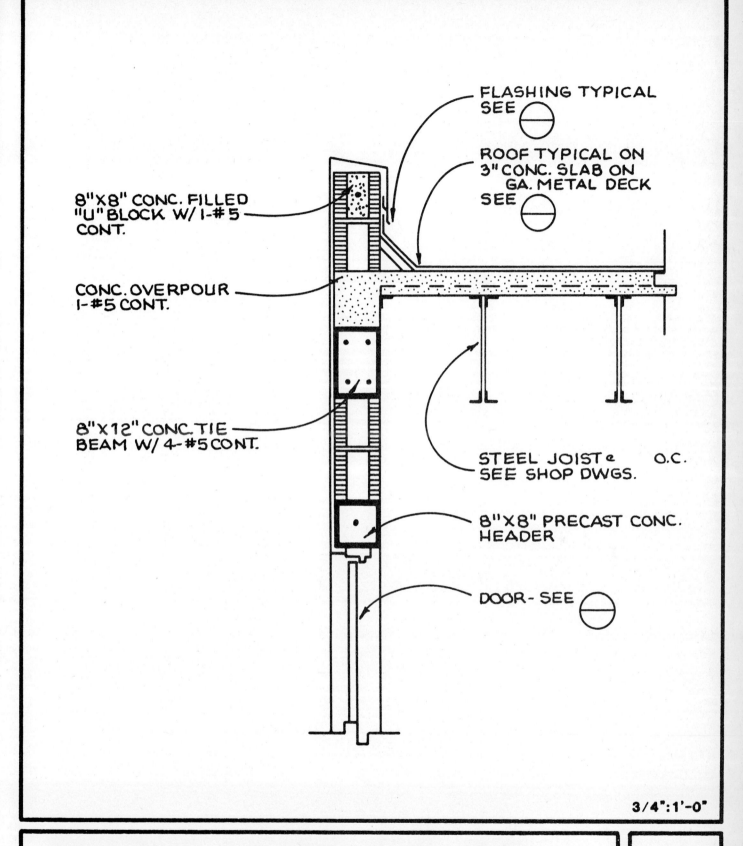

FLASHING TYPICAL SEE ⊘

ROOF TYPICAL ON 3" CONC. SLAB ON GA. METAL DECK SEE ⊘

8"X8" CONC. FILLED "U" BLOCK W/ 1-#5 CONT.

CONC. OVERPOUR 1-#5 CONT.

8"X12" CONC. TIE BEAM W/ 4-#5 CONT.

STEEL JOIST @ O.C. SEE SHOP DWGS.

8"X8" PRECAST CONC. HEADER

DOOR - SEE ⊘

3/4":1'-0"

REINFORCED CONCRETE BEAM: LEVEL STL JOIST & MET ROOF DECK: NO INSULATION

SIDE CONDITION: DOOR

RCE 11

SECTION 6: RC–F

Standard masonry construction with level reinforced concrete tie beam.
Steel joist and metal roof deck with insulation board.

ARCHITECTURAL DETAILING
FOR
COMMERCIAL CONSTRUCTION

6

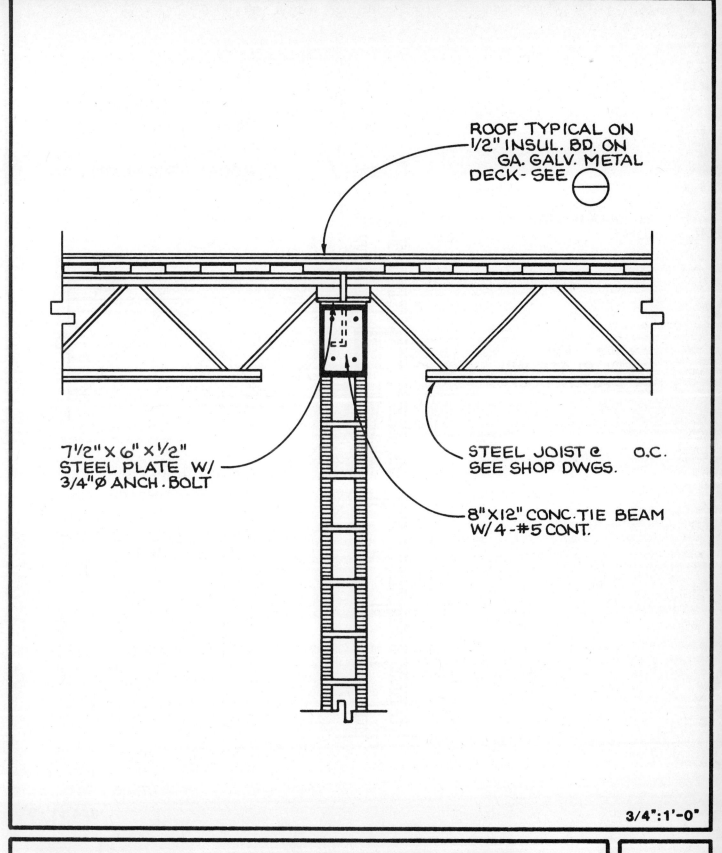

ROOF TYPICAL ON
1/2" INSUL. BD. ON
GA. GALV. METAL
DECK- SEE ⊖

7½" X 6" X ½"
STEEL PLATE W/
3/4"∅ ANCH. BOLT

STEEL JOIST @   O.C.
SEE SHOP DWGS.

8"X12" CONC. TIE BEAM
W/ 4 - #5 CONT.

3/4":1'-0"

**REINFORCED CONCRETE BEAM: LEVEL
STL JOIST & MET ROOF DECK: INSULATION BD
INTERMEDIATE CONDITION: END**

**RCF
1**

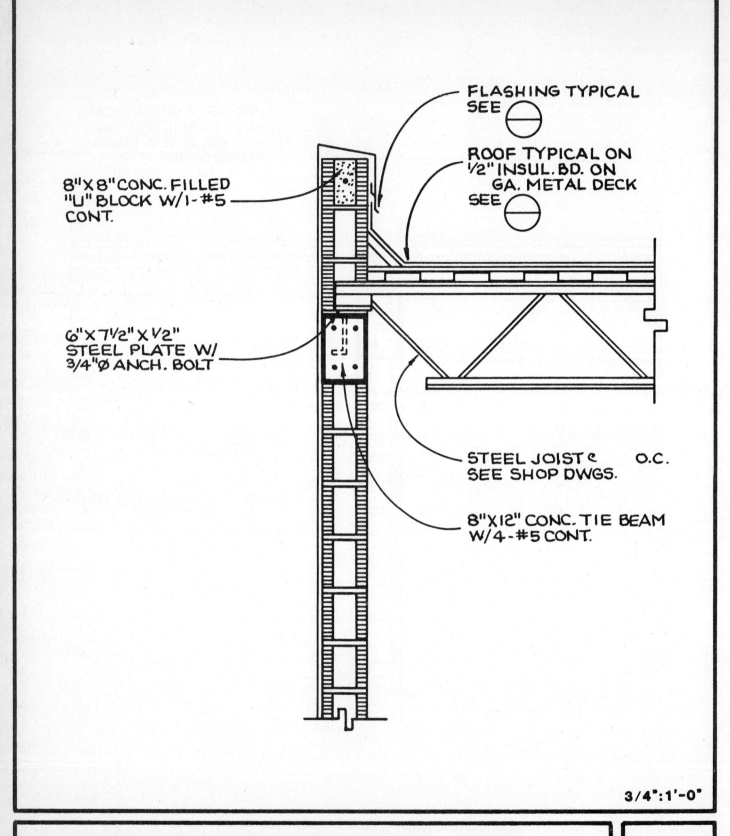

FLASHING TYPICAL
SEE ⊖

ROOF TYPICAL ON
1/2" INSUL. BD. ON
GA. METAL DECK
SEE ⊖

8"X8" CONC. FILLED
"U" BLOCK W/1-#5
CONT.

6"X 7½" X ½"
STEEL PLATE W/
¾"Ø ANCH. BOLT

STEEL JOIST ℄   O.C.
SEE SHOP DWGS.

8"X12" CONC. TIE BEAM
W/4-#5 CONT.

3/4":1'-0"

**REINFORCED CONCRETE BEAM: LEVEL
STL JOIST & MET ROOF DECK: INSULATION BD
END CONDITION**

**RCF
2**

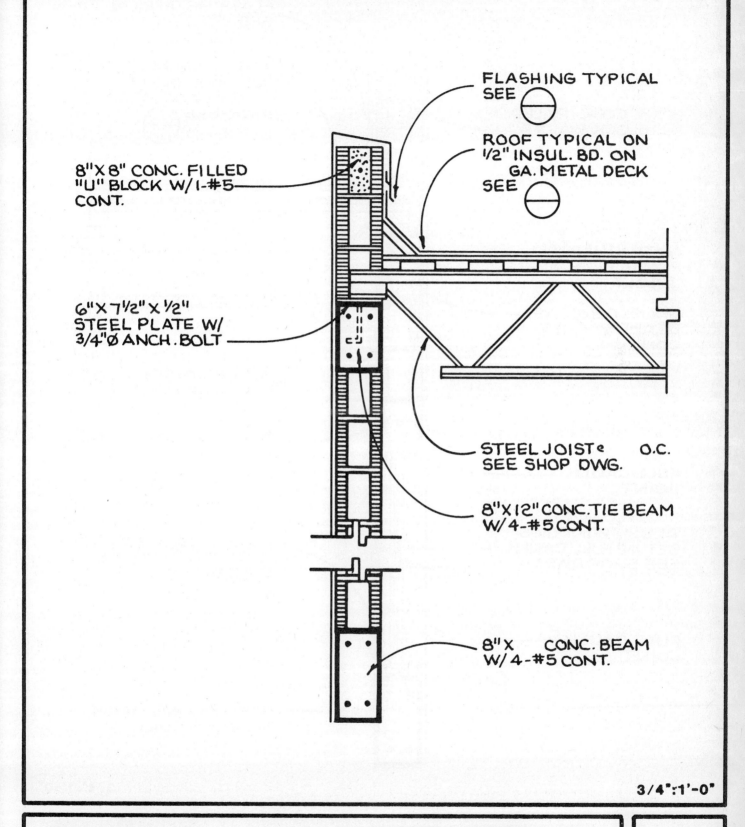

FLASHING TYPICAL
SEE ◯

ROOF TYPICAL ON
½" INSUL. BD. ON
GA. METAL DECK
SEE ◯

8"X 8" CONC. FILLED
"U" BLOCK W/1-#5
CONT.

6"X 7½" X ½"
STEEL PLATE W/
¾"Ø ANCH. BOLT

STEEL JOIST @   O.C.
SEE SHOP DWG.

8"X12" CONC. TIE BEAM
W/ 4-#5 CONT.

8"X   CONC. BEAM
W/ 4-#5 CONT.

3/4":1'-0"

REINFORCED CONCRETE BEAM: LEVEL
STL JOIST & MET ROOF DECK: INSULATION BD
END CONDITION: LOWER BEAM

**RCF
3**

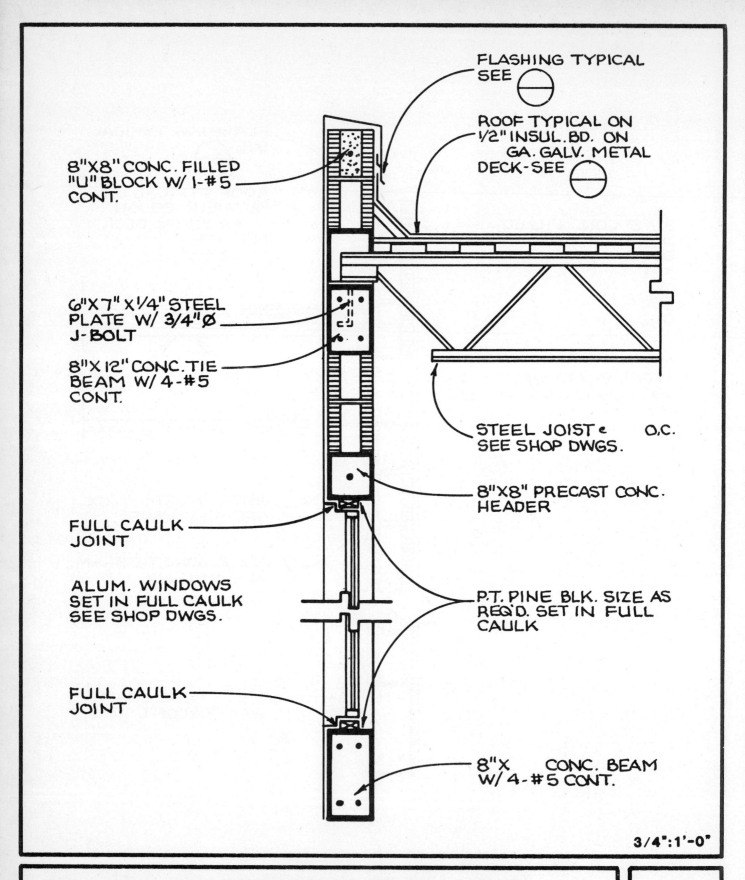

FLASHING TYPICAL SEE ⊖

ROOF TYPICAL ON ½" INSUL. BD. ON GA. GALV. METAL DECK - SEE ⊖

8"X8" CONC. FILLED "U" BLOCK W/ 1-#5 CONT.

6"X7" X¼" STEEL PLATE W/ 3/4"∅ J-BOLT

8"X12" CONC. TIE BEAM W/ 4-#5 CONT.

STEEL JOIST ℮   O.C. SEE SHOP DWGS.

FULL CAULK JOINT

8"X8" PRECAST CONC. HEADER

ALUM. WINDOWS SET IN FULL CAULK SEE SHOP DWGS.

P.T. PINE BLK. SIZE AS REQ'D. SET IN FULL CAULK

FULL CAULK JOINT

8"X   CONC. BEAM W/ 4-#5 CONT.

3/4":1'-0"

REINFORCED CONCRETE BEAM: LEVEL
STL JOIST & MET ROOF DECK: INSULATION BD
END CONDITION: WINDOW

RCF 4

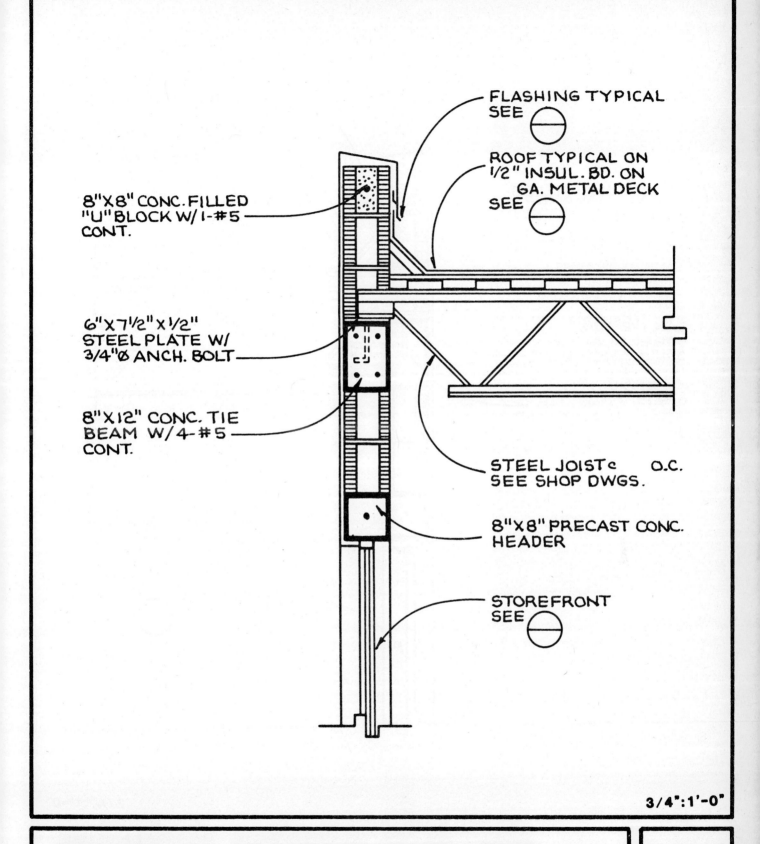

FLASHING TYPICAL
SEE ⊖

ROOF TYPICAL ON
1/2" INSUL. BD. ON
GA. METAL DECK
SEE ⊖

8"X8" CONC. FILLED
"U" BLOCK W/I-#5
CONT.

6"X7½"X½"
STEEL PLATE W/
3/4"Ø ANCH. BOLT

8"X12" CONC. TIE
BEAM W/4-#5
CONT.

STEEL JOIST ᶜ   O.C.
SEE SHOP DWGS.

8"X8" PRECAST CONC.
HEADER

STOREFRONT
SEE ⊖

3/4":1'-0"

| REINFORCED CONCRETE BEAM: LEVEL STL JOIST & MET ROOF DECK: INSULATION BD END CONDITION: STOREFRONT | RCF 5 |

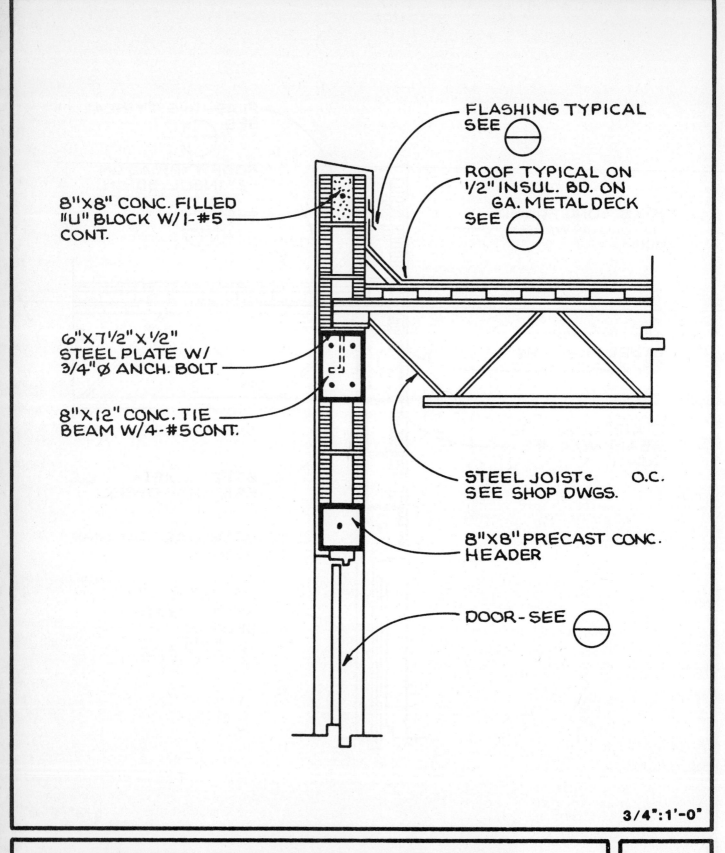

FLASHING TYPICAL
SEE ⊖

ROOF TYPICAL ON
1/2" INSUL. BD. ON
GA. METAL DECK
SEE ⊖

8"X8" CONC. FILLED
"U" BLOCK W/ 1-#5
CONT.

6"X7½"X½"
STEEL PLATE W/
3/4"Ø ANCH. BOLT

8"X12" CONC. TIE
BEAM W/4-#5CONT.

STEEL JOIST ℮   O.C.
SEE SHOP DWGS.

8"X8" PRECAST CONC.
HEADER

DOOR-SEE ⊖

3/4":1'-0"

**REINFORCED CONCRETE BEAM: LEVEL
STL JOIST & MET ROOF DECK: INSULATION BD
END CONDITION: DOOR**

**RCF
6**

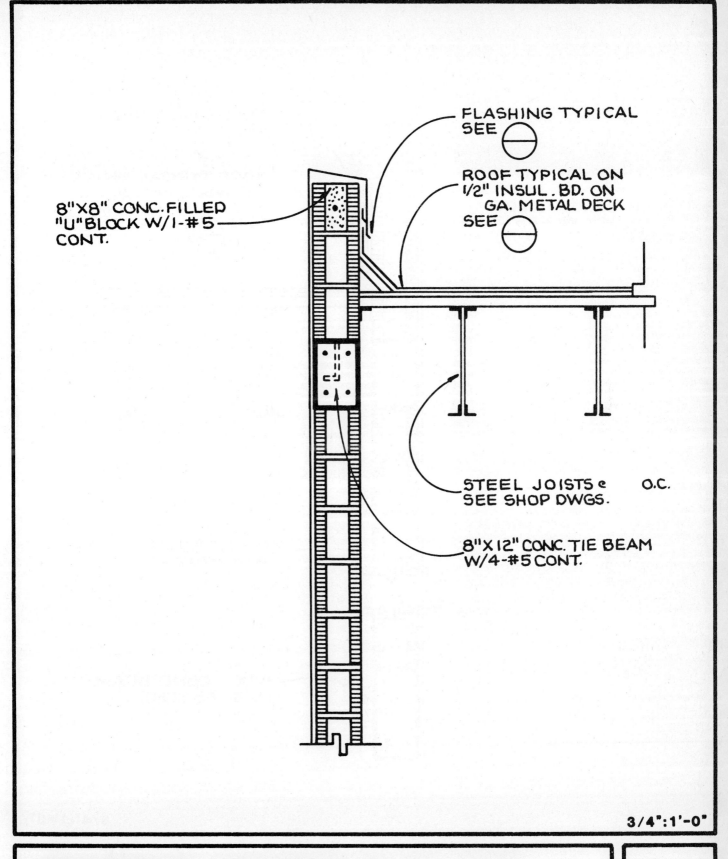

8"X8" CONC. FILLED "U" BLOCK W/1-#5 CONT.

FLASHING TYPICAL SEE ⊖

ROOF TYPICAL ON 1/2" INSUL. BD. ON GA. METAL DECK SEE ⊖

STEEL JOISTS e   O.C. SEE SHOP DWGS.

8"X12" CONC. TIE BEAM W/4-#5 CONT.

3/4":1'-0"

REINFORCED CONCRETE BEAM: LEVEL STL JOIST & MET ROOF DECK: INSULATION BD SIDE CONDITION

RCF 7

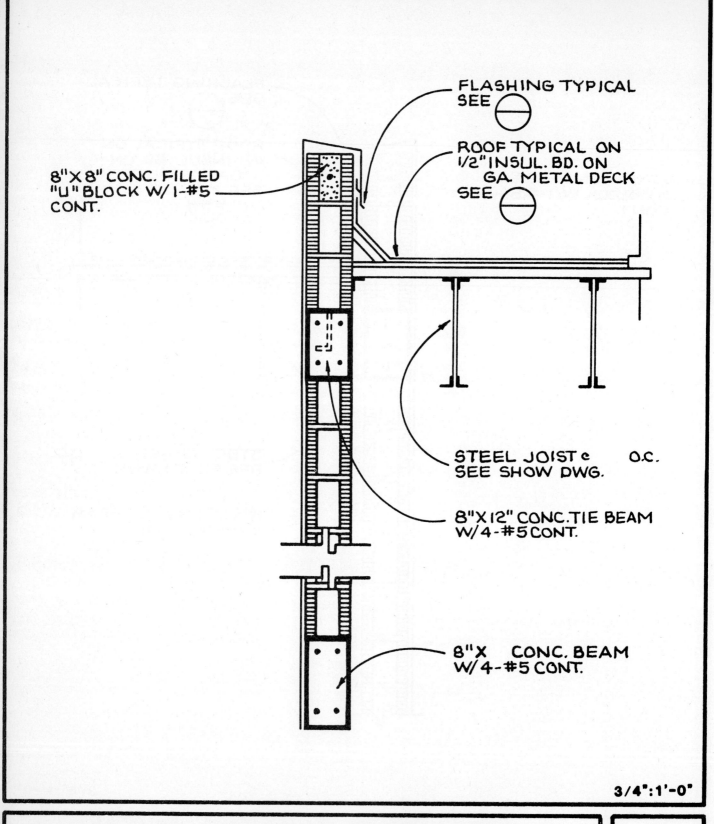

8"X 8" CONC. FILLED
"U" BLOCK W/ 1-#5
CONT.

FLASHING TYPICAL
SEE ⊖

ROOF TYPICAL ON
1/2" INSUL. BD. ON
GA. METAL DECK
SEE ⊖

STEEL JOIST ℮   O.C.
SEE SHOW DWG.

8"X12" CONC. TIE BEAM
W/ 4-#5 CONT.

8"X   CONC. BEAM
W/ 4-#5 CONT.

3/4":1'-0"

REINFORCED CONCRETE BEAM: LEVEL
STL JOIST & MET ROOF DECK: INSULATION BD
SIDE CONDITION: LOWER BEAM

RCF
8

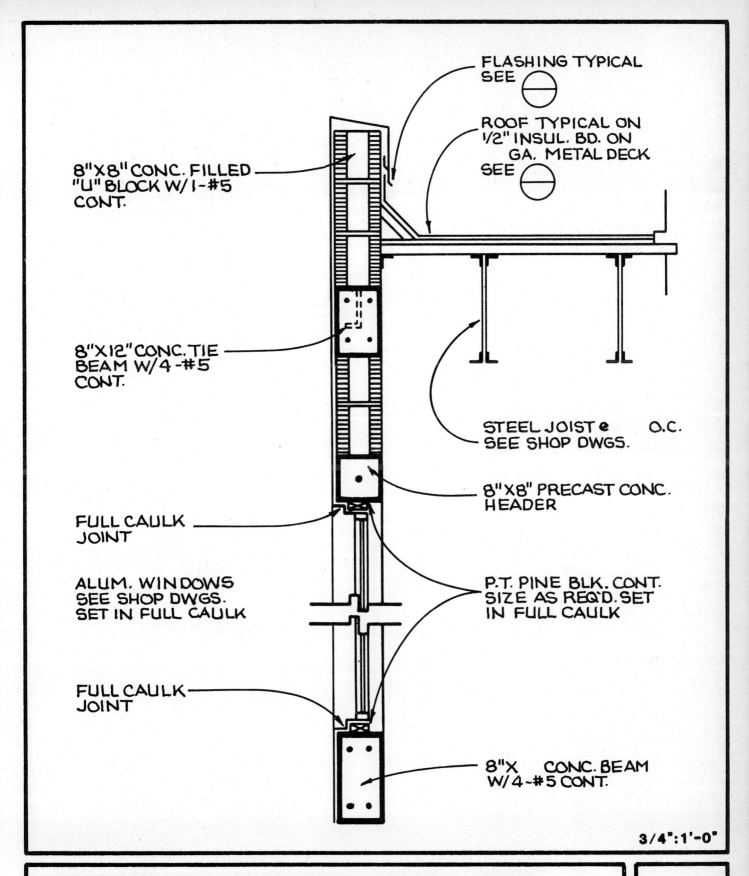

FLASHING TYPICAL
SEE ⊝

ROOF TYPICAL ON
1/2" INSUL. BD. ON
GA. METAL DECK
SEE ⊝

8"X8"CONC. FILLED
"U" BLOCK W/1-#5
CONT.

8"X12"CONC. TIE
BEAM W/4-#5
CONT.

STEEL JOIST @   O.C.
SEE SHOP DWGS.

8"X8" PRECAST CONC.
HEADER

FULL CAULK
JOINT

ALUM. WINDOWS
SEE SHOP DWGS.
SET IN FULL CAULK

P.T. PINE BLK. CONT.
SIZE AS REQ'D. SET
IN FULL CAULK

FULL CAULK
JOINT

8"X   CONC. BEAM
W/4-#5 CONT.

3/4":1'-0"

**REINFORCED CONCRETE BEAM: LEVEL
STL JOIST & MET ROOF DECK: INSULATION BD
SIDE CONDITION: WINDOW**

**RCF
9**

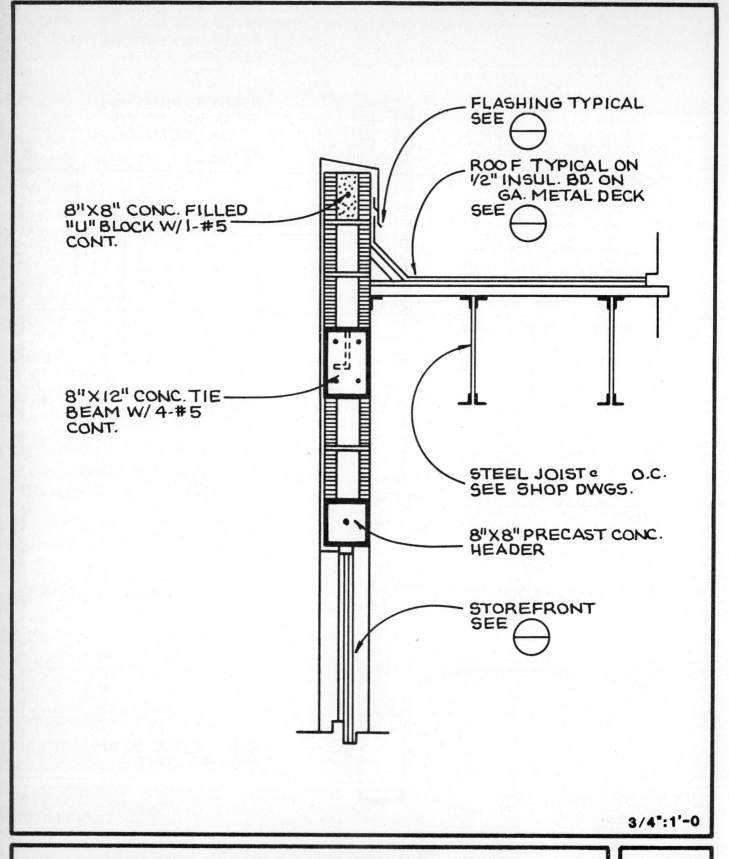

FLASHING TYPICAL
SEE ⊖

ROOF TYPICAL ON
1/2" INSUL. BD. ON
GA. METAL DECK
SEE ⊖

8"X8" CONC. FILLED
"U" BLOCK W/1-#5
CONT.

8"X12" CONC. TIE
BEAM W/ 4-#5
CONT.

STEEL JOIST ℮   O.C.
SEE SHOP DWGS.

8"X8" PRECAST CONC.
HEADER

STOREFRONT
SEE ⊖

3/4":1'-0

**REINFORCED CONCRETE BEAM: LEVEL
STL JOIST & MET ROOF DECK: INSULATION BD
SIDE CONDITION: STOREFRONT**

**RCF
10**

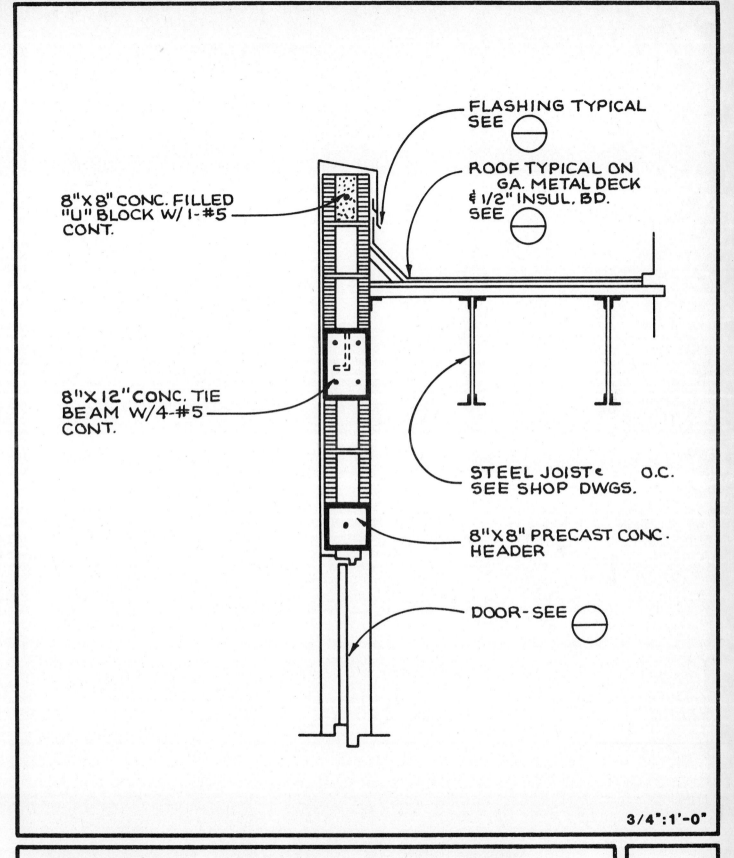

8"X8" CONC. FILLED "U" BLOCK W/ 1-#5 CONT.

8"X12" CONC. TIE BEAM W/4-#5 CONT.

FLASHING TYPICAL SEE ⊖

ROOF TYPICAL ON GA. METAL DECK & 1/2" INSUL. BD. SEE ⊖

STEEL JOIST @ O.C. SEE SHOP DWGS.

8"X8" PRECAST CONC. HEADER

DOOR-SEE ⊖

3/4":1'-0"

REINFORCED CONCRETE BEAM: LEVEL STL JOIST & MET ROOF DECK: INSULATION BD SIDE CONDITION: DOOR

RCF 11

SECTION 7: RC–G

Standard masonry construction with sloped reinforced
concrete tie beam.
Prefabricated wood truss and plywood roof deck with no insulation.

ARCHITECTURAL DETAILING
FOR
COMMERCIAL CONSTRUCTION

7

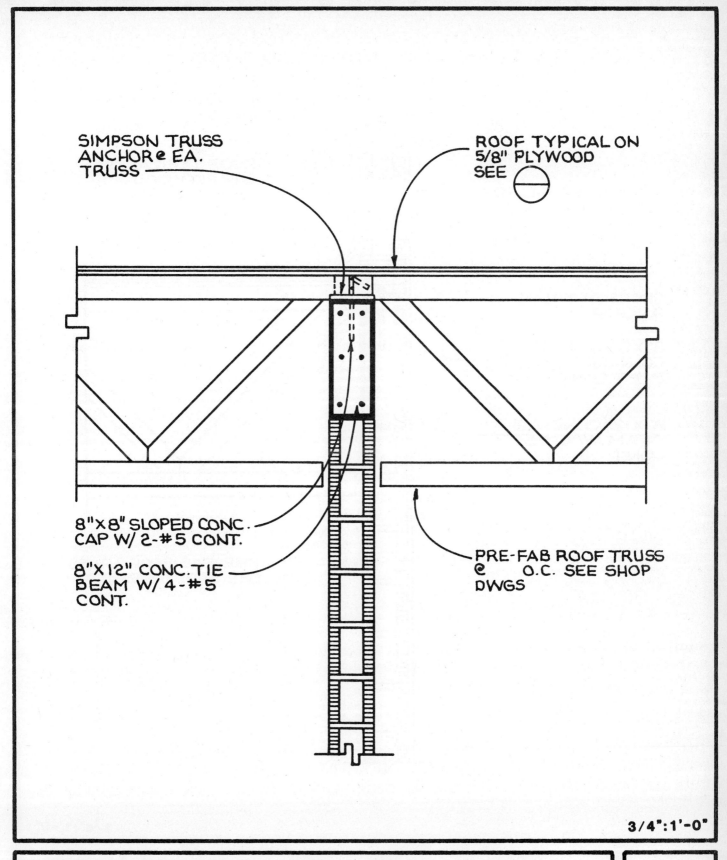

SIMPSON TRUSS ANCHOR @ EA. TRUSS

ROOF TYPICAL ON 5/8" PLYWOOD SEE ⊖

8"x8" SLOPED CONC. CAP W/ 2-#5 CONT.

8"x12" CONC. TIE BEAM W/ 4-#5 CONT.

PRE-FAB ROOF TRUSS @   O.C. SEE SHOP DWGS

3/4":1'-0"

REINFORCED CONCRETE BEAM: SLOPED WD TRUSS & PLYWD ROOF DECK: NO INSUL.

INTERMEDIATE CONDITION: END

RCG 1

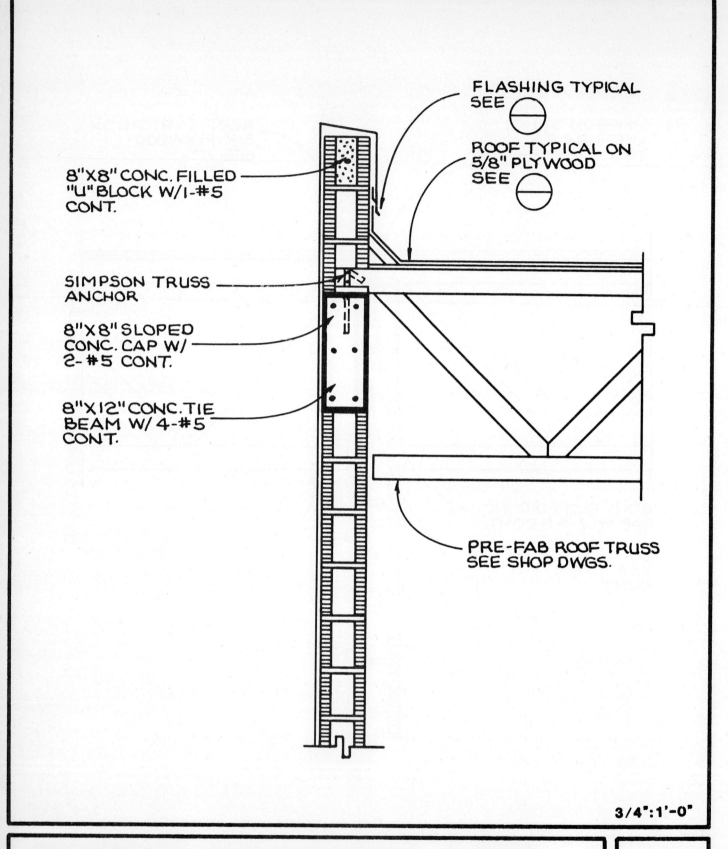

FLASHING TYPICAL
SEE ⊖

ROOF TYPICAL ON
5/8" PLYWOOD
SEE ⊖

8"X8" CONC. FILLED
"U" BLOCK W/1-#5
CONT.

SIMPSON TRUSS
ANCHOR

8"X8" SLOPED
CONC. CAP W/
2-#5 CONT.

8"X12" CONC. TIE
BEAM W/ 4-#5
CONT.

PRE-FAB ROOF TRUSS
SEE SHOP DWGS.

3/4":1'-0"

REINFORCED CONCRETE BEAM: SLOPED WD TRUSS & PLYWD ROOF DECK: NO INSUL.

END CONDITION

RCG
2

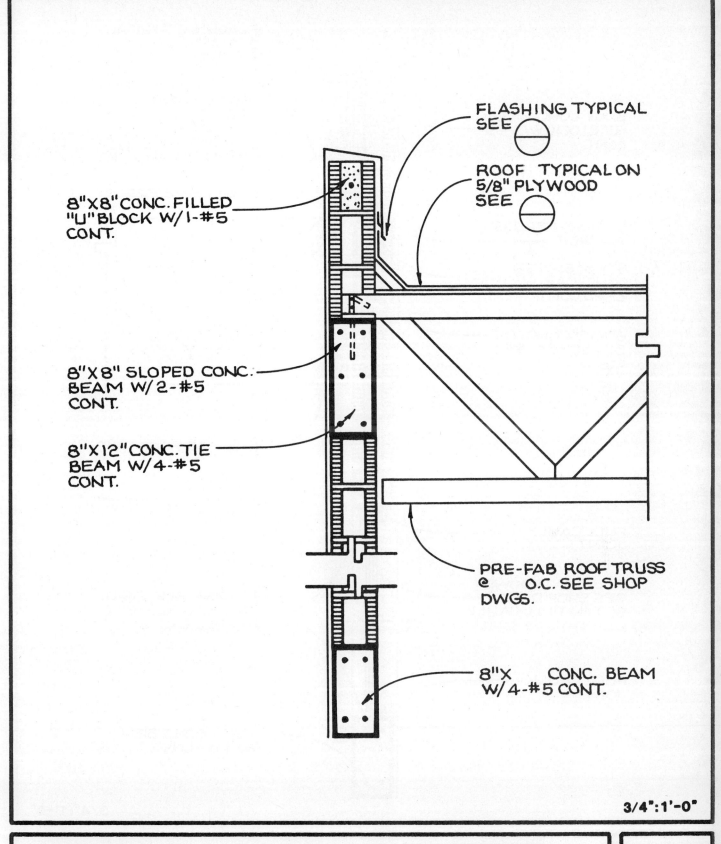

FLASHING TYPICAL
SEE ◯

ROOF TYPICAL ON
5/8" PLYWOOD
SEE ◯

8"X8" CONC. FILLED
"U" BLOCK W/ 1-#5
CONT.

8"X8" SLOPED CONC.
BEAM W/ 2-#5
CONT.

8"X12" CONC. TIE
BEAM W/ 4-#5
CONT.

PRE-FAB ROOF TRUSS
@   O.C. SEE SHOP
DWGS.

8"X   CONC. BEAM
W/ 4-#5 CONT.

3/4":1'-0"

**REINFORCED CONCRETE BEAM: SLOPED
WD TRUSS & PLYWD ROOF DECK: NO INSUL.**

END CONDITION: LOWER BEAM

RCG
3

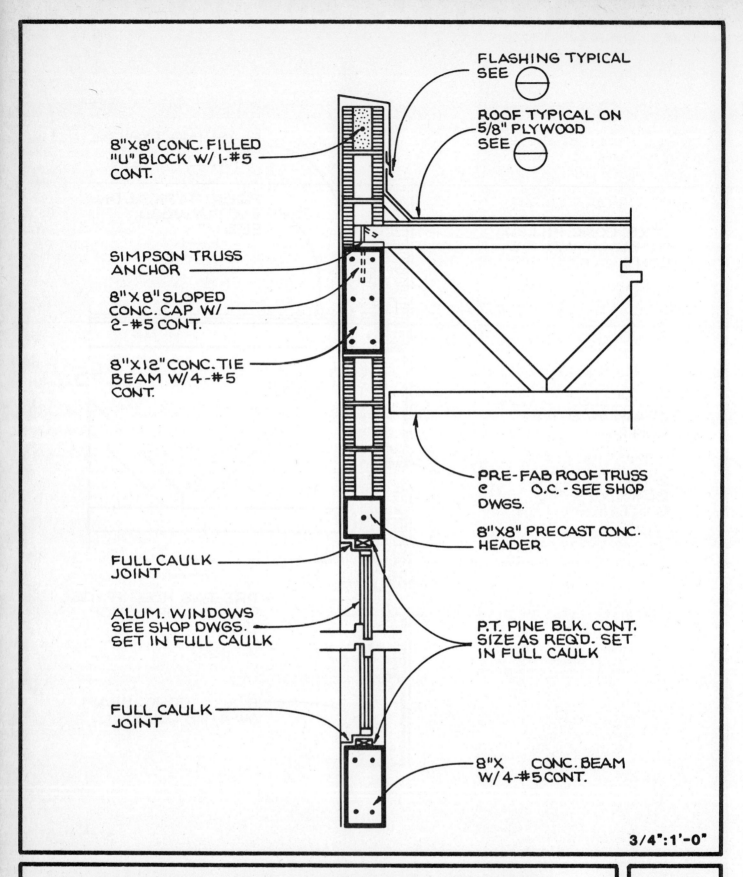

FLASHING TYPICAL
SEE ⊖

ROOF TYPICAL ON
5/8" PLYWOOD
SEE ⊖

8"X8" CONC. FILLED
"U" BLOCK W/ I-#5
CONT.

SIMPSON TRUSS
ANCHOR

8"X8" SLOPED
CONC. CAP W/
2-#5 CONT.

8"X12"CONC.TIE
BEAM W/4-#5
CONT.

PRE-FAB ROOF TRUSS
@   O.C. - SEE SHOP
DWGS.

8"X8" PRECAST CONC.
HEADER

FULL CAULK
JOINT

ALUM. WINDOWS
SEE SHOP DWGS.
SET IN FULL CAULK

P.T. PINE BLK. CONT.
SIZE AS REQ'D. SET
IN FULL CAULK

FULL CAULK
JOINT

8"X   CONC.BEAM
W/4-#5 CONT.

3/4":1'-0"

**REINFORCED CONCRETE BEAM: SLOPED
WD TRUSS & PLYWD ROOF DECK: NO INSUL.
END CONDITION: WINDOW**

**RCG
4**

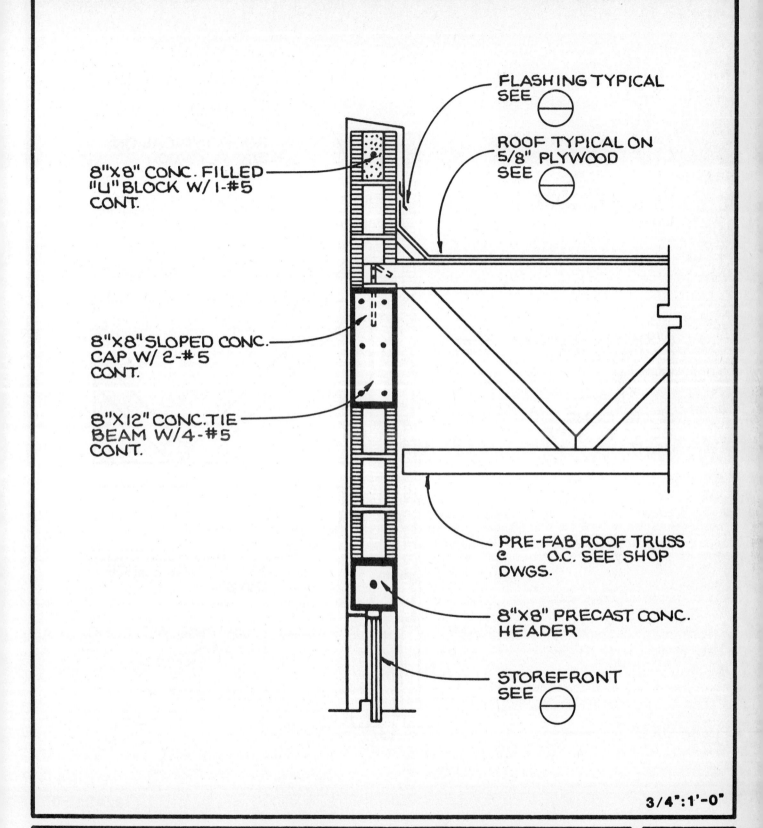

FLASHING TYPICAL
SEE ⊖

ROOF TYPICAL ON
5/8" PLYWOOD
SEE ⊖

8"X8" CONC. FILLED
"U" BLOCK W/ 1-#5
CONT.

8"X8" SLOPED CONC.
CAP W/ 2-#5
CONT.

8"X12" CONC. TIE
BEAM W/ 4-#5
CONT.

PRE-FAB ROOF TRUSS
@   O.C. SEE SHOP
DWGS.

8"X8" PRECAST CONC.
HEADER

STOREFRONT
SEE ⊖

3/4":1'-0"

**REINFORCED CONCRETE BEAM: SLOPED
WD TRUSS & PLYWD ROOF DECK: NO INSUL.**

END CONDITION: STOREFRONT

**RCG
5**

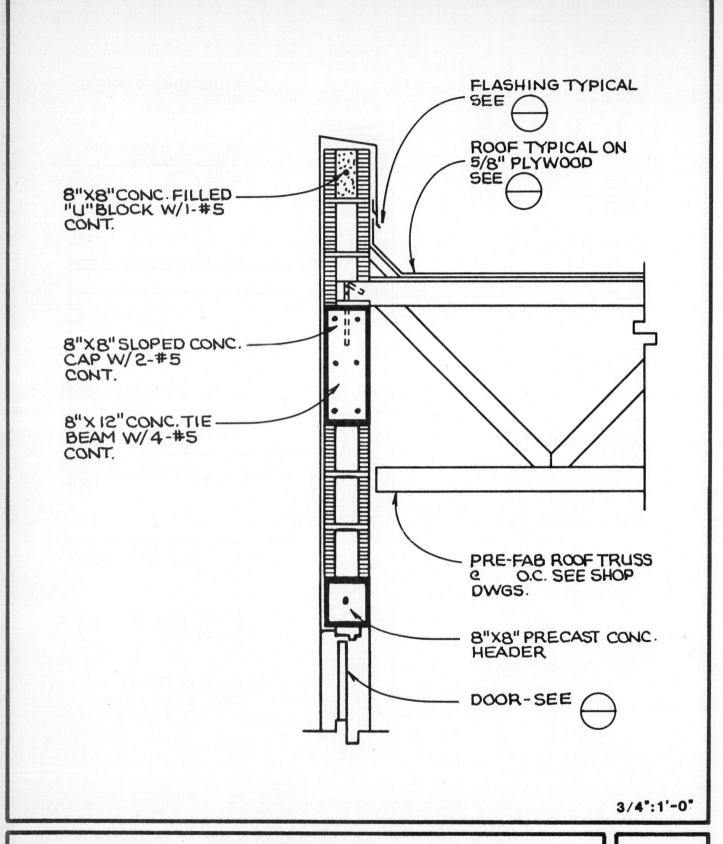

FLASHING TYPICAL
SEE ⊘

ROOF TYPICAL ON
5/8" PLYWOOD
SEE ⊘

8"X8"CONC. FILLED
"U"BLOCK W/1-#5
CONT.

8"X8" SLOPED CONC.
CAP W/2-#5
CONT.

8"X 12" CONC. TIE
BEAM W/4-#5
CONT.

PRE-FAB ROOF TRUSS
℮   O.C. SEE SHOP
DWGS.

8"X8" PRECAST CONC.
HEADER

DOOR-SEE ⊘

3/4":1'-0"

REINFORCED CONCRETE BEAM: SLOPED
WD TRUSS & PLYWD ROOF DECK: NO INSUL.
END CONDITION: DOOR

RCG
6

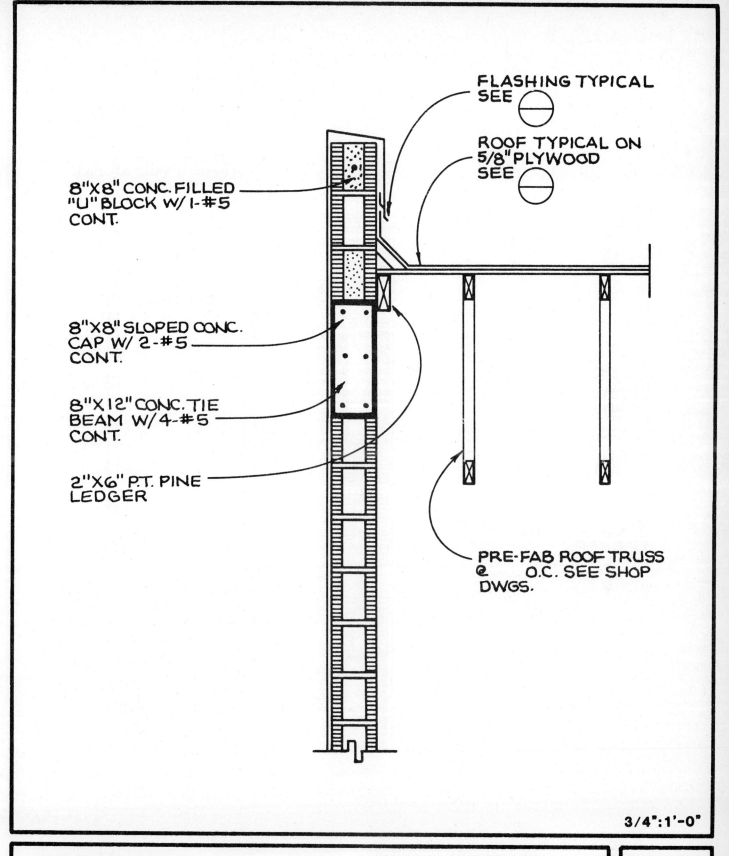

FLASHING TYPICAL
SEE ⊖

ROOF TYPICAL ON
5/8" PLYWOOD
SEE ⊖

8"X8" CONC. FILLED
"U" BLOCK W/ 1-#5
CONT.

8"X8" SLOPED CONC.
CAP W/ 2-#5
CONT.

8"X12" CONC. TIE
BEAM W/ 4-#5
CONT.

2"X6" P.T. PINE
LEDGER

PRE-FAB ROOF TRUSS
@   O.C. SEE SHOP
DWGS.

3/4":1'-0"

**REINFORCED CONCRETE BEAM: SLOPED
WD TRUSS & PLYWD ROOF DECK: NO INSUL.
SIDE CONDITION**

**RCG
7**

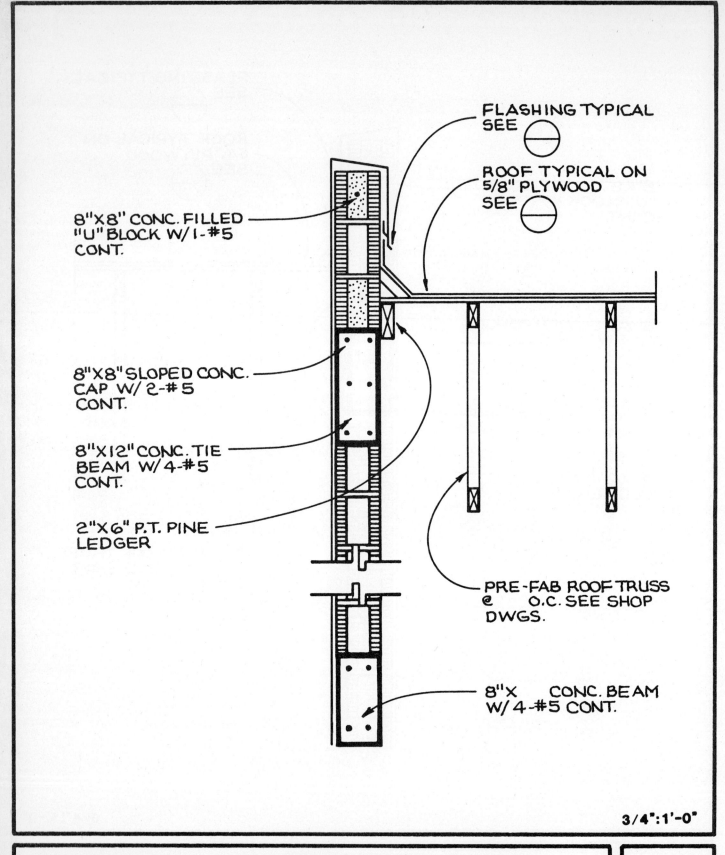

FLASHING TYPICAL
SEE ⊖

ROOF TYPICAL ON
5/8" PLYWOOD
SEE ⊖

8"X8" CONC. FILLED
"U" BLOCK W/1-#5
CONT.

8"X8" SLOPED CONC.
CAP W/ 2-#5
CONT.

8"X12" CONC. TIE
BEAM W/4-#5
CONT.

2"X6" P.T. PINE
LEDGER

PRE-FAB ROOF TRUSS
@   O.C. SEE SHOP
DWGS.

8"X   CONC. BEAM
W/ 4-#5 CONT.

3/4":1'-0"

**REINFORCED CONCRETE BEAM: SLOPED
WD TRUSS & PLYWD ROOF DECK: NO INSUL.**

SIDE CONDITION: LOWER BEAM

**RCG
8**

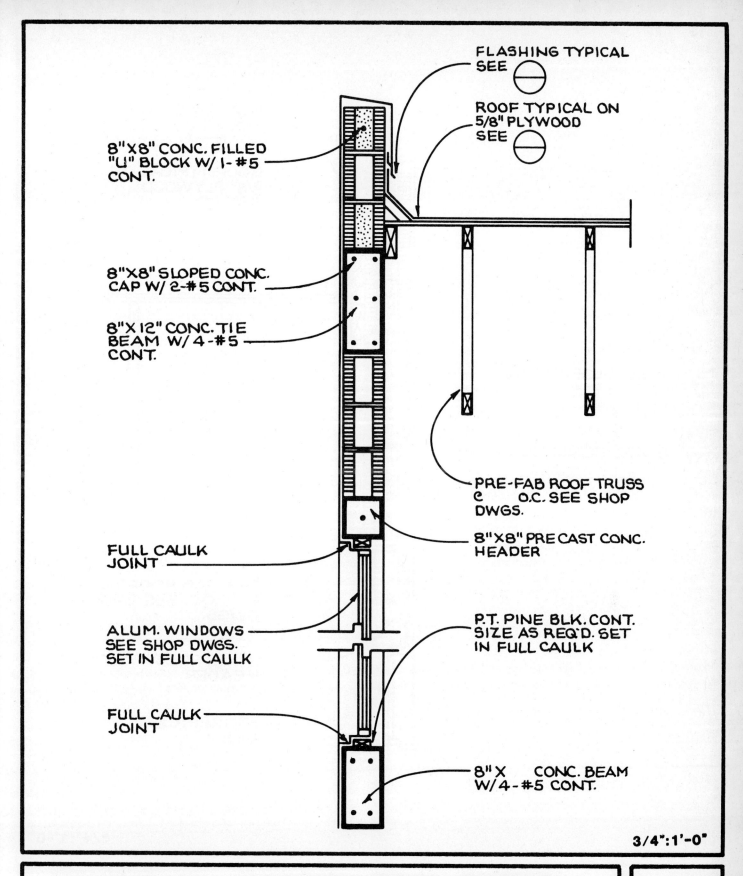

FLASHING TYPICAL
SEE ⊖

ROOF TYPICAL ON
5/8" PLYWOOD
SEE ⊖

8"X8" CONC. FILLED
"U" BLOCK W/ 1-#5
CONT.

8"X8" SLOPED CONC.
CAP W/ 2-#5 CONT.

8"X12" CONC. TIE
BEAM W/ 4-#5
CONT.

FULL CAULK
JOINT

ALUM. WINDOWS
SEE SHOP DWGS.
SET IN FULL CAULK

FULL CAULK
JOINT

PRE-FAB ROOF TRUSS
@   O.C. SEE SHOP
DWGS.

8"X8" PRECAST CONC.
HEADER

P.T. PINE BLK. CONT.
SIZE AS REQ'D. SET
IN FULL CAULK

8"X   CONC. BEAM
W/ 4-#5 CONT.

3/4":1'-0"

REINFORCED CONCRETE BEAM: SLOPED
WD TRUSS & PLYWD ROOF DECK: NO INSUL.

SIDE CONDITION: WINDOW

**RCG
9**

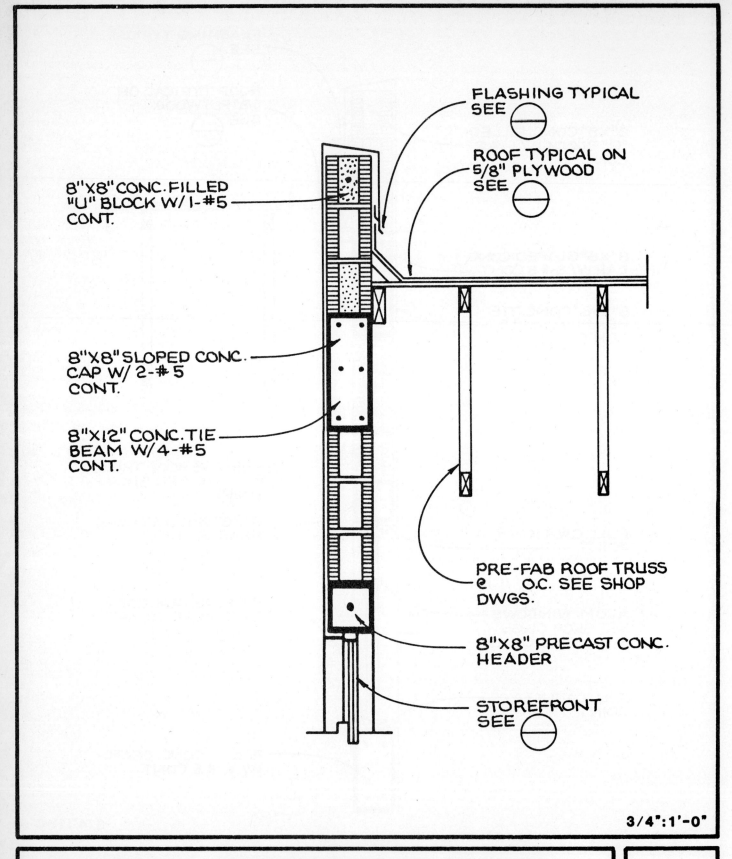

FLASHING TYPICAL
SEE ◯

ROOF TYPICAL ON
5/8" PLYWOOD
SEE ◯

8"X8"CONC.FILLED
"U" BLOCK W/ 1-#5
CONT.

8"X8"SLOPED CONC.
CAP W/ 2-#5
CONT.

8"X12" CONC. TIE
BEAM W/4-#5
CONT.

PRE-FAB ROOF TRUSS
@ O.C. SEE SHOP
DWGS.

8"X8" PRECAST CONC.
HEADER

STOREFRONT
SEE ◯

3/4":1'-0"

REINFORCED CONCRETE BEAM: SLOPED
WD TRUSS & PLYWD ROOF DECK: NO INSUL.

SIDE CONDITION: STOREFRONT

**RCG
10**

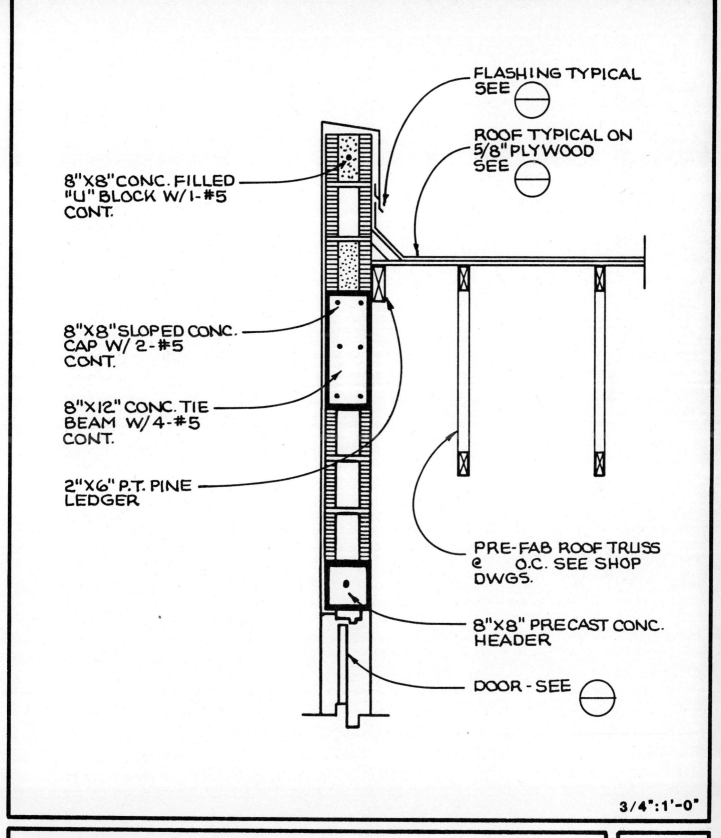

FLASHING TYPICAL
SEE ⊖

ROOF TYPICAL ON
5/8" PLYWOOD
SEE ⊖

8"X8" CONC. FILLED
"U" BLOCK W/ I-#5
CONT.

8"X8" SLOPED CONC.
CAP W/ 2-#5
CONT.

8"X12" CONC. TIE
BEAM W/4-#5
CONT.

2"X6" P.T. PINE
LEDGER

PRE-FAB ROOF TRUSS
@   O.C. SEE SHOP
DWGS.

8"X8" PRECAST CONC.
HEADER

DOOR - SEE ⊖

3/4":1'-0"

**REINFORCED CONCRETE BEAM: SLOPED
WD TRUSS & PLYWD ROOF DECK: NO INSUL.**

SIDE CONDITION: DOOR

**RCG
11**

SECTION 8: RC–H

Standard masonry construction with level reinforced
concrete tie beam.
Wood truss and plywood roof deck with sloped insulation.

ARCHITECTURAL DETAILING
FOR
COMMERCIAL CONSTRUCTION

8

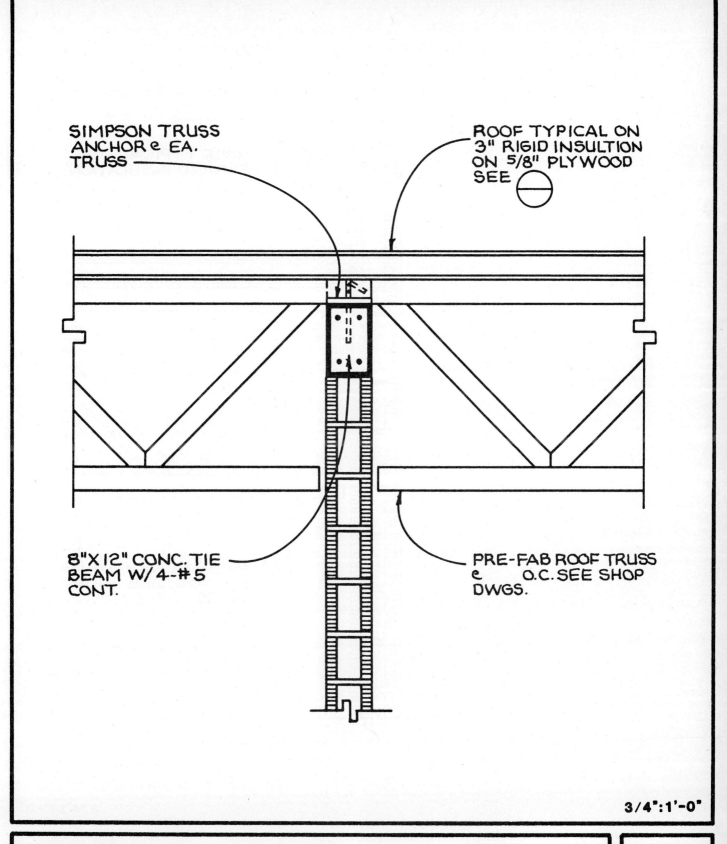

SIMPSON TRUSS ANCHOR e EA. TRUSS —

ROOF TYPICAL ON 3" RIGID INSULTION ON 5/8" PLYWOOD SEE ⊖

8"X 12" CONC. TIE BEAM W/ 4-#5 CONT.

PRE-FAB ROOF TRUSS e   O.C. SEE SHOP DWGS.

3/4":1'-0"

REINFORCED CONCRETE BEAM: LEVEL WD TRUSS & PLYWD ROOF DECK: SLOPED INSUL.

INTERMEDIATE CONDITION: END

RCH 1

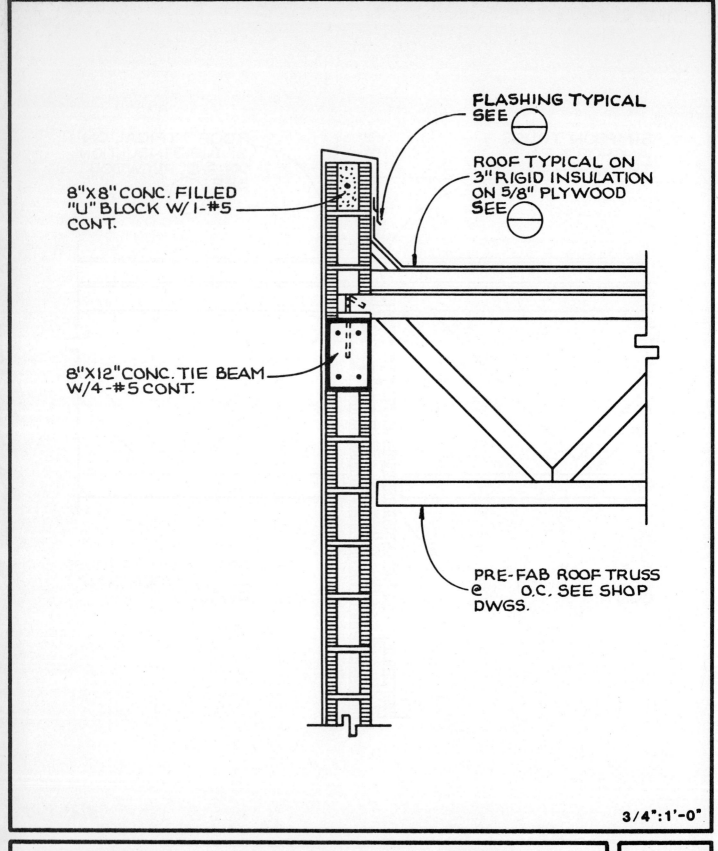

8"X8"CONC. FILLED
"U" BLOCK W/1-#5
CONT.

FLASHING TYPICAL
SEE ⊘

ROOF TYPICAL ON
3" RIGID INSULATION
ON 5/8" PLYWOOD
SEE ⊘

8"X12"CONC. TIE BEAM
W/4-#5 CONT.

PRE-FAB ROOF TRUSS
@   O.C. SEE SHOP
DWGS.

3/4":1'-0"

**REINFORCED CONCRETE BEAM: LEVEL
WD TRUSS & PLYWD ROOF DECK: SLOPED INSUL.
END CONDITION**

**RCH
2**

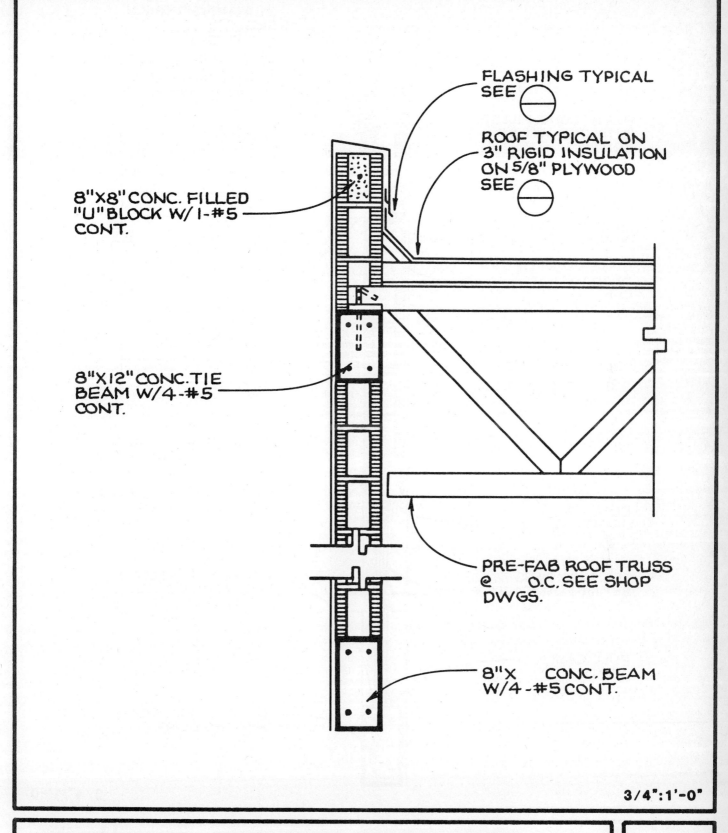

FLASHING TYPICAL
SEE ⊖

ROOF TYPICAL ON
3" RIGID INSULATION
ON 5/8" PLYWOOD
SEE ⊖

8"X8" CONC. FILLED
"U" BLOCK W/ 1-#5
CONT.

8"X 12" CONC. TIE
BEAM W/4-#5
CONT.

PRE-FAB ROOF TRUSS
@   O.C. SEE SHOP
DWGS.

8"X   CONC. BEAM
W/4 -#5 CONT.

3/4":1'-0"

REINFORCED CONCRETE BEAM: LEVEL
WD TRUSS & PLYWD ROOF DECK: SLOPED INSUL.

END CONDITION: LOWER BEAM

RCH 3

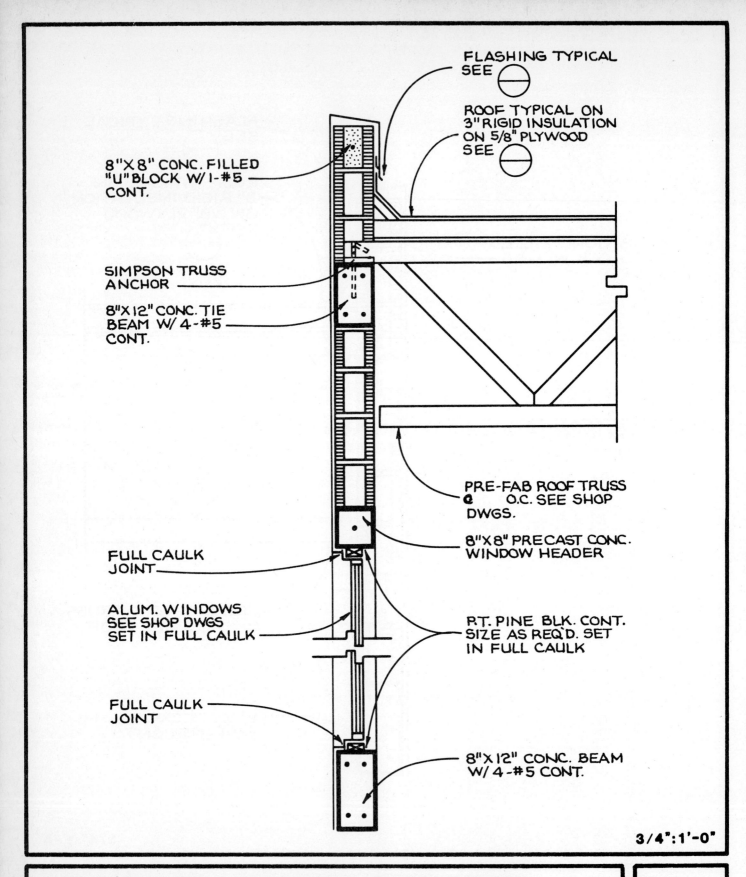

FLASHING TYPICAL
SEE ⊖

ROOF TYPICAL ON
3" RIGID INSULATION
ON 5/8" PLYWOOD
SEE ⊖

8"X8" CONC. FILLED
"U" BLOCK W/ 1-#5
CONT.

SIMPSON TRUSS
ANCHOR

8"X12" CONC. TIE
BEAM W/ 4-#5
CONT.

PRE-FAB ROOF TRUSS
@   O.C. SEE SHOP
DWGS.

8"X8" PRECAST CONC.
WINDOW HEADER

FULL CAULK
JOINT

ALUM. WINDOWS
SEE SHOP DWGS
SET IN FULL CAULK

P.T. PINE BLK. CONT.
SIZE AS REQ'D. SET
IN FULL CAULK

FULL CAULK
JOINT

8"X12" CONC. BEAM
W/ 4-#5 CONT.

3/4":1'-0"

**REINFORCED CONCRETE BEAM: LEVEL
WD TRUSS & PLYWD ROOF DECK: SLOPED INSUL.
END CONDITION: WINDOW**

**RCH
4**

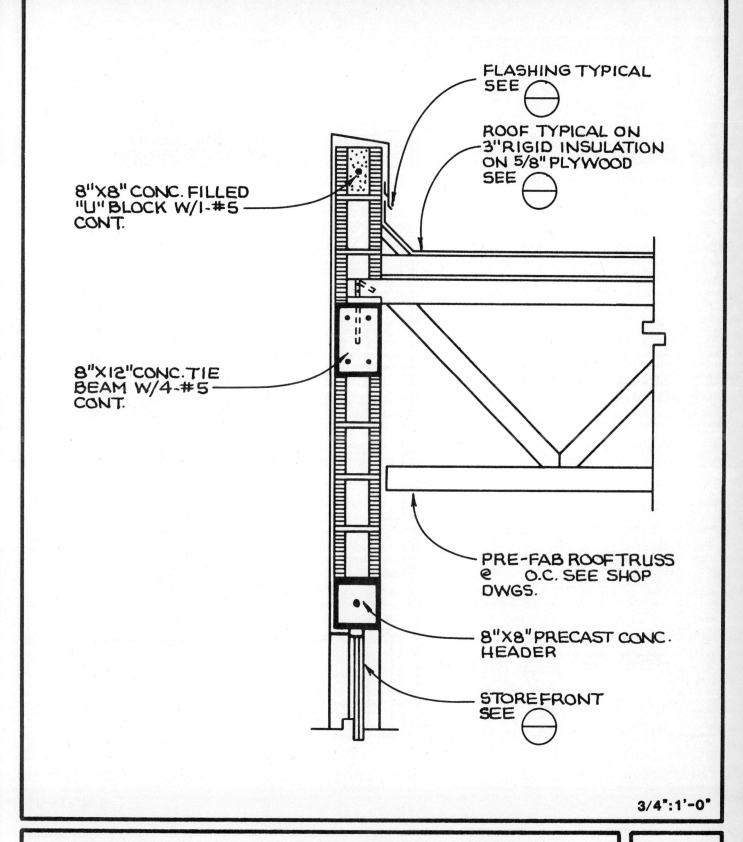

FLASHING TYPICAL
SEE ⊖

ROOF TYPICAL ON
3"RIGID INSULATION
ON 5/8" PLYWOOD
SEE ⊖

8"X8" CONC. FILLED
"U" BLOCK W/1-#5
CONT.

8"X12" CONC. TIE
BEAM W/4-#5
CONT.

PRE-FAB ROOF TRUSS
@   O.C. SEE SHOP
DWGS.

8"X8" PRECAST CONC.
HEADER

STOREFRONT
SEE ⊖

3/4":1'-0"

**REINFORCED CONCRETE BEAM: LEVEL
WD TRUSS & PLYWD ROOF DECK: SLOPED INSUL.
END CONDITION: STOREFRONT**

**RCH
5**

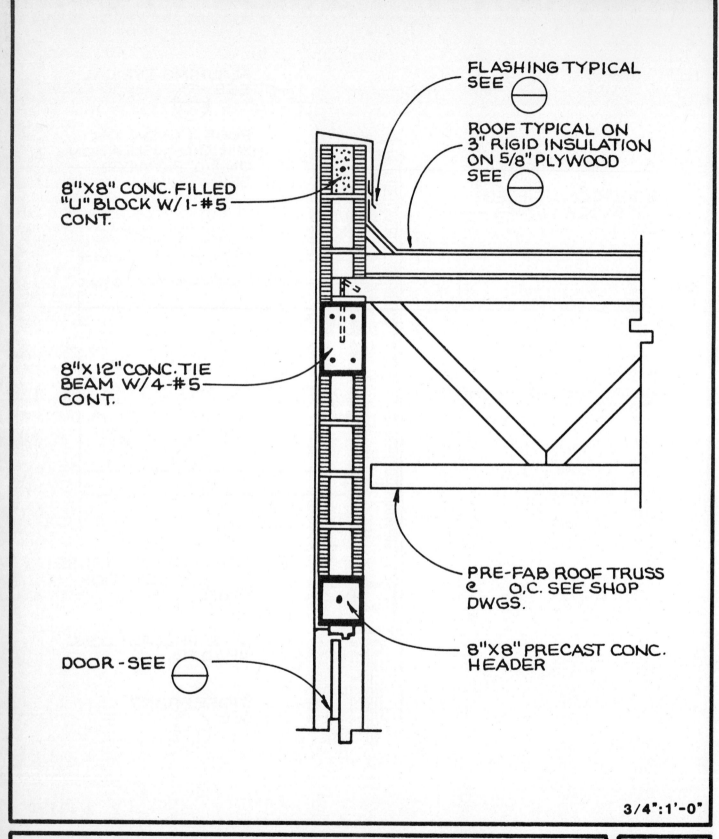

FLASHING TYPICAL SEE ⊖

ROOF TYPICAL ON 3" RIGID INSULATION ON 5/8" PLYWOOD SEE ⊖

8"X8" CONC. FILLED "U" BLOCK W/1-#5 CONT.

8"X12" CONC. TIE BEAM W/4-#5 CONT.

PRE-FAB ROOF TRUSS @   O.C. SEE SHOP DWGS.

8"X8" PRECAST CONC. HEADER

DOOR - SEE ⊖

3/4":1'-0"

REINFORCED CONCRETE BEAM: LEVEL WD TRUSS & PLYWD ROOF DECK: SLOPED INSUL. END CONDITION: DOOR

RCH 6

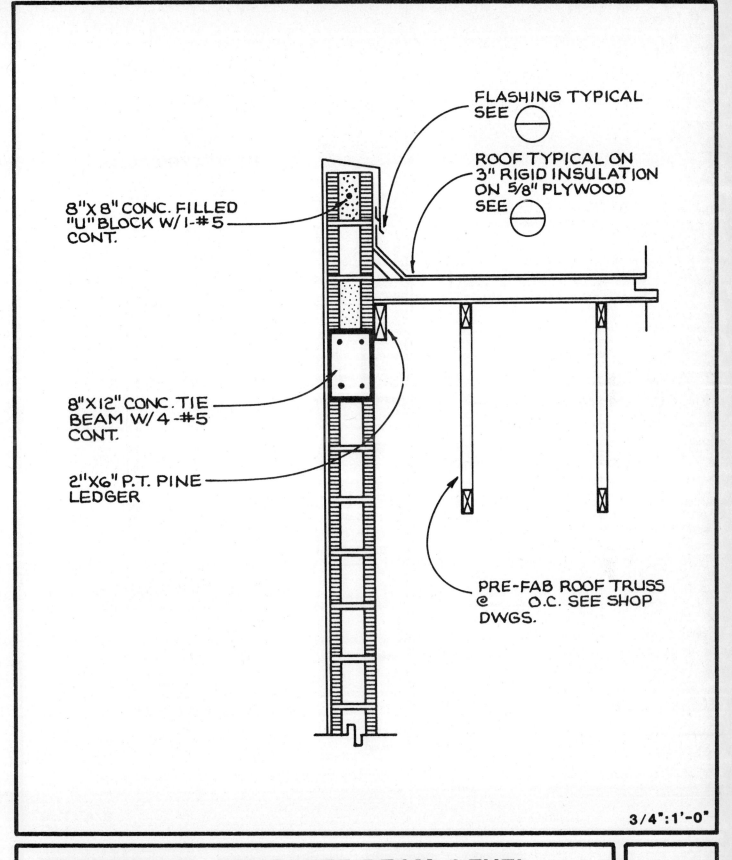

FLASHING TYPICAL
SEE ⊖

ROOF TYPICAL ON
3" RIGID INSULATION
ON 5/8" PLYWOOD
SEE ⊖

8"X 8" CONC. FILLED
"U" BLOCK W/ 1-#5
CONT.

8"X 12" CONC. TIE
BEAM W/ 4 -#5
CONT.

2"X 6" P.T. PINE
LEDGER

PRE-FAB ROOF TRUSS
@   O.C. SEE SHOP
DWGS.

3/4" : 1'-0"

**REINFORCED CONCRETE BEAM: LEVEL
WD TRUSS & PLYWD ROOF DECK: SLOPED INSUL.**

SIDE CONDITION

**RCH
7**

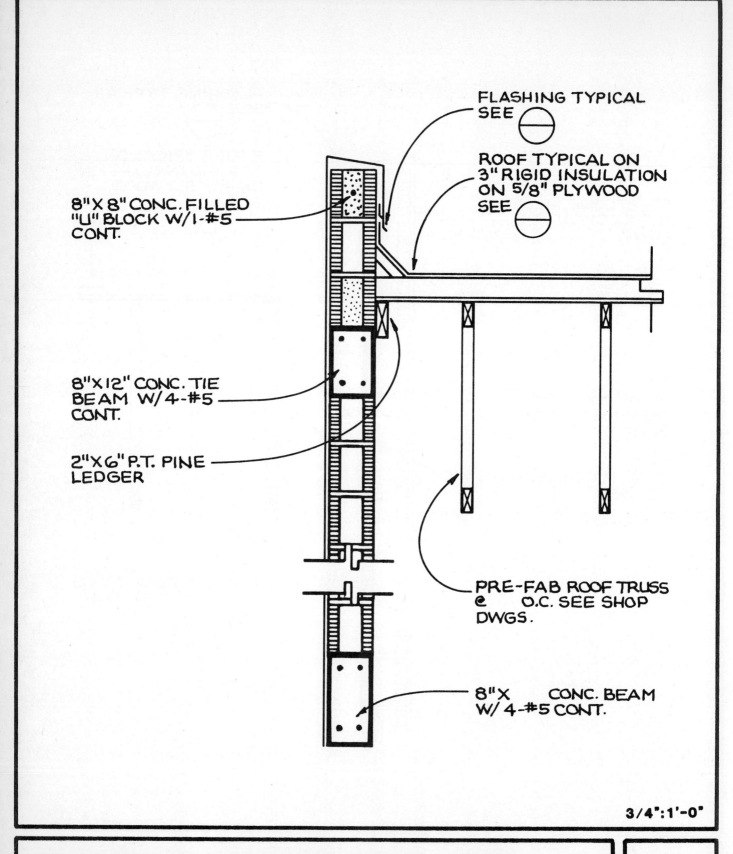

FLASHING TYPICAL
SEE ⊝

ROOF TYPICAL ON
3" RIGID INSULATION
ON 5/8" PLYWOOD
SEE ⊝

8" X 8" CONC. FILLED
"U" BLOCK W/ 1-#5
CONT.

8" X 12" CONC. TIE
BEAM W/ 4-#5
CONT.

2" X 6" P.T. PINE
LEDGER

PRE-FAB ROOF TRUSS
@   O.C. SEE SHOP
DWGS.

8" X   CONC. BEAM
W/ 4-#5 CONT.

3/4":1'-0"

**REINFORCED CONCRETE BEAM: LEVEL
WD TRUSS & PLYWD ROOF DECK: SLOPED INSUL.**

SIDE CONDITION: LOWER BEAM

**RCH
8**

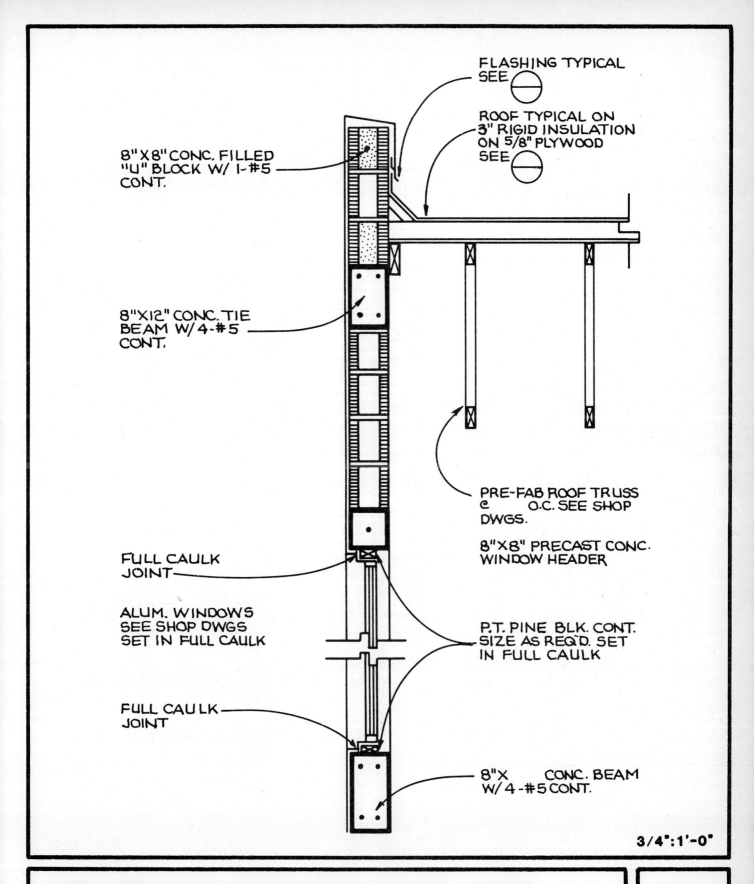

FLASHING TYPICAL
SEE

ROOF TYPICAL ON
3" RIGID INSULATION
ON 5/8" PLYWOOD
SEE

8"X8" CONC. FILLED
"U" BLOCK W/ I-#5
CONT.

8"X12" CONC. TIE
BEAM W/ 4-#5
CONT.

FULL CAULK
JOINT

ALUM. WINDOWS
SEE SHOP DWGS
SET IN FULL CAULK

FULL CAULK
JOINT

PRE-FAB ROOF TRUSS
@   O.C. SEE SHOP
DWGS.

8"X8" PRECAST CONC.
WINDOW HEADER

P.T. PINE BLK. CONT.
SIZE AS REQ'D. SET
IN FULL CAULK

8"X   CONC. BEAM
W/ 4-#5 CONT.

3/4":1'-0"

**REINFORCED CONCRETE BEAM: LEVEL
WD TRUSS & PLYWD ROOF DECK: SLOPED INSUL.
SIDE CONDITION: WINDOW**

**RCH
9**

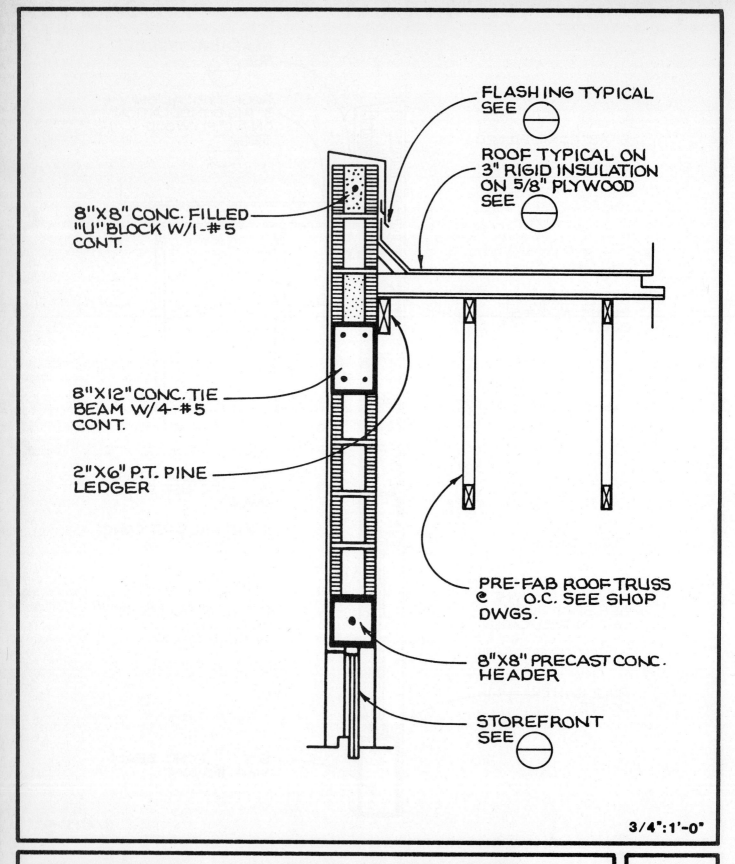

FLASHING TYPICAL
SEE ⊖

ROOF TYPICAL ON
3" RIGID INSULATION
ON 5/8" PLYWOOD
SEE ⊖

8"X8" CONC. FILLED
"U" BLOCK W/ 1-#5
CONT.

8"X12" CONC. TIE
BEAM W/ 4-#5
CONT.

2"X6" P.T. PINE
LEDGER

PRE-FAB ROOF TRUSS
@   O.C. SEE SHOP
DWGS.

8"X8" PRECAST CONC.
HEADER

STOREFRONT
SEE ⊖

3/4":1'-0"

**REINFORCED CONCRETE BEAM: LEVEL
WD TRUSS & PLYWD ROOF DECK: SLOPED INSUL.
SIDE CONDITION: STOREFRONT**

**RCH
10**

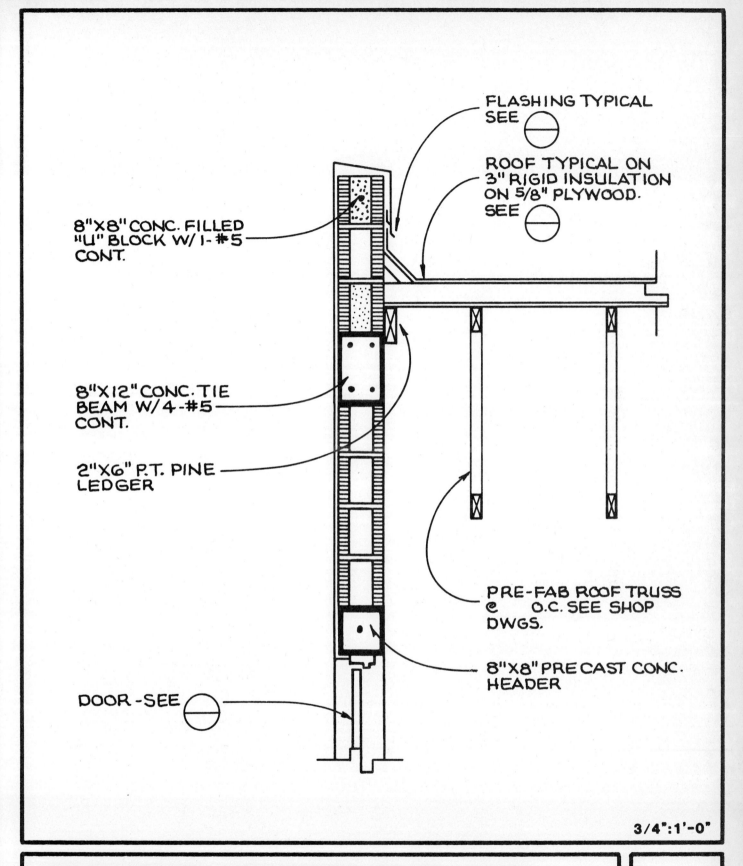

FLASHING TYPICAL
SEE ⊖

ROOF TYPICAL ON
3" RIGID INSULATION
ON 5/8" PLYWOOD.
SEE ⊖

8"X8" CONC. FILLED
"U" BLOCK W/ 1-#5
CONT.

8"X12" CONC. TIE
BEAM W/ 4-#5
CONT.

2"X6" P.T. PINE
LEDGER

PRE-FAB ROOF TRUSS
@   O.C. SEE SHOP
DWGS.

8"X8" PRECAST CONC.
HEADER

DOOR - SEE ⊖

3/4":1'-0"

**REINFORCED CONCRETE BEAM: LEVEL
WD TRUSS & PLYWD ROOF DECK: SLOPED INSUL.**

SIDE CONDITION: DOOR

**RCH
11**

SECTION 9: RM–A

Reinforced masonry construction with sloped beam.
Hollow core concrete roof deck with no insulation.

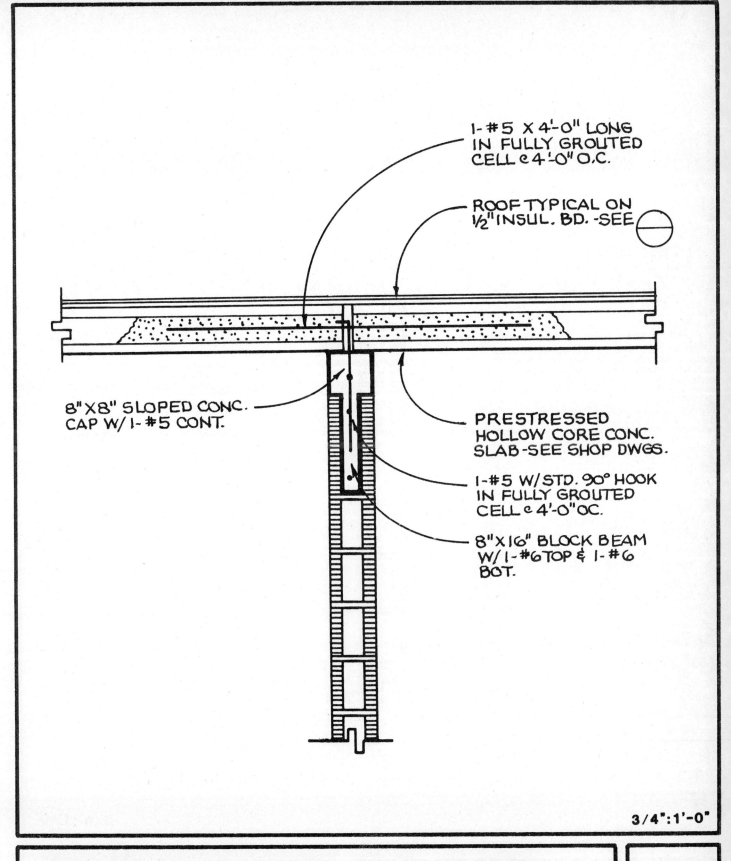

1-#5 X 4'-0" LONG
IN FULLY GROUTED
CELL @ 4'-0" O.C.

ROOF TYPICAL ON
½" INSUL. BD. -SEE ⊘

8"X 8" SLOPED CONC.
CAP W/ 1- #5 CONT.

PRESTRESSED
HOLLOW CORE CONC.
SLAB -SEE SHOP DWGS.

1-#5 W/ STD. 90° HOOK
IN FULLY GROUTED
CELL @ 4'-0" OC.

8"X 16" BLOCK BEAM
W/ 1-#6 TOP & 1- #6
BOT.

3/4":1'-0"

**REINFORCED MASONRY BEAM: SLOPED
HOLLOW CORE ROOF DECK: NO INSULATION**

INTERMEDIATE CONDITION: END

**RMA
1**

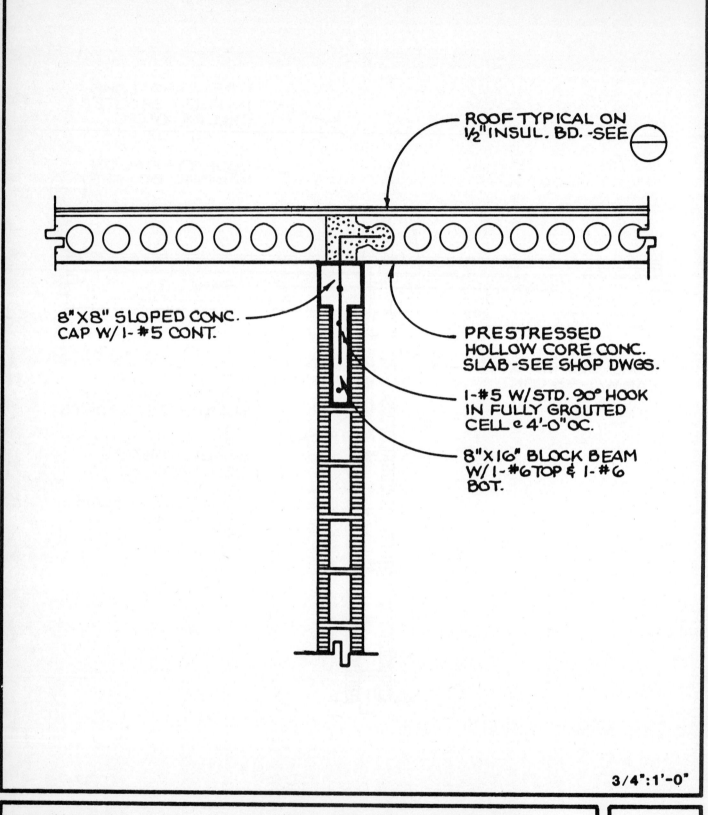

ROOF TYPICAL ON
½" INSUL. BD. -SEE

8"X8" SLOPED CONC.
CAP W/ 1-#5 CONT.

PRESTRESSED
HOLLOW CORE CONC.
SLAB -SEE SHOP DWGS.

1-#5 W/STD. 90° HOOK
IN FULLY GROUTED
CELL @ 4'-0"OC.

8"X16" BLOCK BEAM
W/ 1-#6 TOP & 1-#6
BOT.

3/4":1'-0"

REINFORCED MASONRY BEAM: SLOPED
HOLLOW CORE ROOF DECK: NO INSULATION

INTERMEDIATE CONDITION: SIDE

RMA 2

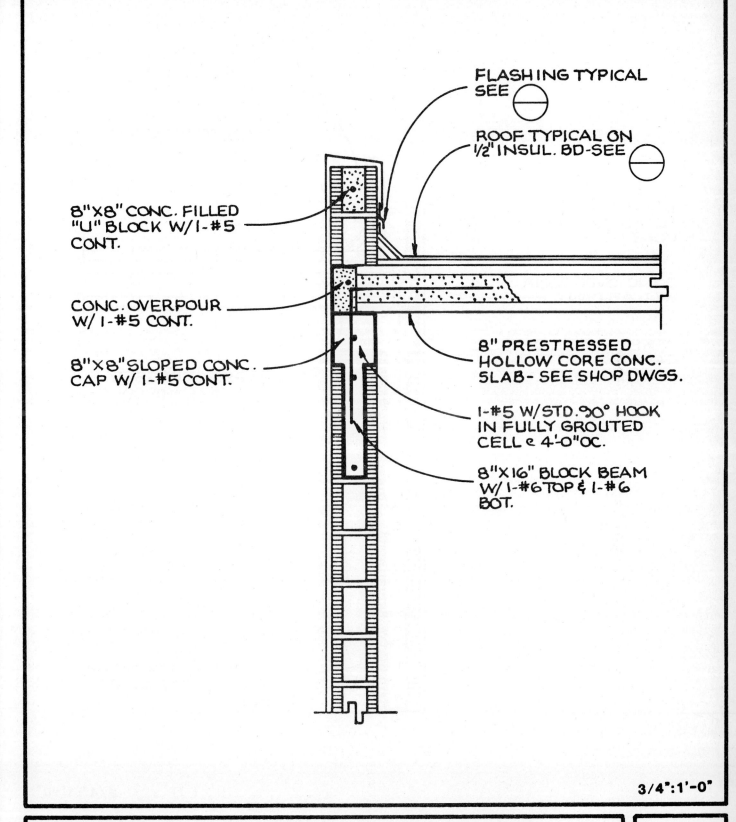

FLASHING TYPICAL
SEE ⊖

ROOF TYPICAL ON
1/2" INSUL. BD-SEE ⊖

8"X8" CONC. FILLED
"U" BLOCK W/1-#5
CONT.

CONC. OVERPOUR
W/1-#5 CONT.

8"X8" SLOPED CONC.
CAP W/1-#5 CONT.

8" PRESTRESSED
HOLLOW CORE CONC.
SLAB- SEE SHOP DWGS.

1-#5 W/STD. 90° HOOK
IN FULLY GROUTED
CELL @ 4'-0" OC.

8"X16" BLOCK BEAM
W/1-#6 TOP & 1-#6
BOT.

3/4":1'-0"

REINFORCED MASONRY BEAM: SLOPED HOLLOW CORE ROOF DECK: NO INSULATION END CONDITION

RMA 3

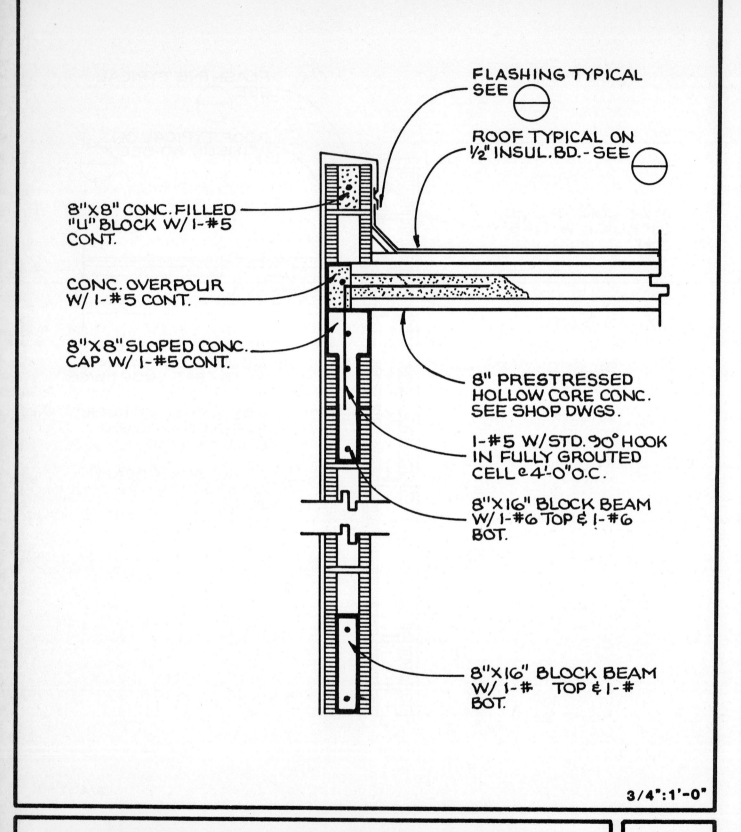

FLASHING TYPICAL
SEE ⊖

ROOF TYPICAL ON
½" INSUL. BD. - SEE ⊖

8"X8" CONC. FILLED
"U" BLOCK W/ 1-#5
CONT.

CONC. OVERPOUR
W/ 1-#5 CONT.

8"X8" SLOPED CONC.
CAP W/ 1-#5 CONT.

8" PRESTRESSED
HOLLOW CORE CONC.
SEE SHOP DWGS.

1-#5 W/ STD. 90° HOOK
IN FULLY GROUTED
CELL @ 4'-0" O.C.

8"X16" BLOCK BEAM
W/ 1-#6 TOP & 1-#6
BOT.

8"X16" BLOCK BEAM
W/ 1-# TOP & 1-#
BOT.

3/4":1'-0"

**REINFORCED MASONRY BEAM: SLOPED
HOLLOW CORE ROOF DECK: NO INSULATION
END CONDITION: LOWER BEAM**

RMA
4

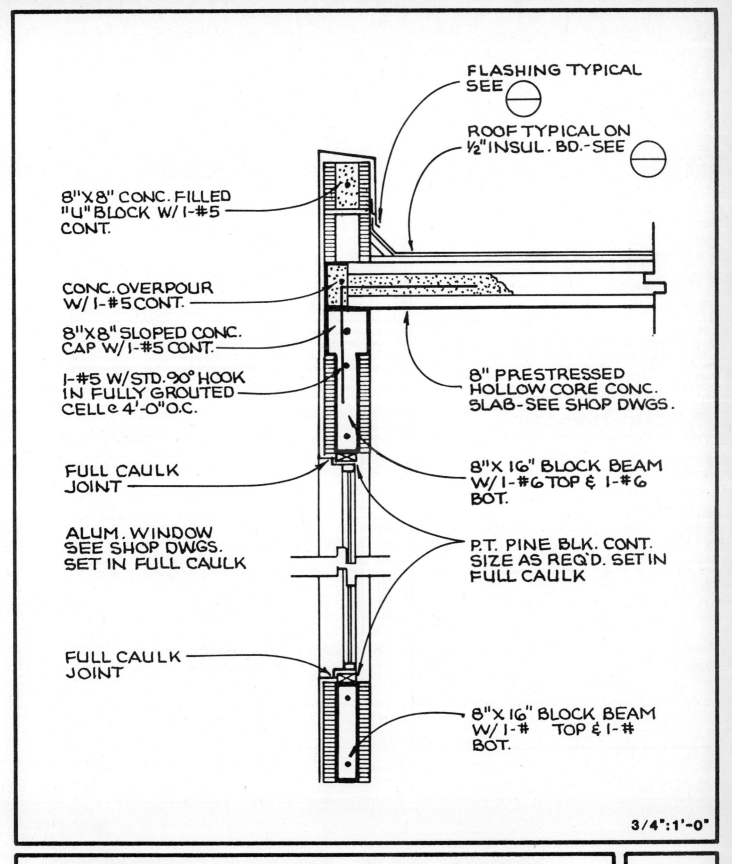

FLASHING TYPICAL
SEE ⊖

ROOF TYPICAL ON
½" INSUL. BD.-SEE ⊖

8"X 8" CONC. FILLED
"U" BLOCK W/ 1-#5
CONT.

CONC. OVERPOUR
W/ 1-#5 CONT.

8"X 8" SLOPED CONC.
CAP W/ 1-#5 CONT.

1-#5 W/STD. 90° HOOK
IN FULLY GROUTED
CELL @ 4'-0" O.C.

FULL CAULK
JOINT

ALUM. WINDOW
SEE SHOP DWGS.
SET IN FULL CAULK

FULL CAULK
JOINT

8" PRESTRESSED
HOLLOW CORE CONC.
SLAB-SEE SHOP DWGS.

8"X 16" BLOCK BEAM
W/ 1-#6 TOP & 1-#6
BOT.

P.T. PINE BLK. CONT.
SIZE AS REQ'D. SET IN
FULL CAULK

8"X 16" BLOCK BEAM
W/ 1-# TOP & 1-#
BOT.

3/4":1'-0"

**REINFORCED MASONRY BEAM: SLOPED
HOLLOW CORE ROOF DECK: NO INSULATION
END CONDITION: WINDOW**

**RMA
5**

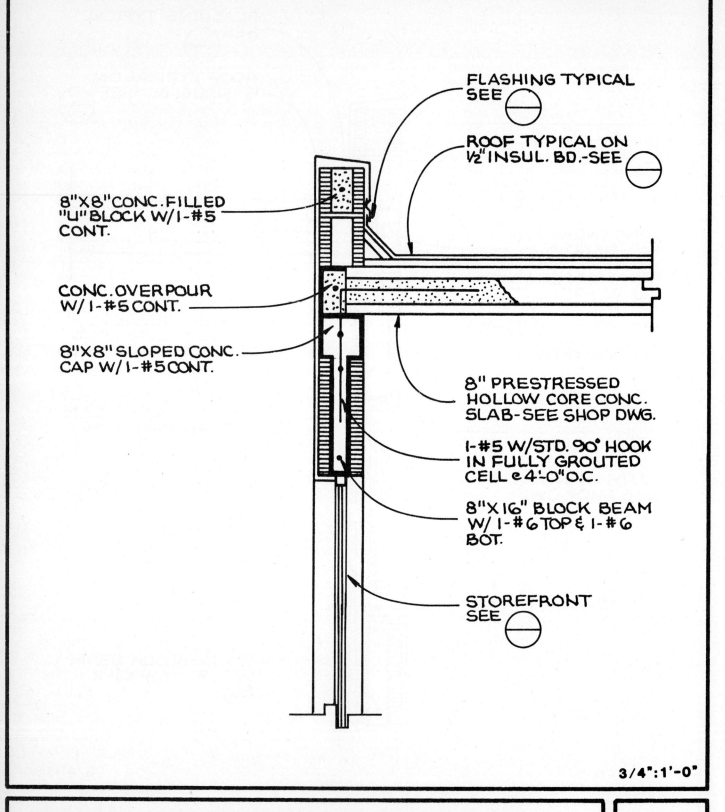

FLASHING TYPICAL SEE ⊖

ROOF TYPICAL ON ½"INSUL. BD.-SEE ⊖

8"X8"CONC.FILLED "U"BLOCK W/1-#5 CONT.

CONC.OVER POUR W/1-#5 CONT.

8"X8" SLOPED CONC. CAP W/1-#5 CONT.

8" PRESTRESSED HOLLOW CORE CONC. SLAB-SEE SHOP DWG.

1-#5 W/STD. 90° HOOK IN FULLY GROUTED CELL @ 4'-0"O.C.

8"X16" BLOCK BEAM W/1-#6 TOP & 1-#6 BOT.

STOREFRONT SEE ⊖

3/4":1'-0"

REINFORCED MASONRY BEAM: SLOPED HOLLOW CORE ROOF DECK: NO INSULATION
END CONDITION: STOREFRONT

RMA 6

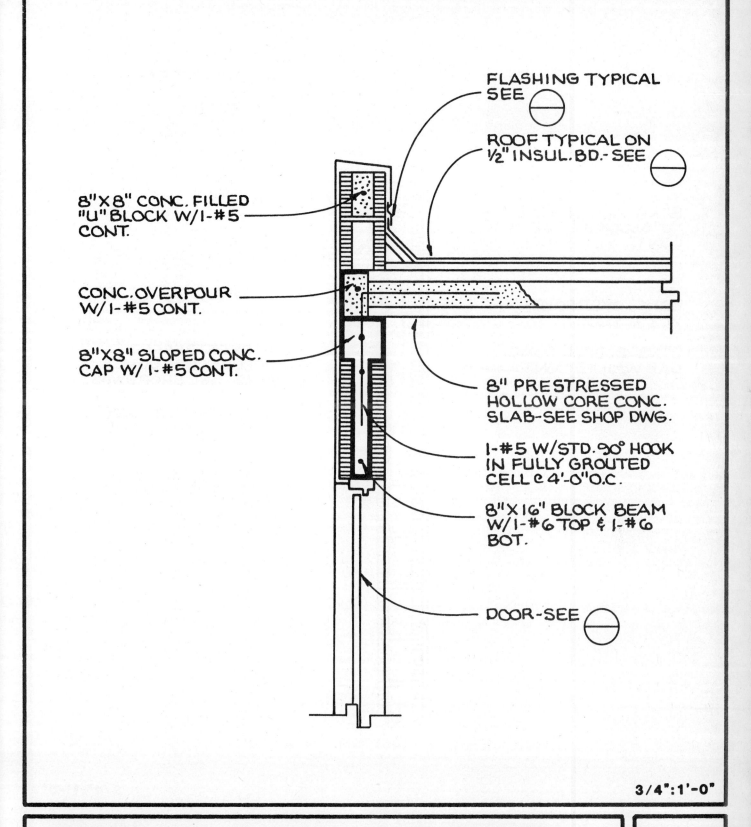

FLASHING TYPICAL SEE ⊘

ROOF TYPICAL ON ½" INSUL. BD.- SEE ⊘

8"X8" CONC. FILLED "U" BLOCK W/1-#5 CONT.

CONC. OVERPOUR W/1-#5 CONT.

8"X8" SLOPED CONC. CAP W/1-#5 CONT.

8" PRESTRESSED HOLLOW CORE CONC. SLAB-SEE SHOP DWG.

1-#5 W/STD. 90° HOOK IN FULLY GROUTED CELL @ 4'-0" O.C.

8"X16" BLOCK BEAM W/1-#6 TOP & 1-#6 BOT.

DOOR-SEE ⊘

3/4":1'-0"

REINFORCED MASONRY BEAM: SLOPED HOLLOW CORE ROOF DECK: NO INSULATION END CONDITION: DOOR

RMA 7

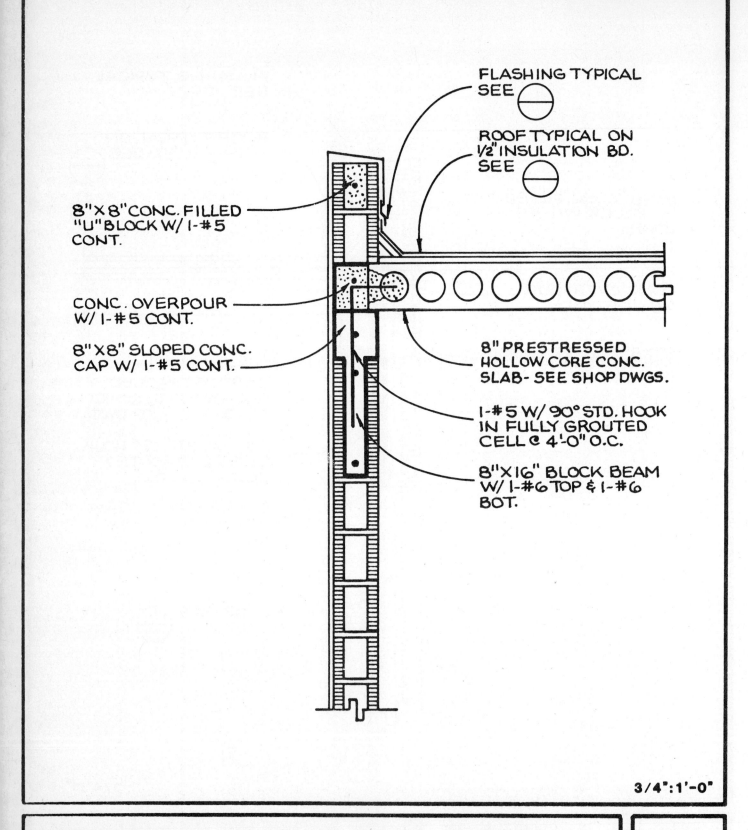

FLASHING TYPICAL SEE ◯

ROOF TYPICAL ON ½" INSULATION BD. SEE ◯

8"X 8" CONC. FILLED "U" BLOCK W/ 1-#5 CONT.

CONC. OVERPOUR W/ 1-#5 CONT.

8"X 8" SLOPED CONC. CAP W/ 1-#5 CONT.

8" PRESTRESSED HOLLOW CORE CONC. SLAB- SEE SHOP DWGS.

1-#5 W/ 90° STD. HOOK IN FULLY GROUTED CELL @ 4'-0" O.C.

8"X16" BLOCK BEAM W/ 1-#6 TOP & 1-#6 BOT.

3/4":1'-0"

REINFORCED MASONRY BEAM: SLOPED HOLLOW CORE ROOF DECK: NO INSULATION SIDE CONDITION

RMA 8

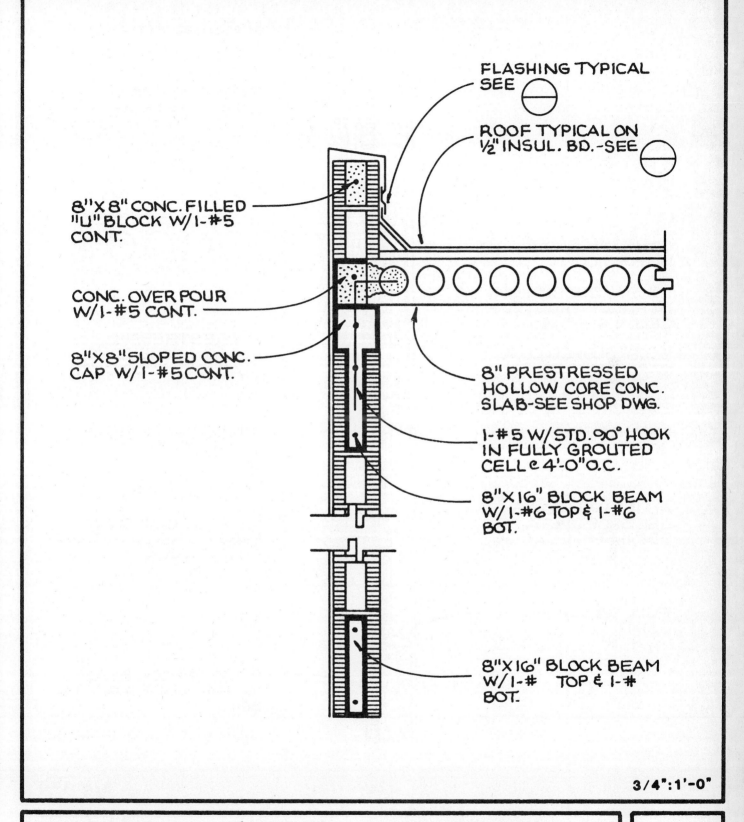

FLASHING TYPICAL
SEE ⊖

ROOF TYPICAL ON
½" INSUL. BD.-SEE
⊖

8"X8" CONC. FILLED
"U" BLOCK W/1-#5
CONT.

CONC. OVER POUR
W/1-#5 CONT.

8"X8" SLOPED CONC.
CAP W/1-#5 CONT.

8" PRESTRESSED
HOLLOW CORE CONC.
SLAB-SEE SHOP DWG.

1-#5 W/STD. 90° HOOK
IN FULLY GROUTED
CELL @ 4'-0" O.C.

8"X16" BLOCK BEAM
W/1-#6 TOP & 1-#6
BOT.

8"X16" BLOCK BEAM
W/1-# TOP & 1-#
BOT.

3/4":1'-0"

**REINFORCED MASONRY BEAM: SLOPED
HOLLOW CORE ROOF DECK: NO INSULATION
SIDE CONDITION: LOWER BEAM**

RMA
9

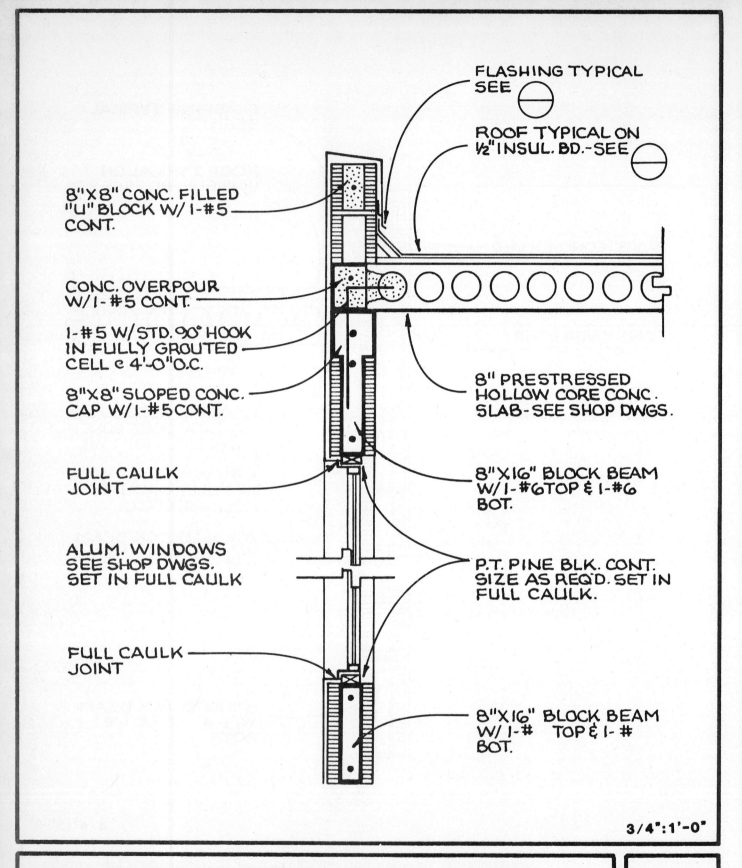

FLASHING TYPICAL
SEE ⊖

ROOF TYPICAL ON
½" INSUL. BD.-SEE ⊖

8"X 8" CONC. FILLED
"U" BLOCK W/ 1-#5
CONT.

CONC. OVERPOUR
W/ 1-#5 CONT.

1-#5 W/ STD. 90° HOOK
IN FULLY GROUTED
CELL @ 4'-0" O.C.

8"X 8" SLOPED CONC.
CAP W/ 1-#5 CONT.

FULL CAULK
JOINT

ALUM. WINDOWS
SEE SHOP DWGS.
SET IN FULL CAULK

FULL CAULK
JOINT

8" PRESTRESSED
HOLLOW CORE CONC.
SLAB- SEE SHOP DWGS.

8"X 16" BLOCK BEAM
W/ 1-#6 TOP & 1-#6
BOT.

P.T. PINE BLK. CONT.
SIZE AS REQ'D. SET IN
FULL CAULK.

8"X 16" BLOCK BEAM
W/ 1-# TOP & 1-#
BOT.

3/4":1'-0"

**REINFORCED MASONRY BEAM: SLOPED
HOLLOW CORE ROOF DECK: NO INSULATION
SIDE CONDITION: WINDOW**

**RMA
10**

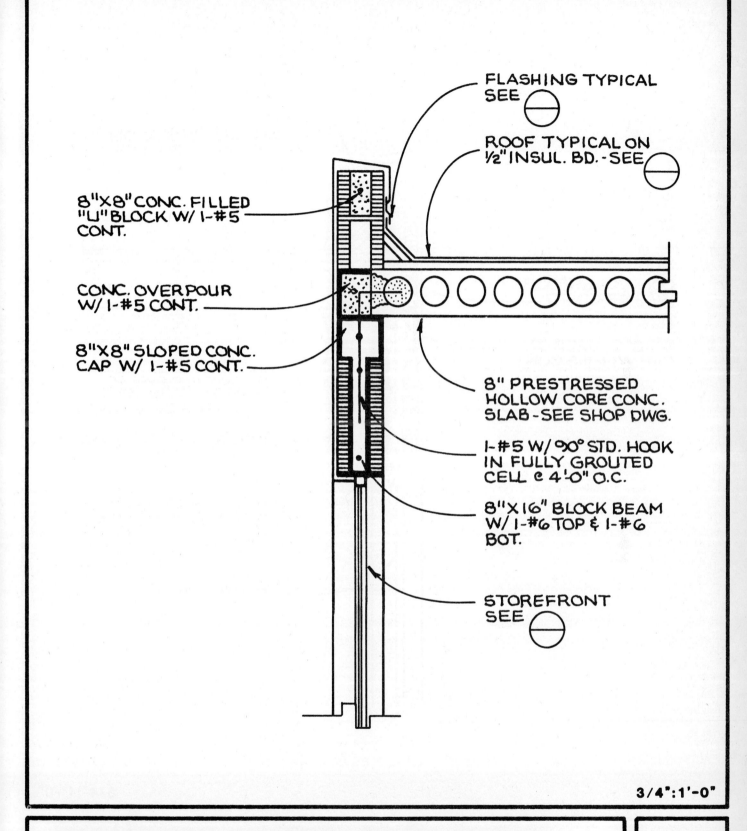

FLASHING TYPICAL
SEE ⊖

ROOF TYPICAL ON
½" INSUL. BD. - SEE ⊖

8"X8" CONC. FILLED
"U" BLOCK W/ 1-#5
CONT.

CONC. OVERPOUR
W/ 1-#5 CONT.

8"X8" SLOPED CONC.
CAP W/ 1-#5 CONT.

8" PRESTRESSED
HOLLOW CORE CONC.
SLAB - SEE SHOP DWG.

1-#5 W/ 90° STD. HOOK
IN FULLY GROUTED
CELL @ 4'-0" O.C.

8"X16" BLOCK BEAM
W/ 1-#6 TOP & 1-#6
BOT.

STOREFRONT
SEE ⊖

3/4":1'-0"

**REINFORCED MASONRY BEAM: SLOPED
HOLLOW CORE ROOF DECK: NO INSULATION
SIDE CONDITION: STOREFRONT**

**RMA
11**

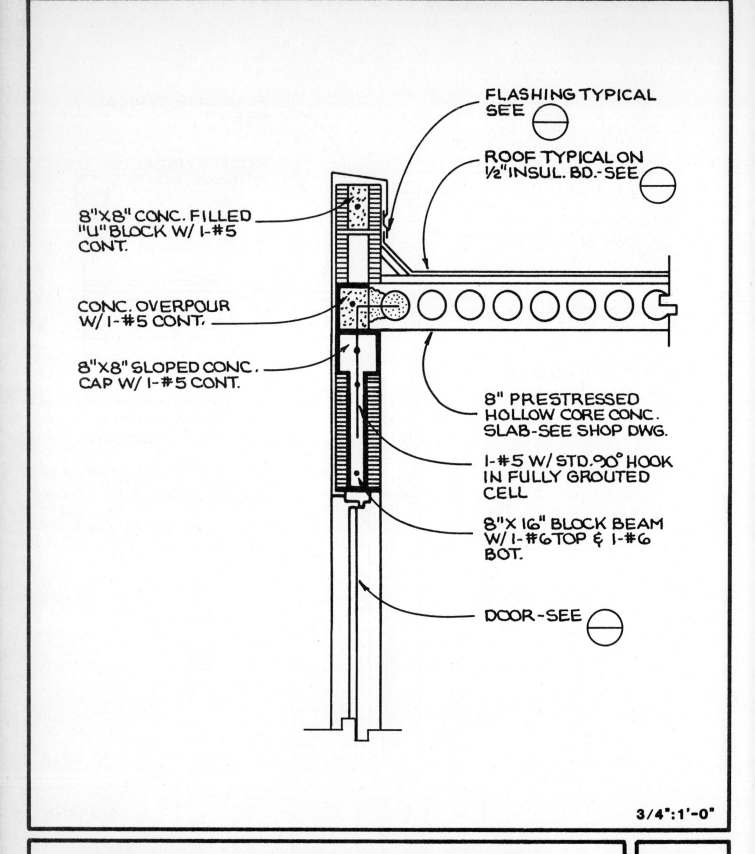

FLASHING TYPICAL SEE ◯

ROOF TYPICAL ON ½"INSUL. BD.-SEE ◯

8"X8" CONC. FILLED "U" BLOCK W/ 1-#5 CONT.

CONC. OVERPOUR W/ 1-#5 CONT.

8"X8" SLOPED CONC. CAP W/ 1-#5 CONT.

8" PRESTRESSED HOLLOW CORE CONC. SLAB-SEE SHOP DWG.

1-#5 W/ STD. 90° HOOK IN FULLY GROUTED CELL

8"X 16" BLOCK BEAM W/ 1-#6 TOP & 1-#6 BOT.

DOOR - SEE ◯

3/4":1'-0"

REINFORCED MASONRY BEAM: SLOPED HOLLOW CORE ROOF DECK: NO INSULATION

SIDE CONDITION: DOOR

RMA 12

SECTION 10: RM—B

Reinforced masonry construction with level beam.
Hollow core concrete roof deck with sloped insulation.

ARCHITECTURAL DETAILING
FOR
COMMERCIAL CONSTRUCTION

10

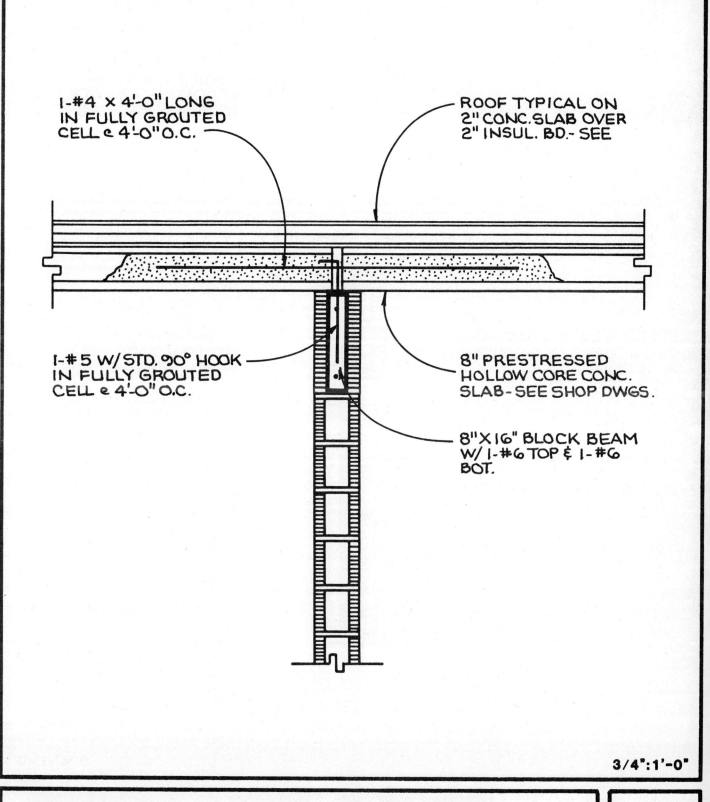

1-#4 × 4'-0" LONG
IN FULLY GROUTED
CELL @ 4'-0" O.C.

ROOF TYPICAL ON
2" CONC. SLAB OVER
2" INSUL. BD.- SEE

1-#5 W/ STD. 90° HOOK
IN FULLY GROUTED
CELL @ 4'-0" O.C.

8" PRESTRESSED
HOLLOW CORE CONC.
SLAB- SEE SHOP DWGS.

8" × 16" BLOCK BEAM
W/ 1-#6 TOP & 1-#6
BOT.

3/4":1'-0"

**REINFORCED MASONRY BEAM: LEVEL
HOLLOW CORE ROOF DECK: SLOPED INSUL.**

INTERMEDIATE CONDITION: END

**RMB
1**

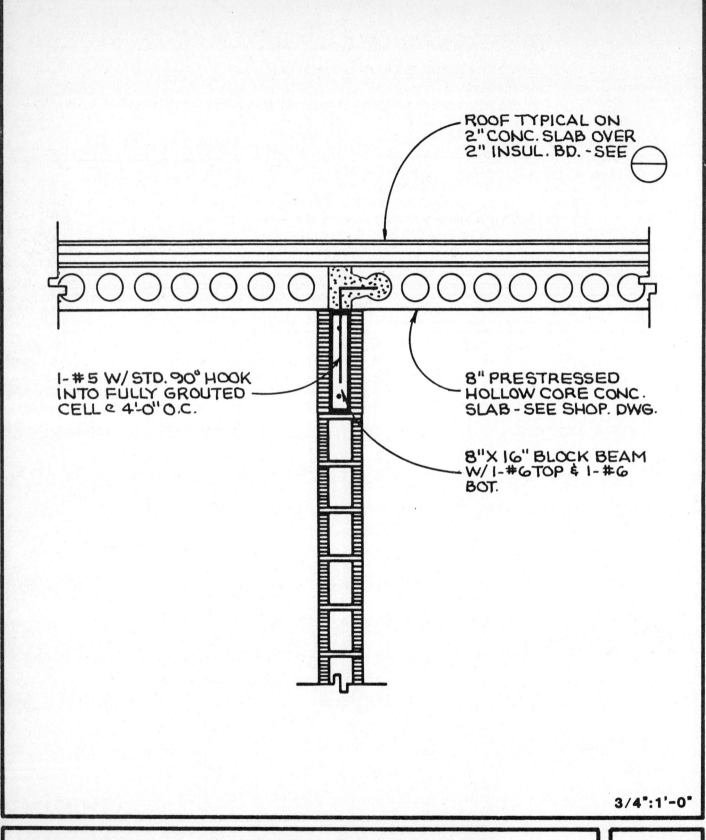

ROOF TYPICAL ON
2" CONC. SLAB OVER
2" INSUL. BD. - SEE ⊖

1- #5 W/ STD. 90° HOOK
INTO FULLY GROUTED
CELL @ 4'-0" O.C.

8" PRESTRESSED
HOLLOW CORE CONC.
SLAB - SEE SHOP. DWG.

8"X 16" BLOCK BEAM
W/ 1-#6 TOP & 1-#6
BOT.

3/4":1'-0"

REINFORCED MASONRY BEAM: LEVEL
HOLLOW CORE ROOF DECK: SLOPED INSUL.

INTERMEDIATE CONDITION: SIDE

RMB
2

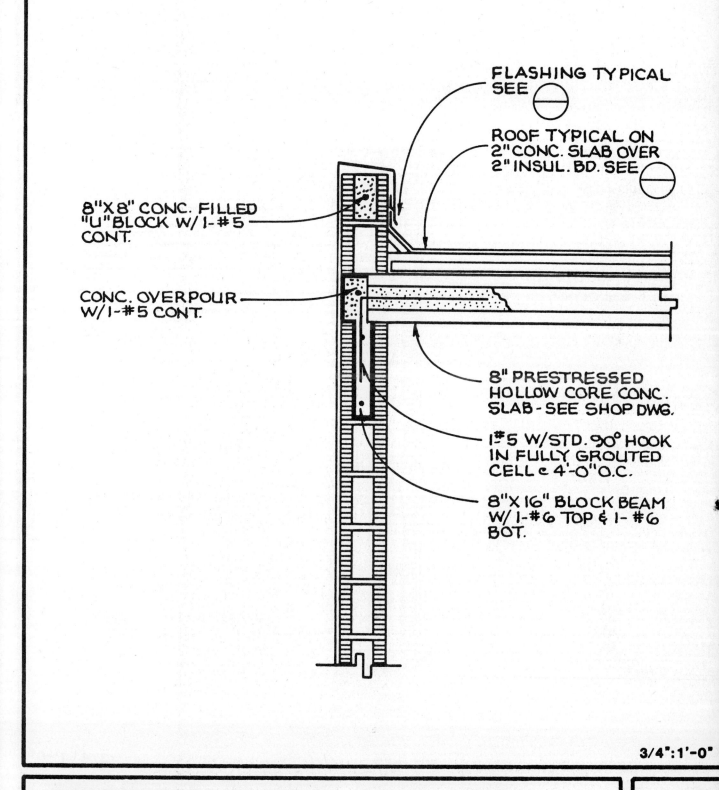

FLASHING TYPICAL SEE ◯

ROOF TYPICAL ON 2" CONC. SLAB OVER 2" INSUL. BD. SEE ◯

8"X8" CONC. FILLED "U" BLOCK W/1-#5 CONT.

CONC. OVERPOUR W/1-#5 CONT.

8" PRESTRESSED HOLLOW CORE CONC. SLAB - SEE SHOP DWG.

1#5 W/STD. 90° HOOK IN FULLY GROUTED CELL @ 4'-0" O.C.

8"X16" BLOCK BEAM W/1-#6 TOP & 1-#6 BOT.

3/4":1'-0"

REINFORCED MASONRY BEAM: LEVEL HOLLOW CORE ROOF DECK: SLOPED INSUL. END CONDITION

RMB 3

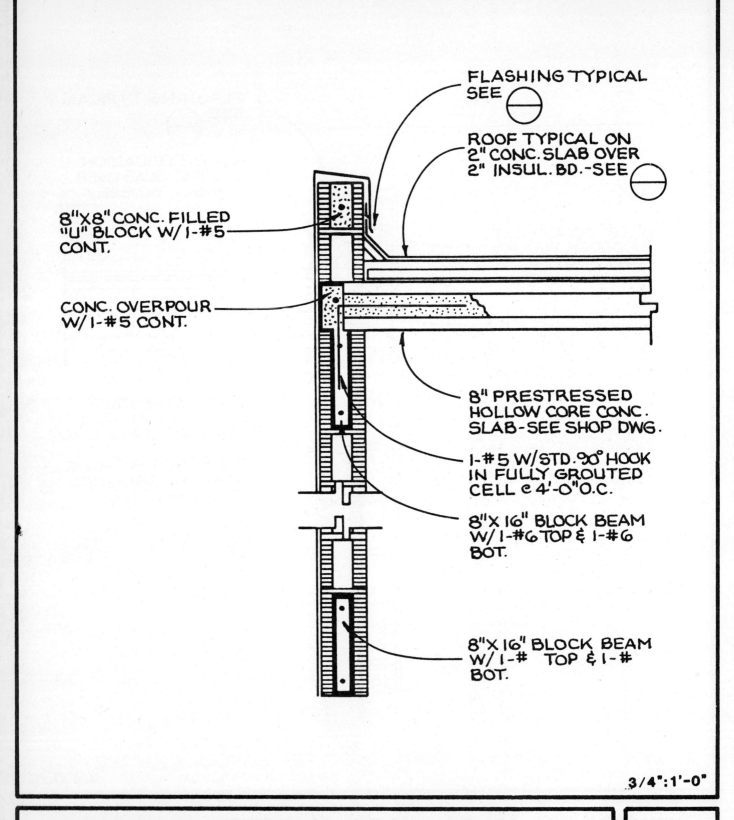

FLASHING TYPICAL SEE ⊖

ROOF TYPICAL ON 2" CONC. SLAB OVER 2" INSUL. BD.-SEE ⊖

8"X8" CONC. FILLED "U" BLOCK W/ 1-#5 CONT.

CONC. OVERPOUR W/ 1-#5 CONT.

8" PRESTRESSED HOLLOW CORE CONC. SLAB-SEE SHOP DWG.

1-#5 W/STD. 90° HOOK IN FULLY GROUTED CELL @ 4'-0" O.C.

8"X 16" BLOCK BEAM W/ 1-#6 TOP & 1-#6 BOT.

8"X 16" BLOCK BEAM W/ 1-# TOP & 1-# BOT.

3/4":1'-0"

REINFORCED MASONRY BEAM: LEVEL HOLLOW CORE ROOF DECK: SLOPED INSUL.

END CONDITION: LOWER BEAM

RMB 4

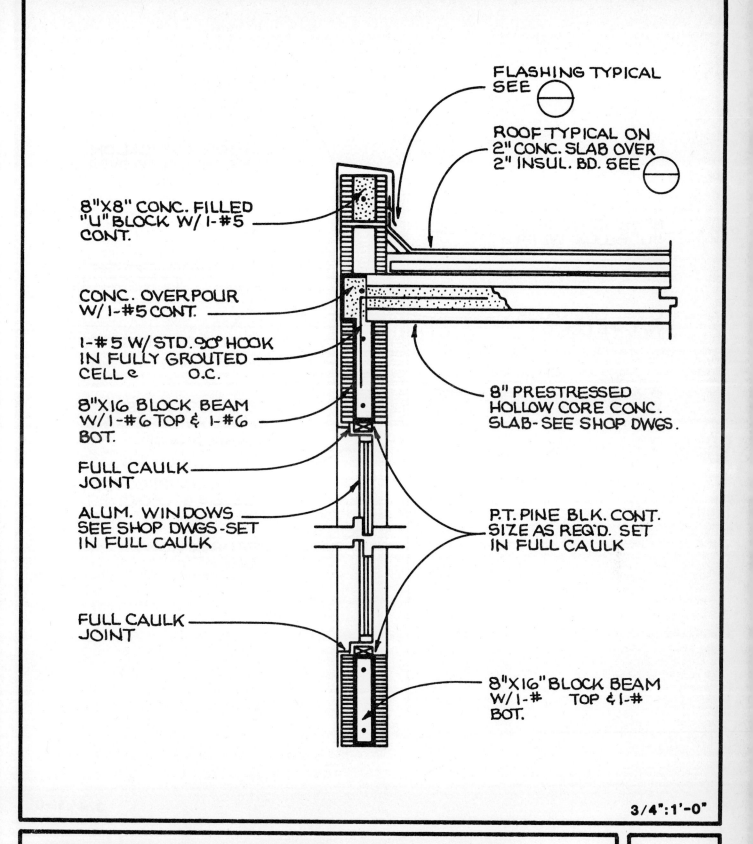

FLASHING TYPICAL SEE ⊖

ROOF TYPICAL ON 2" CONC. SLAB OVER 2" INSUL. BD. SEE ⊖

8"X8" CONC. FILLED "U" BLOCK W/ 1-#5 CONT.

CONC. OVERPOUR W/ 1-#5 CONT.

1-#5 W/ STD. 90° HOOK IN FULLY GROUTED CELL e   O.C.

8"X16 BLOCK BEAM W/ 1-#6 TOP & 1-#6 BOT.

FULL CAULK JOINT

ALUM. WINDOWS SEE SHOP DWGS - SET IN FULL CAULK

FULL CAULK JOINT

8" PRESTRESSED HOLLOW CORE CONC. SLAB - SEE SHOP DWGS.

P.T. PINE BLK. CONT. SIZE AS REQ'D. SET IN FULL CAULK

8"X16" BLOCK BEAM W/ 1-#   TOP & 1-# BOT.

3/4":1'-0"

REINFORCED MASONRY BEAM: LEVEL HOLLOW CORE ROOF DECK: SLOPED INSUL.
END CONDITION: WINDOW

RMB 5

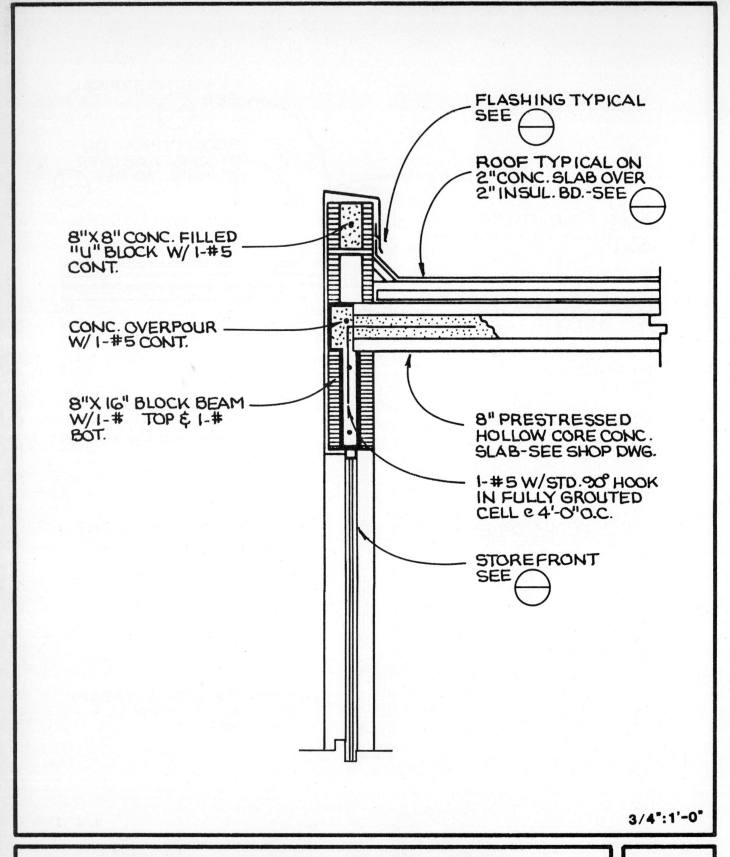

FLASHING TYPICAL
SEE ◯

ROOF TYPICAL ON
2" CONC. SLAB OVER
2" INSUL. BD.-SEE ◯

8" X 8" CONC. FILLED
"U" BLOCK W/ 1-#5
CONT.

CONC. OVERPOUR
W/ 1-#5 CONT.

8" X 16" BLOCK BEAM
W/ 1-# TOP & 1-#
BOT.

8" PRESTRESSED
HOLLOW CORE CONC.
SLAB-SEE SHOP DWG.

1-#5 W/ STD. 90° HOOK
IN FULLY GROUTED
CELL @ 4'-0" O.C.

STOREFRONT
SEE ◯

3/4":1'-0"

**REINFORCED MASONRY BEAM: LEVEL
HOLLOW CORE ROOF DECK: SLOPED INSUL.**

END CONDITION: STOREFRONT

**RMB
6**

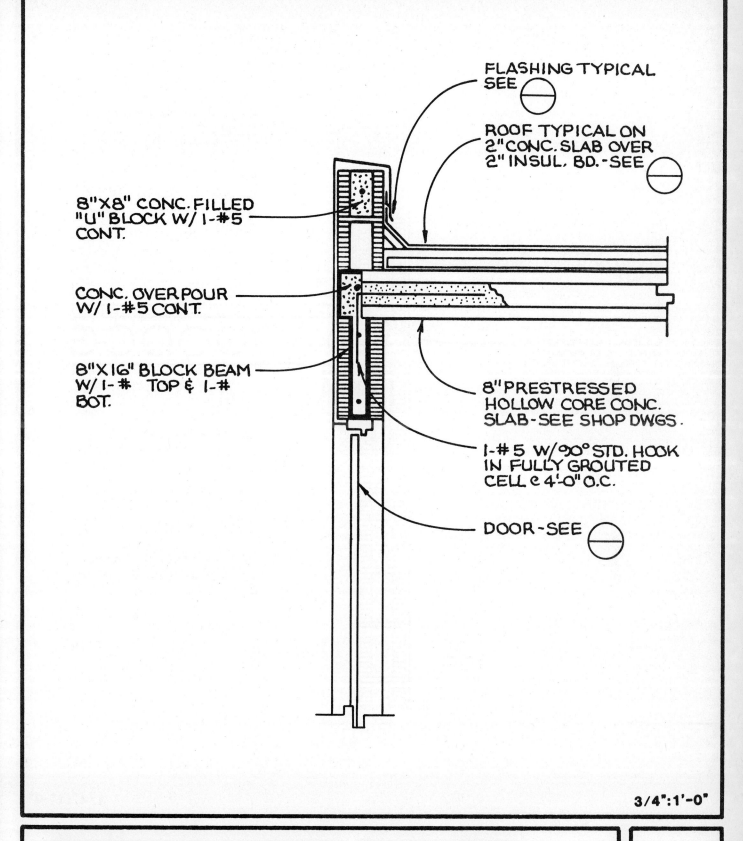

FLASHING TYPICAL
SEE ◯

ROOF TYPICAL ON
2" CONC. SLAB OVER
2" INSUL. BD. - SEE ◯

8"X8" CONC. FILLED
"U" BLOCK W/ I-#5
CONT.

CONC. OVER POUR
W/ I-#5 CONT.

8"X16" BLOCK BEAM
W/ I-# TOP & I-#
BOT.

8" PRESTRESSED
HOLLOW CORE CONC.
SLAB - SEE SHOP DWGS.

I-#5 W/90° STD. HOOK
IN FULLY GROUTED
CELL @ 4'-0" O.C.

DOOR - SEE ◯

3/4":1'-0"

**REINFORCED MASONRY BEAM: LEVEL
HOLLOW CORE ROOF DECK: SLOPED INSUL.**

END CONDITION: DOOR

**RMB
7**

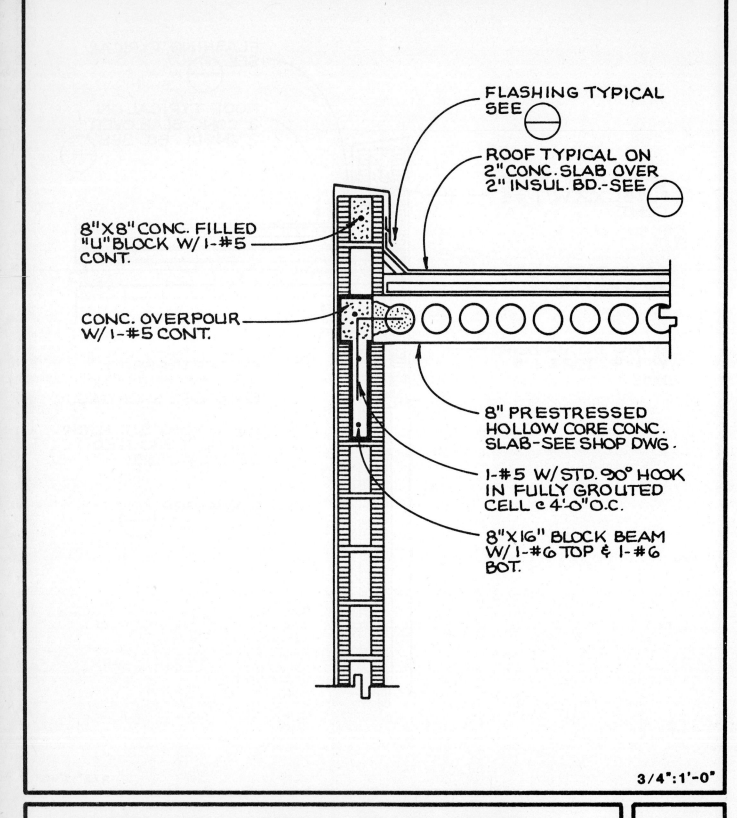

FLASHING TYPICAL
SEE ⊖

ROOF TYPICAL ON
2" CONC. SLAB OVER
2" INSUL. BD.-SEE ⊖

8"X8" CONC. FILLED
"U" BLOCK W/ 1-#5
CONT.

CONC. OVERPOUR
W/ 1-#5 CONT.

8" PRESTRESSED
HOLLOW CORE CONC.
SLAB-SEE SHOP DWG.

1-#5 W/ STD. 90° HOOK
IN FULLY GROUTED
CELL @ 4'-0" O.C.

8"X16" BLOCK BEAM
W/ 1-#6 TOP & 1-#6
BOT.

3/4":1'-0"

**REINFORCED MASONRY BEAM: LEVEL
HOLLOW CORE ROOF DECK: SLOPED INSUL.
SIDE CONDITION**

**RMB
8**

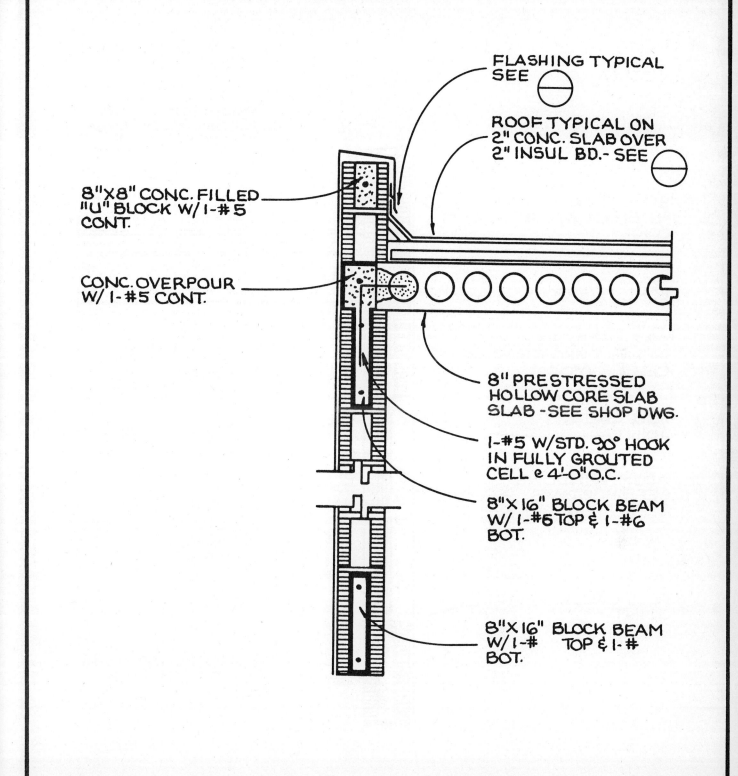

FLASHING TYPICAL
SEE ⊖

ROOF TYPICAL ON
2" CONC. SLAB OVER
2" INSUL BD.- SEE ⊖

8"X8" CONC. FILLED
"U" BLOCK W/ 1-#5
CONT.

CONC. OVERPOUR
W/ 1-#5 CONT.

8" PRESTRESSED
HOLLOW CORE SLAB
SLAB - SEE SHOP DWG.

1-#5 W/STD. 90° HOOK
IN FULLY GROUTED
CELL @ 4'-0" O.C.

8"X16" BLOCK BEAM
W/ 1-#5 TOP & 1-#6
BOT.

8"X16" BLOCK BEAM
W/ 1-#   TOP & 1-#
BOT.

3/4":1'-0"

REINFORCED MASONRY BEAM: LEVEL
HOLLOW CORE ROOF DECK: SLOPED INSUL.

SIDE CONDITION: LOWER BEAM

RMB
9

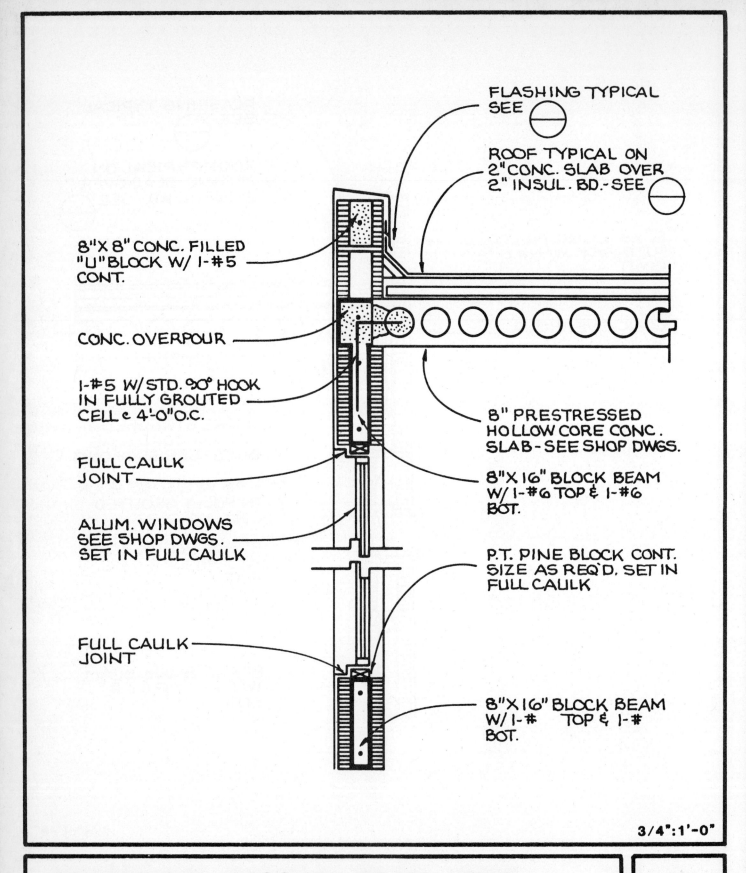

FLASHING TYPICAL SEE ◯

ROOF TYPICAL ON 2" CONC. SLAB OVER 2" INSUL. BD.- SEE ◯

8"X 8" CONC. FILLED "U" BLOCK W/ 1-#5 CONT.

CONC. OVERPOUR

1-#5 W/ STD. 90° HOOK IN FULLY GROUTED CELL @ 4'-0" O.C.

FULL CAULK JOINT

ALUM. WINDOWS SEE SHOP DWGS. SET IN FULL CAULK

FULL CAULK JOINT

8" PRESTRESSED HOLLOW CORE CONC. SLAB - SEE SHOP DWGS.

8"X 16" BLOCK BEAM W/ 1-#6 TOP & 1-#6 BOT.

P.T. PINE BLOCK CONT. SIZE AS REQ'D. SET IN FULL CAULK

8"X 16" BLOCK BEAM W/ 1-# TOP & 1-# BOT.

3/4":1'-0"

REINFORCED MASONRY BEAM: LEVEL HOLLOW CORE ROOF DECK: SLOPED INSUL.

SIDE CONDITION: WINDOW

RMB 10

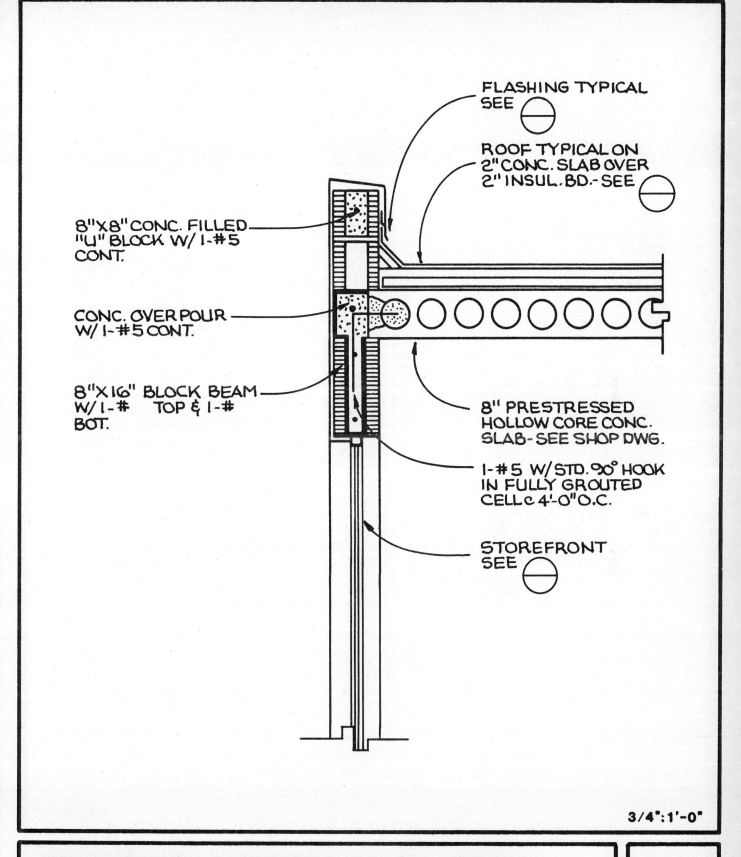

FLASHING TYPICAL
SEE ⊖

ROOF TYPICAL ON
2" CONC. SLAB OVER
2" INSUL. BD.- SEE ⊖

8"X8" CONC. FILLED
"U" BLOCK W/ 1-#5
CONT.

CONC. OVER POUR
W/ 1-#5 CONT.

8"X16" BLOCK BEAM
W/ 1-#   TOP & 1-#
BOT.

8" PRESTRESSED
HOLLOW CORE CONC.
SLAB- SEE SHOP DWG.

1-#5 W/ STD. 90° HOOK
IN FULLY GROUTED
CELL @ 4'-0" O.C.

STOREFRONT
SEE ⊖

3/4":1'-0"

REINFORCED MASONRY BEAM: LEVEL
HOLLOW CORE ROOF DECK: SLOPED INSUL.
SIDE CONDITION: STOREFRONT

**RMB
11**

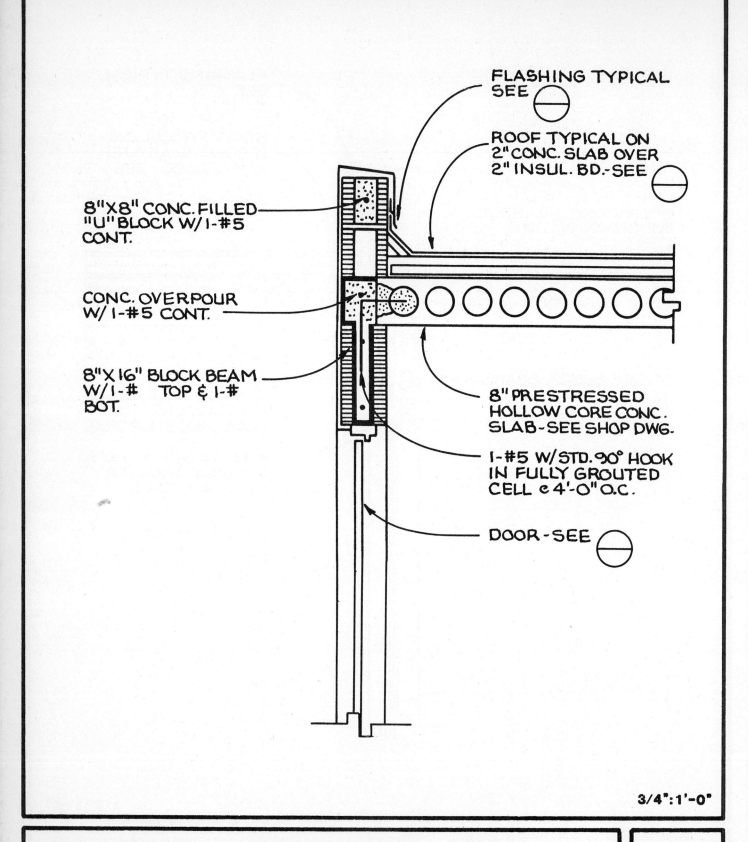

FLASHING TYPICAL
SEE ⊖

ROOF TYPICAL ON
2" CONC. SLAB OVER
2" INSUL. BD.-SEE ⊖

8"X8" CONC. FILLED
"U" BLOCK W/1-#5
CONT.

CONC. OVERPOUR
W/1-#5 CONT.

8"X 16" BLOCK BEAM
W/1-#   TOP & 1-#
BOT.

8" PRESTRESSED
HOLLOW CORE CONC.
SLAB-SEE SHOP DWG.

I-#5 W/STD. 90° HOOK
IN FULLY GROUTED
CELL @ 4'-0" O.C.

DOOR-SEE ⊖

3/4":1'-0"

**REINFORCED MASONRY BEAM: LEVEL
HOLLOW CORE ROOF DECK: SLOPED INSUL.
SIDE CONDITION: DOOR**

**RMB
12**

SECTION 11: RM–C

Reinforced masonry construction with sloped beam.
Prestressed concrete twin tee roof deck with no insulation.

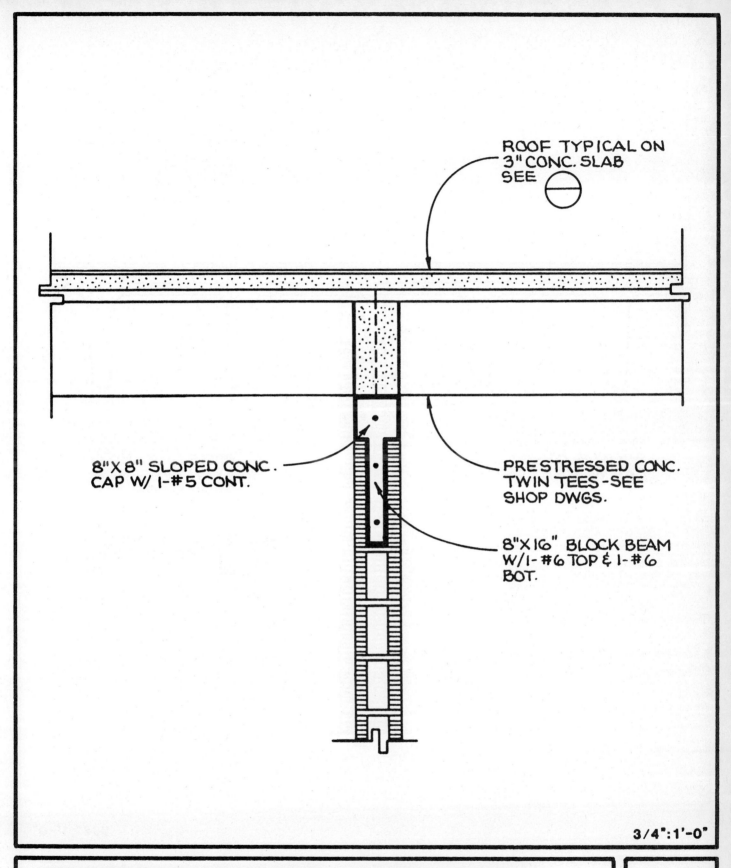

ROOF TYPICAL ON
3" CONC. SLAB
SEE ⊖

8"X 8" SLOPED CONC.
CAP W/ 1-#5 CONT.

PRESTRESSED CONC.
TWIN TEES - SEE
SHOP DWGS.

8"X 16" BLOCK BEAM
W/ 1-#6 TOP & 1-#6
BOT.

3/4":1'-0"

**REINFORCED MASONRY BEAM: SLOPED
TWIN TEE ROOF DECK: NO INSULATION**

INTERMEDIATE CONDITION: END

**RMC
1**

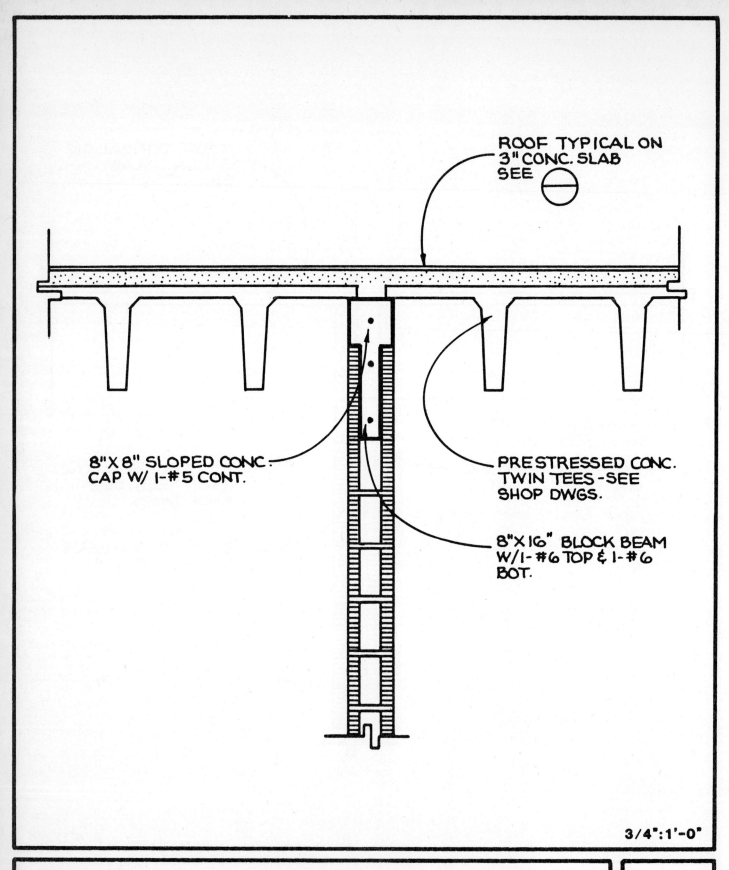

ROOF TYPICAL ON
3" CONC. SLAB
SEE ⊖

8"X 8" SLOPED CONC.
CAP W/ 1-#5 CONT.

PRESTRESSED CONC.
TWIN TEES -SEE
SHOP DWGS.

8"X 16" BLOCK BEAM
W/1-#6 TOP & 1-#6
BOT.

3/4":1'-0"

REINFORCED MASONRY BEAM: SLOPED
TWIN TEE ROOF DECK: NO INSULATION

INTERMEDIATE CONDITION: SIDE

RMC 2

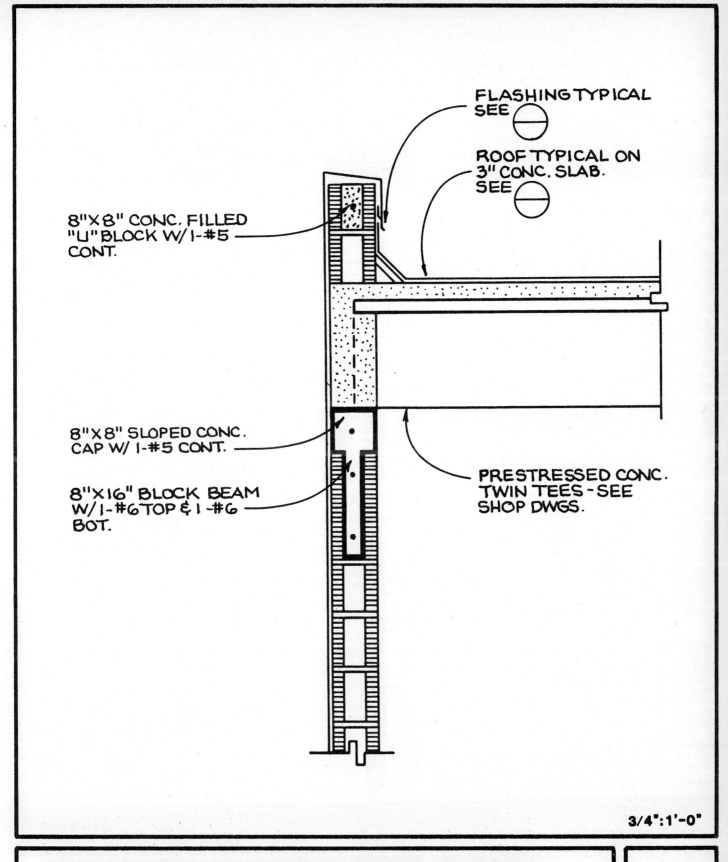

FLASHING TYPICAL
SEE ⊖

ROOF TYPICAL ON
3" CONC. SLAB.
SEE ⊖

8"X 8" CONC. FILLED
"U" BLOCK W/1-#5
CONT.

8"X 8" SLOPED CONC.
CAP W/ 1-#5 CONT.

8"X16" BLOCK BEAM
W/1-#6 TOP & 1-#6
BOT.

PRESTRESSED CONC.
TWIN TEES - SEE
SHOP DWGS.

3/4":1'-0"

**REINFORCED MASONRY BEAM: SLOPED
TWIN TEE ROOF DECK: NO INSULATION
END CONDITION**

**RMC
3**

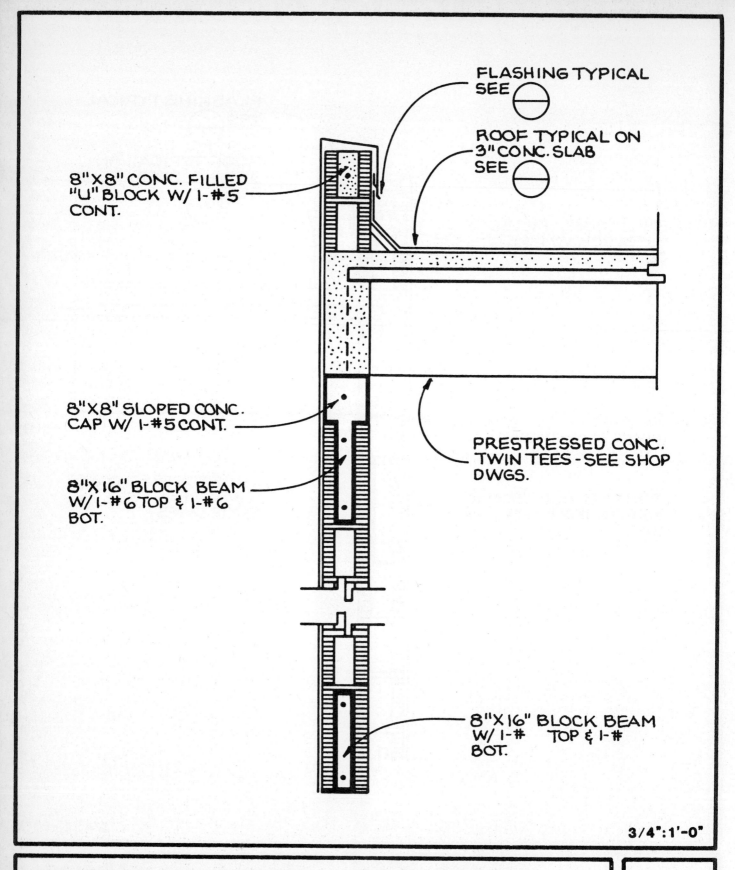

FLASHING TYPICAL
SEE ⊖

ROOF TYPICAL ON
3" CONC. SLAB
SEE ⊖

8"X8" CONC. FILLED
"U" BLOCK W/ 1-#5
CONT.

8"X8" SLOPED CONC.
CAP W/ 1-#5 CONT.

8"X16" BLOCK BEAM
W/ 1-#6 TOP & 1-#6
BOT.

PRESTRESSED CONC.
TWIN TEES - SEE SHOP
DWGS.

8"X16" BLOCK BEAM
W/ 1-# TOP & 1-#
BOT.

3/4":1'-0"

REINFORCED MASONRY BEAM: SLOPED
TWIN TEE ROOF DECK: NO INSULATION

END CONDITION: LOWER BEAM

RMC
4

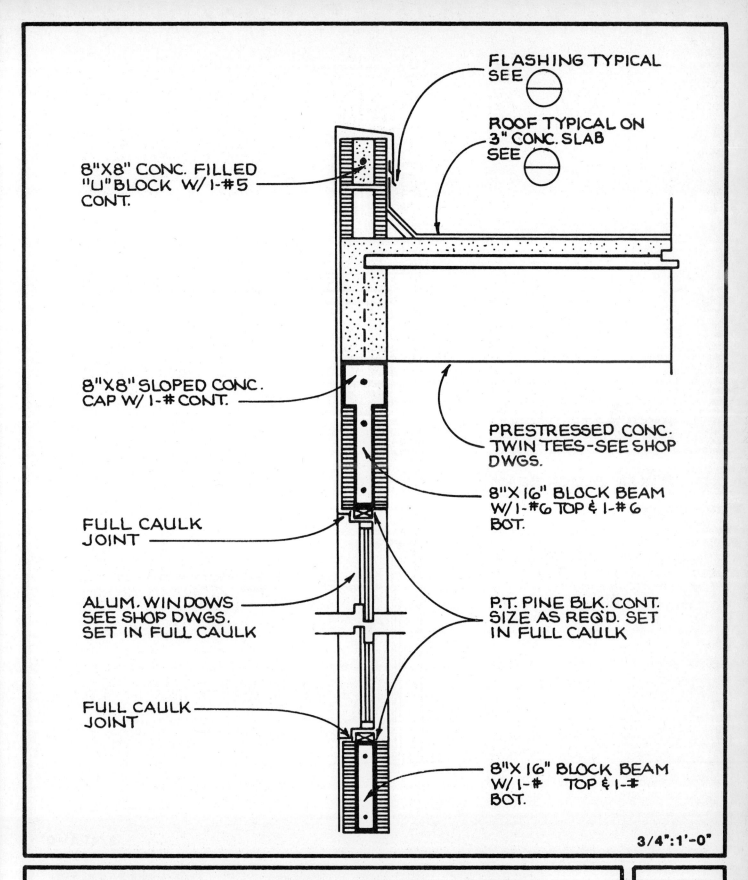

FLASHING TYPICAL
SEE ◯

ROOF TYPICAL ON
3" CONC. SLAB
SEE ◯

8"X8" CONC. FILLED
"U" BLOCK W/ I-#5
CONT.

8"X8" SLOPED CONC.
CAP W/ I-# CONT.

PRESTRESSED CONC.
TWIN TEES-SEE SHOP
DWGS.

8"X 16" BLOCK BEAM
W/ I-#6 TOP & I-#6
BOT.

FULL CAULK
JOINT

ALUM. WINDOWS
SEE SHOP DWGS.
SET IN FULL CAULK

P.T. PINE BLK. CONT.
SIZE AS REQ'D. SET
IN FULL CAULK

FULL CAULK
JOINT

8"X 16" BLOCK BEAM
W/ I-#   TOP & I-#
BOT.

3/4":1'-0"

REINFORCED MASONRY BEAM: SLOPED
TWIN TEE ROOF DECK: NO INSULATION
END CONDITION: WINDOW

RMC
5

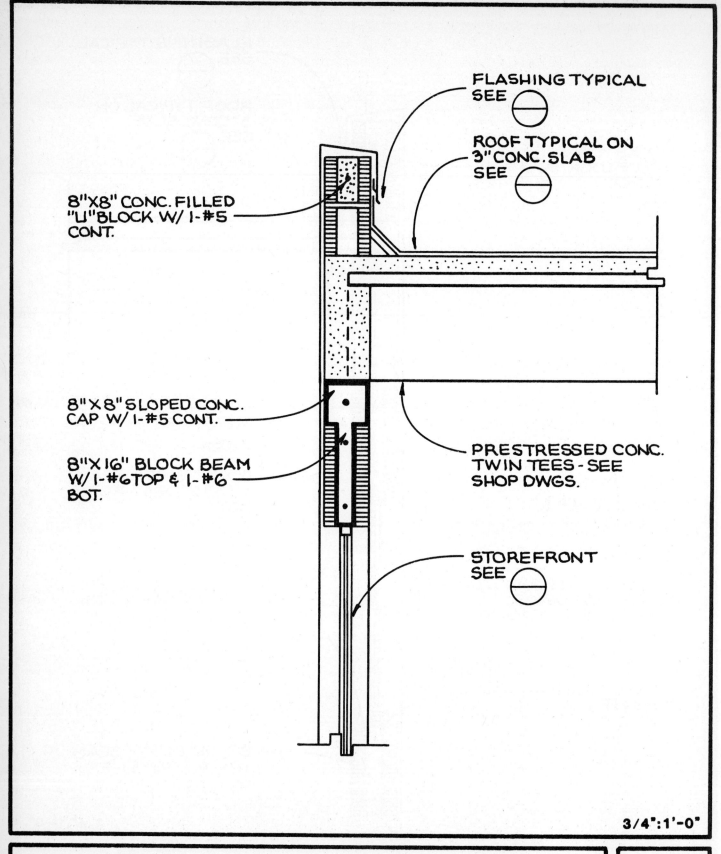

FLASHING TYPICAL
SEE ⊖

ROOF TYPICAL ON
3" CONC. SLAB
SEE ⊖

8"X8" CONC. FILLED
"U" BLOCK W/ 1-#5
CONT.

8"X8" SLOPED CONC.
CAP W/ 1-#5 CONT.

8"X16" BLOCK BEAM
W/ 1-#6 TOP & 1-#6
BOT.

PRESTRESSED CONC.
TWIN TEES - SEE
SHOP DWGS.

STOREFRONT
SEE ⊖

3/4":1'-0"

**REINFORCED MASONRY BEAM: SLOPED
TWIN TEE ROOF DECK: NO INSULATION
END CONDITION: STOREFRONT**

**RMC
6**

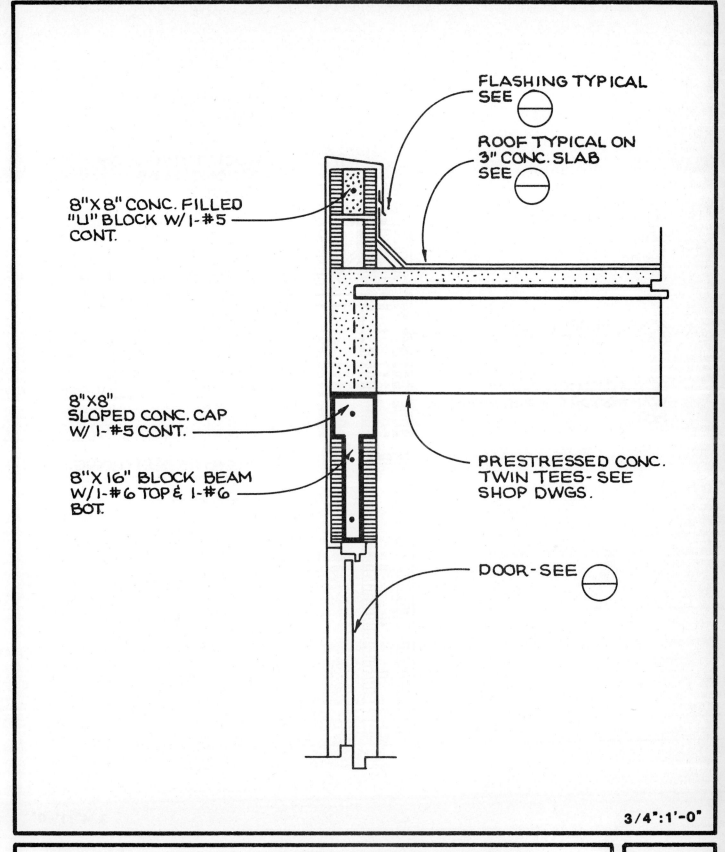

FLASHING TYPICAL
SEE ⊖

ROOF TYPICAL ON
3" CONC. SLAB
SEE ⊖

8"X8" CONC. FILLED
"U" BLOCK W/I-#5
CONT.

8"X8"
SLOPED CONC. CAP
W/ I-#5 CONT.

8"X16" BLOCK BEAM
W/I-#6 TOP & I-#6
BOT.

PRESTRESSED CONC.
TWIN TEES- SEE
SHOP DWGS.

DOOR-SEE ⊖

3/4":1'-0"

**REINFORCED MASONRY BEAM: SLOPED
TWIN TEE ROOF DECK: NO INSULATION
END CONDITION: DOOR**

**RMC
7**

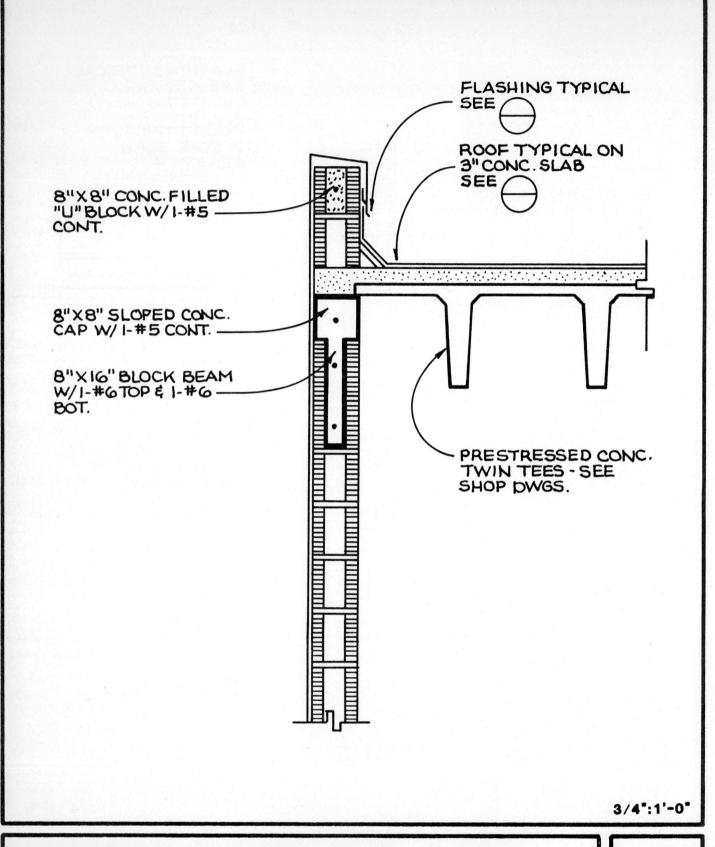

FLASHING TYPICAL
SEE ⊖

ROOF TYPICAL ON
3" CONC. SLAB
SEE ⊖

8"X8" CONC. FILLED
"U" BLOCK W/ 1-#5
CONT.

8"X8" SLOPED CONC.
CAP W/ 1-#5 CONT.

8"X16" BLOCK BEAM
W/ 1-#6 TOP & 1-#6
BOT.

PRESTRESSED CONC.
TWIN TEES - SEE
SHOP DWGS.

3/4":1'-0"

REINFORCED MASONRY BEAM: SLOPED TWIN TEE ROOF DECK: NO INSULATION

SIDE CONDITION

RMC
8

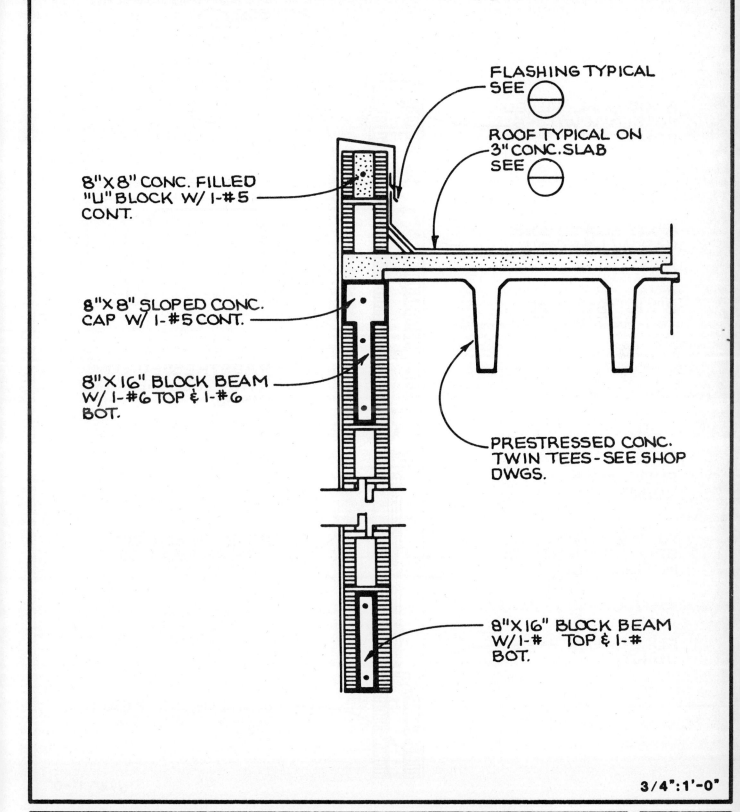

FLASHING TYPICAL
SEE ⊖

ROOF TYPICAL ON
3" CONC. SLAB
SEE ⊖

8"X 8" CONC. FILLED
"U" BLOCK W/ 1-#5
CONT.

8"X 8" SLOPED CONC.
CAP W/ 1-#5 CONT.

8"X 16" BLOCK BEAM
W/ 1-#6 TOP & 1-#6
BOT.

PRESTRESSED CONC.
TWIN TEES - SEE SHOP
DWGS.

8"X 16" BLOCK BEAM
W/ 1-# TOP & 1-#
BOT.

3/4":1'-0"

**REINFORCED MASONRY BEAM: SLOPED
TWIN TEE ROOF DECK: NO INSULATION**

SIDE CONDITION: LOWER BEAM

**RMC
9**

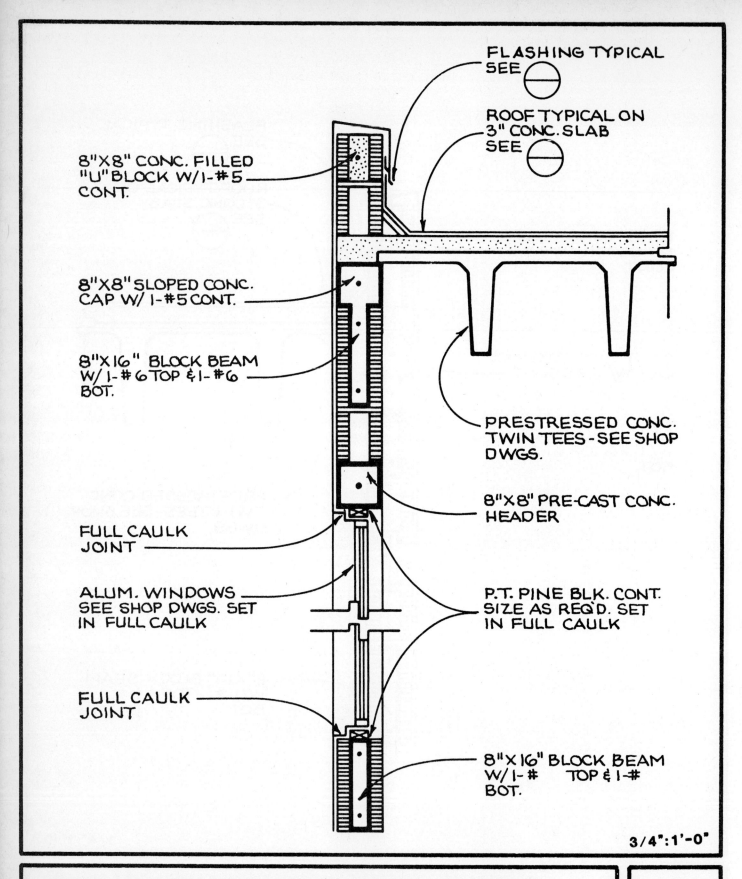

FLASHING TYPICAL
SEE ◯

ROOF TYPICAL ON
3" CONC. SLAB
SEE ◯

8"X8" CONC. FILLED
"U"BLOCK W/1-#5
CONT.

8"X8"SLOPED CONC.
CAP W/ 1-#5 CONT.

8"X16" BLOCK BEAM
W/ 1-#6 TOP &1-#6
BOT.

PRESTRESSED CONC.
TWIN TEES - SEE SHOP
DWGS.

8"X8" PRE-CAST CONC.
HEADER

FULL CAULK
JOINT

ALUM. WINDOWS
SEE SHOP DWGS. SET
IN FULL CAULK

P.T. PINE BLK. CONT.
SIZE AS REQ'D. SET
IN FULL CAULK

FULL CAULK
JOINT

8"X16" BLOCK BEAM
W/ 1-#   TOP & 1-#
BOT.

3/4":1'-0"

**REINFORCED MASONRY BEAM: SLOPED
TWIN TEE ROOF DECK: NO INSULATION**

SIDE CONDITION: WINDOW

**RMC
10**

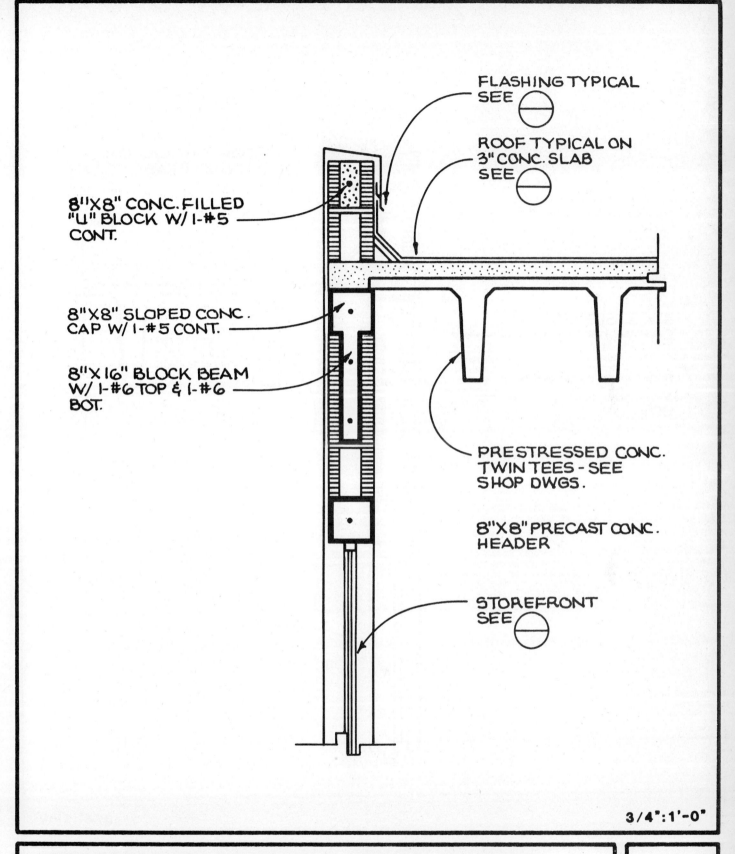

FLASHING TYPICAL
SEE ⊖

ROOF TYPICAL ON
3" CONC. SLAB
SEE ⊖

8"X8" CONC. FILLED
"U" BLOCK W/ I-#5
CONT.

8"X8" SLOPED CONC.
CAP W/ I-#5 CONT.

8"X16" BLOCK BEAM
W/ I-#6 TOP & I-#6
BOT.

PRESTRESSED CONC.
TWIN TEES - SEE
SHOP DWGS.

8"X8" PRECAST CONC.
HEADER

STOREFRONT
SEE ⊖

3/4":1'-0"

**REINFORCED MASONRY BEAM: SLOPED
TWIN TEE ROOF DECK: NO INSULATION**

SIDE CONDITION: STOREFRONT

**RMC
11**

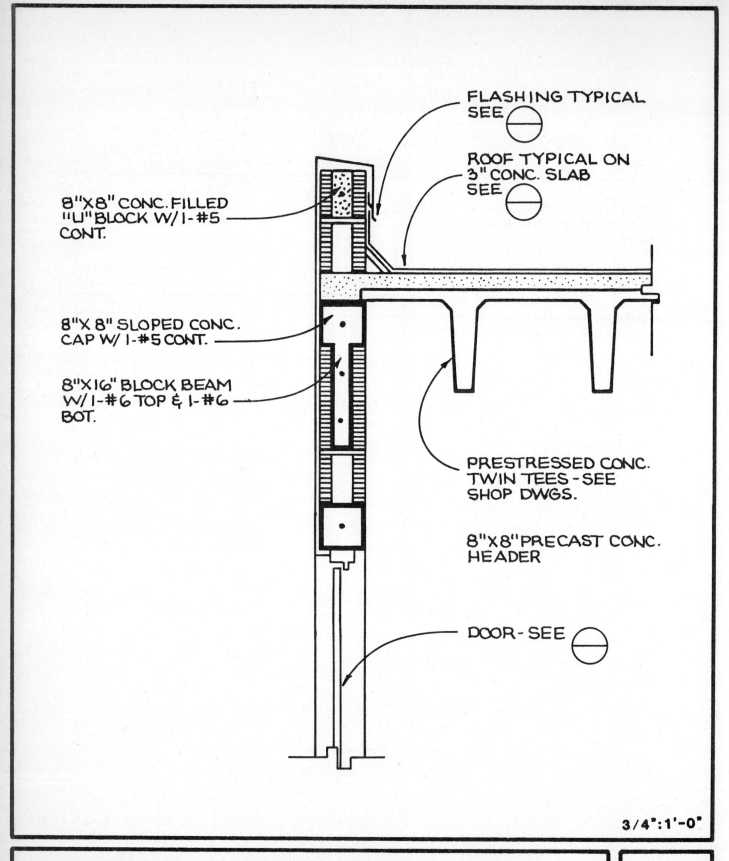

FLASHING TYPICAL SEE ⊖

ROOF TYPICAL ON 3" CONC. SLAB SEE ⊖

8"X8" CONC. FILLED "U" BLOCK W/ 1-#5 CONT.

8"X 8" SLOPED CONC. CAP W/ 1-#5 CONT.

8"X16" BLOCK BEAM W/ 1-#6 TOP & 1-#6 BOT.

PRESTRESSED CONC. TWIN TEES - SEE SHOP DWGS.

8"X8" PRECAST CONC. HEADER

DOOR - SEE ⊖

3/4":1'-0"

REINFORCED MASONRY BEAM: SLOPED
TWIN TEE ROOF DECK: NO INSULATION
SIDE CONDITION: DOOR

RMC
12

SECTION 12: RM–D

Reinforced masonry construction with level beam.
Prestressed concrete twin tee roof deck with sloped insulation.

ARCHITECTURAL DETAILING
FOR
COMMERCIAL CONSTRUCTION

12

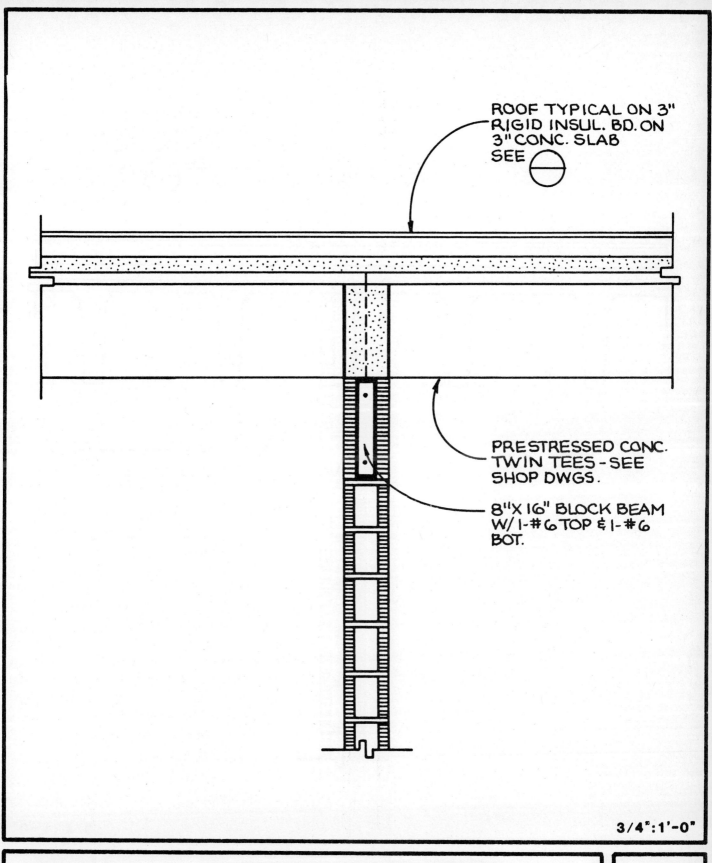

ROOF TYPICAL ON 3"
RIGID INSUL. BD. ON
3" CONC. SLAB
SEE ⊖

PRESTRESSED CONC.
TWIN TEES – SEE
SHOP DWGS.

8" X 16" BLOCK BEAM
W/ 1-#6 TOP & 1-#6
BOT.

3/4":1'-0"

**REINFORCED MASONRY BEAM: LEVEL
TWIN TEE ROOF DECK: SLOPED INSUL.**

INTERMEDIATE CONDITION: END

**RMD
1**

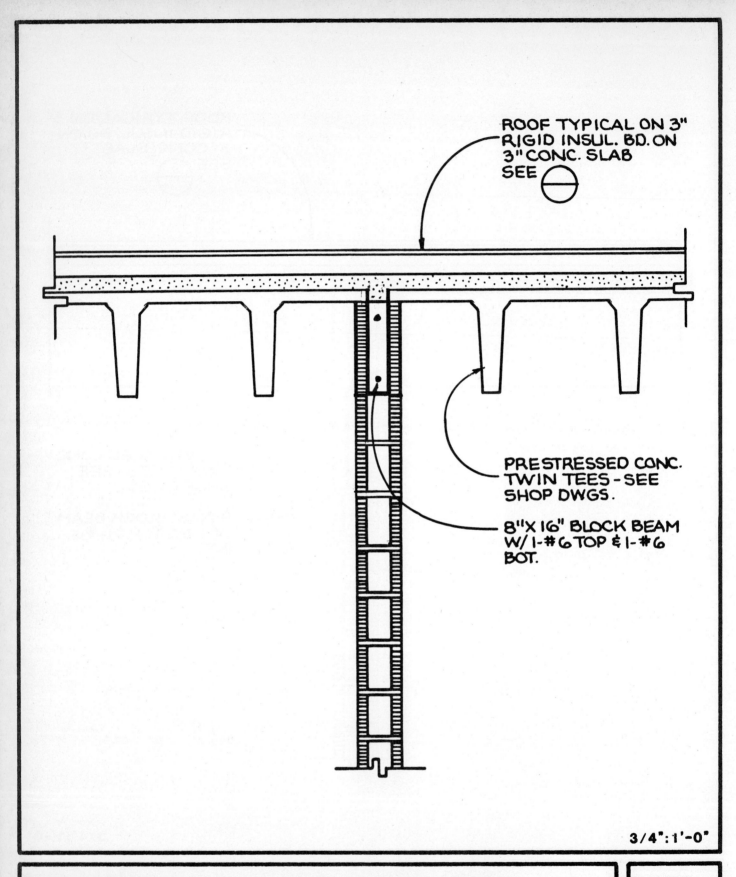

ROOF TYPICAL ON 3"
RIGID INSUL. BD. ON
3" CONC. SLAB
SEE ⊖

PRESTRESSED CONC.
TWIN TEES - SEE
SHOP DWGS.

8"X 16" BLOCK BEAM
W/ 1-#6 TOP & 1-#6
BOT.

3/4":1'-0"

**REINFORCED MASONRY BEAM: LEVEL
TWIN TEE ROOF DECK: SLOPED INSUL.**

INTERMEDIATE CONDITION: SIDE

**RMD
2**

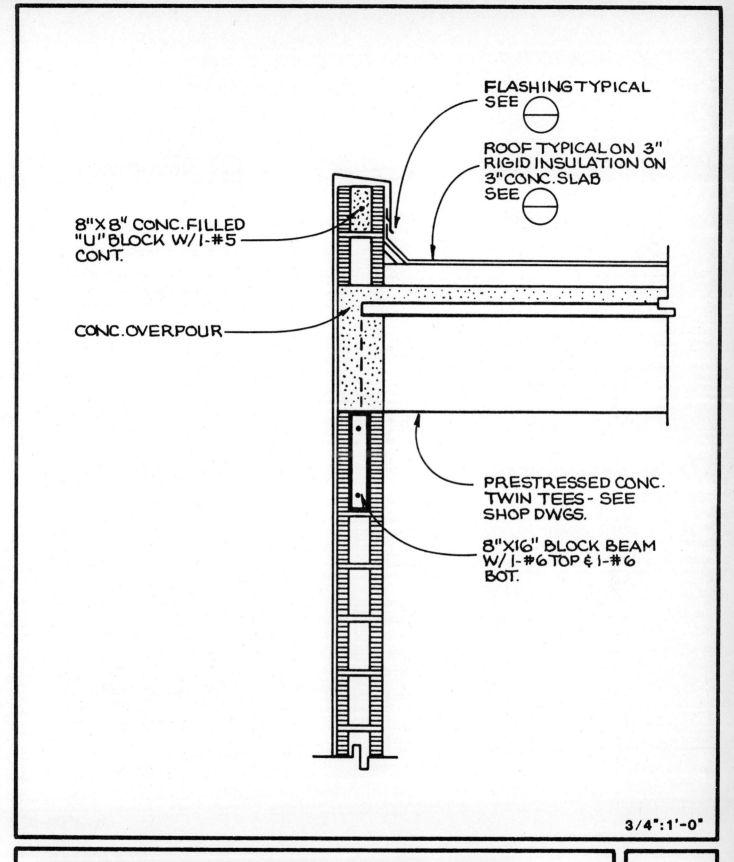

FLASHING TYPICAL
SEE ◯

ROOF TYPICAL ON 3"
RIGID INSULATION ON
3" CONC. SLAB
SEE ◯

8" X 8" CONC. FILLED
"U" BLOCK W/ 1 - #5
CONT.

CONC. OVERPOUR

PRESTRESSED CONC.
TWIN TEES - SEE
SHOP DWGS.

8" X 16" BLOCK BEAM
W/ 1 - #6 TOP & 1 - #6
BOT.

3/4" : 1'-0"

**REINFORCED MASONRY BEAM: LEVEL
TWIN TEE ROOF DECK: SLOPED INSUL.**

END CONDITION

**RMD
3**

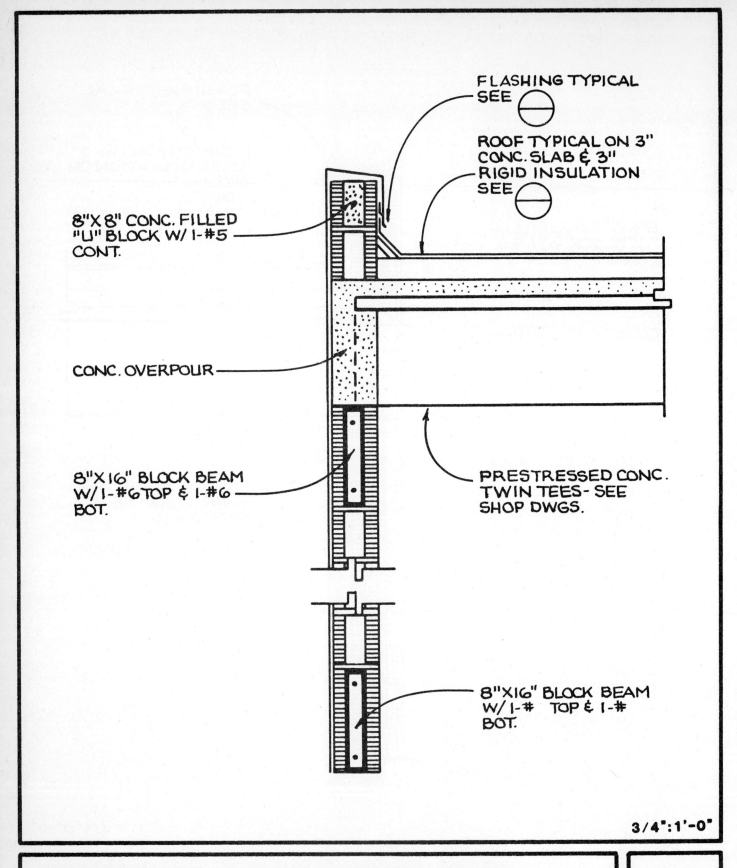

FLASHING TYPICAL
SEE ⊖

ROOF TYPICAL ON 3"
CONC. SLAB & 3"
RIGID INSULATION
SEE ⊖

8"X 8" CONC. FILLED
"U" BLOCK W/ 1-#5
CONT.

CONC. OVERPOUR

8"X16" BLOCK BEAM
W/ 1-#6 TOP & 1-#6
BOT.

PRESTRESSED CONC.
TWIN TEES- SEE
SHOP DWGS.

8"X16" BLOCK BEAM
W/ 1-# TOP & 1-#
BOT.

3/4":1'-0"

REINFORCED MASONRY BEAM: LEVEL
TWIN TEE ROOF DECK: SLOPED INSUL.
END CONDITION: LOWER BEAM

RMD
4

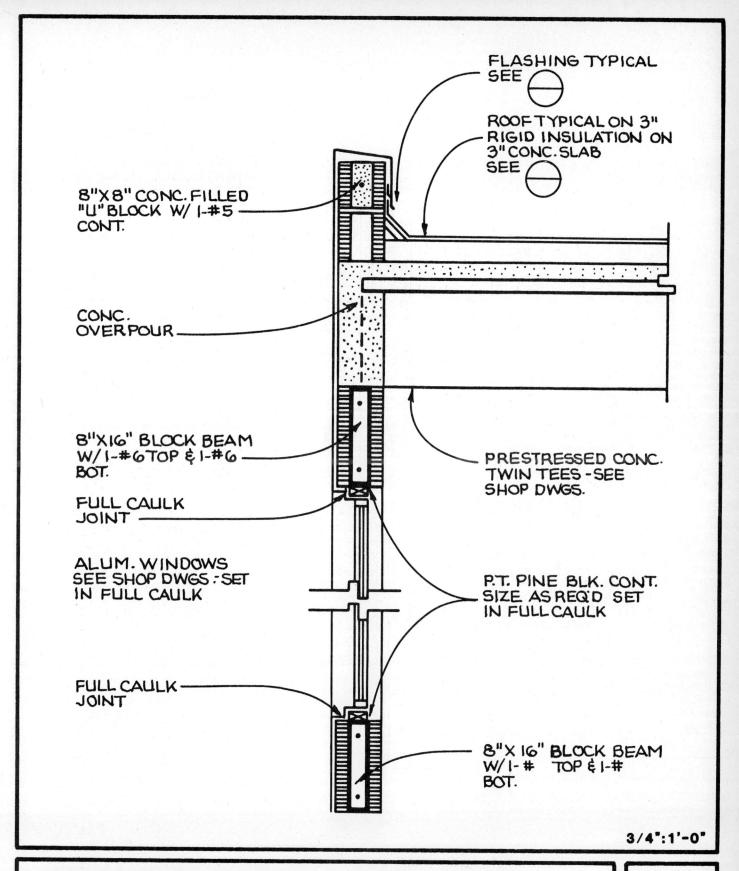

FLASHING TYPICAL
SEE ⊖

ROOF TYPICAL ON 3"
RIGID INSULATION ON
3" CONC. SLAB
SEE ⊖

8"X8" CONC. FILLED
"U" BLOCK W/ 1-#5
CONT.

CONC.
OVERPOUR

8"X16" BLOCK BEAM
W/1-#6 TOP & 1-#6
BOT.

FULL CAULK
JOINT

ALUM. WINDOWS
SEE SHOP DWGS : SET
IN FULL CAULK

PRESTRESSED CONC.
TWIN TEES - SEE
SHOP DWGS.

P.T. PINE BLK. CONT.
SIZE AS REQ'D SET
IN FULL CAULK

FULL CAULK
JOINT

8"X 16" BLOCK BEAM
W/ 1-# TOP & 1-#
BOT.

3/4":1'-0"

**REINFORCED MASONRY BEAM: LEVEL
TWIN TEE ROOF DECK: SLOPED INSUL.**

END CONDITION: WINDOW

**RMD
5**

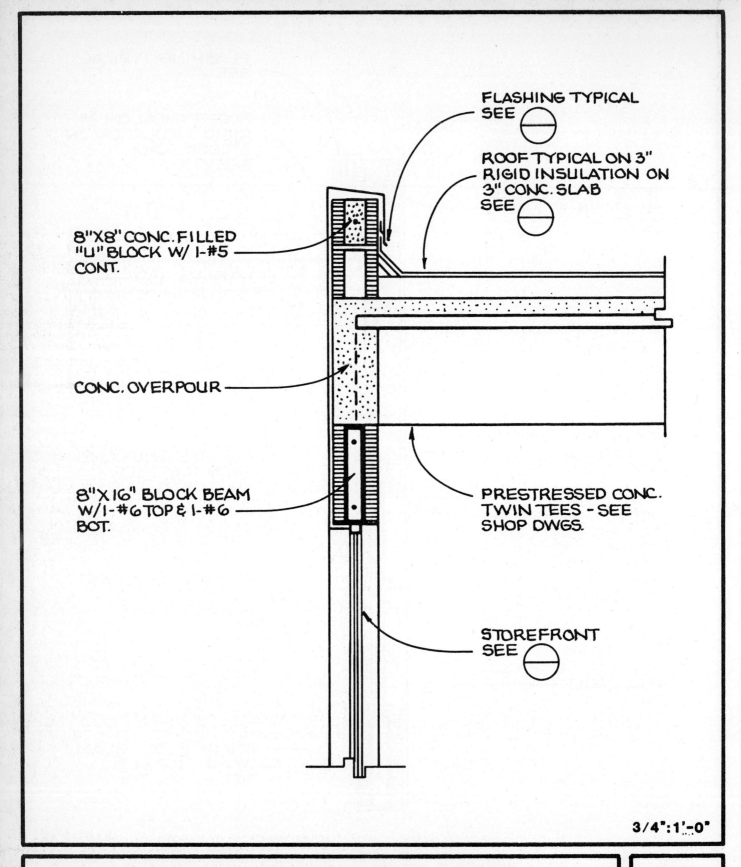

FLASHING TYPICAL
SEE ⊖

ROOF TYPICAL ON 3"
RIGID INSULATION ON
3" CONC. SLAB
SEE ⊖

8"X8" CONC. FILLED
"U" BLOCK W/ 1-#5
CONT.

CONC. OVERPOUR

8"X16" BLOCK BEAM
W/ 1-#6 TOP & 1-#6
BOT.

PRESTRESSED CONC.
TWIN TEES - SEE
SHOP DWGS.

STOREFRONT
SEE ⊖

3/4":1'-0"

**REINFORCED MASONRY BEAM: LEVEL
TWIN TEE ROOF DECK: SLOPED INSUL.
END CONDITION: STOREFRONT**

**RMD
6**

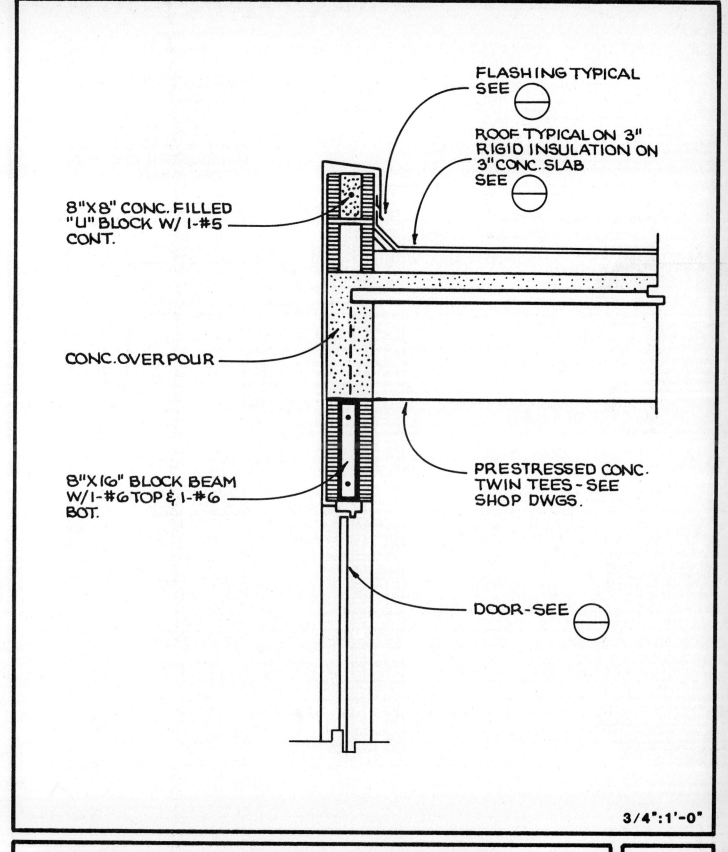

FLASHING TYPICAL
SEE ⊘

ROOF TYPICAL ON 3"
RIGID INSULATION ON
3" CONC. SLAB
SEE ⊘

8"X8" CONC. FILLED
"U" BLOCK W/ 1-#5
CONT.

CONC. OVER POUR

8"X16" BLOCK BEAM
W/ 1-#6 TOP & 1-#6
BOT.

PRESTRESSED CONC.
TWIN TEES - SEE
SHOP DWGS.

DOOR - SEE ⊘

3/4":1'-0"

REINFORCED MASONRY BEAM: LEVEL
TWIN TEE ROOF DECK: SLOPED INSUL.
END CONDITION: DOOR

RMD
7

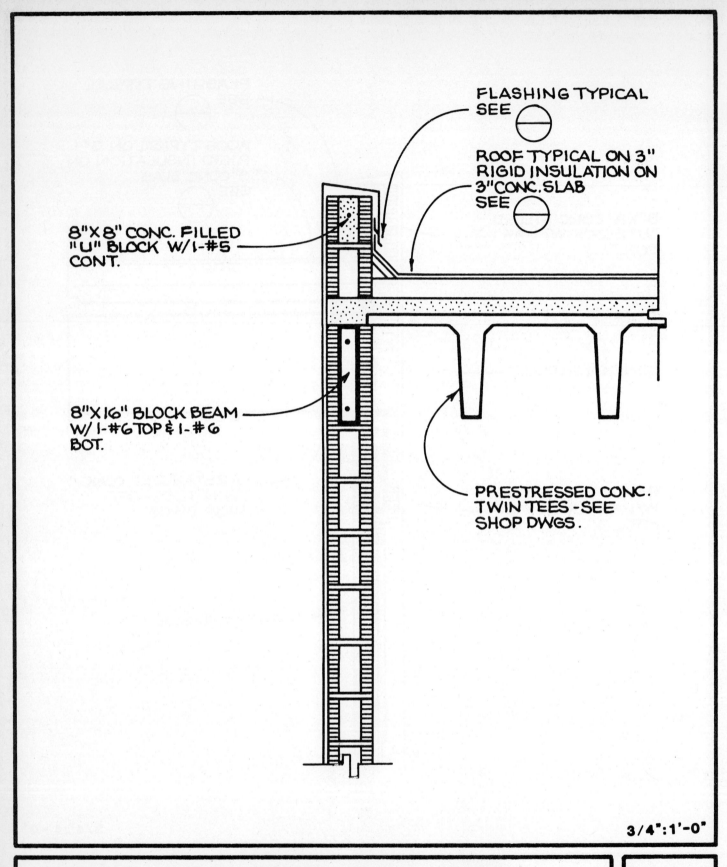

FLASHING TYPICAL SEE ⊖

ROOF TYPICAL ON 3" RIGID INSULATION ON 3" CONC. SLAB SEE ⊖

8"X 8" CONC. FILLED "U" BLOCK W/ 1-#5 CONT.

8"X 16" BLOCK BEAM W/ 1-#6 TOP & 1-#6 BOT.

PRESTRESSED CONC. TWIN TEES - SEE SHOP DWGS.

3/4":1'-0"

REINFORCED MASONRY BEAM: LEVEL TWIN TEE ROOF DECK: SLOPED INSUL.

SIDE CONDITION

RMD 8

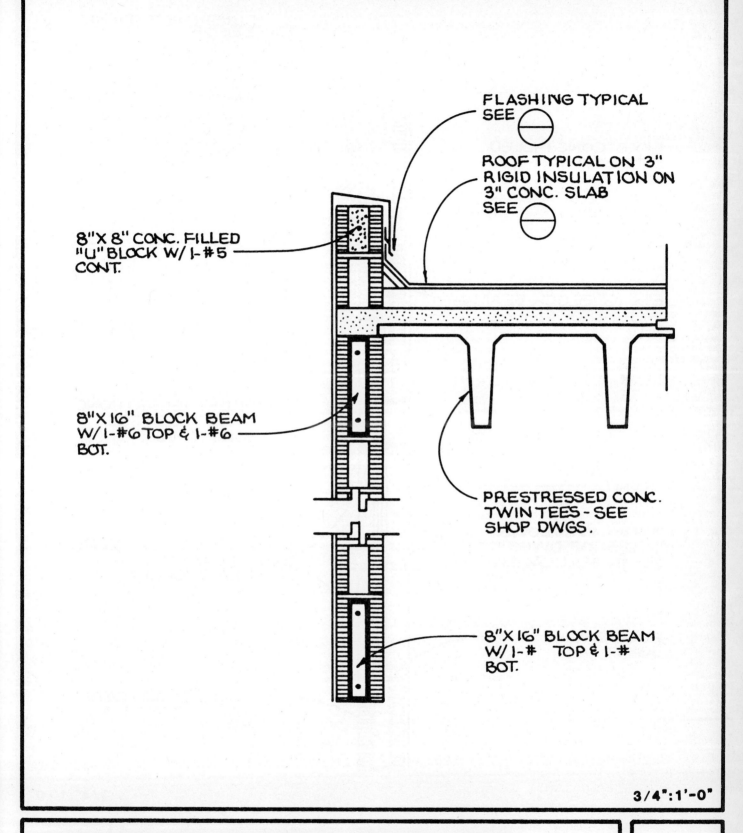

FLASHING TYPICAL
SEE ◯

ROOF TYPICAL ON 3"
RIGID INSULATION ON
3" CONC. SLAB
SEE ◯

8"X 8" CONC. FILLED
"U" BLOCK W/ 1-#5
CONT.

8"X 16" BLOCK BEAM
W/ 1-#6 TOP & 1-#6
BOT.

PRESTRESSED CONC.
TWIN TEES - SEE
SHOP DWGS.

8"X 16" BLOCK BEAM
W/ 1-# TOP & 1-#
BOT.

3/4":1'-0"

**REINFORCED MASONRY BEAM: LEVEL
TWIN TEE ROOF DECK: SLOPED INSUL.**

SIDE CONDITION: LOWER BEAM

**RMD
9**

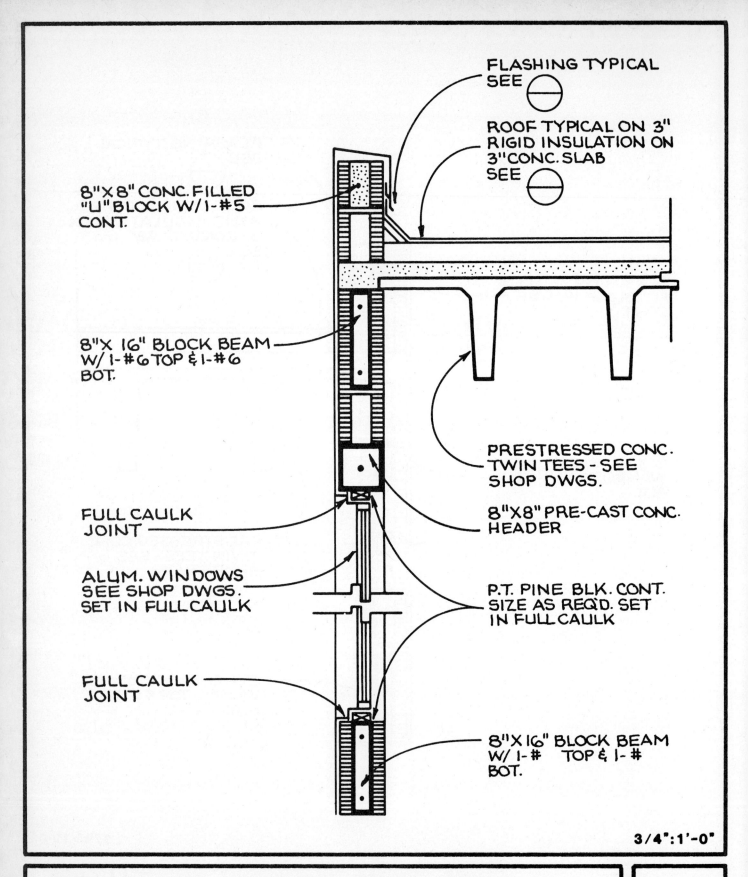

FLASHING TYPICAL SEE ⊖

ROOF TYPICAL ON 3" RIGID INSULATION ON 3" CONC. SLAB SEE ⊖

8"X 8" CONC. FILLED "U" BLOCK W/ 1-#5 CONT.

8"X 16" BLOCK BEAM W/ 1-#6 TOP & 1-#6 BOT.

FULL CAULK JOINT

ALUM. WINDOWS SEE SHOP DWGS. SET IN FULL CAULK

FULL CAULK JOINT

PRESTRESSED CONC. TWIN TEES - SEE SHOP DWGS.

8"X8" PRE-CAST CONC. HEADER

P.T. PINE BLK. CONT. SIZE AS REQ'D. SET IN FULL CAULK

8"X 16" BLOCK BEAM W/ 1-# TOP & 1-# BOT.

3/4":1'-0"

REINFORCED MASONRY BEAM: LEVEL TWIN TEE ROOF DECK: SLOPED INSUL.

SIDE CONDITION: WINDOW

RMD 10

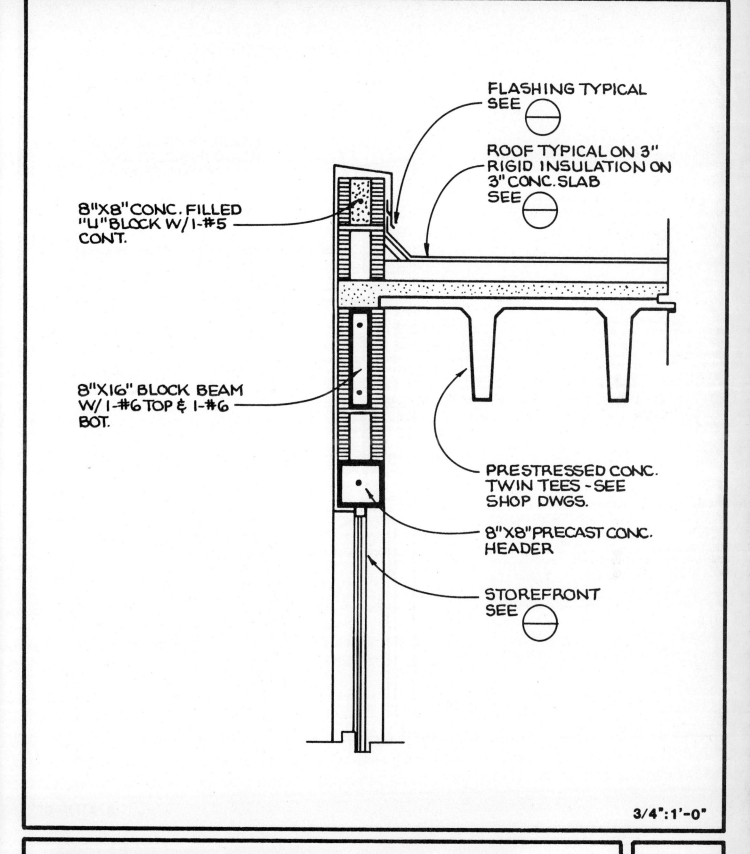

FLASHING TYPICAL
SEE ◯

ROOF TYPICAL ON 3"
RIGID INSULATION ON
3" CONC. SLAB
SEE ◯

8"X8"CONC. FILLED
"U"BLOCK W/1-#5
CONT.

8"X16" BLOCK BEAM
W/ 1-#6 TOP & 1-#6
BOT.

PRESTRESSED CONC.
TWIN TEES - SEE
SHOP DWGS.

8"X8"PRECAST CONC.
HEADER

STOREFRONT
SEE ◯

3/4":1'-0"

REINFORCED MASONRY BEAM: LEVEL
TWIN TEE ROOF DECK: SLOPED INSUL.

SIDE CONDITION: STOREFRONT

RMD
11

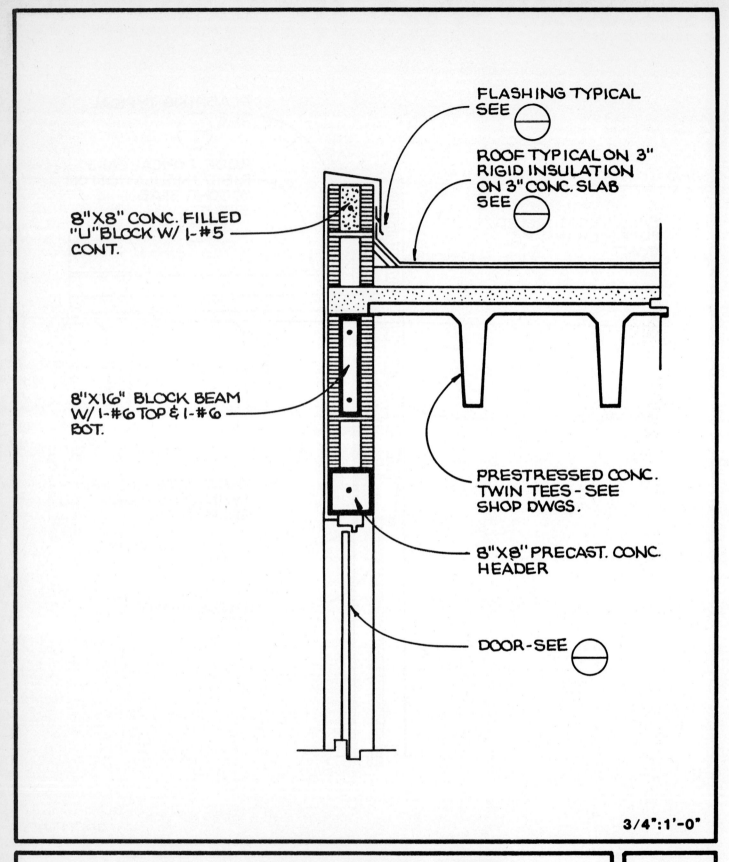

FLASHING TYPICAL
SEE ⊖

ROOF TYPICAL ON 3"
RIGID INSULATION
ON 3" CONC. SLAB
SEE ⊖

8"X8" CONC. FILLED
"U" BLOCK W/ 1-#5
CONT.

8"X16" BLOCK BEAM
W/ 1-#6 TOP & 1-#6
BOT.

PRESTRESSED CONC.
TWIN TEES - SEE
SHOP DWGS.

8"X8" PRECAST. CONC.
HEADER

DOOR - SEE ⊖

3/4":1'-0"

**REINFORCED MASONRY BEAM: LEVEL
TWIN TEE ROOF DECK: SLOPED INSUL.**

SIDE CONDITION: DOOR

**RMD
12**

SECTION 13: RM–E

Reinforced masonry construction with level beam.
Steel joist and metal roof deck with no insulation.

ARCHITECTURAL DETAILING
FOR
COMMERCIAL CONSTRUCTION

13

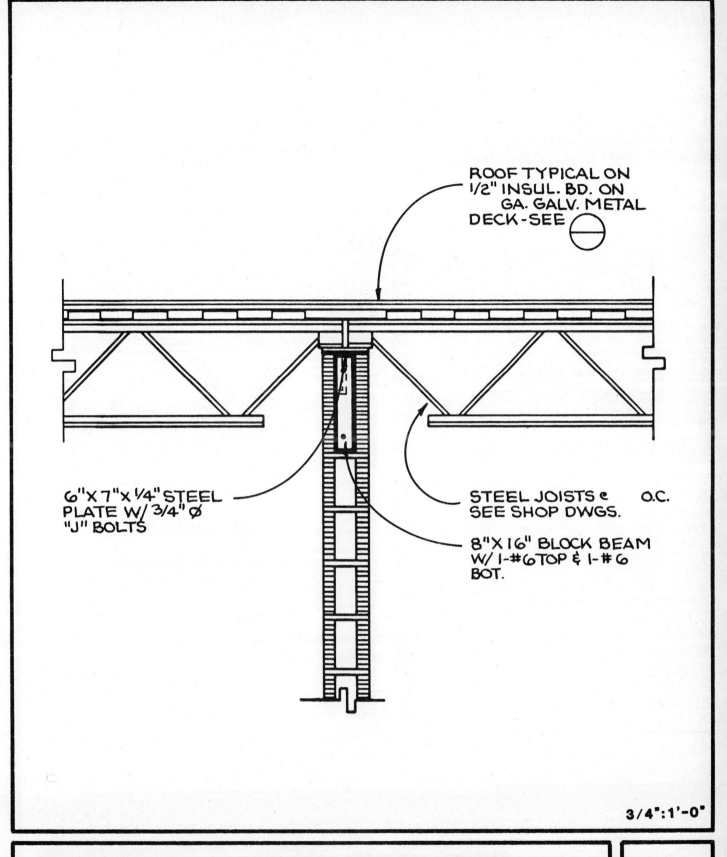

ROOF TYPICAL ON
1/2" INSUL. BD. ON
GA. GALV. METAL
DECK - SEE ⊖

6"X 7"X 1/4" STEEL
PLATE W/ 3/4" ∅
"J" BOLTS

STEEL JOISTS @   O.C.
SEE SHOP DWGS.

8"X 16" BLOCK BEAM
W/ 1-#6 TOP & 1-# 6
BOT.

3/4":1'-0"

REINFORCED MASONRY BEAM: LEVEL
STL JOIST & MET ROOF DECK: NO INSULATION.
INTERMEDIATE CONDITION: END

**RME
1**

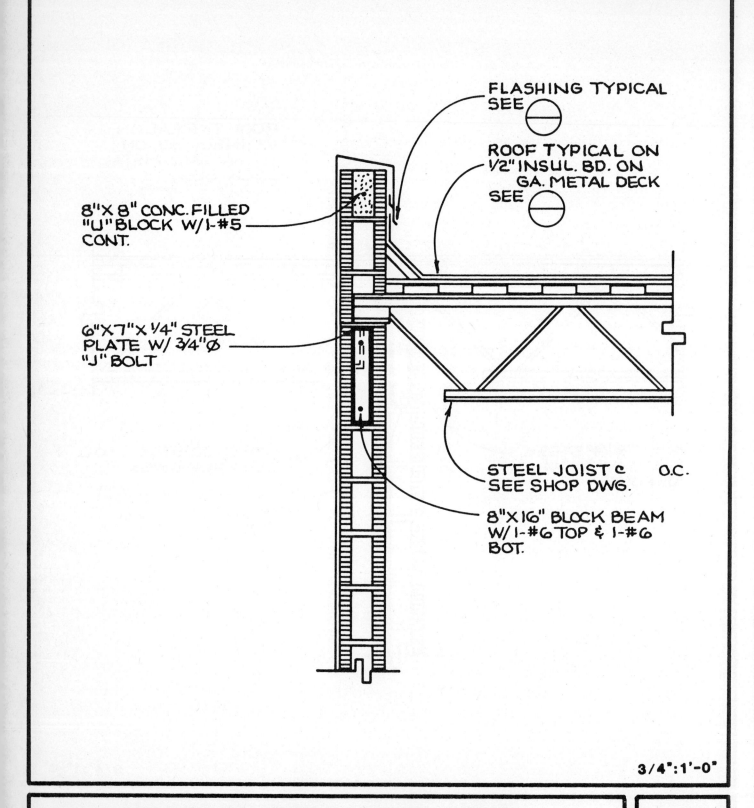

FLASHING TYPICAL
SEE ⊘

ROOF TYPICAL ON
½" INSUL. BD. ON
GA. METAL DECK
SEE ⊘

8"X 8" CONC. FILLED
"U" BLOCK W/I-#5
CONT.

6"X7"X ¼" STEEL
PLATE W/ ¾"∅
"J" BOLT

STEEL JOIST ℄   O.C.
SEE SHOP DWG.

8"X16" BLOCK BEAM
W/I-#6 TOP & I-#6
BOT.

3/4":1'-0"

**REINFORCED MASONRY BEAM: LEVEL
STL JOIST & MET ROOF DECK: NO INSULATION
END CONDITION**

**RME
2**

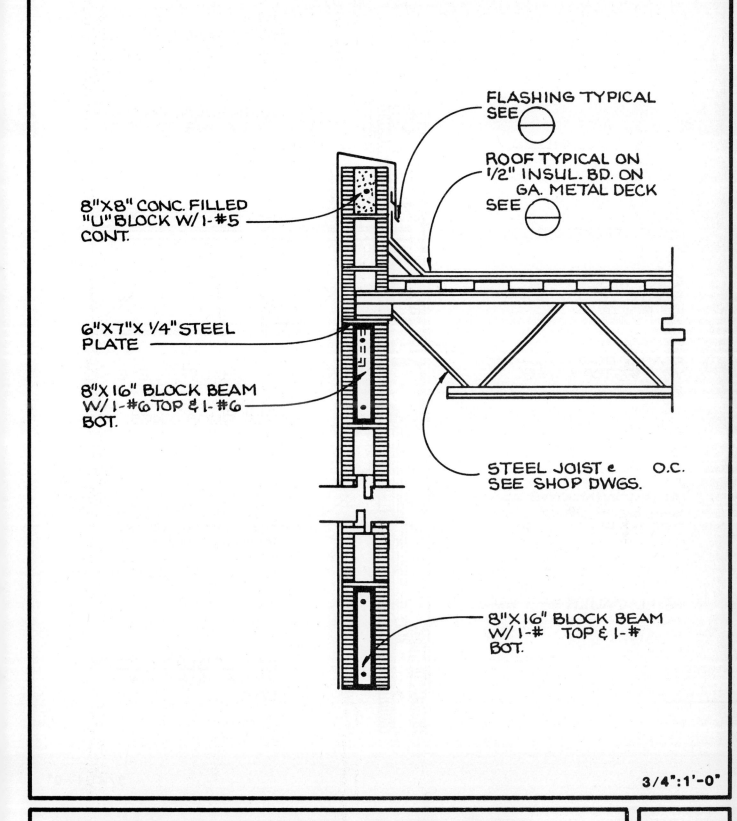

FLASHING TYPICAL
SEE ◯

ROOF TYPICAL ON
1/2" INSUL. BD. ON
GA. METAL DECK
SEE ◯

8"X8" CONC. FILLED
"U" BLOCK W/ 1-#5
CONT.

6"X7"X 1/4" STEEL
PLATE

8"X16" BLOCK BEAM
W/ 1-#6 TOP & 1-#6
BOT.

STEEL JOIST @   O.C.
SEE SHOP DWGS.

8"X16" BLOCK BEAM
W/ 1-#   TOP & 1-#
BOT.

3/4":1'-0"

**REINFORCED MASONRY BEAM: LEVEL
STL JOIST & MET ROOF DECK: NO INSULATION
END CONDITION: LOWER BEAM**

**RME
3**

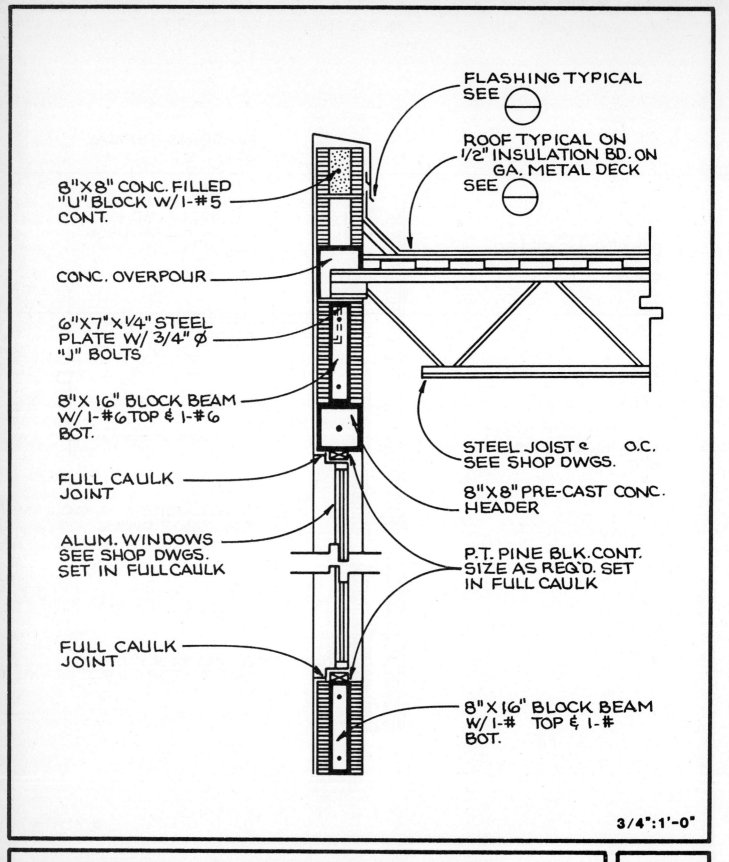

FLASHING TYPICAL SEE ⊘

ROOF TYPICAL ON 1/2" INSULATION BD. ON GA. METAL DECK SEE ⊘

8"X8" CONC. FILLED "U" BLOCK W/ 1-#5 CONT.

CONC. OVERPOUR

6"X7"X1/4" STEEL PLATE W/ 3/4" Ø "J" BOLTS

8"X 16" BLOCK BEAM W/ 1-#6 TOP & 1-#6 BOT.

FULL CAULK JOINT

ALUM. WINDOWS SEE SHOP DWGS. SET IN FULL CAULK

FULL CAULK JOINT

STEEL JOIST e   O.C. SEE SHOP DWGS.

8"X8" PRE-CAST CONC. HEADER

P.T. PINE BLK. CONT. SIZE AS REQ'D. SET IN FULL CAULK

8"X 16" BLOCK BEAM W/ 1-# TOP & 1-# BOT.

3/4":1'-0"

REINFORCED MASONRY BEAM: LEVEL
STL JOIST & MET ROOF DECK: NO INSULATION
END CONDITION: WINDOW

RME 4

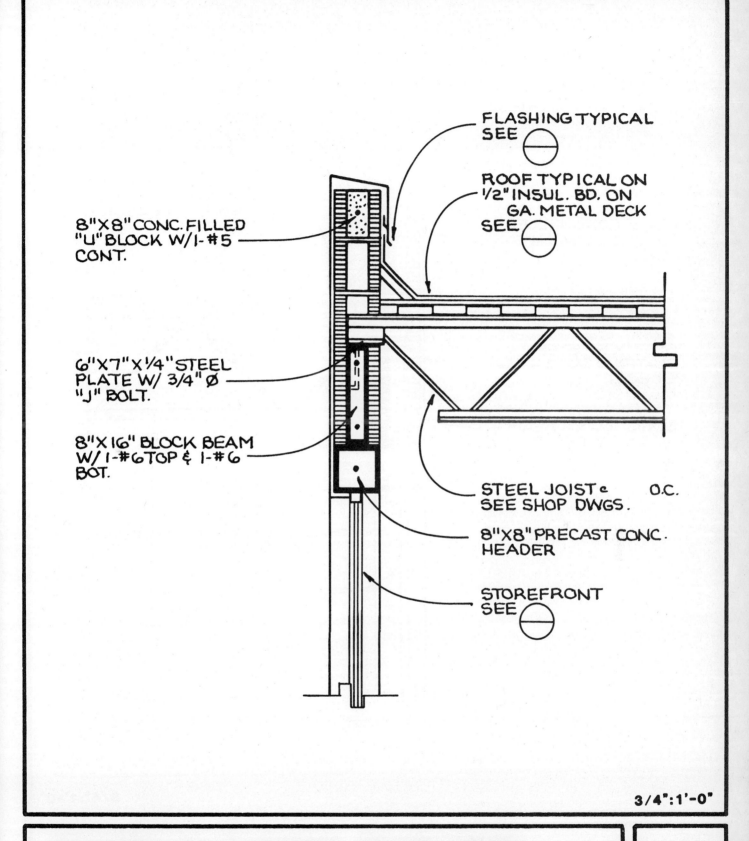

FLASHING TYPICAL
SEE ⊖

ROOF TYPICAL ON
1/2"INSUL. BD. ON
GA. METAL DECK
SEE ⊖

8"X8"CONC. FILLED
"U"BLOCK W/1-#5
CONT.

6"X7"X1/4"STEEL
PLATE W/ 3/4" ∅
"J" BOLT.

8"X16" BLOCK BEAM
W/1-#6TOP & 1-#6
BOT.

STEEL JOIST ℮   O.C.
SEE SHOP DWGS.

8"X8"PRECAST CONC.
HEADER

STOREFRONT
SEE ⊖

3/4":1'-0"

REINFORCED MASONRY BEAM: LEVEL
STL JOIST & MET ROOF DECK: NO INSULATION
END CONDITION: STOREFRONT

**RME
5**

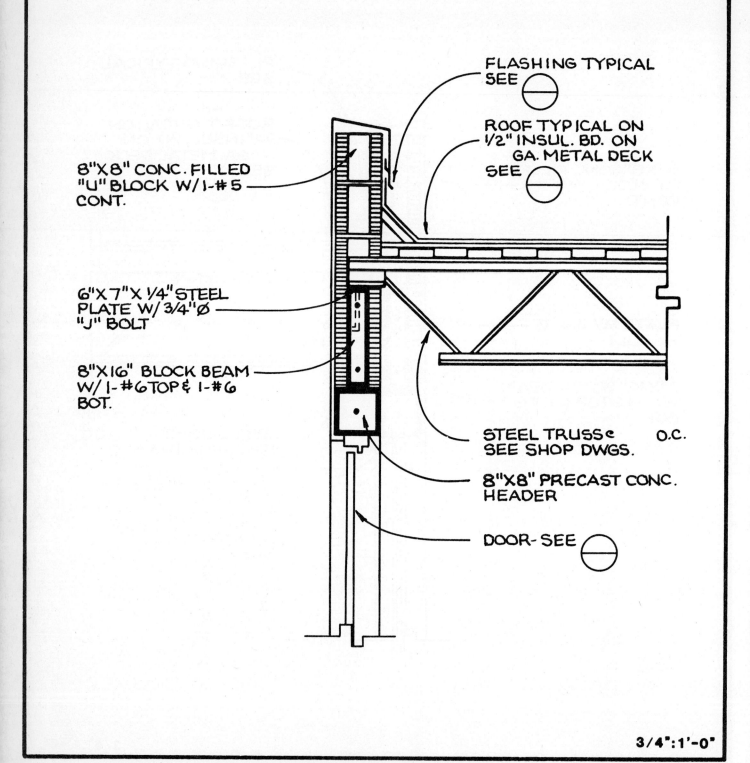

FLASHING TYPICAL
SEE ⊘

ROOF TYPICAL ON
1/2" INSUL. BD. ON
GA. METAL DECK
SEE ⊘

8"X8" CONC. FILLED
"U" BLOCK W/1-#5
CONT.

6"X7"X1/4"STEEL
PLATE W/3/4"∅
"J" BOLT

8"X16" BLOCK BEAM
W/1-#6TOP&1-#6
BOT.

STEEL TRUSS ℮   O.C.
SEE SHOP DWGS.

8"X8" PRECAST CONC.
HEADER

DOOR- SEE ⊘

3/4":1'-0"

REINFORCED MASONRY BEAM: LEVEL
STL JOIST & MET ROOF DECK: NO INSULATION
END CONDITION: DOOR

RME
6

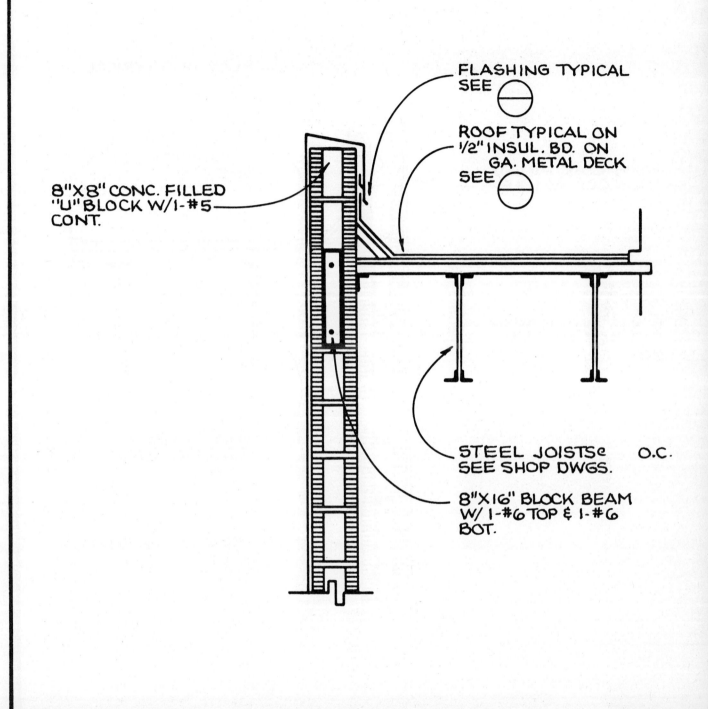

FLASHING TYPICAL
SEE ◯

ROOF TYPICAL ON
½" INSUL. BD. ON
GA. METAL DECK
SEE ◯

8"X8" CONC. FILLED
"U" BLOCK W/1-#5
CONT.

STEEL JOISTS ℓ   O.C.
SEE SHOP DWGS.

8"X16" BLOCK BEAM
W/ 1-#6 TOP & 1-#6
BOT.

3/4":1'-0"

**REINFORCED MASONRY BEAM: LEVEL
STL JOIST & MET ROOF DECK: NO INSULATION
SIDE CONDITION**

**RME
7**

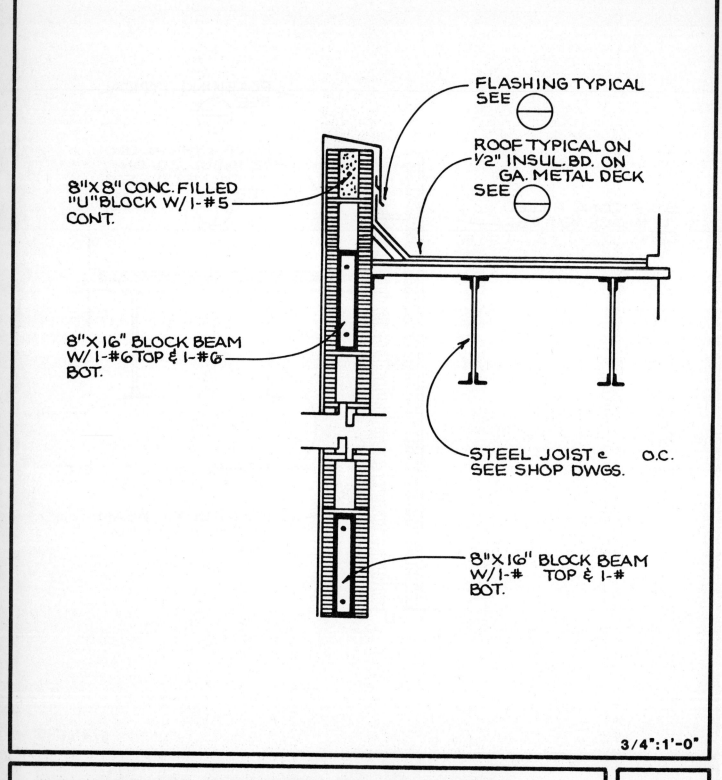

FLASHING TYPICAL
SEE ⊖

ROOF TYPICAL ON
1/2" INSUL. BD. ON
GA. METAL DECK
SEE ⊖

8"X 8" CONC. FILLED
"U" BLOCK W/ 1-#5
CONT.

8"X 16" BLOCK BEAM
W/ 1-#6 TOP & 1-#6
BOT.

STEEL JOIST ℓ   O.C.
SEE SHOP DWGS.

8"X 16" BLOCK BEAM
W/ 1-#   TOP & 1-#
BOT.

3/4":1'-0"

**REINFORCED MASONRY BEAM: LEVEL
STL JOIST & MET ROOF DECK: NO INSULATION.
SIDE CONDITION: LOWER BEAM**

**RME
8**

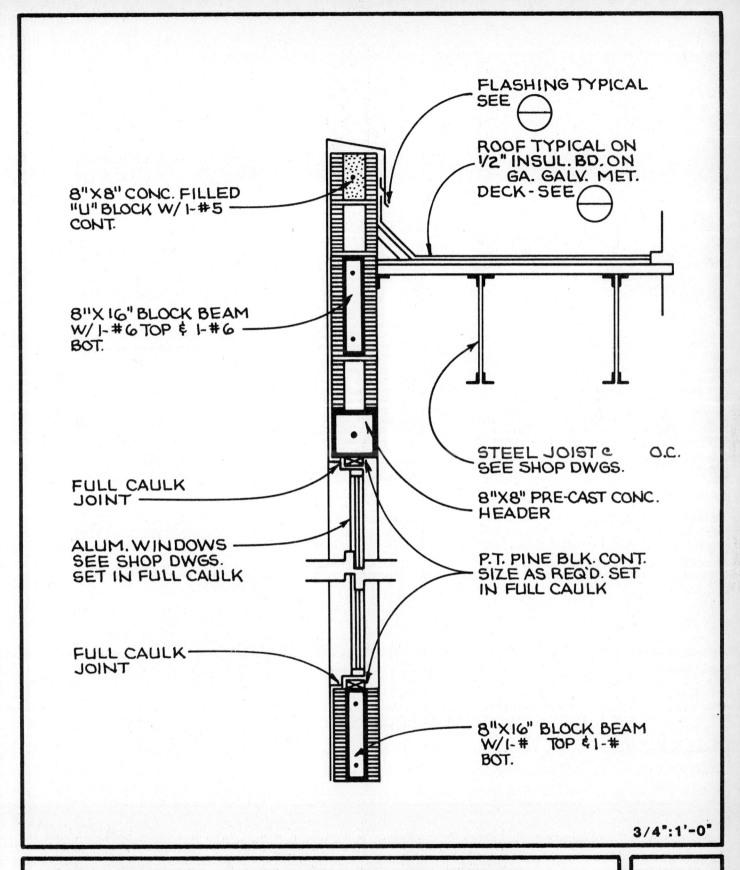

FLASHING TYPICAL SEE ⊘

ROOF TYPICAL ON ½" INSUL. BD. ON GA. GALV. MET. DECK - SEE ⊘

8"X8" CONC. FILLED "U" BLOCK W/1-#5 CONT.

8"X16" BLOCK BEAM W/1-#6 TOP & 1-#6 BOT.

FULL CAULK JOINT

ALUM. WINDOWS SEE SHOP DWGS. SET IN FULL CAULK

FULL CAULK JOINT

STEEL JOIST ℄   O.C. SEE SHOP DWGS.

8"X8" PRE-CAST CONC. HEADER

P.T. PINE BLK. CONT. SIZE AS REQ'D. SET IN FULL CAULK

8"X16" BLOCK BEAM W/1-#   TOP & 1-# BOT.

3/4":1'-0"

REINFORCED MASONRY BEAM: LEVEL STL JOIST & MET ROOF DECK: NO INSULATION SIDE CONDITION: WINDOW

RME 9

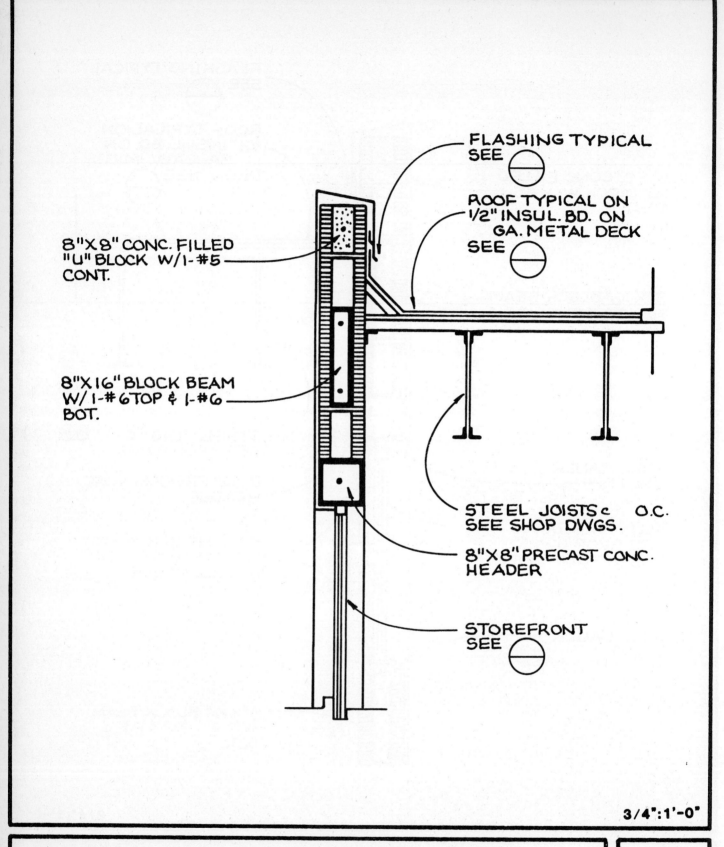

FLASHING TYPICAL
SEE ⊘

ROOF TYPICAL ON
1/2" INSUL. BD. ON
GA. METAL DECK
SEE ⊘

8"X8" CONC. FILLED
"U" BLOCK W/1-#5
CONT.

8"X16" BLOCK BEAM
W/1-#6 TOP & 1-#6
BOT.

STEEL JOISTS ∈   O.C.
SEE SHOP DWGS.

8"X8" PRECAST CONC.
HEADER

STOREFRONT
SEE ⊘

3/4":1'-0"

REINFORCED MASONRY BEAM: LEVEL
STL JOIST & MET ROOF DECK: NO INSULATION.
SIDE CONDITION: STOREFRONT

RME
10

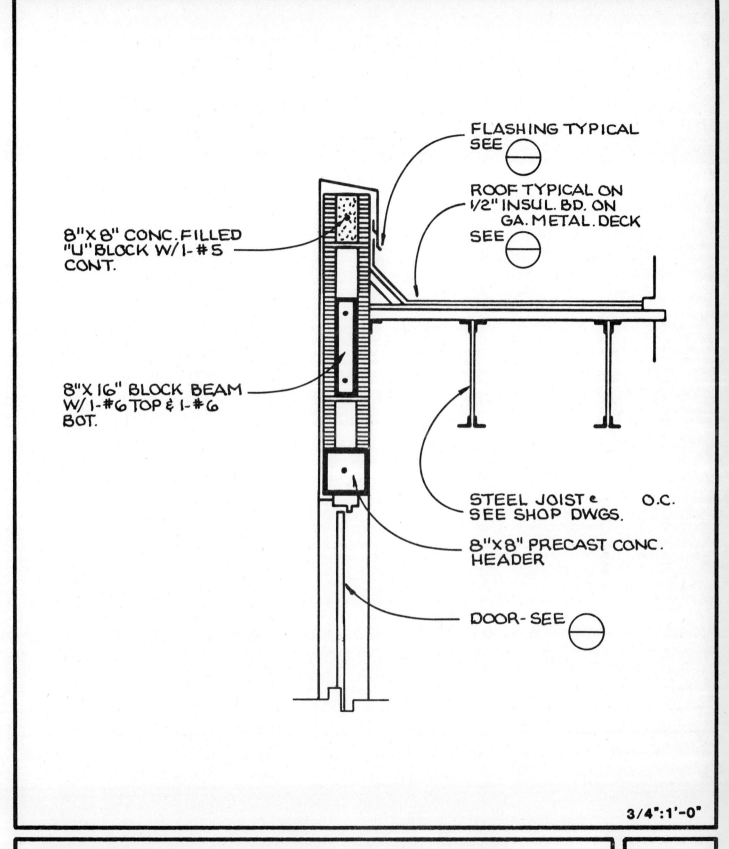

FLASHING TYPICAL
SEE ⊖

ROOF TYPICAL ON
1/2" INSUL. BD. ON
GA. METAL. DECK
SEE ⊖

8"X 8" CONC. FILLED
"U" BLOCK W/ I-#5
CONT.

8"X 16" BLOCK BEAM
W/ I-#6 TOP & I-#6
BOT.

STEEL JOIST ℓ   O.C.
SEE SHOP DWGS.

8"X 8" PRECAST CONC.
HEADER

DOOR- SEE ⊖

3/4":1'-0"

**REINFORCED MASONRY BEAM: LEVEL
STL JOIST & MET ROOF DECK: NO INSULATION
SIDE CONDITION: DOOR**

**RME
11**

SECTION 14: RM–F

Reinforced masonry construction with level beam.
Steel joist and metal roof deck with insulation board.

ARCHITECTURAL DETAILING
FOR
COMMERCIAL CONSTRUCTION

14

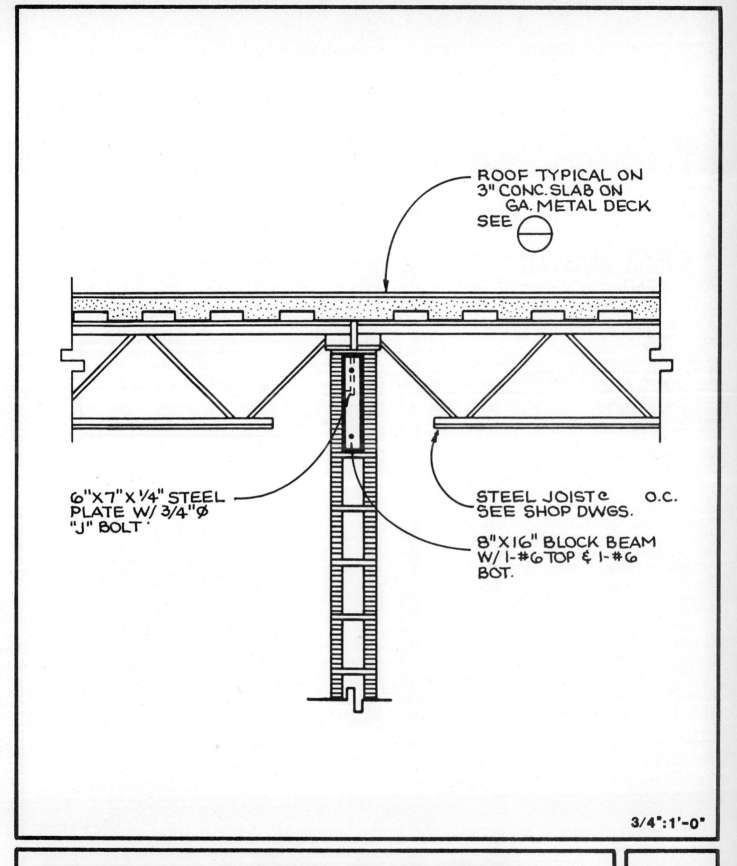

ROOF TYPICAL ON
3" CONC. SLAB ON
GA. METAL DECK
SEE ⊖

6"X7"X¼" STEEL
PLATE W/ 3/4"∅
"J" BOLT :

STEEL JOIST ℓ   O.C.
SEE SHOP DWGS.

8"X16" BLOCK BEAM
W/ 1-#6 TOP & 1-#6
BOT.

3/4":1'-0"

**REINFORCED MASONRY BEAM: LEVEL
STL JOIST & MET ROOF DECK: INSULATION BD**

INTERMEDIATE CONDITION: END

RMF
1

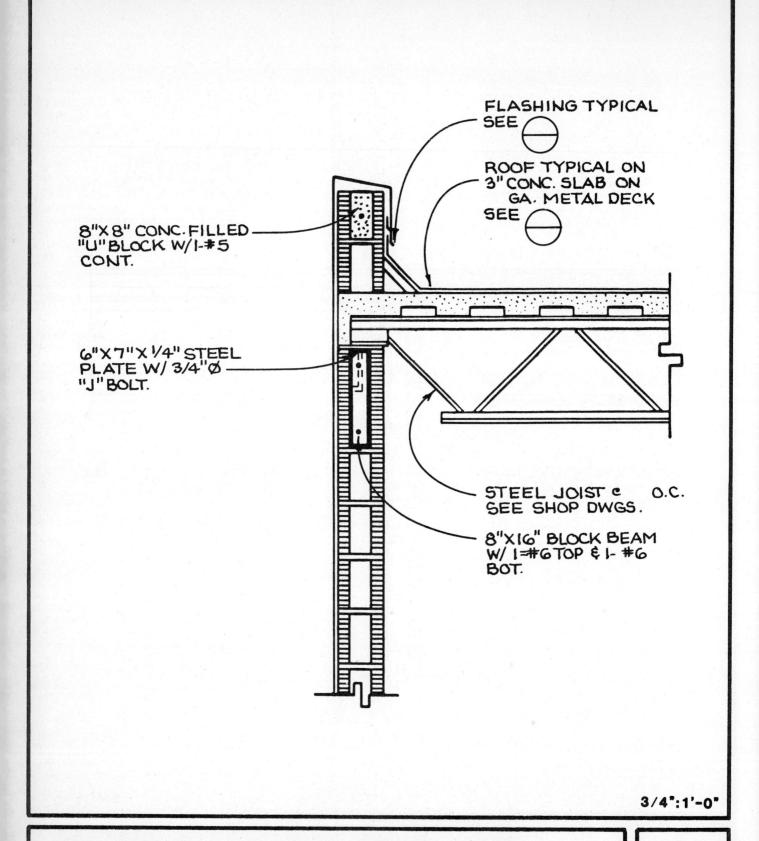

FLASHING TYPICAL
SEE ⊖

ROOF TYPICAL ON
3" CONC. SLAB ON
GA. METAL DECK
SEE ⊖

8"X 8" CONC. FILLED
"U" BLOCK W/ 1-#5
CONT.

6"X 7"X 1/4" STEEL
PLATE W/ 3/4"∅
"J" BOLT.

STEEL JOIST ℄   O.C.
SEE SHOP DWGS.

8"X16" BLOCK BEAM
W/ 1=#6 TOP & 1- #6
BOT.

3/4":1'-0"

REINFORCED MASONRY BEAM: LEVEL
STL JOIST & MET ROOF DECK: INSULATION BD
END CONDITION

RMF
2

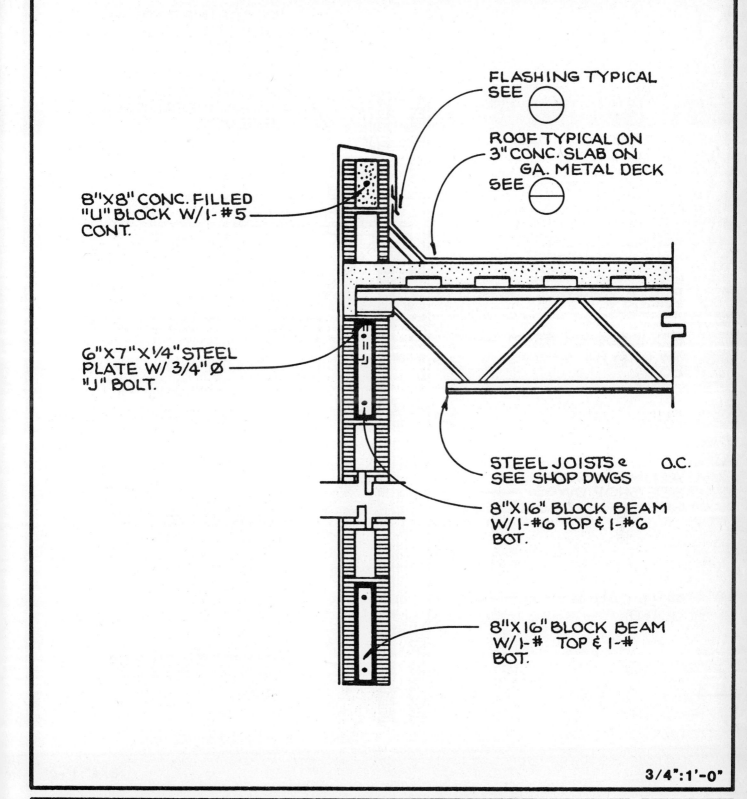

FLASHING TYPICAL
SEE ⊖

ROOF TYPICAL ON
3" CONC. SLAB ON
GA. METAL DECK
SEE ⊖

8"X8" CONC. FILLED
"U" BLOCK W/1-#5
CONT.

6"X7"X1/4" STEEL
PLATE W/ 3/4" Ø
"J" BOLT.

STEEL JOISTS @   O.C.
SEE SHOP DWGS

8"X16" BLOCK BEAM
W/1-#6 TOP & 1-#6
BOT.

8"X16" BLOCK BEAM
W/1-#   TOP & 1-#
BOT.

3/4":1'-0"

**REINFORCED MASONRY BEAM: LEVEL
STL JOIST & MET ROOF DECK: INSULATION BD
END CONDITION: LOWER BEAM**

**RMF
3**

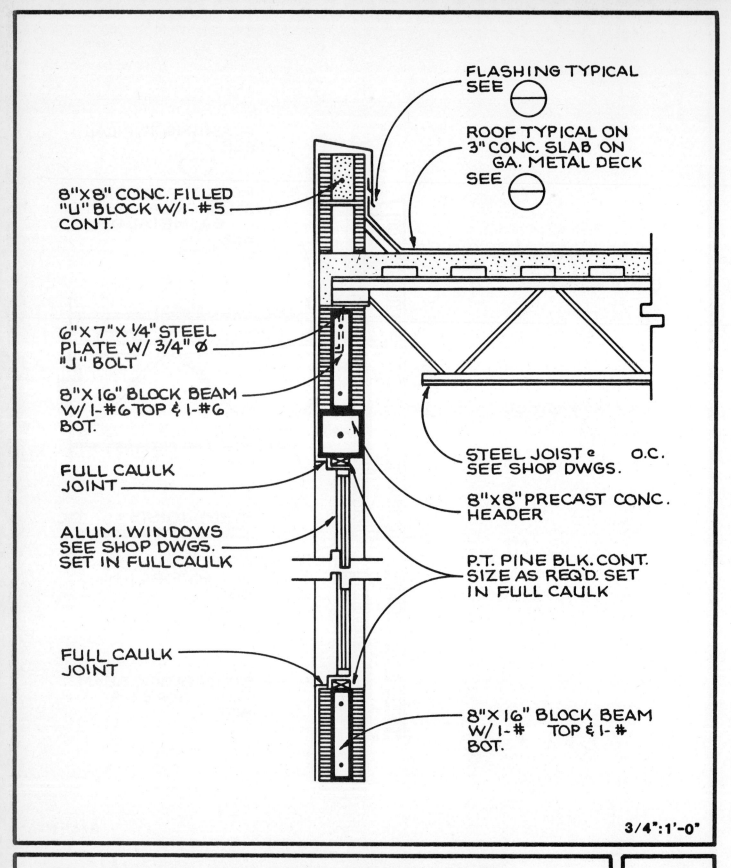

FLASHING TYPICAL
SEE ⊖

ROOF TYPICAL ON
3" CONC. SLAB ON
GA. METAL DECK
SEE ⊖

8"X8" CONC. FILLED
"U" BLOCK W/ 1-#5
CONT.

6"X7"X ¼" STEEL
PLATE W/ 3/4" Ø
"J" BOLT

8"X16" BLOCK BEAM
W/ 1-#6 TOP & 1-#6
BOT.

FULL CAULK
JOINT

ALUM. WINDOWS
SEE SHOP DWGS.
SET IN FULL CAULK

FULL CAULK
JOINT

STEEL JOIST e   O.C.
SEE SHOP DWGS.

8"X8" PRECAST CONC.
HEADER

P.T. PINE BLK. CONT.
SIZE AS REQ'D. SET
IN FULL CAULK

8"X16" BLOCK BEAM
W/ 1-#   TOP & 1-#
BOT.

3/4":1'-0"

REINFORCED MASONRY BEAM: LEVEL
STL JOIST & MET ROOF DECK: INSULATION BD
END CONDITION: WINDOW

RMF
4

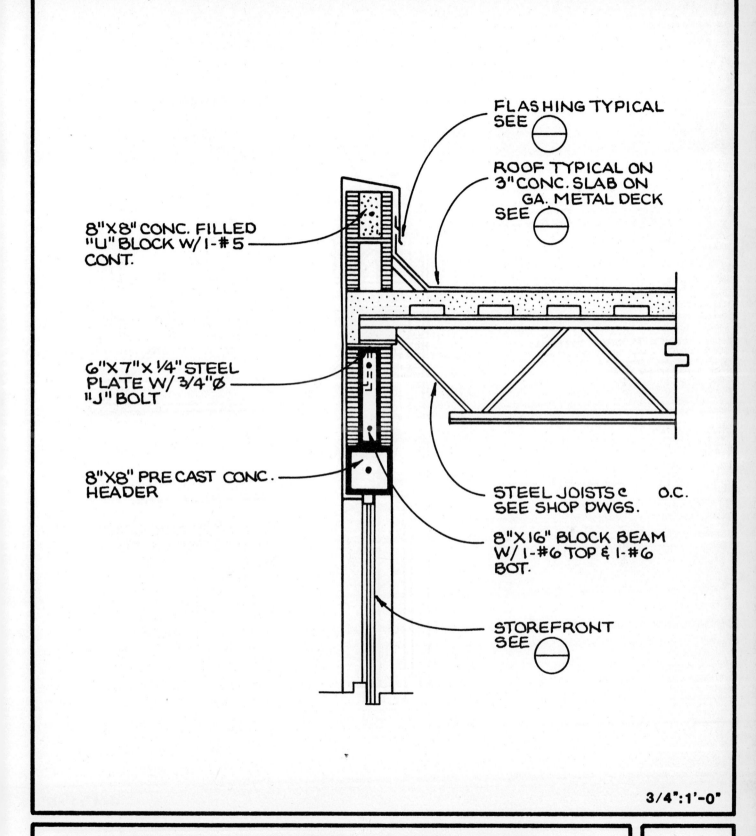

FLASHING TYPICAL
SEE ◯

ROOF TYPICAL ON
3" CONC. SLAB ON
GA. METAL DECK
SEE ◯

8"X8" CONC. FILLED
"U" BLOCK W/ 1-#5
CONT.

6"X7"X ¼" STEEL
PLATE W/ ¾"∅
"J" BOLT

8"X8" PRE CAST CONC.
HEADER

STEEL JOISTS ℄   O.C.
SEE SHOP DWGS.

8"X16" BLOCK BEAM
W/ 1-#6 TOP & 1-#6
BOT.

STOREFRONT
SEE ◯

3/4":1'-0"

**REINFORCED MASONRY BEAM: LEVEL
STL JOIST & MET ROOF DECK: INSULATION BD
END CONDITION: STOREFRONT**

**RMF
5**

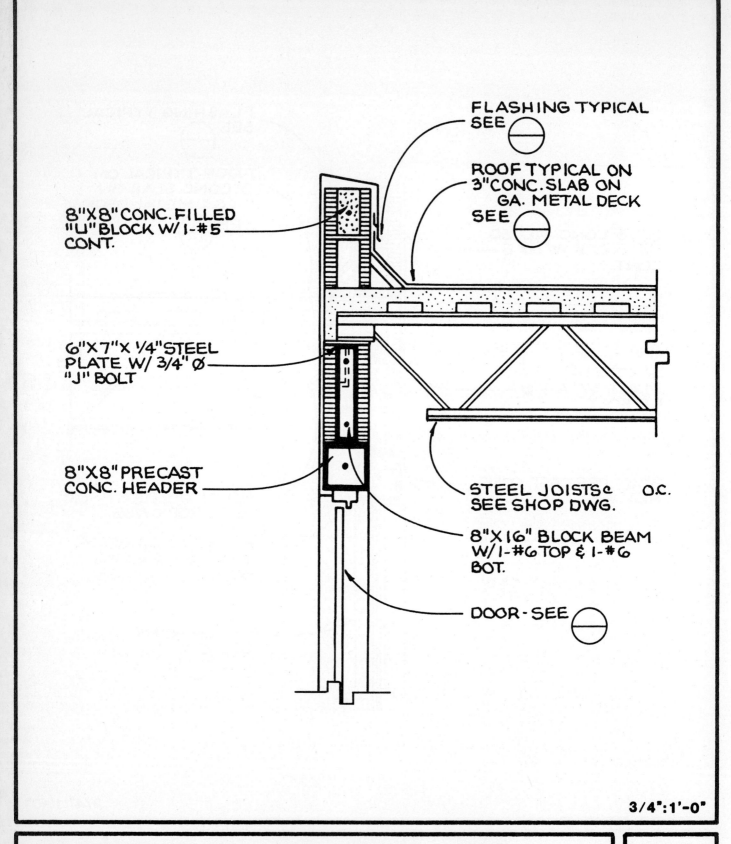

FLASHING TYPICAL
SEE ⊖

ROOF TYPICAL ON
3"CONC.SLAB ON
GA. METAL DECK
SEE ⊖

8"X8"CONC.FILLED
"U"BLOCK W/1-#5
CONT.

6"X7"X ¼"STEEL
PLATE W/ ¾" Ø
"J" BOLT

8"X8"PRECAST
CONC. HEADER

STEEL JOISTS⊄   O.C.
SEE SHOP DWG.

8"X16" BLOCK BEAM
W/1-#6 TOP & 1-#6
BOT.

DOOR-SEE ⊖

3/4":1'-0"

**REINFORCED MASONRY BEAM: LEVEL
STL JOIST & MET ROOF DECK: INSULATION BD
END CONDITION: DOOR**

**RMF
6**

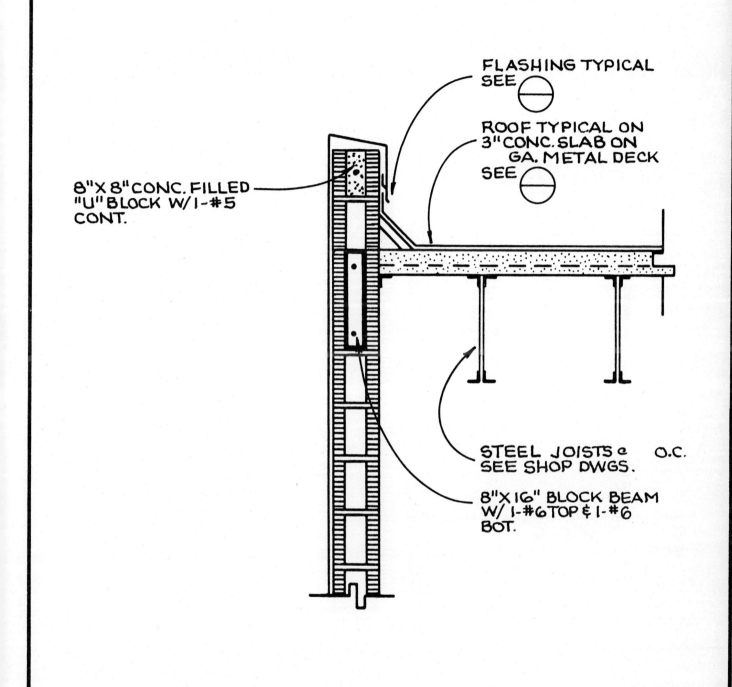

FLASHING TYPICAL
SEE ⊖

ROOF TYPICAL ON
3" CONC. SLAB ON
GA. METAL DECK
SEE ⊖

8" X 8" CONC. FILLED
"U" BLOCK W/ 1 - #5
CONT.

STEEL JOISTS @   O.C.
SEE SHOP DWGS.

8" X 16" BLOCK BEAM
W/ 1 - #6 TOP & 1 - #6
BOT.

3/4":1'-0"

**REINFORCED MASONRY BEAM: LEVEL
STL JOIST & MET ROOF DECK: INSULATION BD
SIDE CONDITION**

**RMF
7**

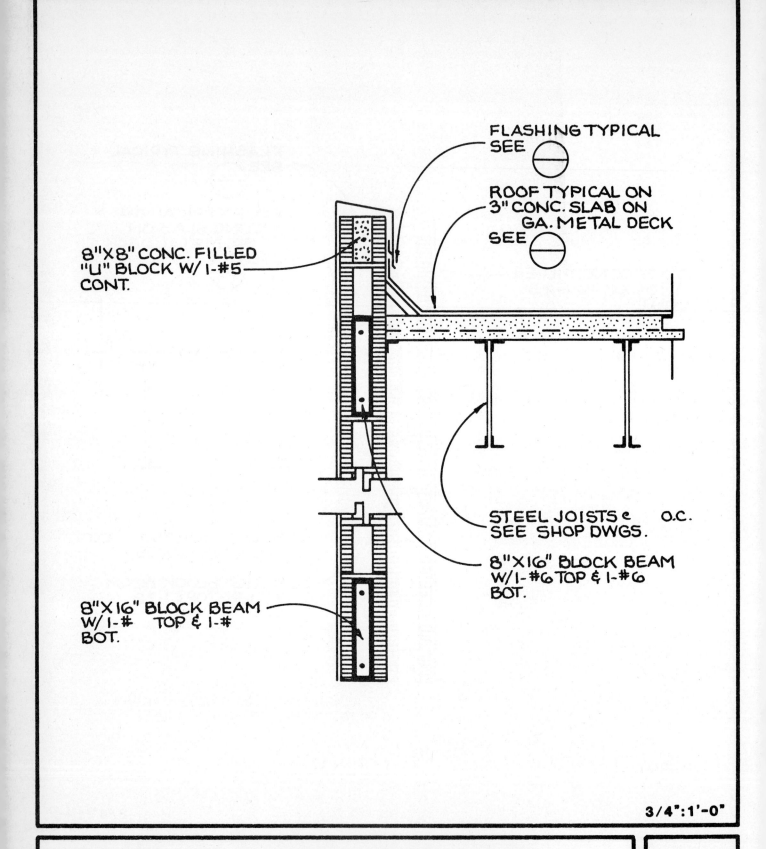

FLASHING TYPICAL
SEE ⊖

ROOF TYPICAL ON
3" CONC. SLAB ON
GA. METAL DECK
SEE ⊖

8"X8" CONC. FILLED
"U" BLOCK W/ 1-#5
CONT.

STEEL JOISTS ℮   O.C.
SEE SHOP DWGS.

8"X16" BLOCK BEAM
W/ 1-#6 TOP & 1-#6
BOT.

8"X16" BLOCK BEAM
W/ 1-#   TOP & 1-#
BOT.

3/4":1'-0"

**REINFORCED MASONRY BEAM: LEVEL
STL JOIST & MET ROOF DECK: INSULATION BD
SIDE CONDITION: LOWER BEAM**

**RMF
8**

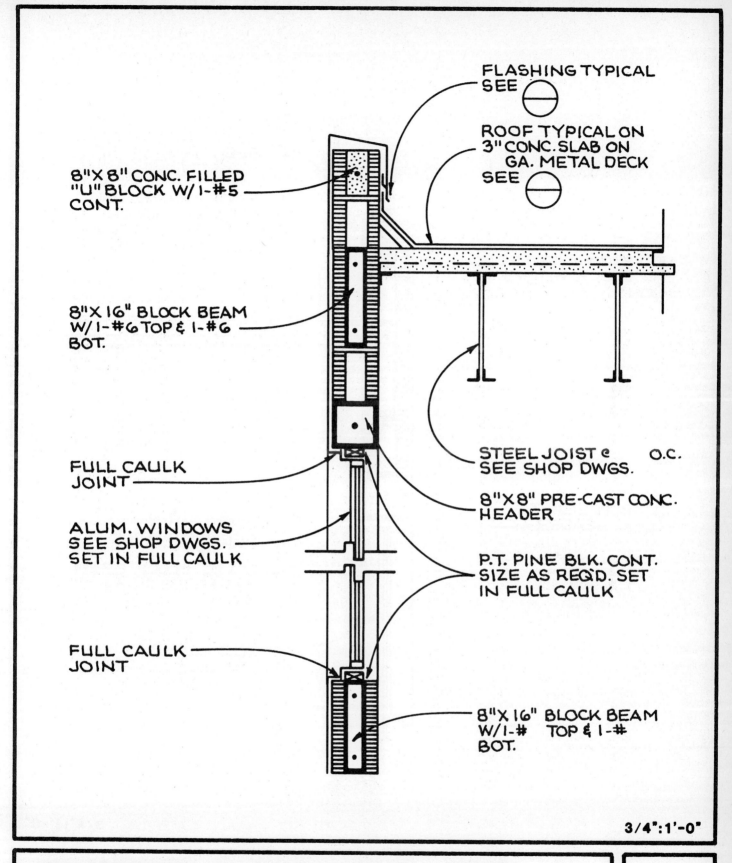

FLASHING TYPICAL SEE ⊖

ROOF TYPICAL ON 3" CONC. SLAB ON GA. METAL DECK SEE ⊖

8"X 8" CONC. FILLED "U" BLOCK W/ 1-#5 CONT.

8"X 16" BLOCK BEAM W/ 1-#6 TOP & 1-#6 BOT.

FULL CAULK JOINT

ALUM. WINDOWS SEE SHOP DWGS. SET IN FULL CAULK

FULL CAULK JOINT

STEEL JOIST @   O.C. SEE SHOP DWGS.

8"X 8" PRE-CAST CONC. HEADER

P.T. PINE BLK. CONT. SIZE AS REQ'D. SET IN FULL CAULK

8"X 16" BLOCK BEAM W/ 1-#   TOP & 1-#   BOT.

3/4":1'-0"

REINFORCED MASONRY BEAM: LEVEL
STL JOIST & MET ROOF DECK: INSULATION BD
SIDE CONDITION: WINDOW

**RMF
9**

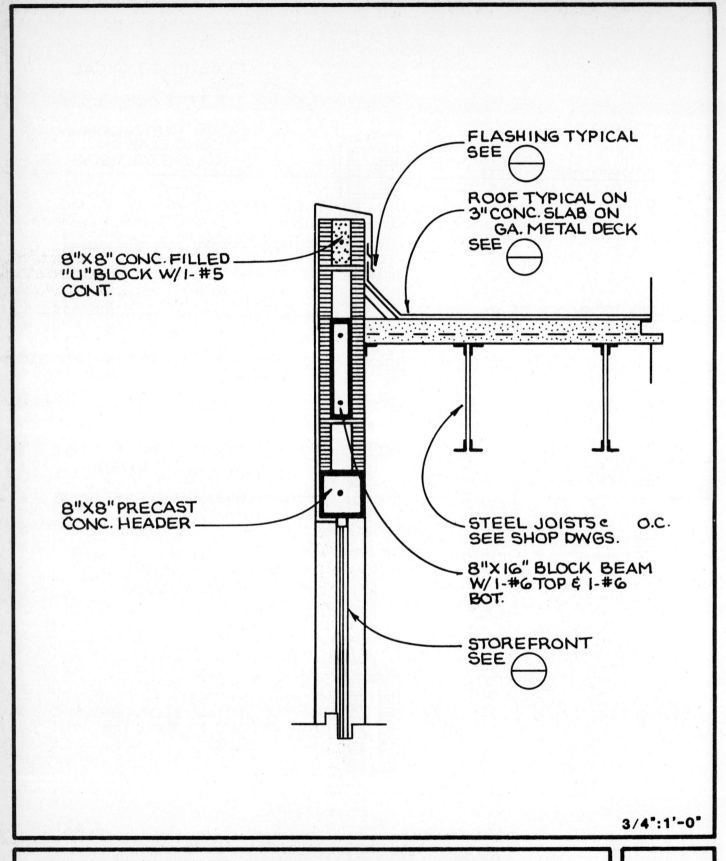

FLASHING TYPICAL SEE ⊖

ROOF TYPICAL ON 3"CONC. SLAB ON GA. METAL DECK SEE ⊖

8"X8"CONC. FILLED "U"BLOCK W/1-#5 CONT.

8"X8"PRECAST CONC. HEADER

STEEL JOISTS ⊂ O.C. SEE SHOP DWGS.

8"X16" BLOCK BEAM W/1-#6 TOP & 1-#6 BOT.

STOREFRONT SEE ⊖

3/4":1'-0"

REINFORCED MASONRY BEAM: LEVEL
STL JOIST & MET ROOF DECK: INSULATION BD
SIDE CONDITION: STOREFRONT

RMF 10

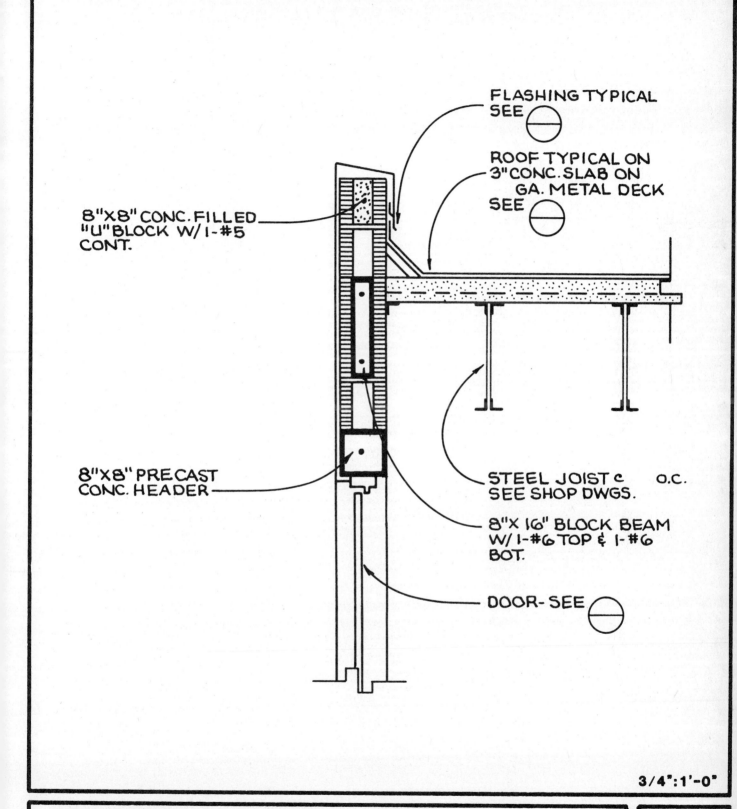

FLASHING TYPICAL
SEE ⊖

ROOF TYPICAL ON
3" CONC. SLAB ON
GA. METAL DECK
SEE ⊖

8"X8" CONC. FILLED
"U" BLOCK W/ 1-#5
CONT.

8"X8" PRECAST
CONC. HEADER

STEEL JOIST ⊂   O.C.
SEE SHOP DWGS.

8"X 16" BLOCK BEAM
W/ 1-#6 TOP & 1-#6
BOT.

DOOR- SEE ⊖

3/4":1'-0"

**REINFORCED MASONRY BEAM: LEVEL
STL JOIST & MET ROOF DECK: INSULATION BD
SIDE CONDITION: DOOR**

**RMF
11**

SECTION 15: RM–G

Reinforced masonry construction with sloped beam.
Prefabricated wood truss and plywood roof deck with no insulation.

RMG 1   Intermediate condition: End
RMG 2   End condition
RMG 3   End condition with lower beam
RMG 4   End condition with window
RMG 5   End condition with storefront
RMG 6   End condition with door
RMG 7   Side condition
RMG 8   Side condition with lower beam
RMG 9   Side condition with window
RMG 10 Side condition with storefront
RMG 11 Side condition with door

ARCHITECTURAL DETAILING
FOR
COMMERCIAL CONSTRUCTION

15

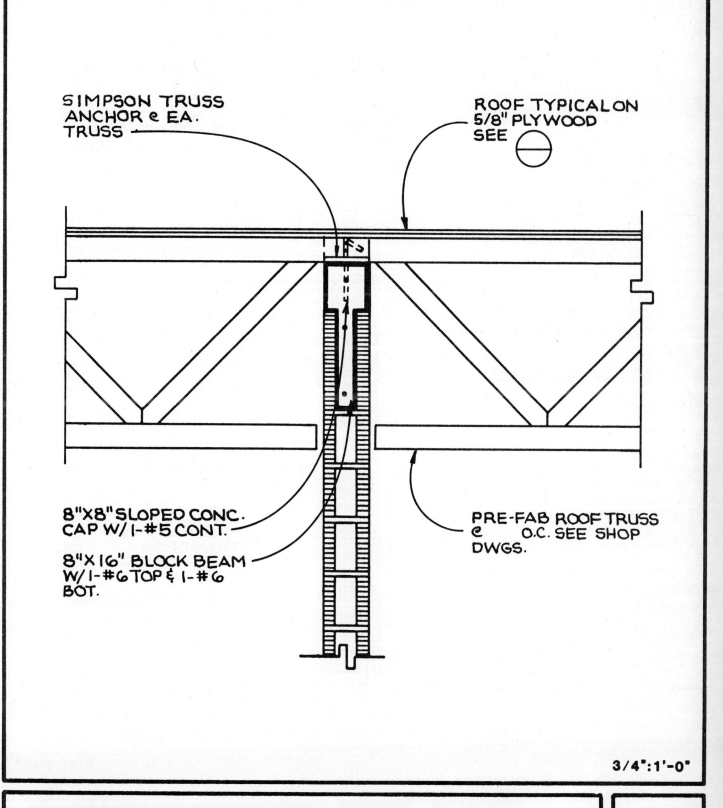

SIMPSON TRUSS ANCHOR @ EA. TRUSS

ROOF TYPICAL ON 5/8" PLYWOOD SEE ⊖

8"X8" SLOPED CONC. CAP W/ 1-#5 CONT.

8"X16" BLOCK BEAM W/ 1-#6 TOP & 1-#6 BOT.

PRE-FAB ROOF TRUSS @ O.C. SEE SHOP DWGS.

3/4":1'-0"

REINFORCED MASONRY BEAM: SLOPED WD TRUSS & PLYWD ROOF DECK: NO INSUL.

INTERMEDIATE CONDITION: END

RMG 1

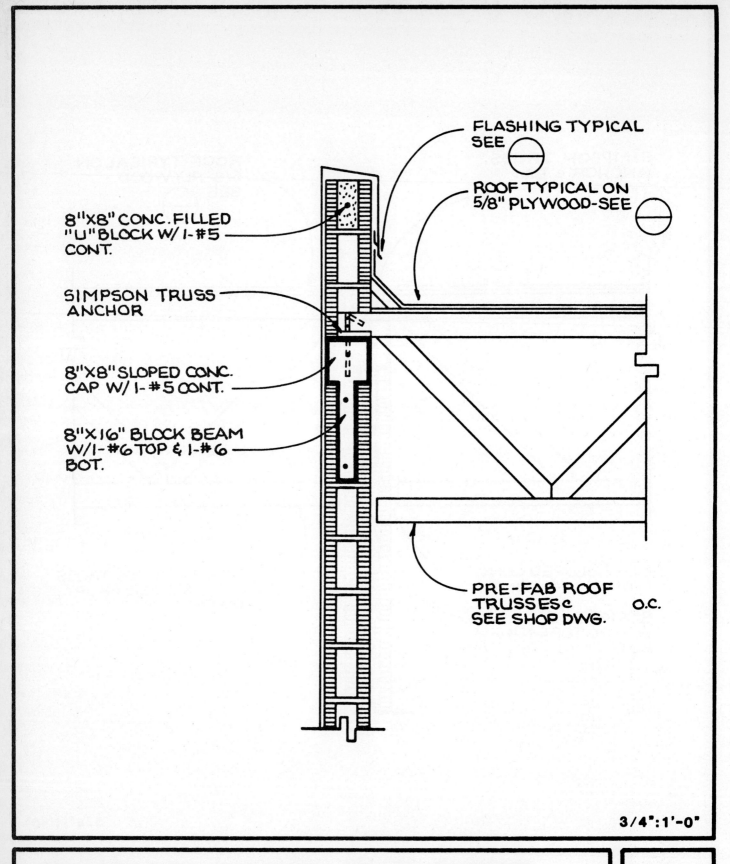

FLASHING TYPICAL SEE ⊖

ROOF TYPICAL ON 5/8" PLYWOOD-SEE ⊖

8"X8" CONC. FILLED "U" BLOCK W/ 1-#5 CONT.

SIMPSON TRUSS ANCHOR

8"X8" SLOPED CONC. CAP W/ 1-#5 CONT.

8"X16" BLOCK BEAM W/ 1-#6 TOP & 1-#6 BOT.

PRE-FAB ROOF TRUSSES ℅ SEE SHOP DWG. O.C.

3/4":1'-0"

REINFORCED MASONRY BEAM: SLOPED WD TRUSS & PLYWD ROOF DECK: NO INSUL. END CONDITION

RMG 2

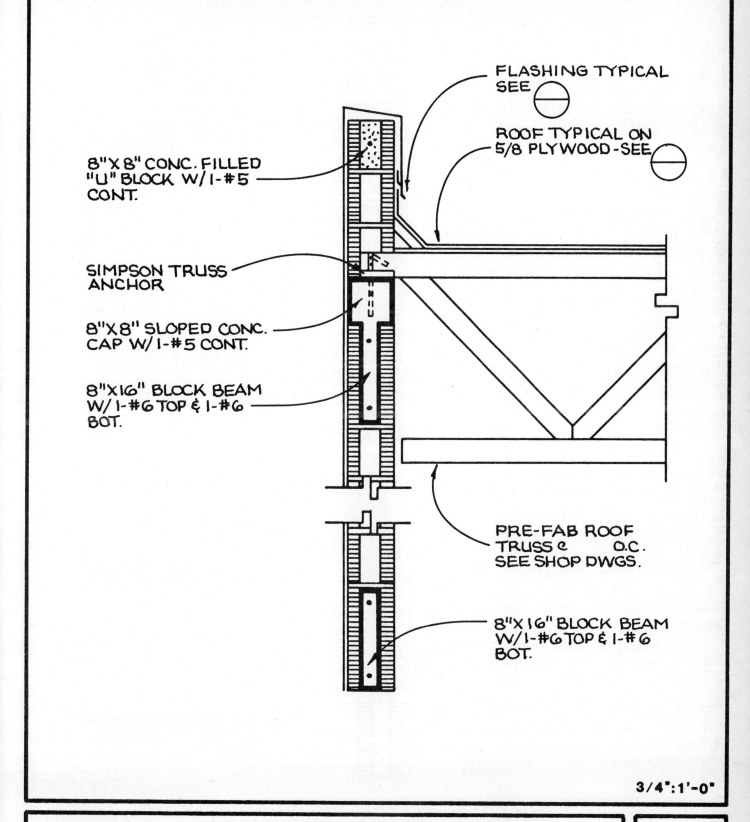

8"X 8" CONC. FILLED "U" BLOCK W/ 1-#5 CONT.

SIMPSON TRUSS ANCHOR

8"X 8" SLOPED CONC. CAP W/ 1-#5 CONT.

8"X16" BLOCK BEAM W/ 1-#6 TOP & 1-#6 BOT.

FLASHING TYPICAL SEE

ROOF TYPICAL ON 5/8 PLYWOOD-SEE

PRE-FAB ROOF TRUSS @   O.C. SEE SHOP DWGS.

8"X16" BLOCK BEAM W/ 1-#6 TOP & 1-#6 BOT.

3/4":1'-0"

REINFORCED MASONRY BEAM: SLOPED
WD TRUSS & PLYWD ROOF DECK: NO INSUL.
END CONDITION: LOWER BEAM

RMG
3

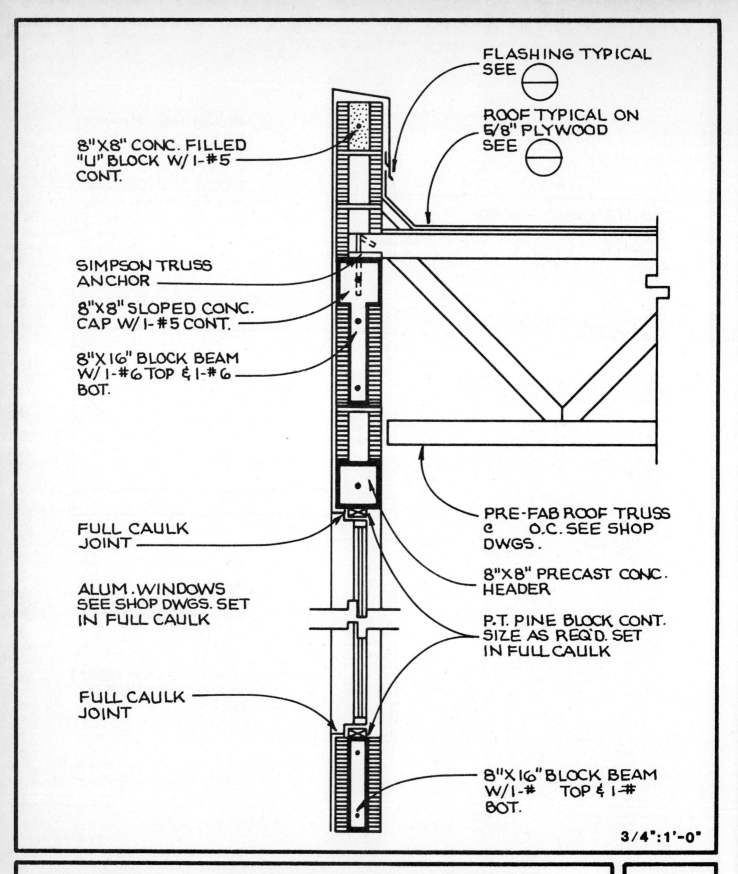

FLASHING TYPICAL
SEE ◯

ROOF TYPICAL ON
5/8" PLYWOOD
SEE ◯

8"X8" CONC. FILLED
"U" BLOCK W/ I-#5
CONT.

SIMPSON TRUSS
ANCHOR

8"X8" SLOPED CONC.
CAP W/ I-#5 CONT.

8"X16" BLOCK BEAM
W/ I-#6 TOP & I-#6
BOT.

FULL CAULK
JOINT

ALUM. WINDOWS
SEE SHOP DWGS. SET
IN FULL CAULK

FULL CAULK
JOINT

PRE-FAB ROOF TRUSS
@   O.C. SEE SHOP
DWGS.

8"X8" PRECAST CONC.
HEADER

P.T. PINE BLOCK CONT.
SIZE AS REQ'D. SET
IN FULL CAULK

8"X16" BLOCK BEAM
W/ I-#   TOP & I-#
BOT.

3/4":1'-0"

REINFORCED MASONRY BEAM: SLOPED
WD TRUSS & PLYWD ROOF DECK: NO INSUL.
END CONDITION: WINDOW

**RMG
4**

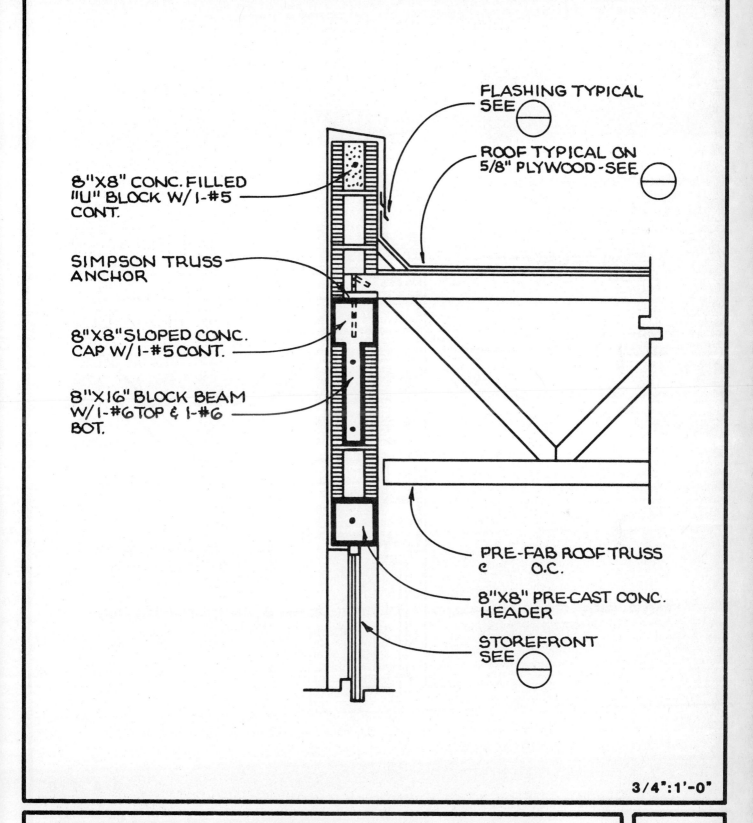

FLASHING TYPICAL
SEE ⊘

ROOF TYPICAL ON
5/8" PLYWOOD - SEE ⊘

8"X8" CONC. FILLED
"U" BLOCK W/ 1-#5
CONT.

SIMPSON TRUSS
ANCHOR

8"X8" SLOPED CONC.
CAP W/ 1-#5 CONT.

8"X16" BLOCK BEAM
W/ 1-#6 TOP & 1-#6
BOT.

PRE-FAB ROOF TRUSS
@   O.C.

8"X8" PRE-CAST CONC.
HEADER

STOREFRONT
SEE ⊘

3/4":1'-0"

**REINFORCED MASONRY BEAM: SLOPED
WD TRUSS & PLYWD ROOF DECK: NO INSUL.**

END CONDITION: STOREFRONT

**RMG
5**

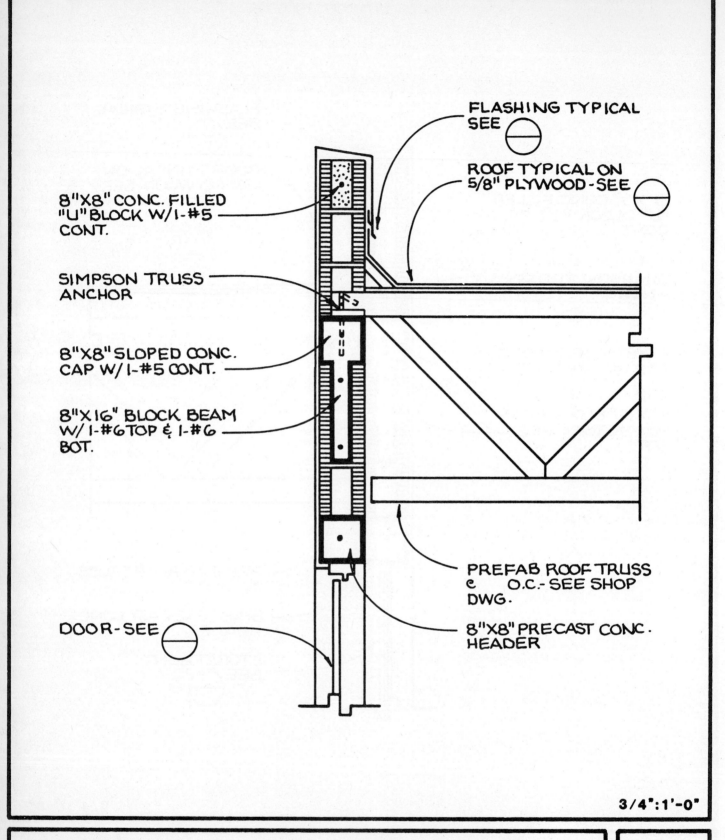

FLASHING TYPICAL SEE ◯

ROOF TYPICAL ON 5/8" PLYWOOD - SEE ◯

8"X8" CONC. FILLED "U" BLOCK W/ 1-#5 CONT.

SIMPSON TRUSS ANCHOR

8"X8" SLOPED CONC. CAP W/ 1-#5 CONT.

8"X16" BLOCK BEAM W/ 1-#6 TOP & 1-#6 BOT.

DOOR - SEE ◯

PREFAB ROOF TRUSS @   O.C. - SEE SHOP DWG.

8"X8" PRECAST CONC. HEADER

3/4":1'-0"

REINFORCED MASONRY BEAM: SLOPED WD TRUSS & PLYWD ROOF DECK: NO INSUL.

END CONDITION: DOOR

RMG 6

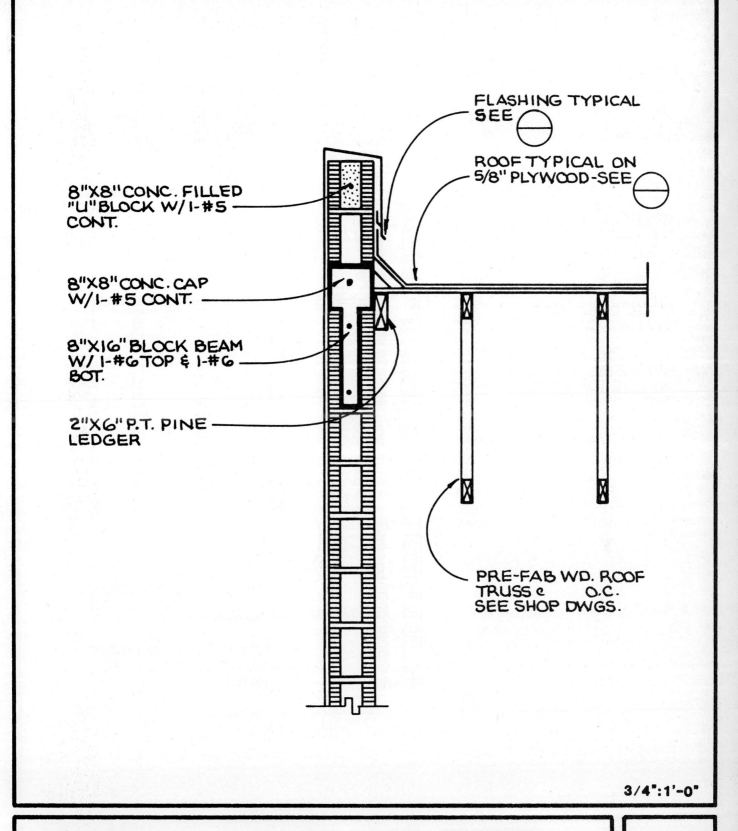

FLASHING TYPICAL
SEE ⊘

ROOF TYPICAL ON
5/8" PLYWOOD-SEE ⊘

8"X8"CONC. FILLED
"U" BLOCK W/ 1-#5
CONT.

8"X8" CONC. CAP
W/ 1-#5 CONT.

8"X16" BLOCK BEAM
W/ 1-#6 TOP & 1-#6
BOT.

2"X6" P.T. PINE
LEDGER

PRE-FAB WD. ROOF
TRUSS ℓ   O.C.
SEE SHOP DWGS.

3/4":1'-0"

**REINFORCED MASONRY BEAM: SLOPED
WD TRUSS & PLYWD ROOF DECK: NO INSUL.**

SIDE CONDITION

**RMG
7**

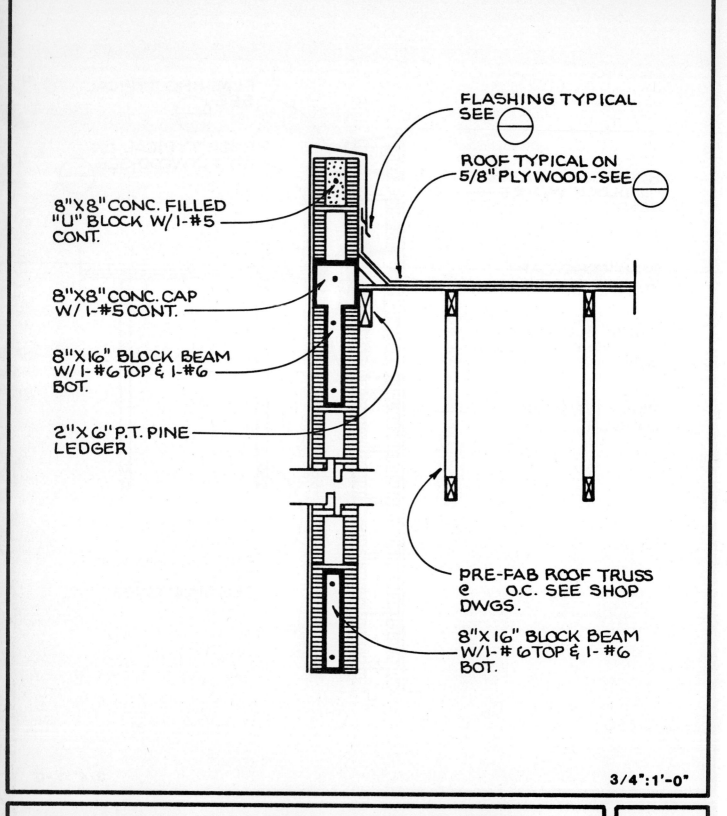

FLASHING TYPICAL SEE ⊖

ROOF TYPICAL ON 5/8" PLYWOOD-SEE ⊖

8"X8" CONC. FILLED "U" BLOCK W/I-#5 CONT.

8"X8" CONC. CAP W/I-#5 CONT.

8"X16" BLOCK BEAM W/I-#6 TOP & I-#6 BOT.

2"X6" P.T. PINE LEDGER

PRE-FAB ROOF TRUSS @   O.C. SEE SHOP DWGS.

8"X16" BLOCK BEAM W/I-#6 TOP & I-#6 BOT.

3/4":1'-0"

REINFORCED MASONRY BEAM: SLOPED WD TRUSS & PLYWD ROOF DECK: NO INSUL.

SIDE CONDITION: LOWER BEAM

RMG 8

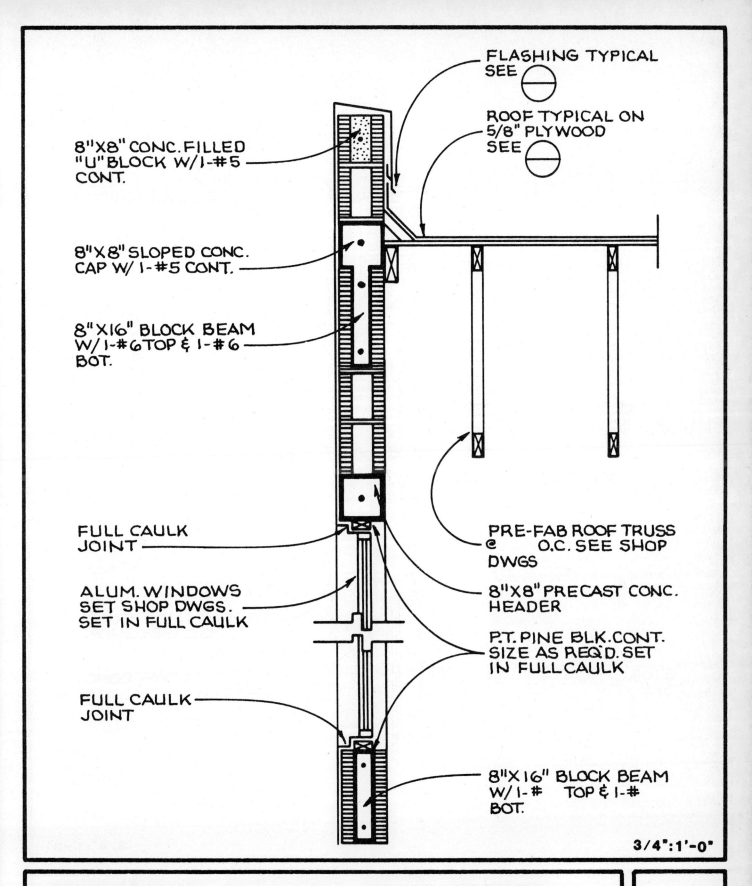

8"X8" CONC. FILLED "U" BLOCK W/1-#5 CONT.

8"X8" SLOPED CONC. CAP W/ 1-#5 CONT.

8"X16" BLOCK BEAM W/1-#6 TOP & 1-#6 BOT.

FULL CAULK JOINT

ALUM. WINDOWS SET SHOP DWGS. SET IN FULL CAULK

FULL CAULK JOINT

FLASHING TYPICAL SEE ⊖

ROOF TYPICAL ON 5/8" PLYWOOD SEE ⊖

PRE-FAB ROOF TRUSS @ O.C. SEE SHOP DWGS

8"X8" PRECAST CONC. HEADER

P.T. PINE BLK. CONT. SIZE AS REQ'D. SET IN FULL CAULK

8"X16" BLOCK BEAM W/1-# TOP & 1-# BOT.

3/4":1'-0"

REINFORCED MASONRY BEAM: SLOPED WD TRUSS & PLYWD ROOF DECK: NO INSUL.

SIDE CONDITION: WINDOW

RMG 9

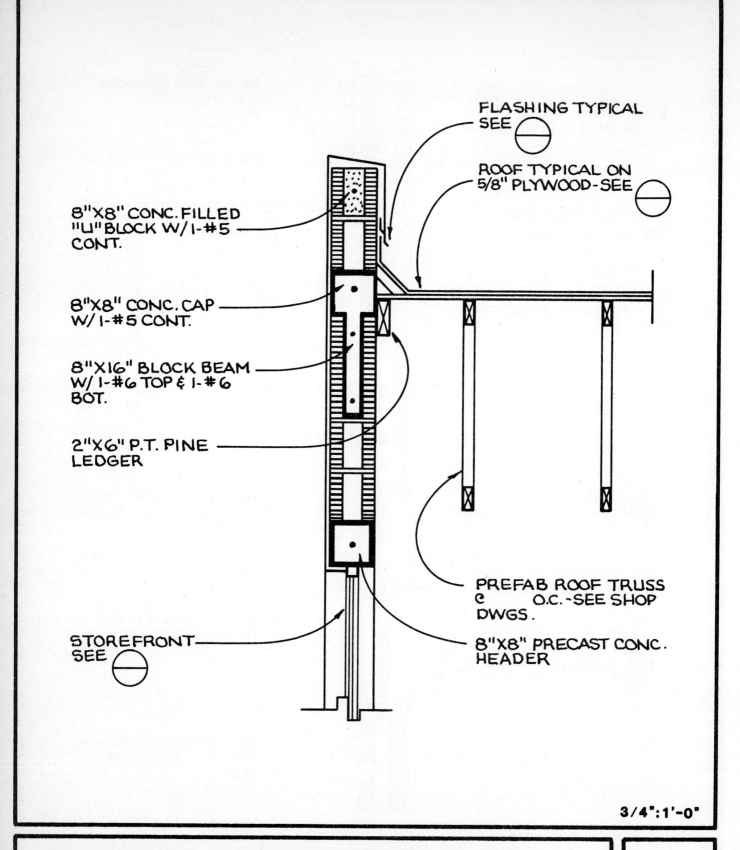

FLASHING TYPICAL
SEE ⊘

ROOF TYPICAL ON
5/8" PLYWOOD-SEE ⊘

8"X8" CONC. FILLED
"U" BLOCK W/ 1-#5
CONT.

8"X8" CONC. CAP
W/ 1-#5 CONT.

8"X16" BLOCK BEAM
W/ 1-#6 TOP & 1-#6
BOT.

2"X6" P.T. PINE
LEDGER

STOREFRONT
SEE ⊘

PREFAB ROOF TRUSS
@   O.C.-SEE SHOP
DWGS.

8"X8" PRECAST CONC.
HEADER

3/4":1'-0"

REINFORCED MASONRY BEAM: SLOPED
WD TRUSS & PLYWD ROOF DECK: NO INSUL.

SIDE CONDITION: STOREFRONT

RMG
10

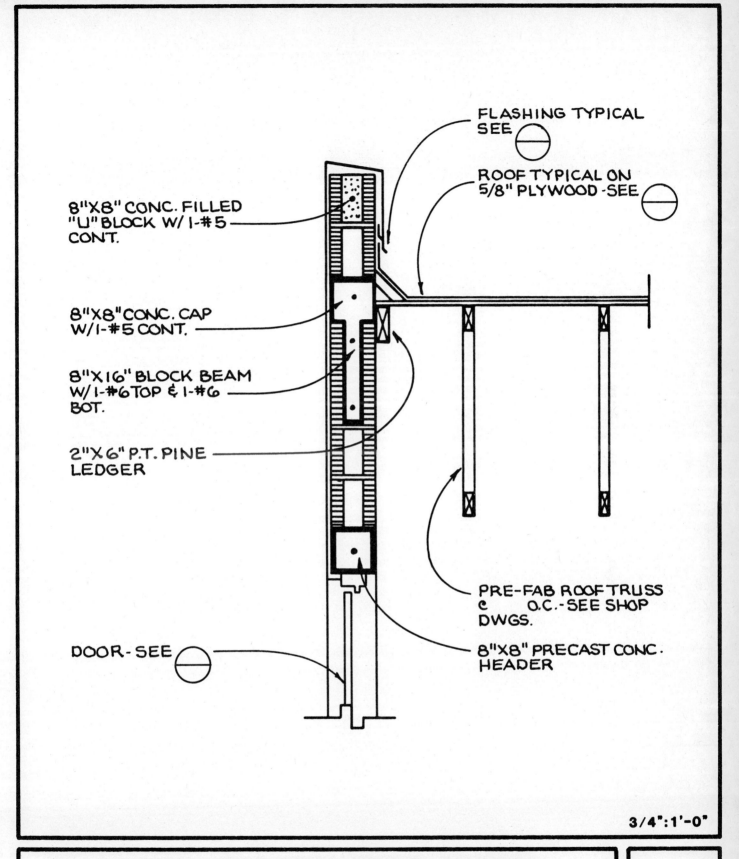

FLASHING TYPICAL
SEE ⊖

ROOF TYPICAL ON
5/8" PLYWOOD - SEE ⊖

8"X8" CONC. FILLED
"U" BLOCK W/ 1-#5
CONT.

8"X8" CONC. CAP
W/ 1-#5 CONT.

8"X16" BLOCK BEAM
W/ 1-#6 TOP & 1-#6
BOT.

2"X6" P.T. PINE
LEDGER

PRE-FAB ROOF TRUSS
@   O.C. - SEE SHOP
DWGS.

DOOR - SEE ⊖

8"X8" PRECAST CONC.
HEADER

3/4":1'-0"

**REINFORCED MASONRY BEAM: SLOPED
WD TRUSS & PLYWD ROOF DECK: NO INSUL.**

SIDE CONDITION: DOOR

**RMG
11**

SECTION 16: RM–H

Reinforced masonry construction with level beam.
Wood truss and plywood roof deck with sloped insulation.

ARCHITECTURAL DETAILING
FOR
COMMERCIAL CONSTRUCTION

16

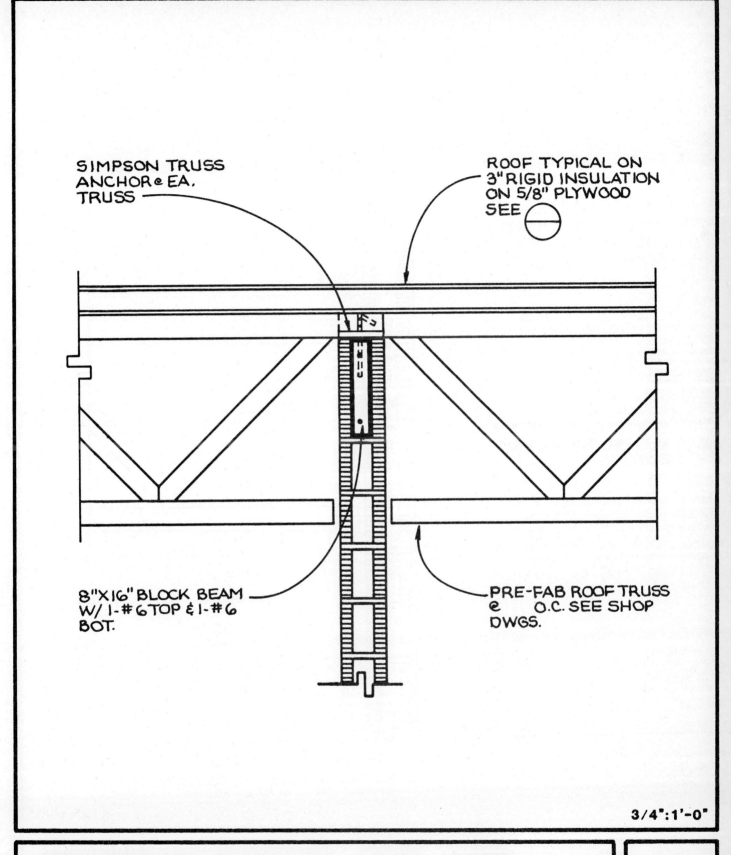

SIMPSON TRUSS ANCHOR e EA. TRUSS

ROOF TYPICAL ON 3" RIGID INSULATION ON 5/8" PLYWOOD SEE ⊘

8"X16" BLOCK BEAM W/ 1-#6 TOP & 1-#6 BOT.

PRE-FAB ROOF TRUSS e ___ O.C. SEE SHOP DWGS.

3/4":1'-0"

**REINFORCED MASONRY BEAM: LEVEL
WD TRUSS & PLYWD ROOF DECK: SLOPED INSUL.**

INTERMEDIATE CONDITION: END

**RMH
1**

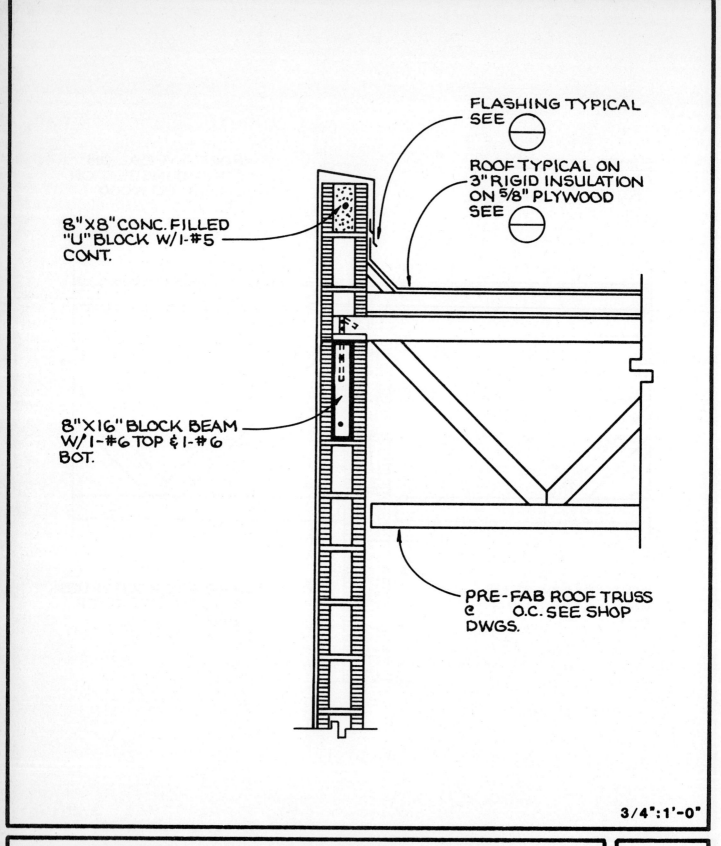

FLASHING TYPICAL
SEE ⊖

ROOF TYPICAL ON
3" RIGID INSULATION
ON 5/8" PLYWOOD
SEE ⊖

8"X8"CONC. FILLED
"U" BLOCK W/1-#5
CONT.

8"X16"BLOCK BEAM
W/1-#6 TOP & 1-#6
BOT.

PRE-FAB ROOF TRUSS
@   O.C. SEE SHOP
DWGS.

3/4":1'-0"

REINFORCED MASONRY BEAM: LEVEL
WD TRUSS & PLYWD ROOF DECK: SLOPED INSUL.
END CONDITION

RMH
2

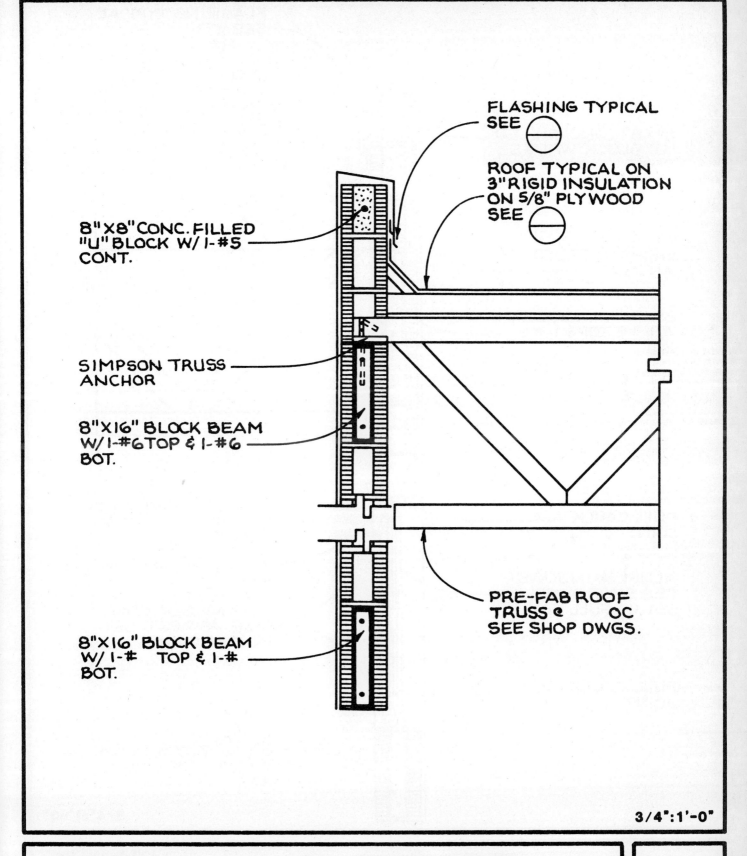

FLASHING TYPICAL
SEE ⊖

ROOF TYPICAL ON
3" RIGID INSULATION
ON 5/8" PLYWOOD
SEE ⊖

8"X8" CONC. FILLED
"U" BLOCK W/ 1-#5
CONT.

SIMPSON TRUSS
ANCHOR

8"X16" BLOCK BEAM
W/1-#6 TOP & 1-#6
BOT.

8"X16" BLOCK BEAM
W/ 1-#   TOP & 1-#
BOT.

PRE-FAB ROOF
TRUSS @   OC
SEE SHOP DWGS.

3/4":1'-0"

**REINFORCED MASONRY BEAM: LEVEL
WD TRUSS & PLYWD ROOF DECK: SLOPED INSUL.**

END CONDITION: LOWER BEAM

RMH
3

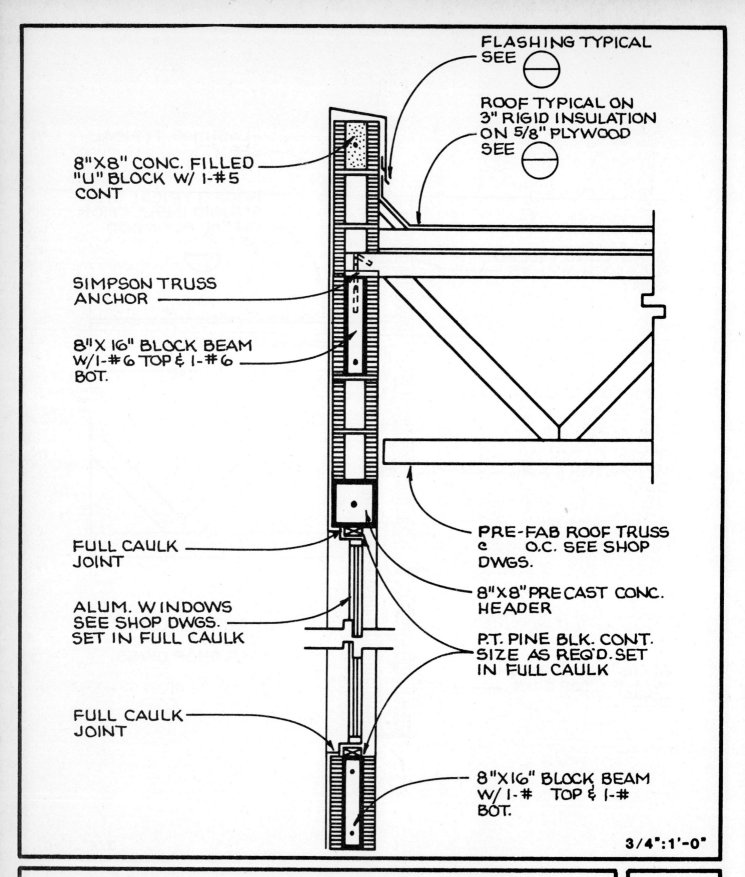

FLASHING TYPICAL
SEE ⊖

ROOF TYPICAL ON
3" RIGID INSULATION
ON 5/8" PLYWOOD
SEE ⊖

8"X8" CONC. FILLED
"U" BLOCK W/ 1-#5
CONT

SIMPSON TRUSS
ANCHOR

8"X16" BLOCK BEAM
W/1-#6 TOP & 1-#6
BOT.

FULL CAULK
JOINT

ALUM. WINDOWS
SEE SHOP DWGS.
SET IN FULL CAULK

FULL CAULK
JOINT

PRE-FAB ROOF TRUSS
ℓ   O.C. SEE SHOP
DWGS.

8"X8" PRECAST CONC.
HEADER

P.T. PINE BLK. CONT.
SIZE AS REQ'D. SET
IN FULL CAULK

8"X16" BLOCK BEAM
W/ 1-# TOP & 1-#
BOT.

3/4":1'-0"

**REINFORCED MASONRY BEAM: LEVEL
WD TRUSS & PLYWD ROOF DECK: SLOPED INSUL.
END CONDITION: WINDOW**

**RMH
4**

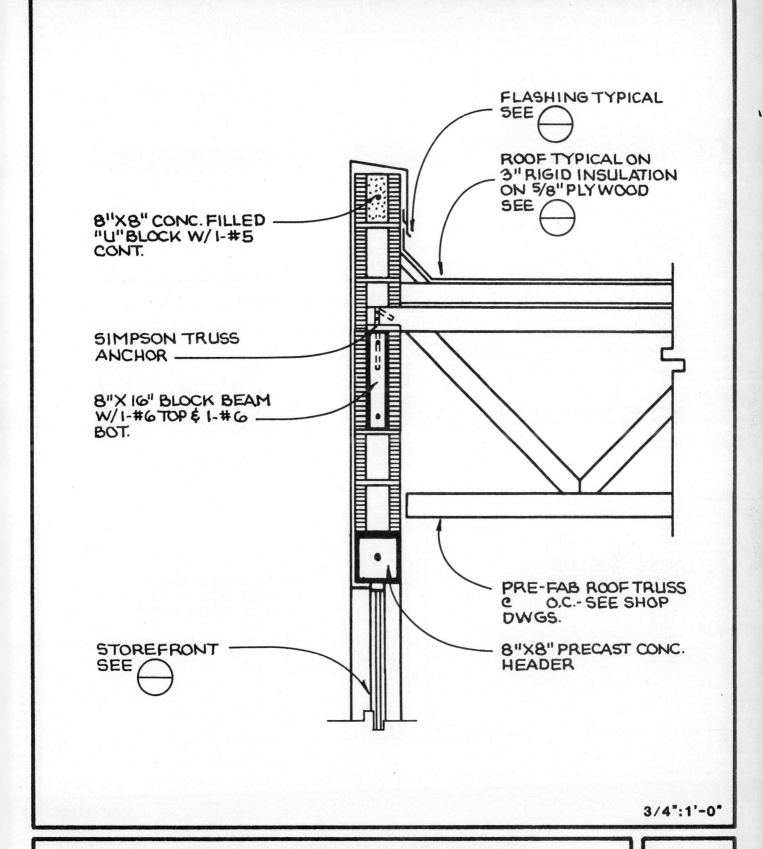

FLASHING TYPICAL
SEE ⊖

ROOF TYPICAL ON
3" RIGID INSULATION
ON 5/8" PLYWOOD
SEE ⊖

8"X8" CONC. FILLED
"U" BLOCK W/ 1-#5
CONT.

SIMPSON TRUSS
ANCHOR

8"X 16" BLOCK BEAM
W/ 1-#6 TOP & 1-#6
BOT.

STOREFRONT
SEE ⊖

PRE-FAB ROOF TRUSS
@   O.C.- SEE SHOP
DWGS.

8"X8" PRECAST CONC.
HEADER

3/4":1'-0"

REINFORCED MASONRY BEAM: LEVEL
WD TRUSS & PLYWD ROOF DECK: SLOPED INSUL.
END CONDITION: STOREFRONT

**RMH
5**

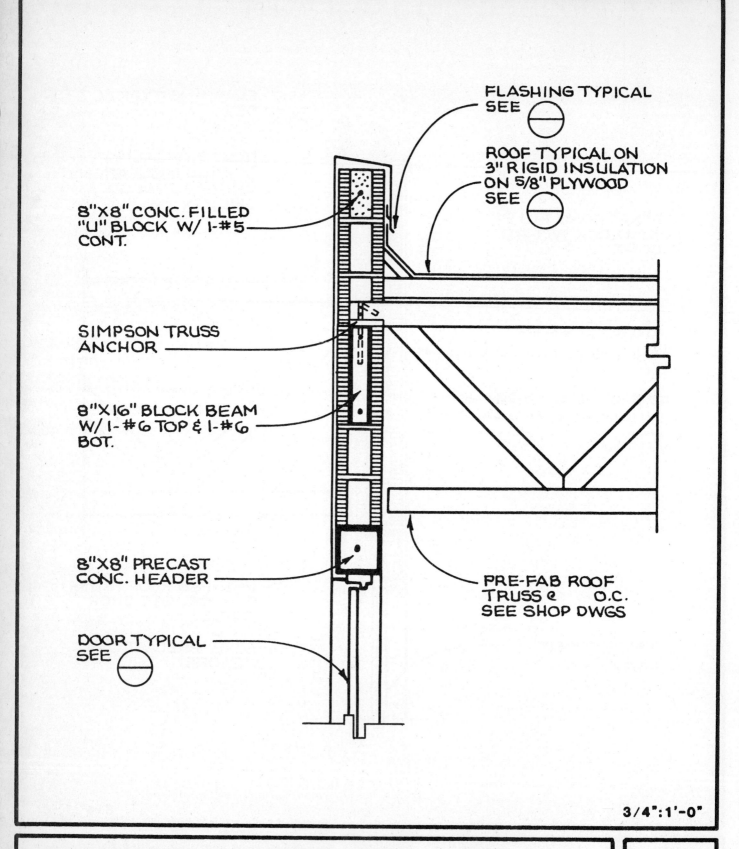

FLASHING TYPICAL
SEE ⊖

ROOF TYPICAL ON
3" RIGID INSULATION
ON 5/8" PLYWOOD
SEE ⊖

8"X8" CONC. FILLED
"U" BLOCK W/ 1-#5
CONT.

SIMPSON TRUSS
ANCHOR

8"X16" BLOCK BEAM
W/ 1-#6 TOP & 1-#6
BOT.

8"X8" PRECAST
CONC. HEADER

PRE-FAB ROOF
TRUSS @   O.C.
SEE SHOP DWGS

DOOR TYPICAL
SEE ⊖

3/4":1'-0"

REINFORCED MASONRY BEAM: LEVEL
WD TRUSS & PLYWD ROOF DECK: SLOPED INSUL.

END CONDITION: DOOR

RMH
6

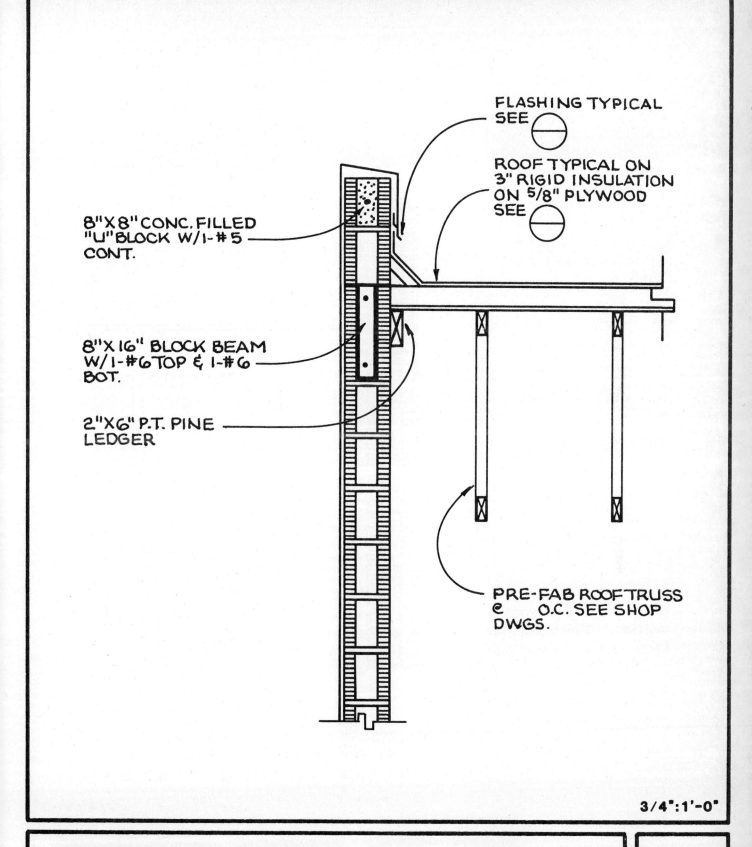

FLASHING TYPICAL
SEE ⊖

ROOF TYPICAL ON
3" RIGID INSULATION
ON 5/8" PLYWOOD
SEE ⊖

8"X8" CONC. FILLED
"U" BLOCK W/1-#5
CONT.

8"X16" BLOCK BEAM
W/1-#6 TOP & 1-#6
BOT.

2"X6" P.T. PINE
LEDGER

PRE-FAB ROOF TRUSS
@   O.C. SEE SHOP
DWGS.

3/4":1'-0"

**REINFORCED MASONRY BEAM: LEVEL
WD TRUSS & PLYWD ROOF DECK: SLOPED INSUL.
SIDE CONDITION**

**RMH
7**

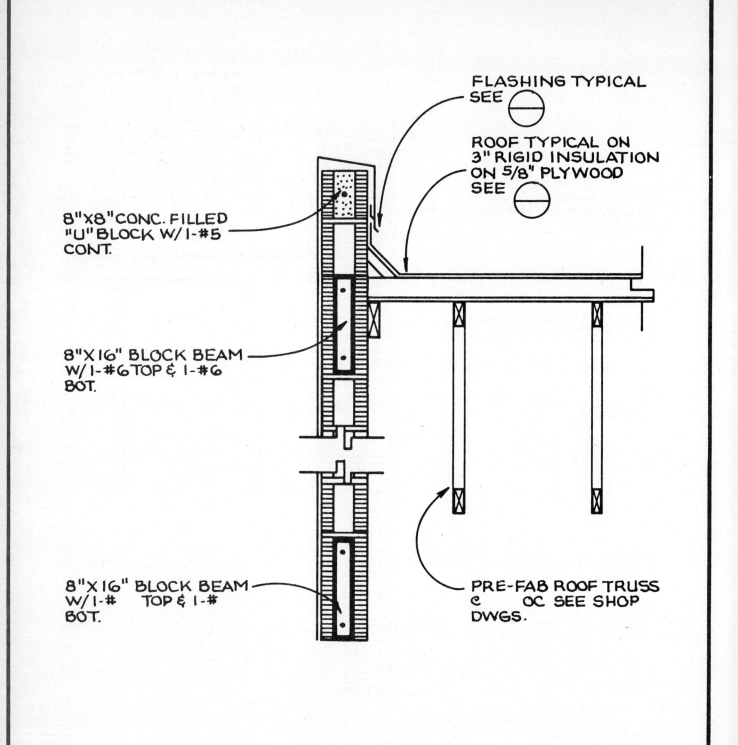

FLASHING TYPICAL
SEE ⊖

ROOF TYPICAL ON
3" RIGID INSULATION
ON 5/8" PLYWOOD
SEE ⊖

8"x8"CONC. FILLED
"U"BLOCK W/1-#5
CONT.

8"X16" BLOCK BEAM
W/1-#6 TOP & 1-#6
BOT.

8"X16" BLOCK BEAM
W/1-#   TOP & 1-#
BOT.

PRE-FAB ROOF TRUSS
℃   OC SEE SHOP
DWGS.

3/4":1'-0"

**REINFORCED MASONRY BEAM: LEVEL
WD TRUSS & PLYWD ROOF DECK: SLOPED INSUL.**

SIDE CONDITION: LOWER BEAM

**RMH
8**

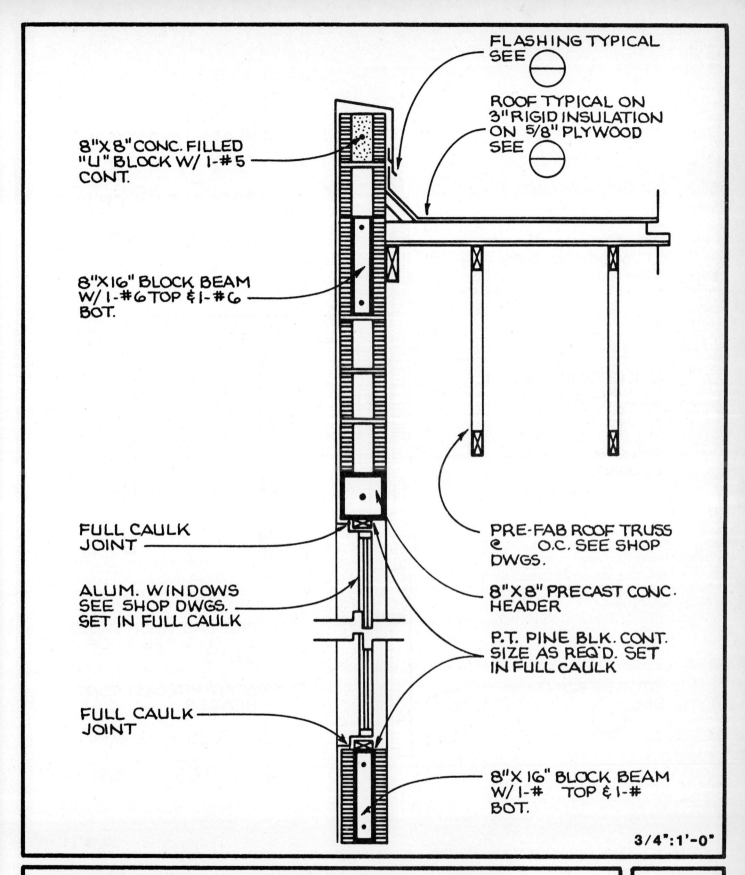

FLASHING TYPICAL SEE ◯

ROOF TYPICAL ON 3" RIGID INSULATION ON 5/8" PLYWOOD SEE ◯

8"X 8" CONC. FILLED "U" BLOCK W/ 1-#5 CONT.

8"X16" BLOCK BEAM W/ 1-#6 TOP & 1-#6 BOT.

FULL CAULK JOINT

ALUM. WINDOWS SEE SHOP DWGS. SET IN FULL CAULK

FULL CAULK JOINT

PRE-FAB ROOF TRUSS @ O.C. SEE SHOP DWGS.

8"X 8" PRECAST CONC. HEADER

P.T. PINE BLK. CONT. SIZE AS REQ'D. SET IN FULL CAULK

8"X 16" BLOCK BEAM W/ 1-# TOP & 1-# BOT.

3/4":1'-0"

REINFORCED MASONRY BEAM: LEVEL WD TRUSS & PLYWD ROOF DECK: SLOPED INSUL.

SIDE CONDITION: WINDOW

RMH 9

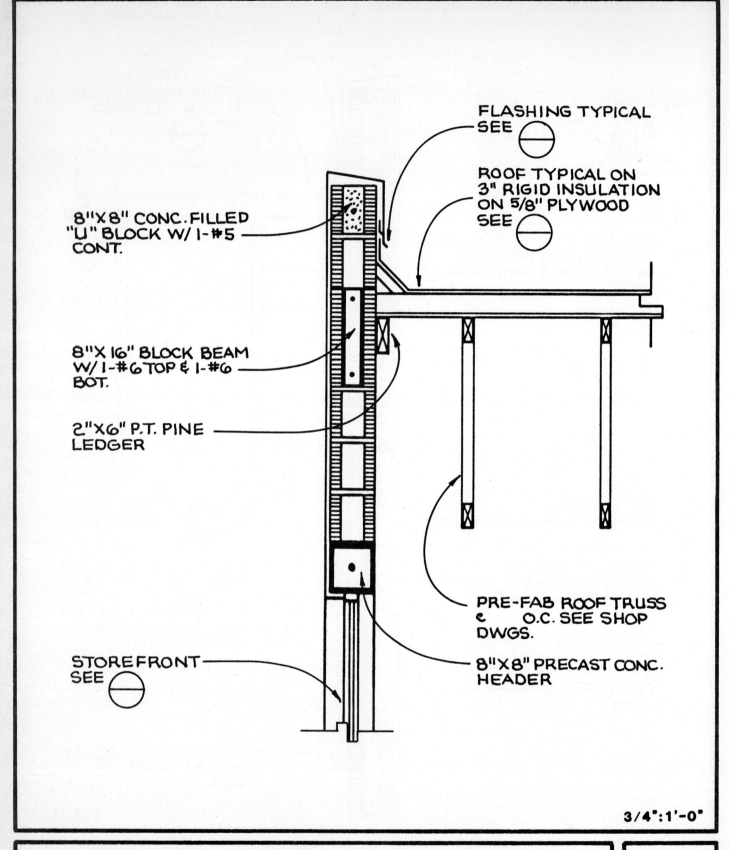

FLASHING TYPICAL
SEE ◯

ROOF TYPICAL ON
3" RIGID INSULATION
ON 5/8" PLYWOOD
SEE ◯

8"X8" CONC. FILLED
"U" BLOCK W/ 1-#5
CONT.

8"X 16" BLOCK BEAM
W/ 1-#6 TOP & 1-#6
BOT.

2"X6" P.T. PINE
LEDGER

PRE-FAB ROOF TRUSS
&   O.C. SEE SHOP
DWGS.

STOREFRONT
SEE ◯

8"X8" PRECAST CONC.
HEADER

3/4":1'-0"

**REINFORCED MASONRY BEAM: LEVEL
WD TRUSS & PLYWD ROOF DECK: SLOPED INSUL.**

SIDE CONDITION: STOREFRONT

**RMH
10**

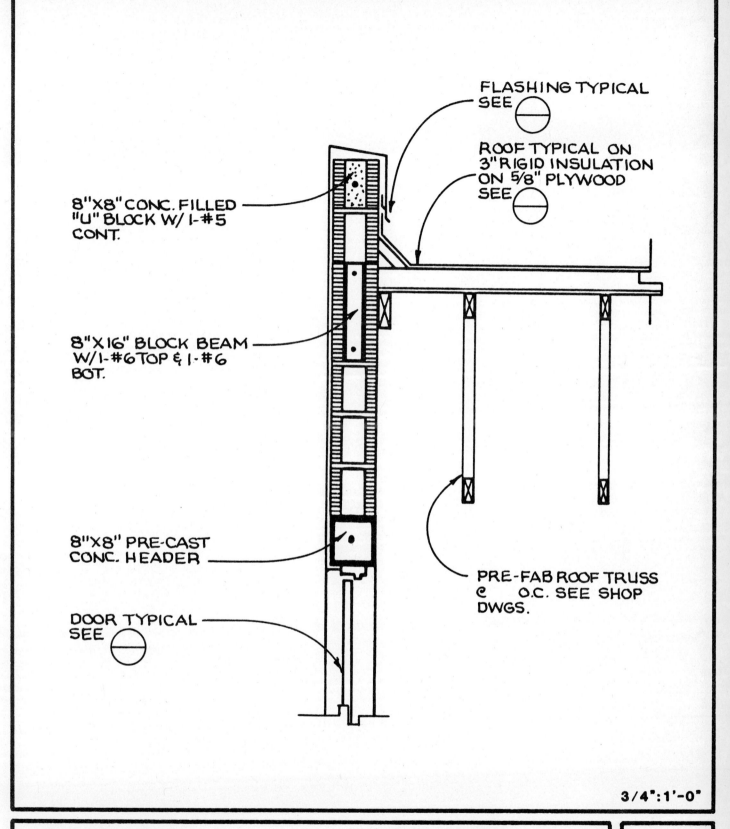

FLASHING TYPICAL
SEE ⊖

ROOF TYPICAL ON
3" RIGID INSULATION
ON 5/8" PLYWOOD
SEE ⊖

8"X8" CONC. FILLED
"U" BLOCK W/ 1-#5
CONT.

8"X16" BLOCK BEAM
W/ 1-#6 TOP & 1-#6
BOT.

8"X8" PRE-CAST
CONC. HEADER

PRE-FAB ROOF TRUSS
@ O.C. SEE SHOP
DWGS.

DOOR TYPICAL
SEE ⊖

3/4":1'-0"

**REINFORCED MASONRY BEAM: LEVEL
WD TRUSS & PLYWD ROOF DECK: SLOPED INSUL.
SIDE CONDITION: DOOR**

**RMH
11**

SECTION 17: FOOTINGS

SECTION 17: FOOTINGS

ARCHITECTURAL DETAILING
FOR
COMMERCIAL CONSTRUCTION

17

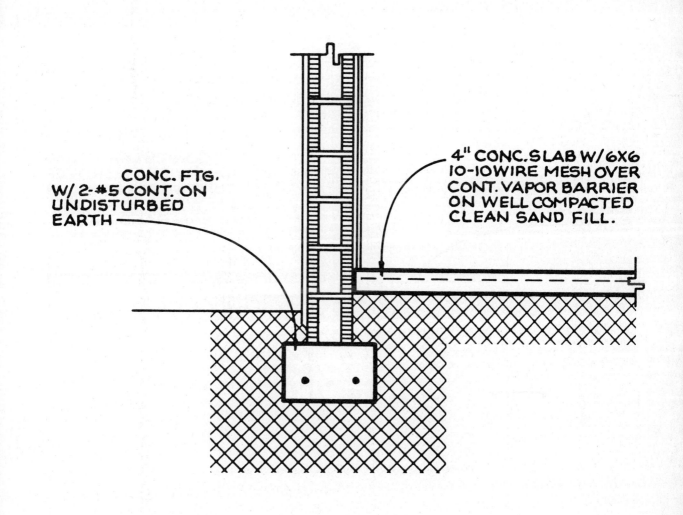

CONC. FTG.
W/ 2-#5 CONT. ON
UNDISTURBED
EARTH

4" CONC. SLAB W/ 6X6
10-10 WIRE MESH OVER
CONT. VAPOR BARRIER
ON WELL COMPACTED
CLEAN SAND FILL.

3/4": 1'-0"

SPREAD FOOTING: END

F 1

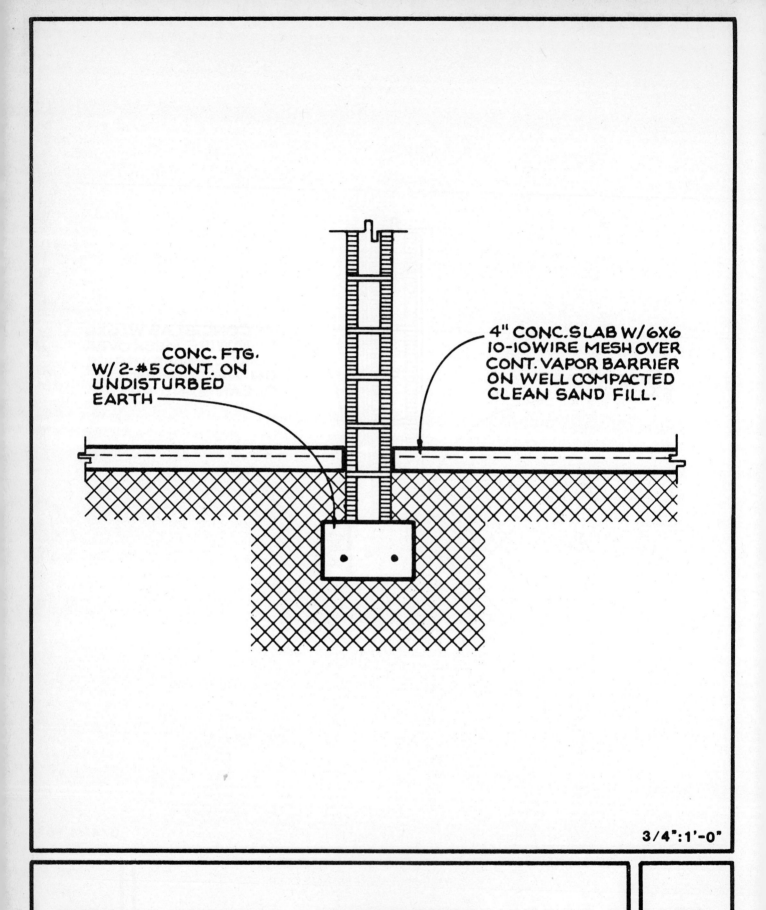

CONC. FTG.
W/ 2-#5 CONT. ON
UNDISTURBED
EARTH

4" CONC. SLAB W/ 6X6
10-10 WIRE MESH OVER
CONT. VAPOR BARRIER
ON WELL COMPACTED
CLEAN SAND FILL.

3/4":1'-0"

SPREAD FOOTING: INTERMEDIATE

F 2

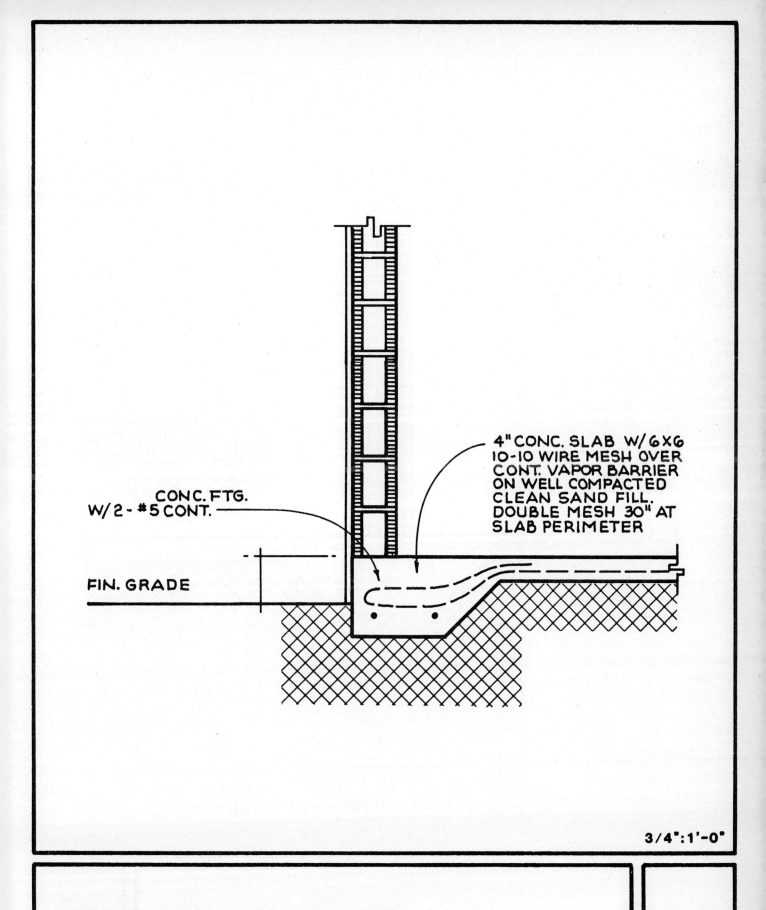

4" CONC. SLAB W/ 6X6
10-10 WIRE MESH OVER
CONT. VAPOR BARRIER
ON WELL COMPACTED
CLEAN SAND FILL.
DOUBLE MESH 30" AT
SLAB PERIMETER

CONC. FTG.
W/ 2 - #5 CONT.

FIN. GRADE

3/4":1'-0"

MONOLITHIC FOOTING: END

F 3

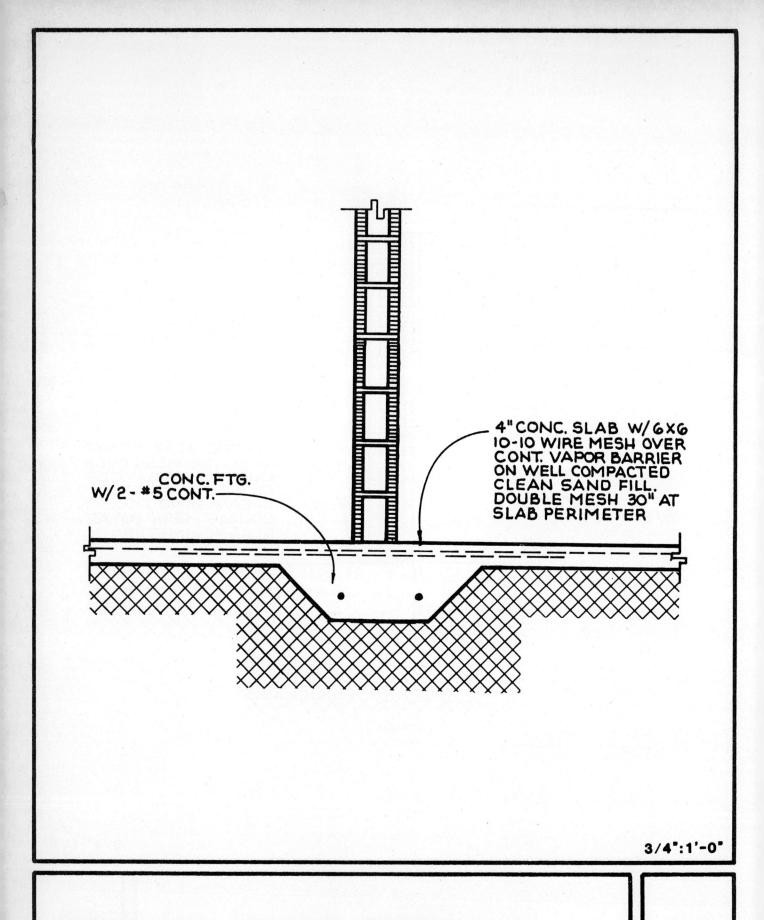

CONC. FTG.
W/ 2 - #5 CONT.

4" CONC. SLAB W/ 6X6
10-10 WIRE MESH OVER
CONT. VAPOR BARRIER
ON WELL COMPACTED
CLEAN SAND FILL.
DOUBLE MESH 30" AT
SLAB PERIMETER

3/4":1'-0"

MONOLITHIC FOOTING: INTERMEDIATE

F 4

SECTION 18: CONCRETE

SECTION 18: CONCRETE

ARCHITECTURAL DETAILING
FOR
COMMERCIAL CONSTRUCTION

18

BEAM SCHEDULE

NO.	A	B	D	C	E	#3 STIRRUPS	REMARKS

C 1

FOOTING SCHEDULE

NO.	SIZE	REINFORCING

FOOTING SCHEDULE

C 2

COLUMN SCHEDULE

NO.	SIZE	REINFORCING

COLUMN SCHEDULE

C 3

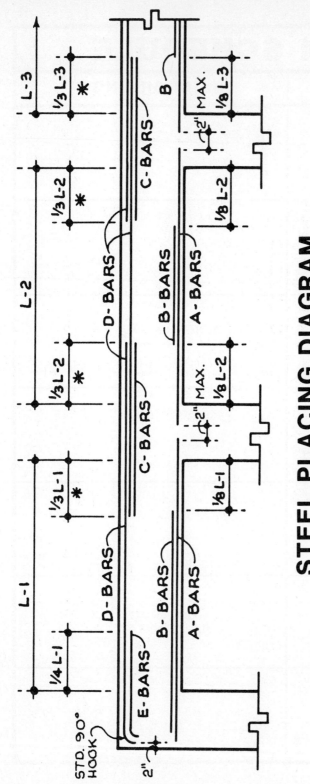

STEEL PLACING DIAGRAM

TOP STEEL : CLEAR COVER

BEAMS :   2"
FOOTINGS :   3"
SLABS :   1"
SLABS ON GRADE :   1"
GRADE BEAMS :   3"

BOTTOM STEEL : CLEAR COVER

BEAMS :   2"
FOOTINGS :   3"
SLABS :   1"
SLABS ON GRADE :   2"
GRADE BEAMS :   3"

* WHICHEVER IS GREATER IN TWO CONSECUTIVE SPANS
  PROVIDE #3 TIES @12"OC IN ALL BEAMS UNLESS NOTED OTHERWISE.

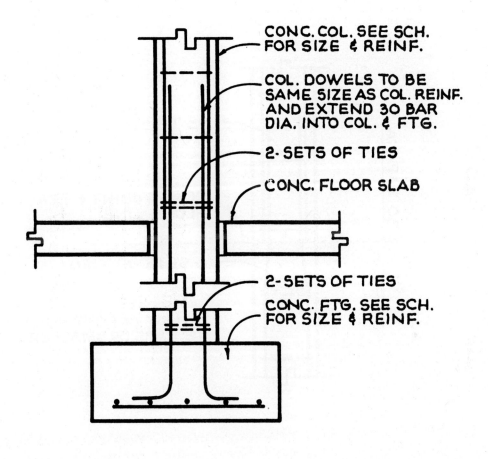

CONC. COL. SEE SCH. FOR SIZE & REINF.

COL. DOWELS TO BE SAME SIZE AS COL. REINF. AND EXTEND 30 BAR DIA. INTO COL. & FTG.

2·SETS OF TIES

CONC. FLOOR SLAB

2·SETS OF TIES

CONC. FTG. SEE SCH. FOR SIZE & REINF.

NO SCALE

COLUMN REINFORCING: FOUNDATION

C 5

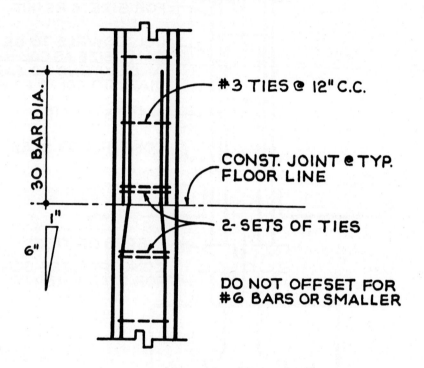

#3 TIES @ 12" C.C.

CONST. JOINT @ TYP. FLOOR LINE

2- SETS OF TIES

DO NOT OFFSET FOR #6 BARS OR SMALLER

30 BAR DIA.

1"

6"

NO SCALE

COLUMN REINFORCING: INTERMEDIATE SPLICE

C 6

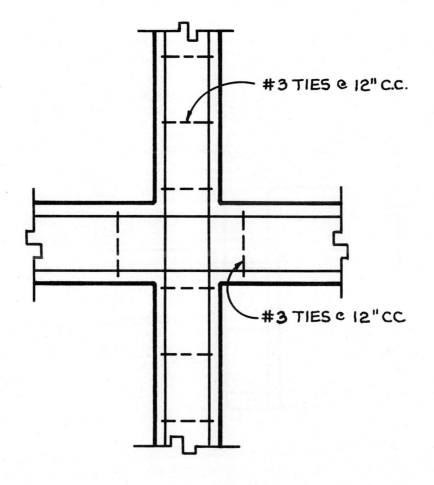

#3 TIES @ 12" C.C.

#3 TIES @ 12" CC

NO SCALE

COLUMN REINFORCING: INTERMEDIATE BEAM | **C 7**

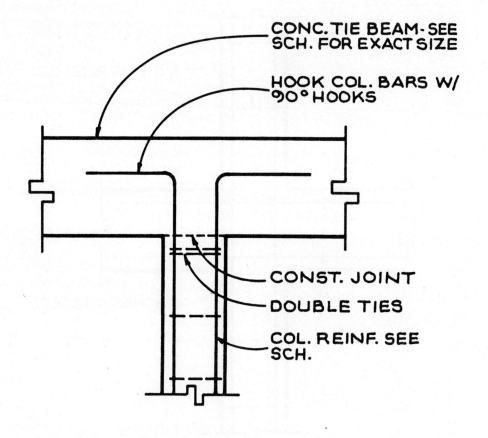

CONC. TIE BEAM - SEE
SCH. FOR EXACT SIZE

HOOK COL. BARS W/
90° HOOKS

CONST. JOINT

DOUBLE TIES

COL. REINF. SEE
SCH.

NO SCALE

COLUMN REINFORCING: TIE BEAM

C 8

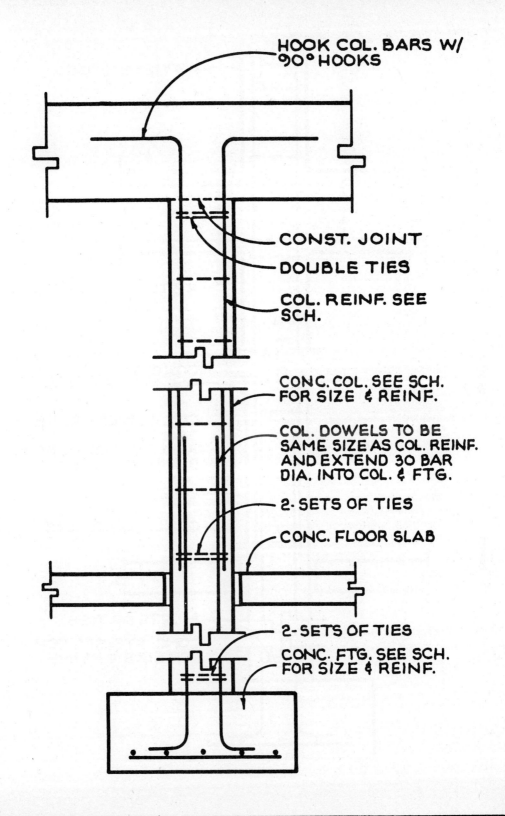

HOOK COL. BARS W/ 90° HOOKS

CONST. JOINT

DOUBLE TIES

COL. REINF. SEE SCH.

CONC. COL. SEE SCH. FOR SIZE & REINF.

COL. DOWELS TO BE SAME SIZE AS COL. REINF. AND EXTEND 30 BAR DIA. INTO COL. & FTG.

2- SETS OF TIES

CONC. FLOOR SLAB

2- SETS OF TIES

CONC. FTG. SEE SCH. FOR SIZE & REINF.

NO SCALE

COLUMN REINFORCING: FOUNDATION TO TIE BEAM

C 9

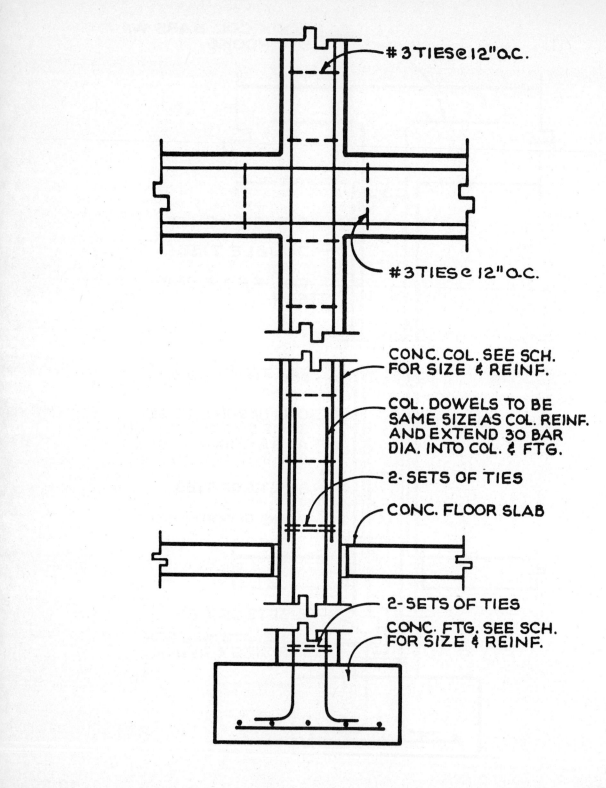

#3 TIES @ 12" O.C.

#3 TIES @ 12" O.C.

CONC. COL. SEE SCH. FOR SIZE & REINF.

COL. DOWELS TO BE SAME SIZE AS COL. REINF. AND EXTEND 30 BAR DIA. INTO COL. & FTG.

2· SETS OF TIES

CONC. FLOOR SLAB

2· SETS OF TIES

CONC. FTG. SEE SCH. FOR SIZE & REINF.

NO SCALE

COLUMN REINFORCING: FOUNDATION TO INTERMEDIATE BEAM

C 10

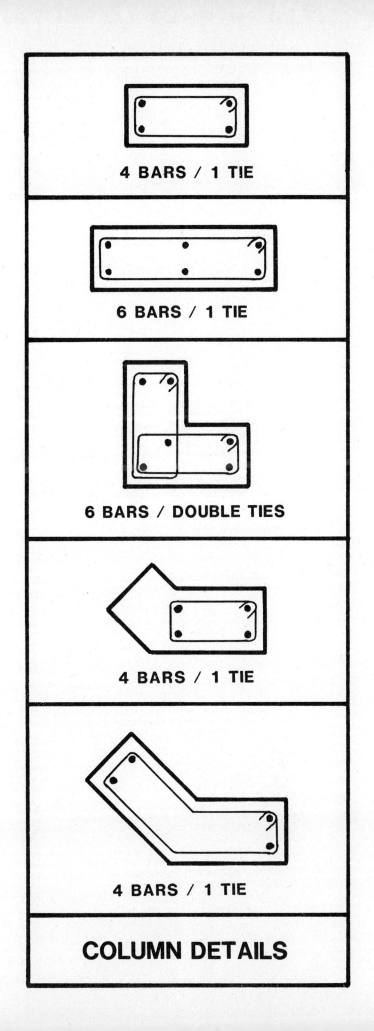

4 BARS / 1 TIE

6 BARS / 1 TIE

6 BARS / DOUBLE TIES

4 BARS / 1 TIE

4 BARS / 1 TIE

COLUMN DETAILS

C 11

SECTION 19: STEEL

ARCHITECTURAL DETAILING
FOR
COMMERCIAL CONSTRUCTION

19

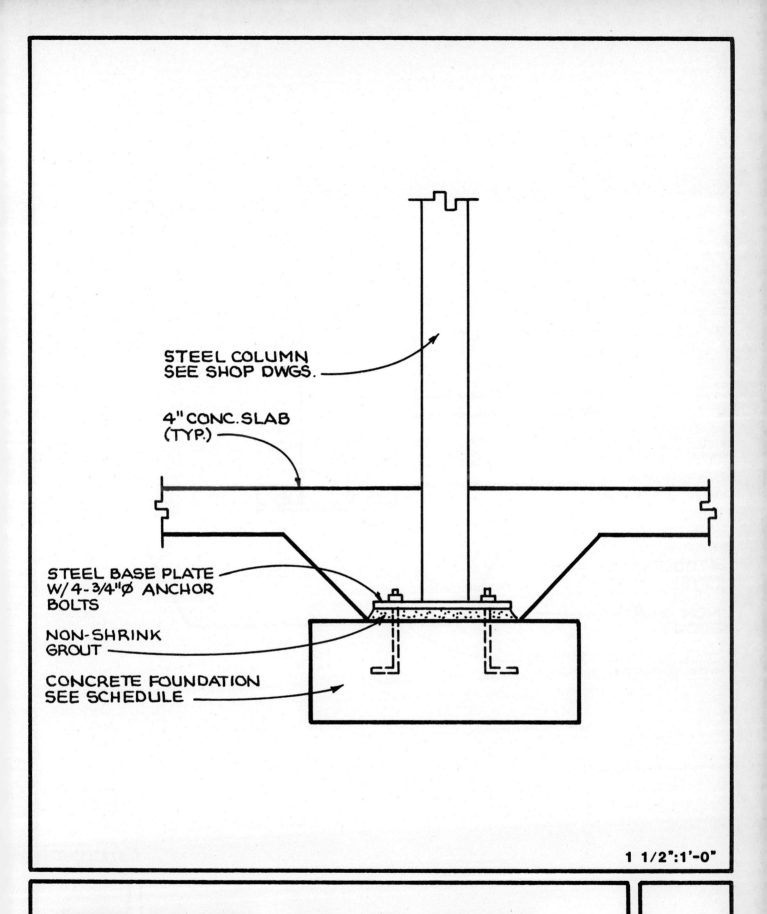

STEEL COLUMN
SEE SHOP DWGS.

4" CONC. SLAB
(TYP.)

STEEL BASE PLATE
W/ 4-3/4"Ø ANCHOR
BOLTS

NON-SHRINK
GROUT

CONCRETE FOUNDATION
SEE SCHEDULE

1 1/2":1'-0"

STEEL COLUMN / ISOLATED FOOTING CONNECTION

S 1

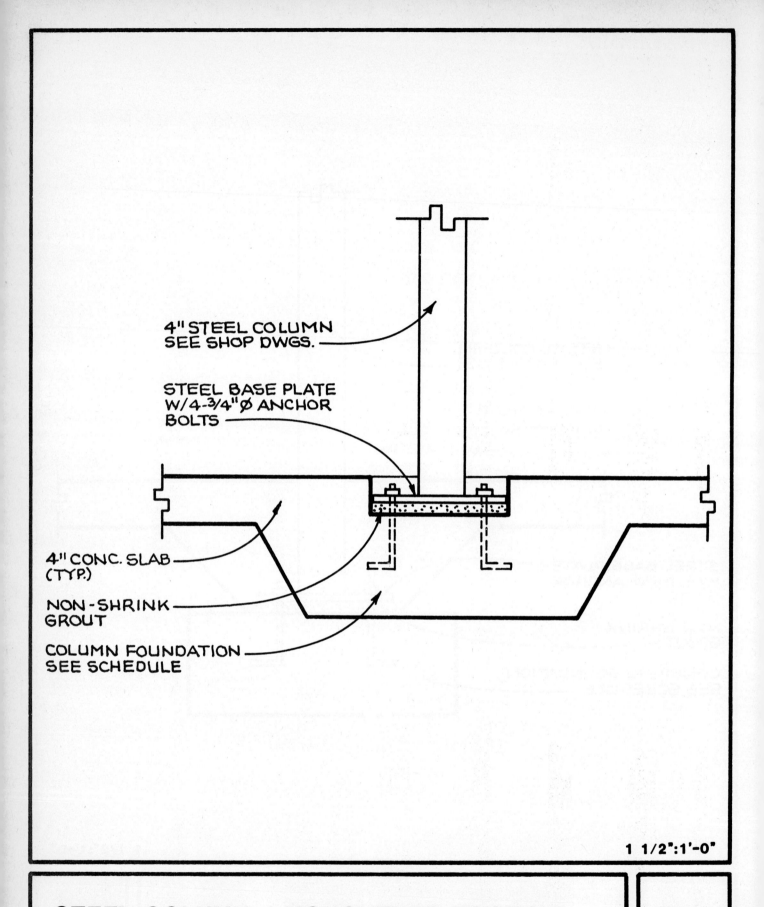

4" STEEL COLUMN
SEE SHOP DWGS.

STEEL BASE PLATE
W/4-¾"Ø ANCHOR
BOLTS

4" CONC. SLAB
(TYP.)

NON-SHRINK
GROUT

COLUMN FOUNDATION
SEE SCHEDULE

1 1/2":1'-0"

STEEL COLUMN / MONOLITHIC FOOTING CONNECTION

S 2

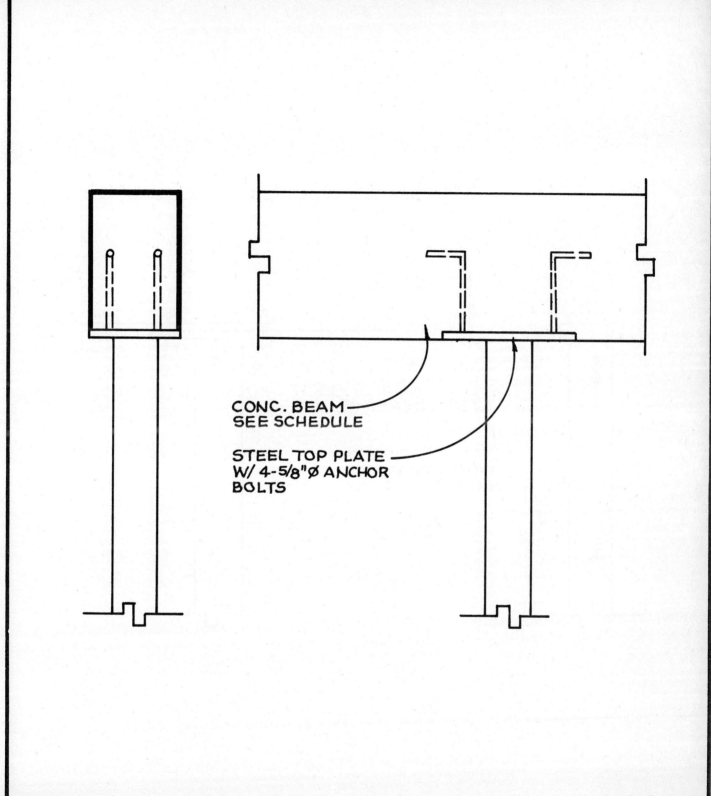

CONC. BEAM
SEE SCHEDULE

STEEL TOP PLATE
W/ 4-5/8"∅ ANCHOR
BOLTS

1 1/2":1'-0"

**STEEL COLUMN / CONCRETE BEAM
CONNECTION**

S 3

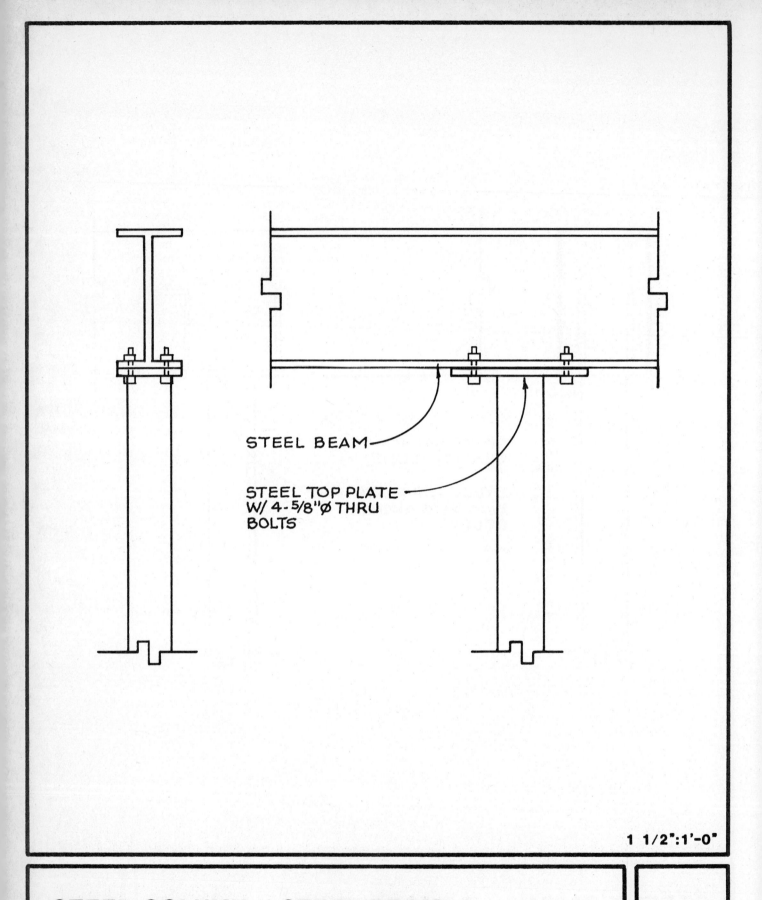

STEEL BEAM

STEEL TOP PLATE
W/ 4-5/8"Ø THRU
BOLTS

1 1/2":1'-0"

**STEEL COLUMN / STEEL BEAM
CONNECTION**

S 4

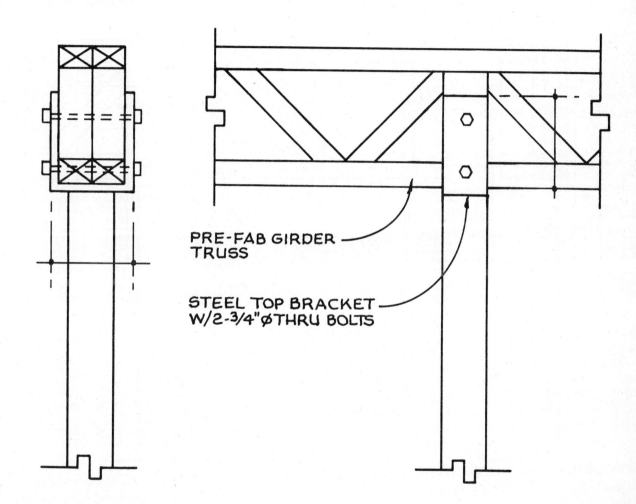

PRE-FAB GIRDER
TRUSS

STEEL TOP BRACKET
W/2-3/4"ØTHRU BOLTS

1 1/2":1'-0"

STEEL COLUMN / WOOD TRUSS CONNECTION

S 5

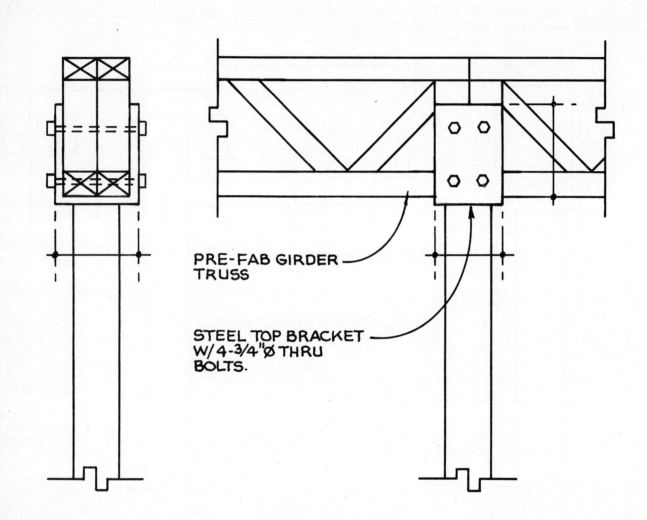

PRE-FAB GIRDER TRUSS

STEEL TOP BRACKET W/ 4-3/4"Ø THRU BOLTS.

1 1/2":1'-0"

STEEL COLUMN / WOOD TRUSS SPLICE CONNECTION

S 6

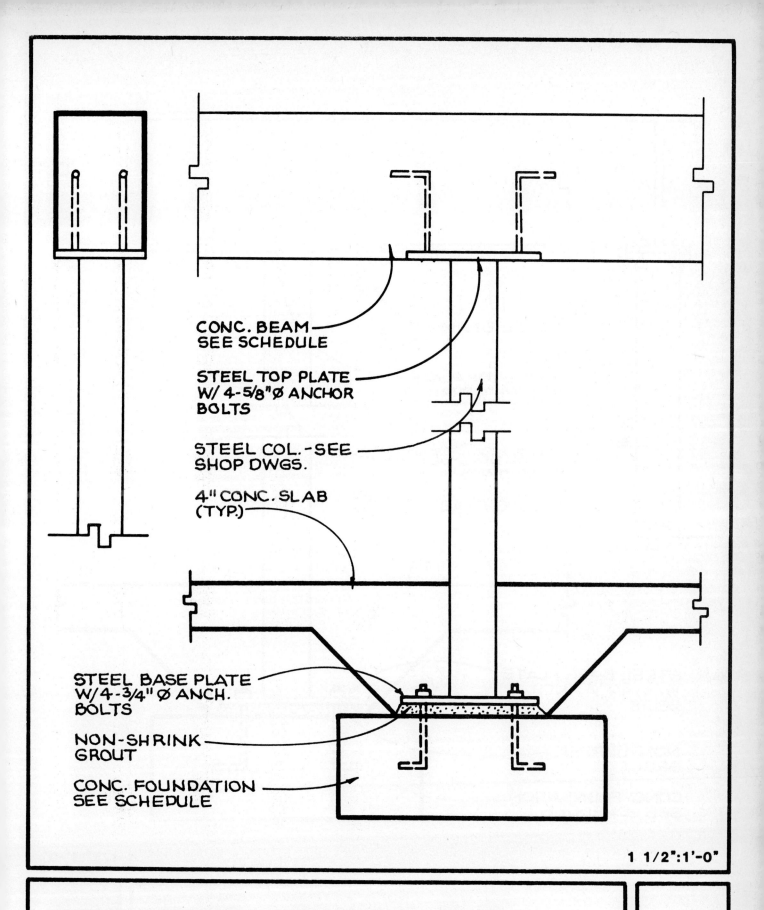

CONC. BEAM
SEE SCHEDULE

STEEL TOP PLATE
W/ 4-5/8"∅ ANCHOR
BOLTS

STEEL COL.-SEE
SHOP DWGS.

4" CONC. SLAB
(TYP.)

STEEL BASE PLATE
W/4-3/4"∅ ANCH.
BOLTS

NON-SHRINK
GROUT

CONC. FOUNDATION
SEE SCHEDULE

1 1/2":1'-0"

STEEL COLUMN / CONCRETE BEAM
ISOLATED FOOTING

S 7

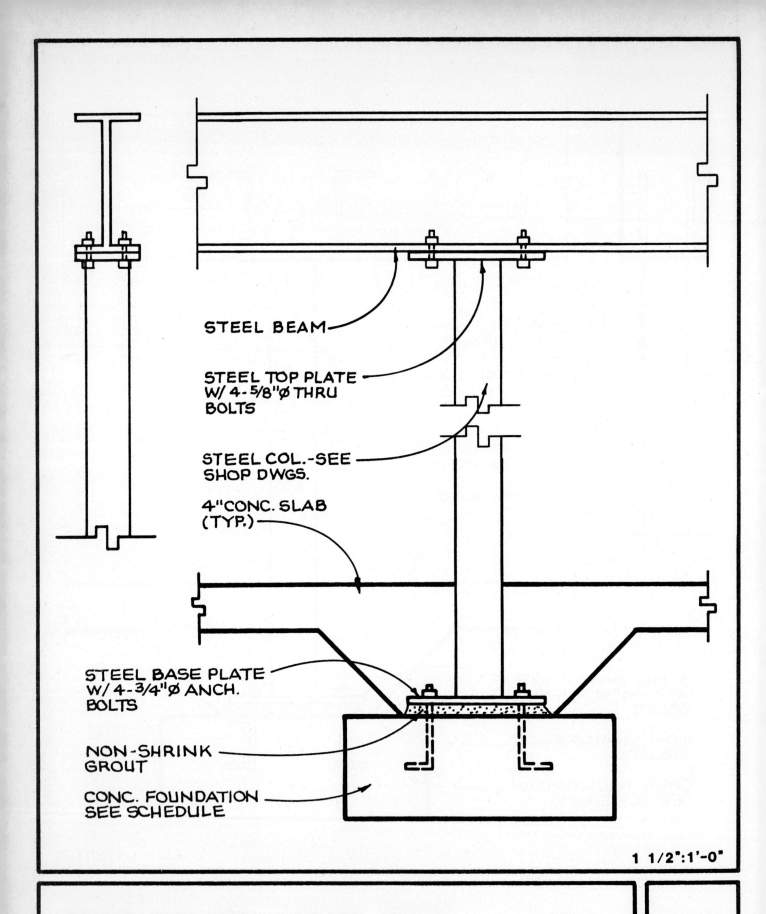

STEEL BEAM

STEEL TOP PLATE
W/ 4-5/8"Ø THRU
BOLTS

STEEL COL.-SEE
SHOP DWGS.

4" CONC. SLAB
(TYP.)

STEEL BASE PLATE
W/ 4-3/4"Ø ANCH.
BOLTS

NON-SHRINK
GROUT

CONC. FOUNDATION
SEE SCHEDULE

1 1/2":1'-0"

STEEL COLUMN / STEEL BEAM
ISOLATED FOOTING

S 8

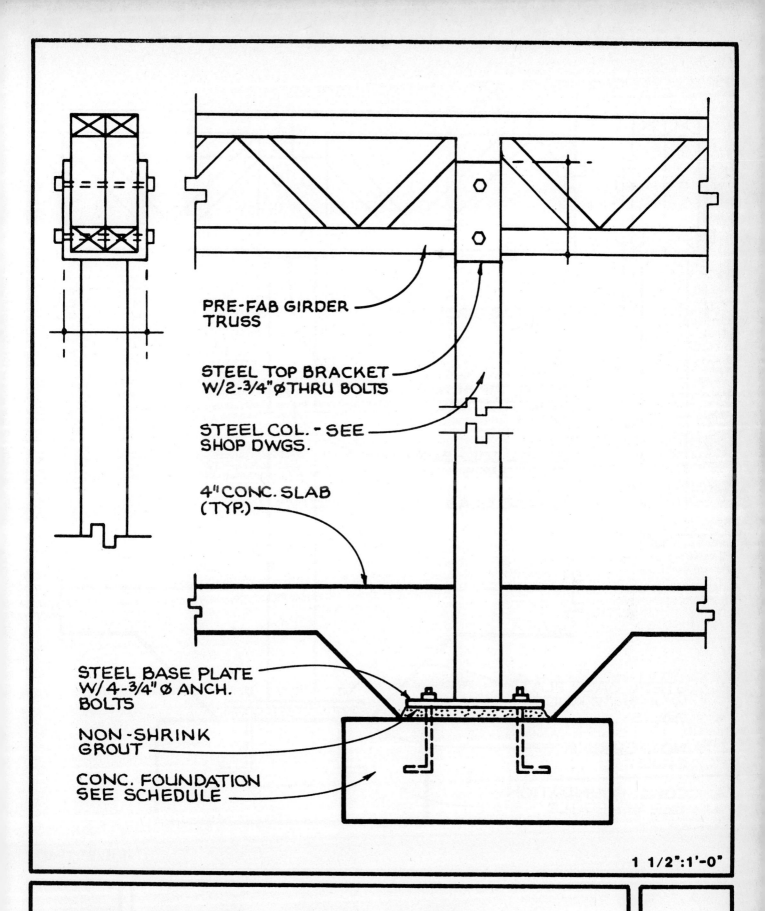

PRE-FAB GIRDER TRUSS

STEEL TOP BRACKET W/2-3/4"Ø THRU BOLTS

STEEL COL. - SEE SHOP DWGS.

4" CONC. SLAB (TYP.)

STEEL BASE PLATE W/ 4-3/4" Ø ANCH. BOLTS

NON-SHRINK GROUT

CONC. FOUNDATION SEE SCHEDULE

1 1/2":1'-0"

STEEL COLUMN / WOOD TRUSS ISOLATED FOOTING

S 9

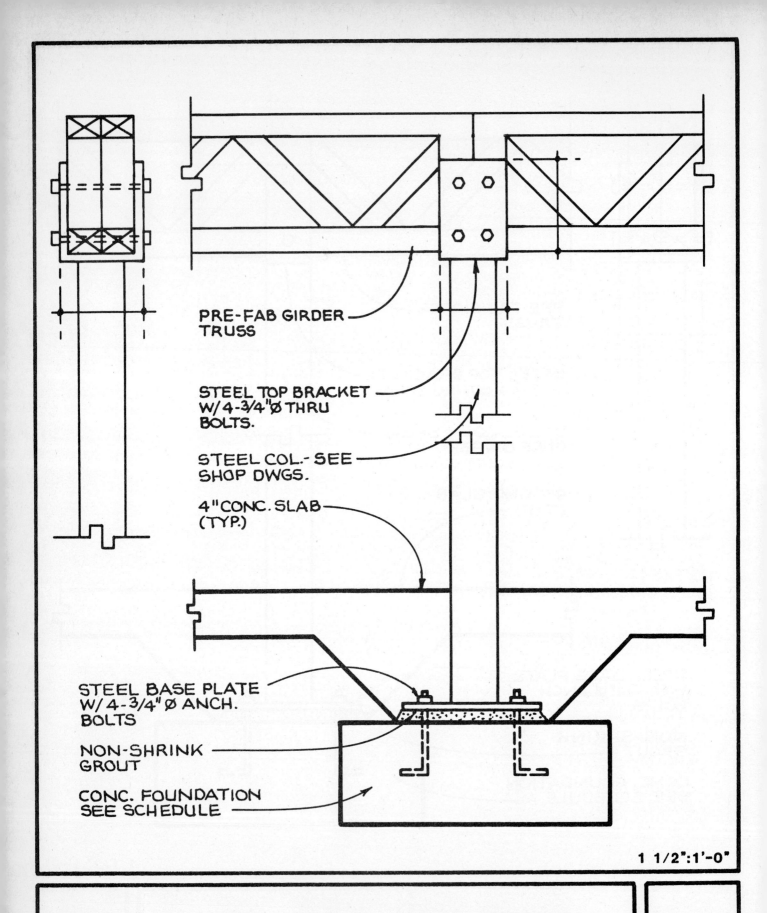

PRE-FAB GIRDER TRUSS

STEEL TOP BRACKET W/ 4-3/4"∅ THRU BOLTS.

STEEL COL.- SEE SHOP DWGS.

4" CONC. SLAB (TYP.)

STEEL BASE PLATE W/ 4-3/4"∅ ANCH. BOLTS

NON-SHRINK GROUT

CONC. FOUNDATION SEE SCHEDULE

1 1/2":1'-0"

STEEL COLUMN / WOOD TRUSS SPLICE ISOLATED FOOTING

S 10

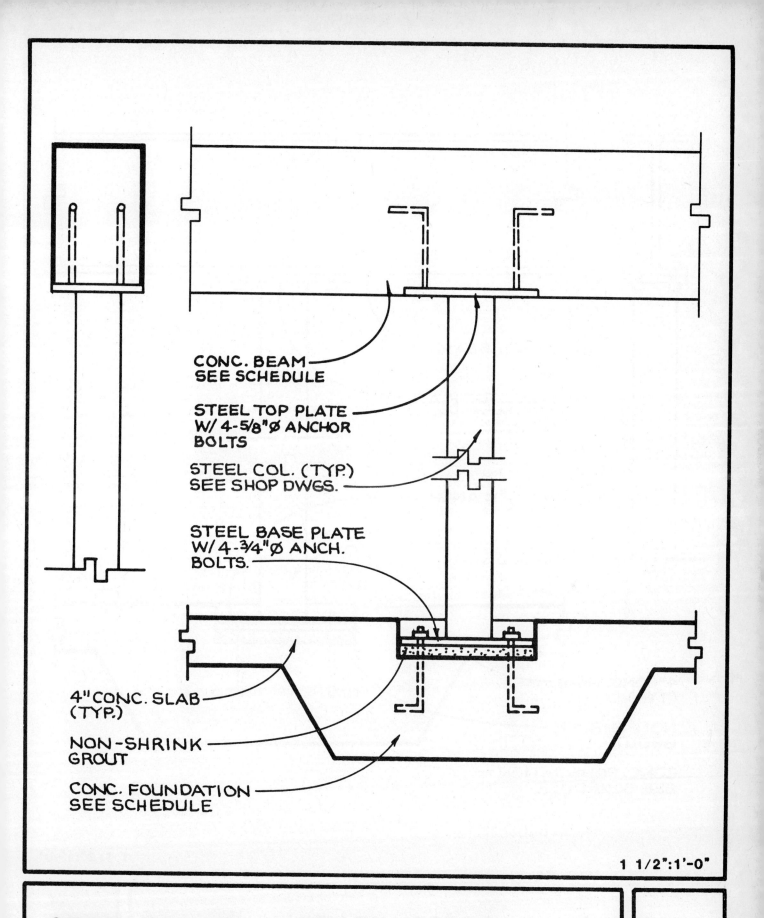

CONC. BEAM
SEE SCHEDULE

STEEL TOP PLATE
W/ 4-5/8"∅ ANCHOR
BOLTS

STEEL COL. (TYP.)
SEE SHOP DWGS.

STEEL BASE PLATE
W/ 4-3/4"∅ ANCH.
BOLTS.

4" CONC. SLAB
(TYP.)

NON-SHRINK
GROUT

CONC. FOUNDATION
SEE SCHEDULE

1 1/2":1'-0"

STEEL COLUMN / CONCRETE BEAM MONOLITHIC FOOTING

S 11

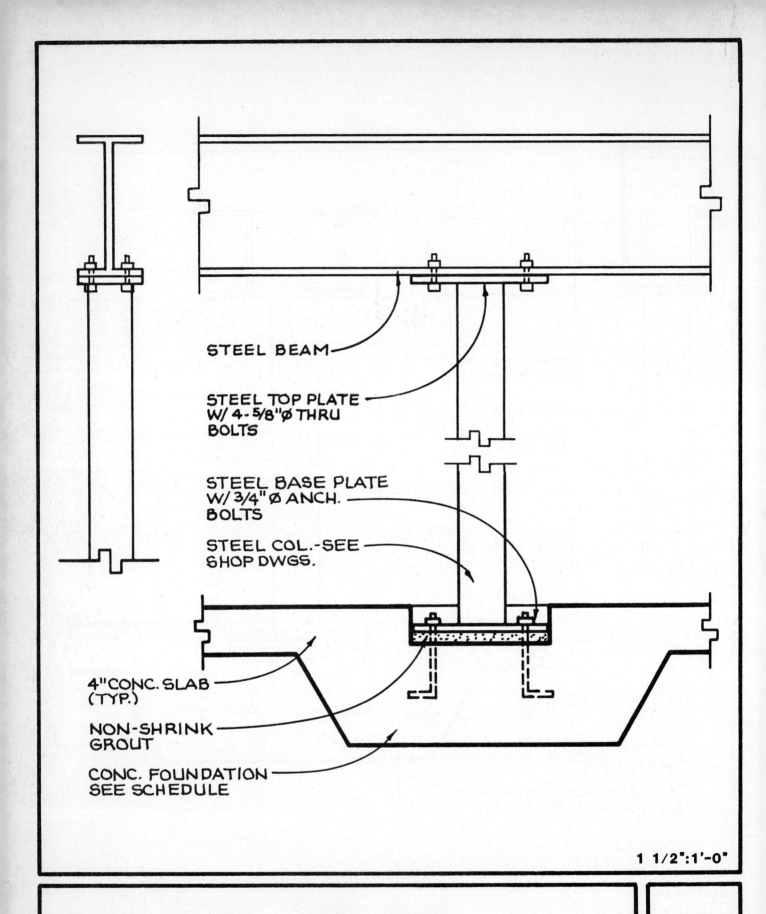

STEEL BEAM

STEEL TOP PLATE
W/ 4-5/8"∅ THRU
BOLTS

STEEL BASE PLATE
W/ 3/4"∅ ANCH.
BOLTS

STEEL COL.-SEE
SHOP DWGS.

4"CONC. SLAB
(TYP.)

NON-SHRINK
GROUT

CONC. FOUNDATION
SEE SCHEDULE

1 1/2":1'-0"

STEEL COLUMN / STEEL BEAM
MONOLITHIC FOOTING

S 12

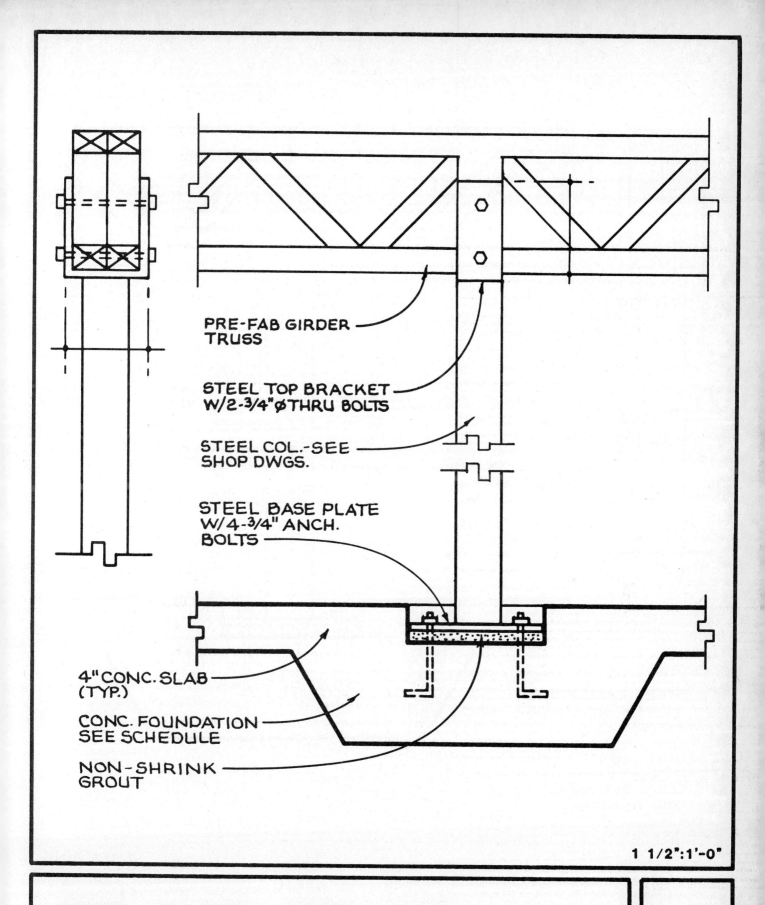

PRE-FAB GIRDER TRUSS

STEEL TOP BRACKET W/2-¾"Ø THRU BOLTS

STEEL COL.-SEE SHOP DWGS.

STEEL BASE PLATE W/4-¾" ANCH. BOLTS

4" CONC. SLAB (TYP.)

CONC. FOUNDATION SEE SCHEDULE

NON-SHRINK GROUT

1 1/2":1'-0"

STEEL COLUMN / WOOD TRUSS MONOLITHIC FOOTING

S 13

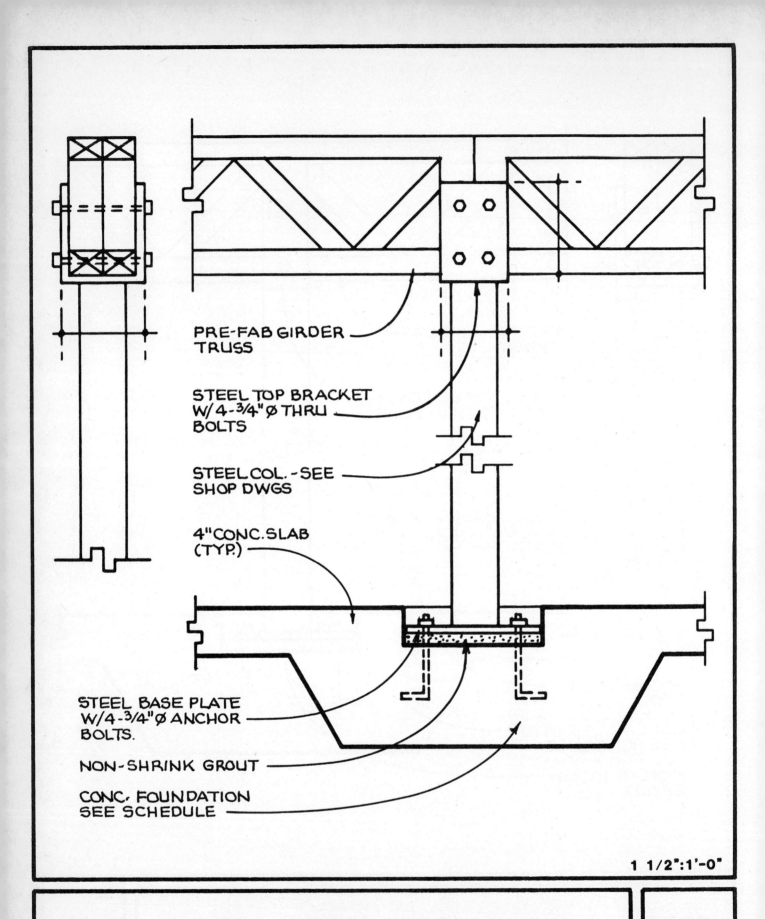

PRE-FAB GIRDER TRUSS

STEEL TOP BRACKET W/ 4-3/4"Ø THRU BOLTS

STEEL COL. - SEE SHOP DWGS

4" CONC. SLAB (TYP.)

STEEL BASE PLATE W/ 4-3/4"Ø ANCHOR BOLTS.

NON-SHRINK GROUT

CONC. FOUNDATION SEE SCHEDULE

1 1/2":1'-0"

STEEL COLUMN / WOOD TRUSS SPLICE MONOLITHIC FOOTING

S 14

SECTION 20: WOOD

SECTION 20: WOOD

ARCHITECTURAL DETAILING
FOR
COMMERCIAL CONSTRUCTION

20

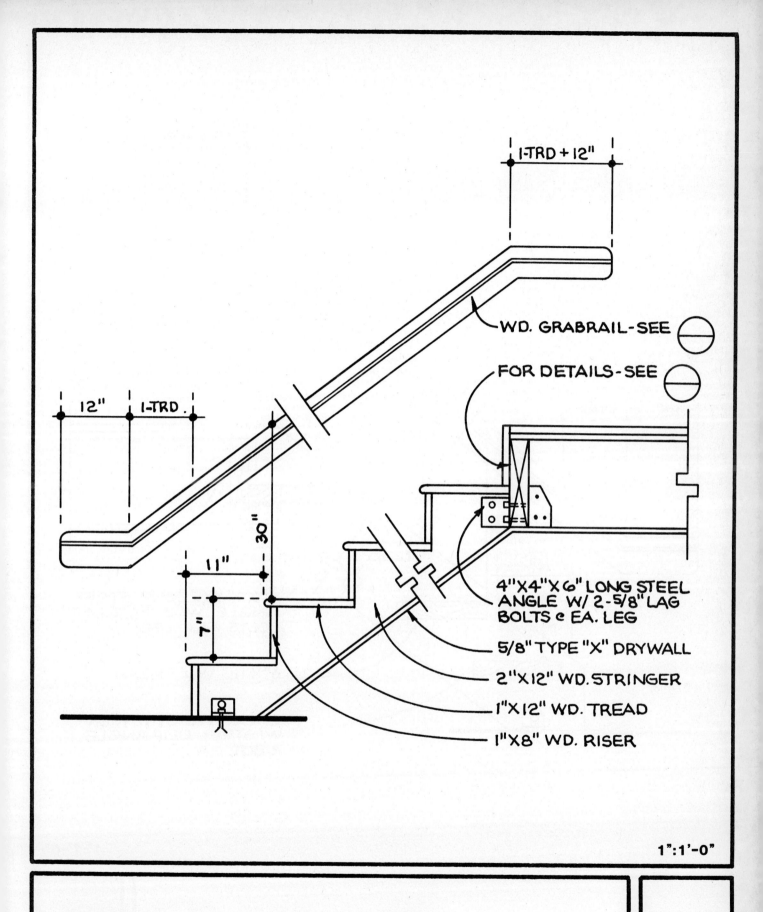

1-TRD + 12"

WD. GRABRAIL-SEE

FOR DETAILS-SEE

12" 1-TRD .

30"

11"

7"

4"X4"X6" LONG STEEL
ANGLE W/ 2-5/8" LAG
BOLTS @ EA. LEG

5/8" TYPE "X" DRYWALL

2"X12" WD.STRINGER

1"X12" WD. TREAD

1"X8" WD. RISER

1":1'-0"

WOOD STAIR: CLOSED RISER

W 1

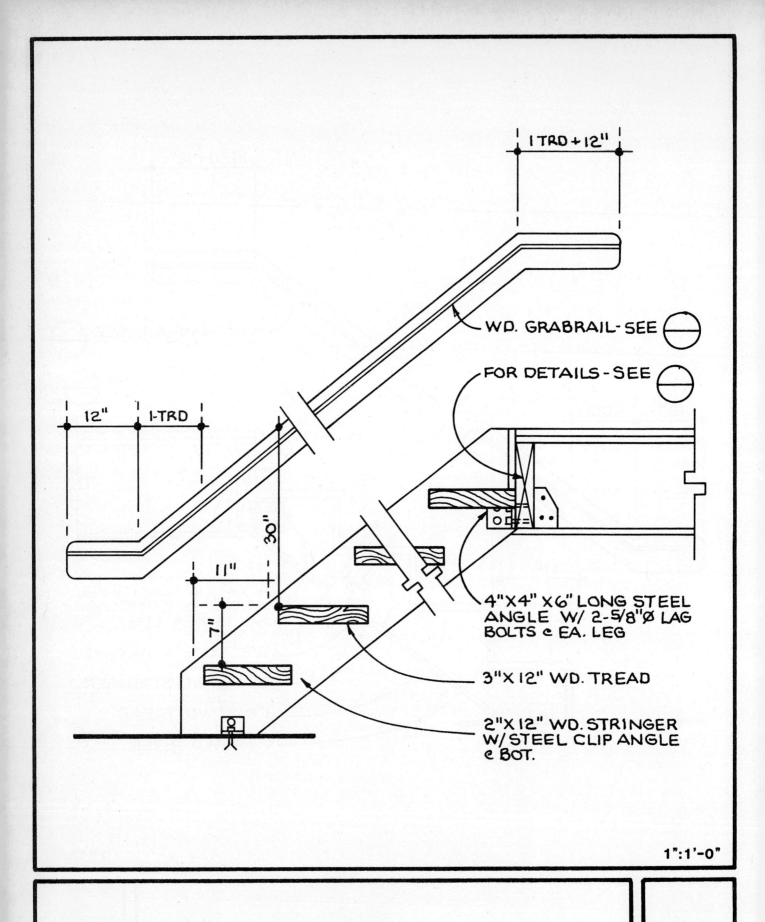

1 TRD + 12"

12" | 1-TRD

30"

11"

7"

WD. GRABRAIL-SEE ⊘

FOR DETAILS-SEE ⊘

4"X4" X6" LONG STEEL
ANGLE W/ 2-5/8"Ø LAG
BOLTS ℮ EA. LEG

3"X 12" WD. TREAD

2"X 12" WD. STRINGER
W/ STEEL CLIP ANGLE
℮ BOT.

1":1'-0"

WOOD STAIR: OPEN RISER

W 2

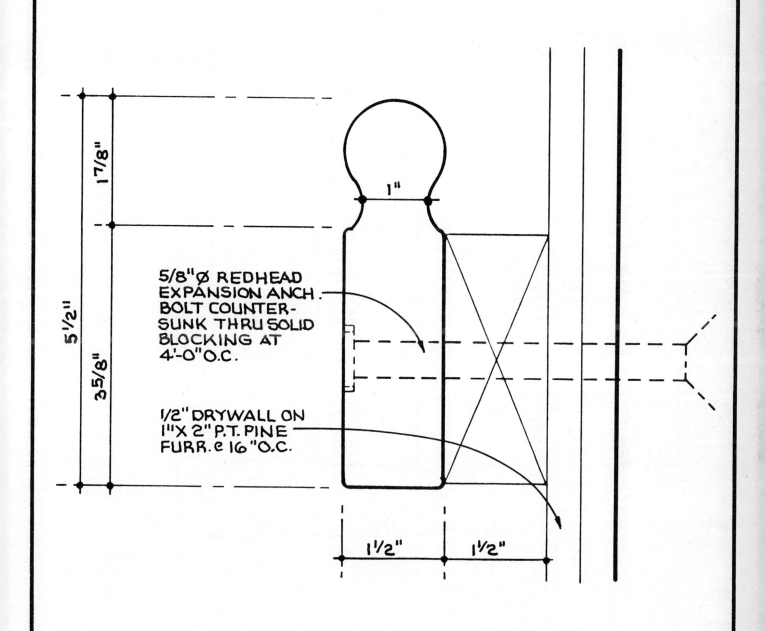

17/8"

5 1/2"

3 5/8"

5/8"Ø REDHEAD
EXPANSION ANCH.
BOLT COUNTER-
SUNK THRU SOLID
BLOCKING AT
4'-0"O.C.

1"

1/2"DRYWALL ON
1"X 2" P.T. PINE
FURR.@16"O.C.

1 1/2"   1 1/2"

1 1/2":1'-0"

WOOD GRABRAIL AT CONCRETE WALL

W 3

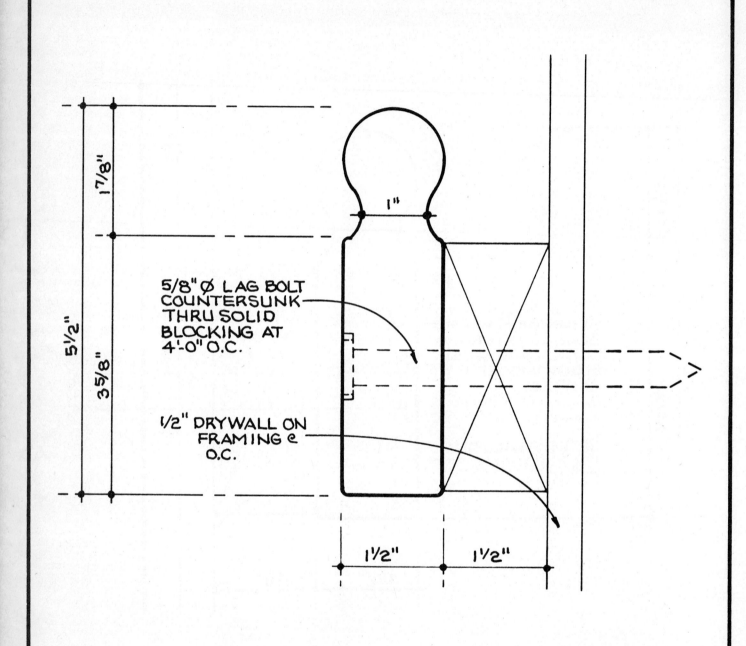

1⁷/₈"

5½"

3⅝"

5/8" Ø LAG BOLT
COUNTERSUNK
THRU SOLID
BLOCKING AT
4'-0" O.C.

1"

1/2" DRYWALL ON
FRAMING @
O.C.

1½"

1½"

1 1/2":1'-0"

WOOD GRABRAIL AT WD FRAME WALL

W 4

SECTION 21: ROOFING

R 1   Built-up roof with painted topcoat over hollow core with a concrete slab over insulation

R 2   Built-up roof with painted topcoat over twin tees with insulation over concrete slab

R 3   Built-up roof with painted topcoat over steel joists with concrete slab over metal deck

R 4   Built-up roof with painted topcoat over wood trusses with insulation on plywood deck

R 5   Built-up roof with gravel topcoat over hollow core with a concrete slab over insulation

R 6   Built-up roof with gravel topcoat over twin tees with insulation over concrete slab

R 7   Built-up roof with gravel topcoat over steel joists with concrete slab over metal deck

R 8   Built-up roof with gravel topcoat over wood trusses with insulation on plywood deck

R 9   Built-up roof with painted topcoat over hollow core with ½" insulation board

R 10   Built-up roof with painted topcoat over twin tees with ½" insulation board

R 11   Built-up roof with painted topcoat over steel joists with ½" insulation board on metal deck

R 12   Built-up roof with painted topcoat over wood trusses with plywood deck

R 13   Built-up roof with gravel topcoat over hollow core with ½" insulation board

R 14   Built-up roof with gravel topcoat over twin tees with ½" insulation board

R 15   Built-up roof with gravel topcoat over steel joists with ½" insulation board on metal deck

R 16   Built-up roof with gravel topcoat over wood trusses with plywood deck

R 17   Roof flashing at concrete block parapet

R 18   Roof flashing at wood frame parapet

R 19   Plumbing vent flashing: Over top

R 20   Plumbing vent flashing: Collar

ARCHITECTURAL DETAILING
FOR
COMMERCIAL CONSTRUCTION

21

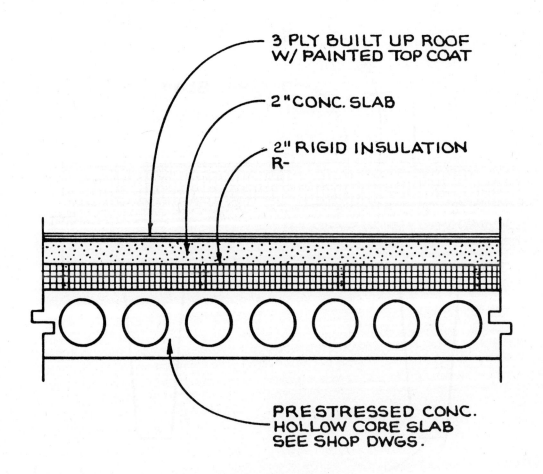

3 PLY BUILT UP ROOF
W/ PAINTED TOP COAT

2" CONC. SLAB

2" RIGID INSULATION
R-

PRE STRESSED CONC.
HOLLOW CORE SLAB
SEE SHOP DWGS.

1 1/2":1'-0"

**BUILT UP ROOF: PAINTED TOP COAT
HOLLOW CORE W/ CONC. SLAB OVER INSUL.**

R 1

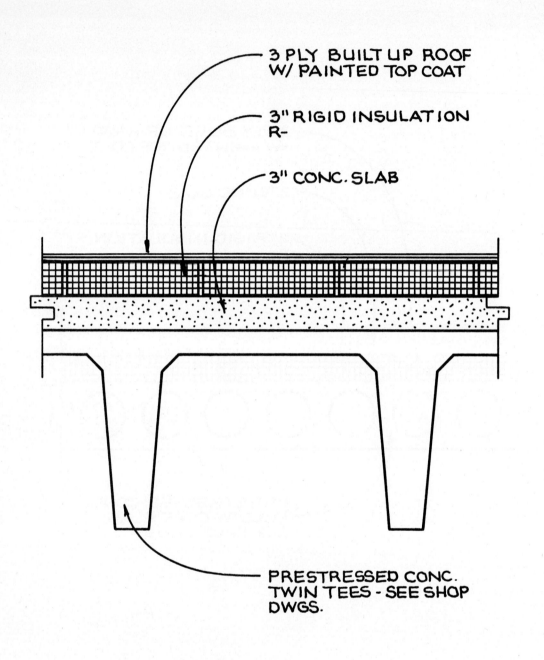

3 PLY BUILT UP ROOF
W/ PAINTED TOP COAT

3" RIGID INSULATION
R-

3" CONC. SLAB

PRESTRESSED CONC.
TWIN TEES - SEE SHOP
DWGS.

**BUILT UP ROOF: PAINTED TOP COAT
TWIN TEES W/ INSUL. OVER CONC. SLAB**

R 2

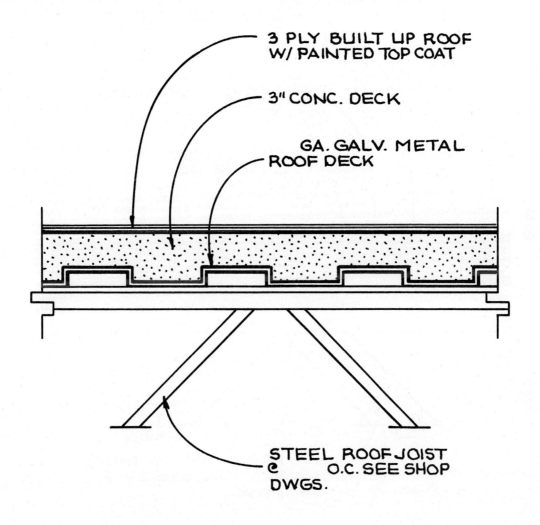

3 PLY BUILT UP ROOF
W/ PAINTED TOP COAT

3" CONC. DECK

GA. GALV. METAL
ROOF DECK

STEEL ROOF JOIST
@   O.C. SEE SHOP
DWGS.

1 1/2":1'-0"

BUILT UP ROOF: PAINTED TOP COAT
CONCRETE SLAB ON METAL DECK

R 3

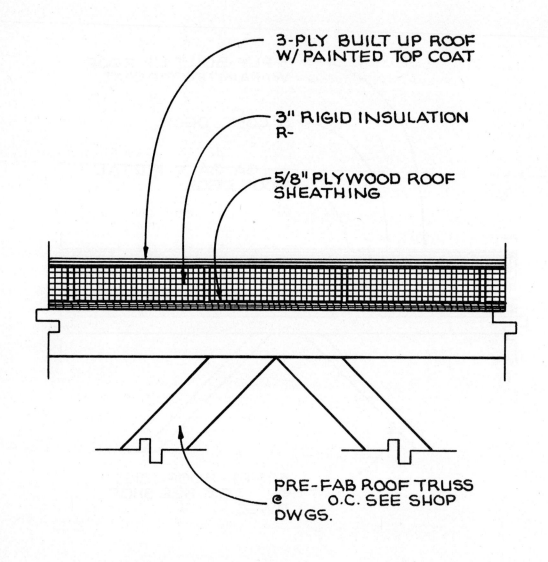

3-PLY BUILT UP ROOF
W/ PAINTED TOP COAT

3" RIGID INSULATION
R-

5/8" PLYWOOD ROOF
SHEATHING

PRE-FAB ROOF TRUSS
@   O.C. SEE SHOP
DWGS.

1 1/2":1'-0"

**BUILT UP ROOF: PAINTED TOP COAT
WOOD TRUSSES W/ INSUL. OVER PLYWOOD**

R 4

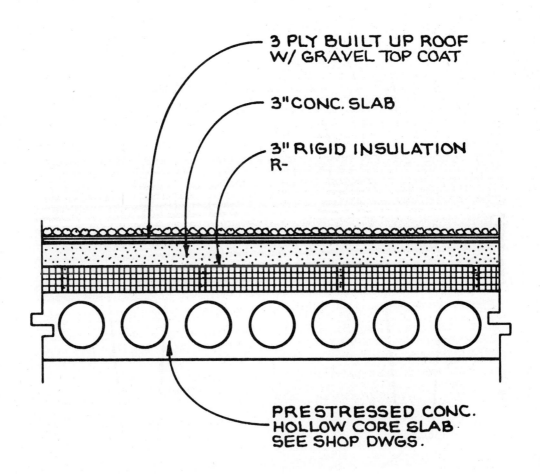

3 PLY BUILT UP ROOF
W/ GRAVEL TOP COAT

3" CONC. SLAB

3" RIGID INSULATION
R-

PRESTRESSED CONC.
HOLLOW CORE SLAB.
SEE SHOP DWGS.

1 1/2":1'-0"

BUILT UP ROOF: GRAVEL TOP COAT
HOLLOW CORE W/ CONC. SLAB OVER INSUL.

R 5

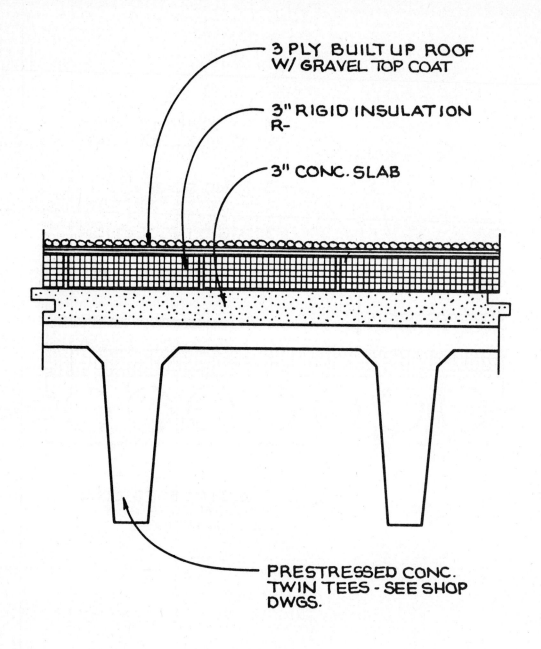

3 PLY BUILT UP ROOF
W/ GRAVEL TOP COAT

3" RIGID INSULATION
R-

3" CONC. SLAB

PRESTRESSED CONC.
TWIN TEES - SEE SHOP
DWGS.

BUILT UP ROOF: GRAVEL TOP COAT
TWIN TEES W/ INSUL. OVER CONC. SLAB

R 6

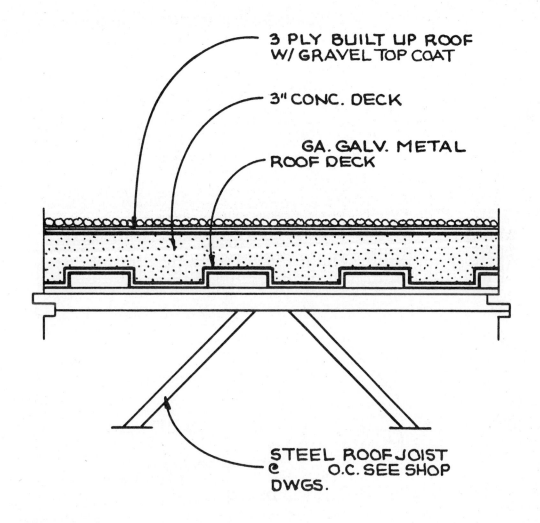

3 PLY BUILT UP ROOF
W/ GRAVEL TOP COAT

3" CONC. DECK

GA. GALV. METAL
ROOF DECK

STEEL ROOF JOIST
@   O.C. SEE SHOP
DWGS.

1 1/2":1'-0"

**BUILT UP ROOF: GRAVEL TOP COAT
CONCRETE SLAB ON METAL DECK**

R 7

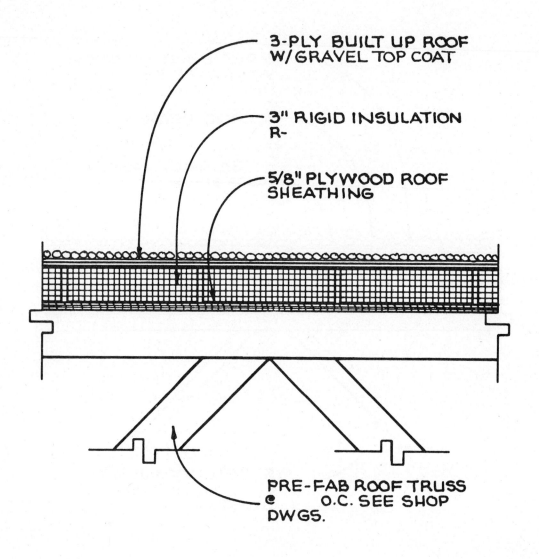

3-PLY BUILT UP ROOF
W/GRAVEL TOP COAT

3" RIGID INSULATION
R-

5/8" PLYWOOD ROOF
SHEATHING

PRE-FAB ROOF TRUSS
@   O.C. SEE SHOP
DWGS.

1 1/2":1'-0"

BUILT UP ROOF: GRAVEL TOP COAT
WOOD TRUSSES W/ INSUL. OVER PLYWOOD

R 8

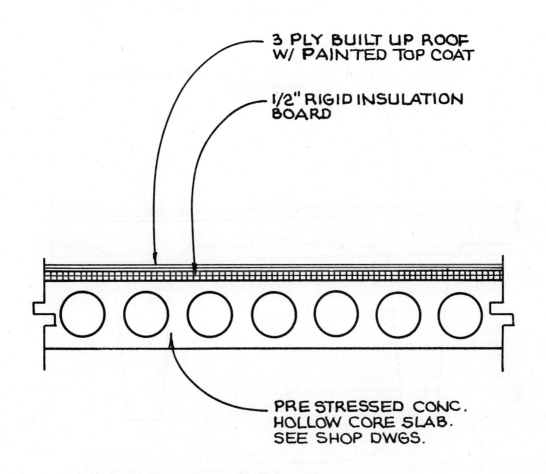

3 PLY BUILT UP ROOF
W/ PAINTED TOP COAT

1/2" RIGID INSULATION
BOARD

PRE STRESSED CONC.
HOLLOW CORE SLAB.
SEE SHOP DWGS.

1 1/2":1'-0"

BUILT UP ROOF: PAINTED TOP COAT
HOLLOW CORE W/ 1/2" INSULATION BD.

R 9

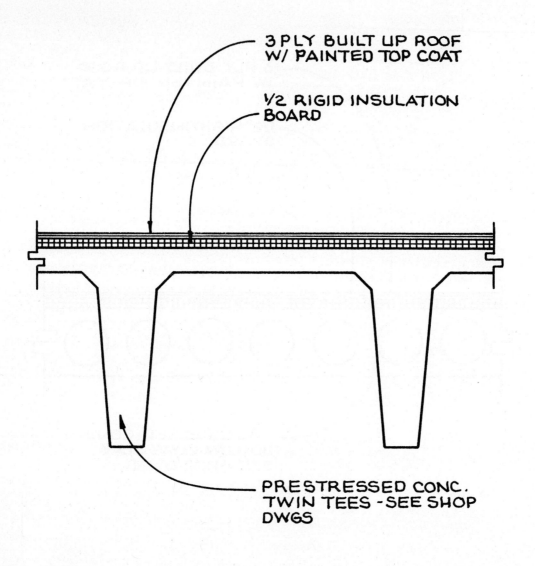

3 PLY BUILT UP ROOF
W/ PAINTED TOP COAT

½ RIGID INSULATION
BOARD

PRESTRESSED CONC.
TWIN TEES - SEE SHOP
DWGS

1 1/2":1'-0"

**BUILT UP ROOF: PAINTED TOP COAT
TWIN TEES W/ 1/2" INSULATION BD.**

R 10

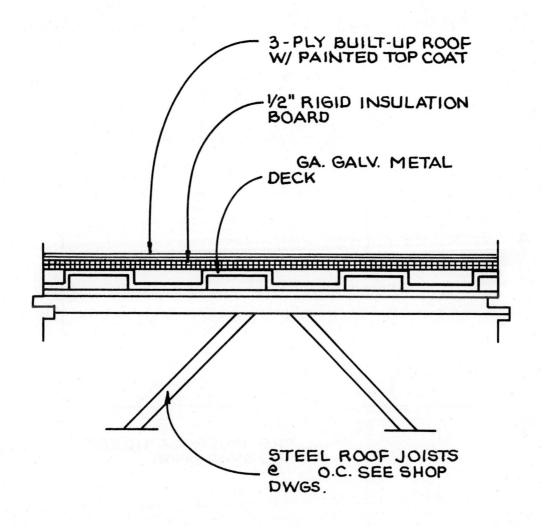

3-PLY BUILT-UP ROOF
W/ PAINTED TOP COAT

1/2" RIGID INSULATION
BOARD

GA. GALV. METAL
DECK

STEEL ROOF JOISTS
@   O.C. SEE SHOP
DWGS.

1 1/2":1'-0"

**BUILT UP ROOF: PAINTED TOP COAT
METAL DECK W/ 1/2" INSULATION BD.**

R 11

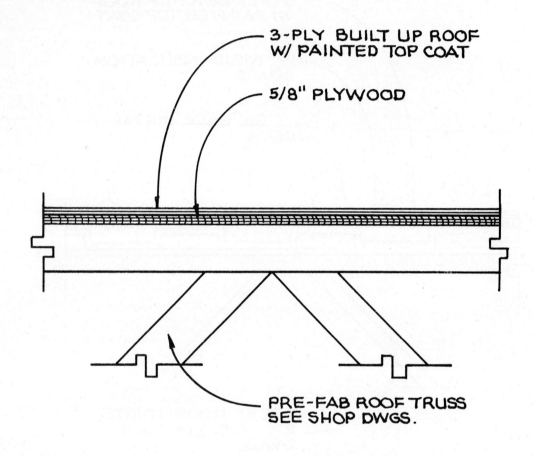

3-PLY BUILT UP ROOF
W/ PAINTED TOP COAT

5/8" PLYWOOD

PRE-FAB ROOF TRUSS
SEE SHOP DWGS.

1 1/2":1'-0"

**BUILT UP ROOF: PAINTED TOP COAT
WOOD TRUSSES W/ PLYWOOD**

R 12

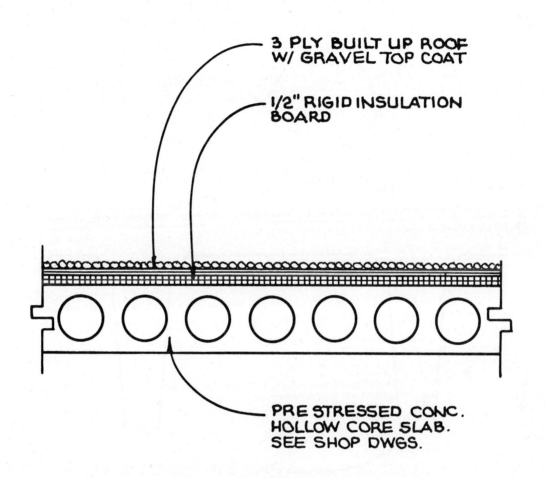

3 PLY BUILT UP ROOF
W/ GRAVEL TOP COAT

1/2" RIGID INSULATION
BOARD

PRE STRESSED CONC.
HOLLOW CORE SLAB.
SEE SHOP DWGS.

1 1/2":1'-0"

**BUILT UP ROOF: GRAVEL TOP COAT
HOLLOW CORE W/ 1/2" INSULATION BD.**

R 13

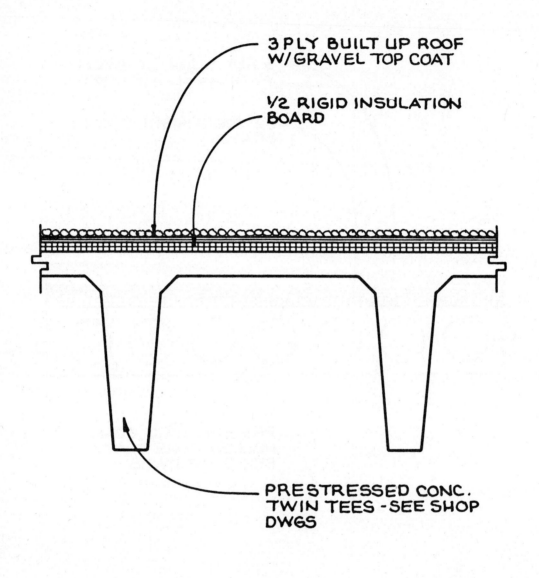

3 PLY BUILT UP ROOF
W/GRAVEL TOP COAT

1/2 RIGID INSULATION
BOARD

PRESTRESSED CONC.
TWIN TEES - SEE SHOP
DWGS

1 1/2":1'-0"

BUILT UP ROOF: GRAVEL TOP COAT
TWIN TEES W/ 1/2" INSULATION BD.

R 14

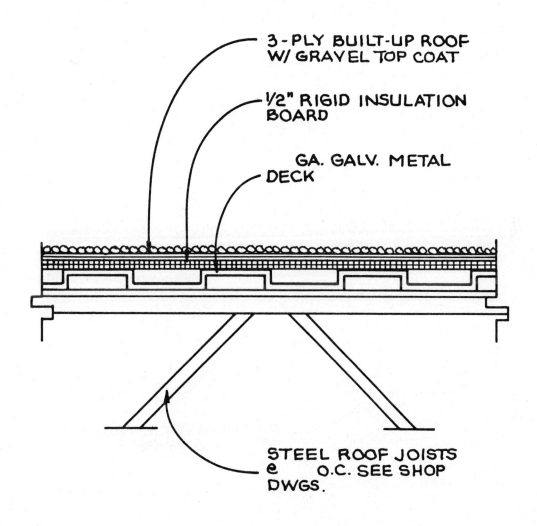

3-PLY BUILT-UP ROOF
W/ GRAVEL TOP COAT

1/2" RIGID INSULATION
BOARD

GA. GALV. METAL
DECK

STEEL ROOF JOISTS
@   O.C. SEE SHOP
DWGS.

1 1/2":1'-0"

**BUILT UP ROOF: GRAVEL TOP COAT
METAL DECK W/ 1/2" INSULATION BD.**

R 15

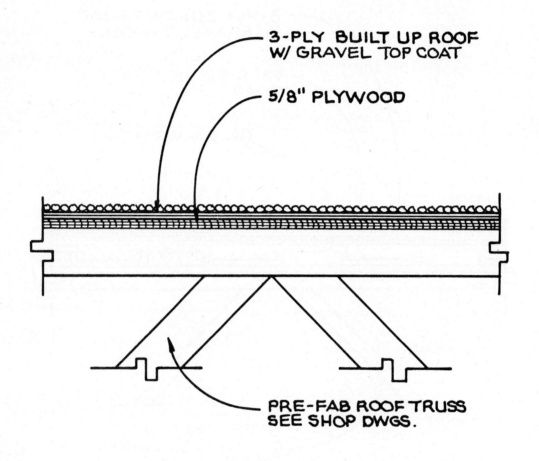

3-PLY BUILT UP ROOF
W/ GRAVEL TOP COAT

5/8" PLYWOOD

PRE-FAB ROOF TRUSS
SEE SHOP DWGS.

1 1/2":1'-0"

BUILT UP ROOF: GRAVEL TOP COAT
WOOD TRUSSES W/ PLYWOOD

R 16

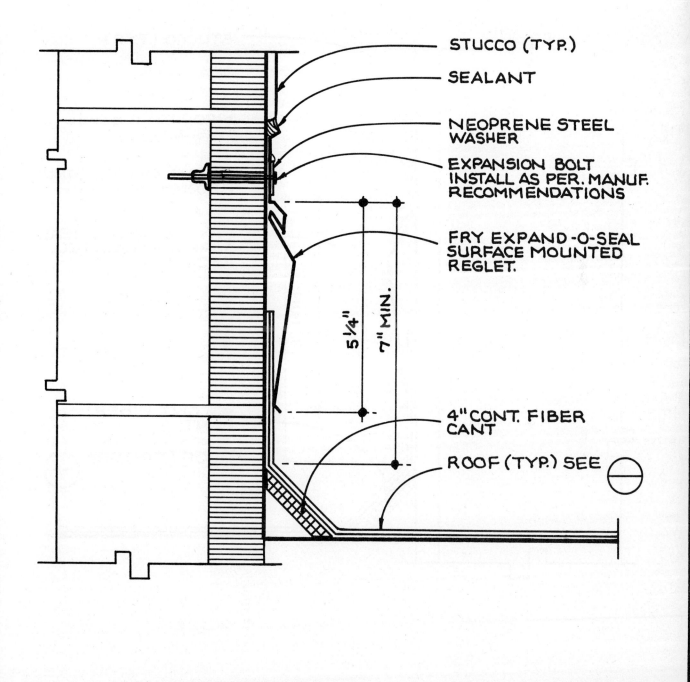

STUCCO (TYP.)

SEALANT

NEOPRENE STEEL WASHER

EXPANSION BOLT INSTALL AS PER. MANUF. RECOMMENDATIONS

FRY EXPAND-O-SEAL SURFACE MOUNTED REGLET.

5¼"

7" MIN.

4" CONT. FIBER CANT

ROOF (TYP.) SEE

NO SCALE

ROOF FLASHING: CONCRETE BLOCK PARAPET

R 17

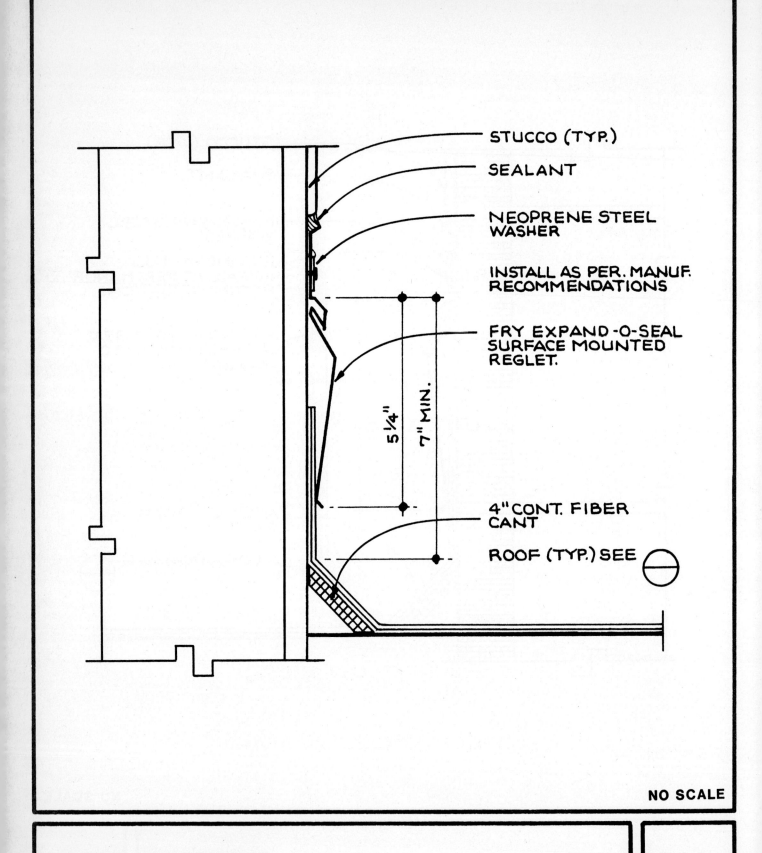

STUCCO (TYP.)

SEALANT

NEOPRENE STEEL WASHER

INSTALL AS PER. MANUF. RECOMMENDATIONS

FRY EXPAND-O-SEAL SURFACE MOUNTED REGLET.

5¼"

7" MIN.

4" CONT. FIBER CANT

ROOF (TYP.) SEE ⊖

NO SCALE

ROOF FLASHING: WOOD FRAME PARAPET

R 18

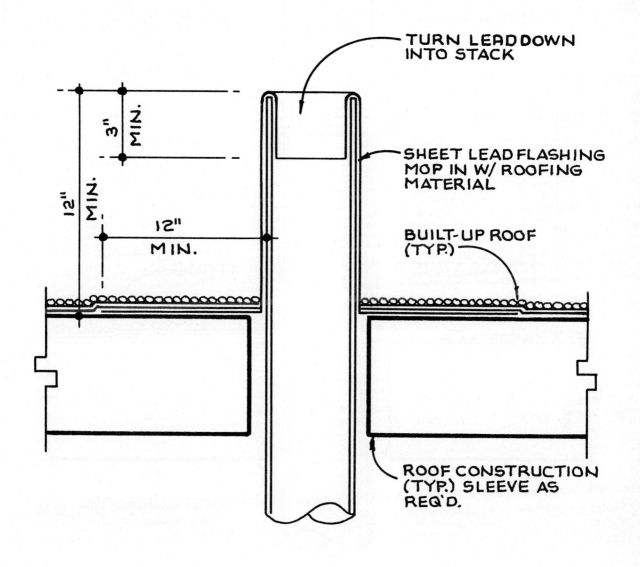

TURN LEAD DOWN
INTO STACK

3" MIN.

12" MIN.

12"
MIN.

SHEET LEAD FLASHING
MOP IN W/ ROOFING
MATERIAL

BUILT-UP ROOF
(TYP.)

ROOF CONSTRUCTION
(TYP.) SLEEVE AS
REQ'D.

NO SCALE

PLUMBING VENT FLASHING: OVER TOP

R 19

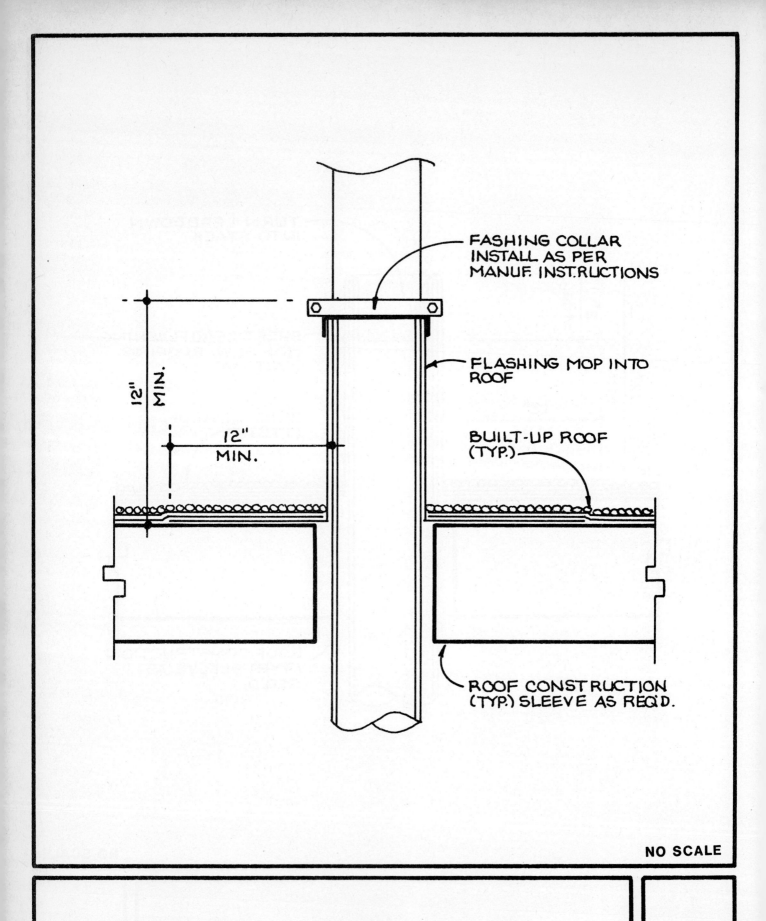

FASHING COLLAR
INSTALL AS PER
MANUF. INSTRUCTIONS

FLASHING MOP INTO
ROOF

BUILT-UP ROOF
(TYP.)

12" MIN.

12" MIN.

ROOF CONSTRUCTION
(TYP.) SLEEVE AS REQ'D.

NO SCALE

PLUMBING VENT FLASHING: COLLAR

R 20

SECTION 22: DOORS, WINDOWS, AND INTERIORS

ARCHITECTURAL DETAILING
FOR
COMMERCIAL CONSTRUCTION

22

FINISH SCHEDULE

ROOM	FLOOR	BASE	WALLS	CEILING	CLG.HT.

DWI 1

DOOR SCHEDULE

NO.	LOCATION	WID.	HGT.	TK.	OPERAT	CONST.	MATER.	FINISH	JAMB

WINDOW SCHEDULE

NO.	TYPE	SIZE	GLASS	FRAME	SILL	HEAD HT.

DWI 3

FINISH SCHEDULE

ROOM	FLOOR		BASE		WALLS		CEILING		CLG.HT.

DOOR SCHEDULE

NO.	LOCATION	WID.	HGT.	TK.	OPERAT	CONST.	MATER.	FINISH	JAMB

WINDOW SCHEDULE

NO.	TYPE	SIZE	GLASS	FRAME	SILL	HEAD HT.

FINISH SCHEDULE

ROOM	FLOOR	BASE	WALLS	CEILING	CLG.HT.

DOOR SCHEDULE

NO.	LOCATION	WID.	HGT.	TK.	OPERAT	CONST.	MATER.	FINISH	JAMB

DWI 5

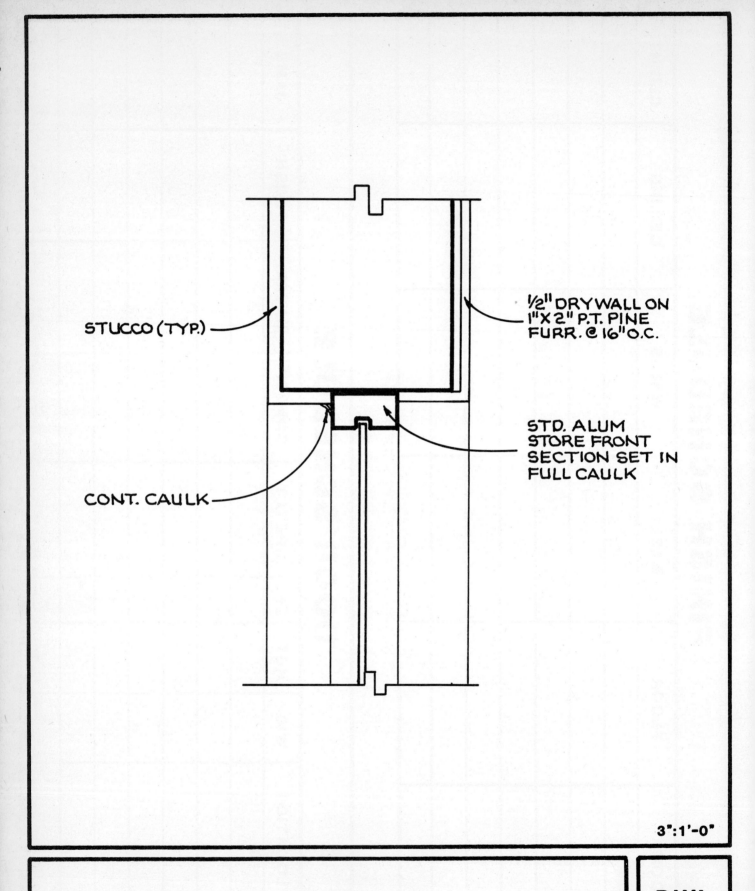

STUCCO (TYP.)

½" DRYWALL ON
1" X 2" P.T. PINE
FURR. @ 16" O.C.

CONT. CAULK

STD. ALUM
STORE FRONT
SECTION SET IN
FULL CAULK

3":1'-0"

STOREFRONT: GLASS HEADER

DWI 6

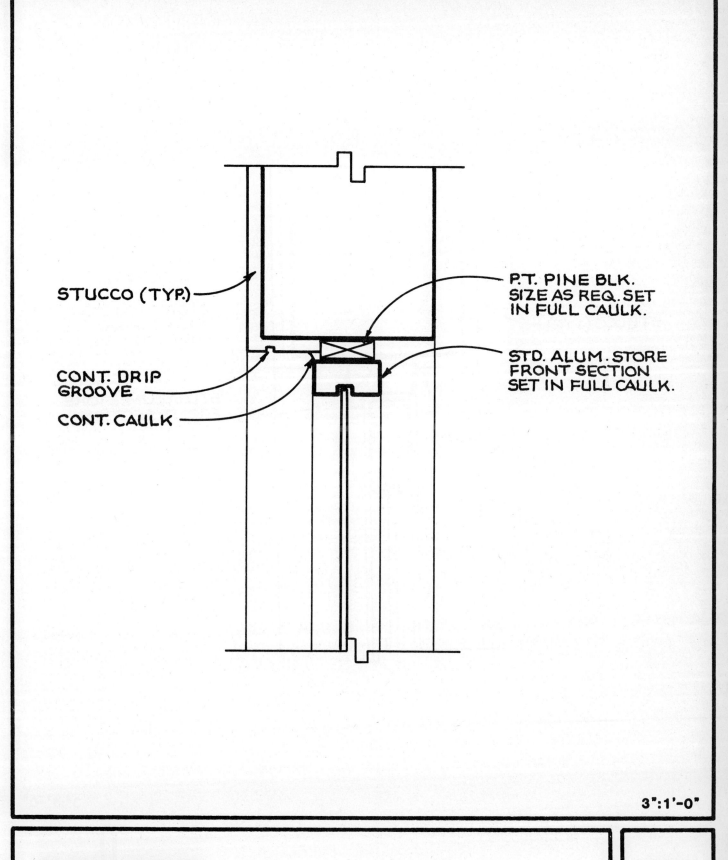

STUCCO (TYP.)

P.T. PINE BLK.
SIZE AS REQ. SET
IN FULL CAULK.

STD. ALUM. STORE
FRONT SECTION
SET IN FULL CAULK.

CONT. DRIP
GROOVE

CONT. CAULK

3":1'-0"

STOREFRONT:
GLASS HEADER WITH WOOD BLOCK

DWI
7

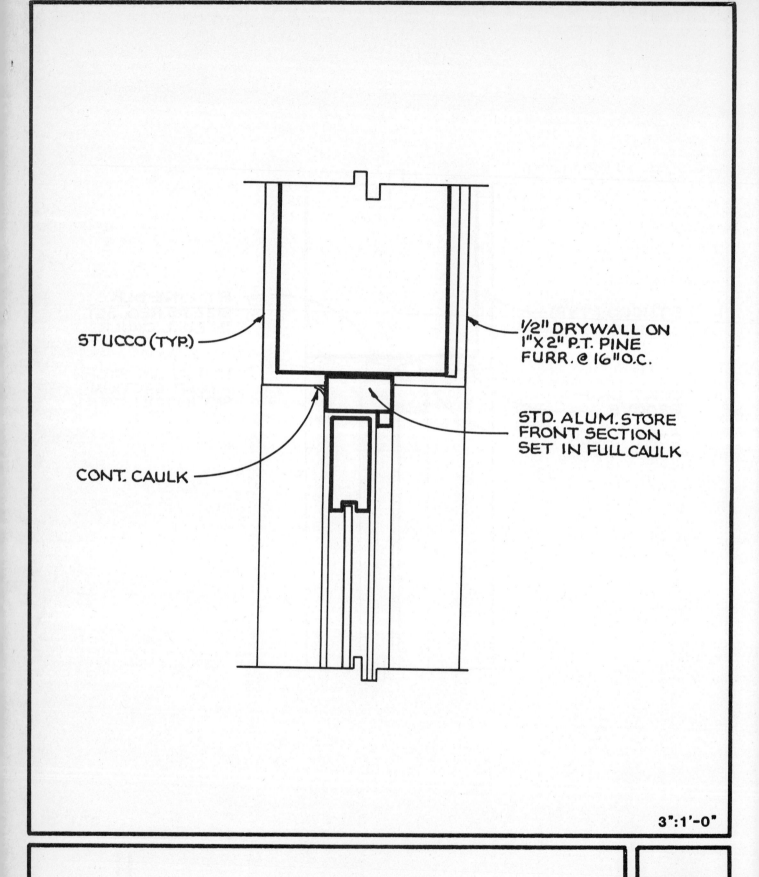

STUCCO (TYP.)

1/2" DRYWALL ON
1" X 2" P.T. PINE
FURR. @ 16" O.C.

STD. ALUM. STORE
FRONT SECTION
SET IN FULL CAULK

CONT. CAULK

3":1'-0"

STOREFRONT: DOOR HEADER

DWI
8

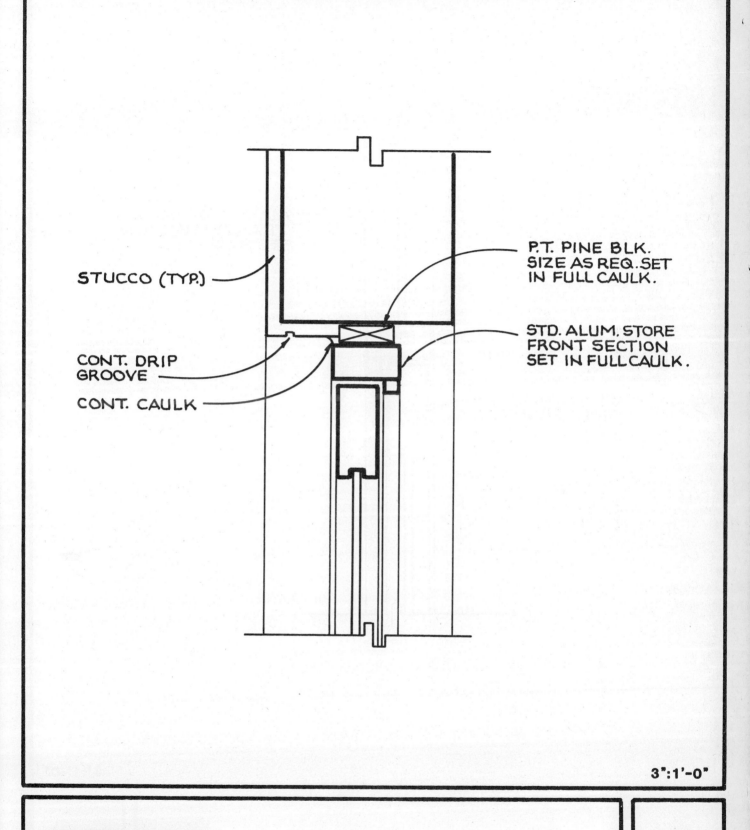

STUCCO (TYP.)

P.T. PINE BLK.
SIZE AS REQ..SET
IN FULL CAULK.

STD. ALUM. STORE
FRONT SECTION
SET IN FULL CAULK.

CONT. DRIP
GROOVE

CONT. CAULK

3":1'-0"

STOREFRONT:
DOOR HEADER WITH WOOD BLOCK

DWI
9

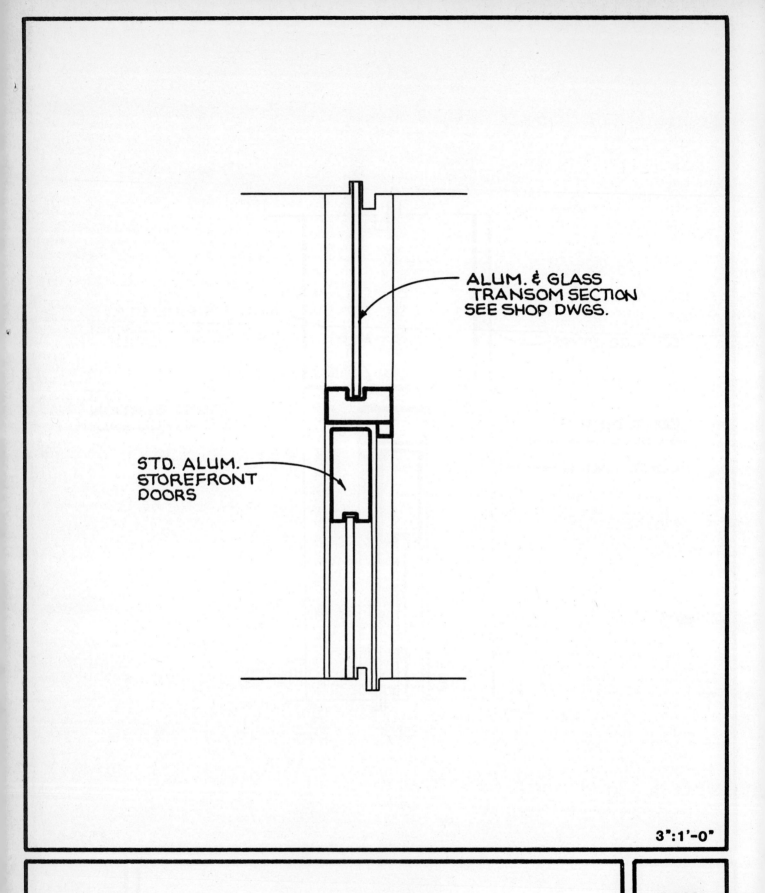

ALUM. & GLASS
TRANSOM SECTION
SEE SHOP DWGS.

STD. ALUM.
STOREFRONT
DOORS

3":1'-0"

STOREFRONT: DOOR TRANSOM

DWI
10

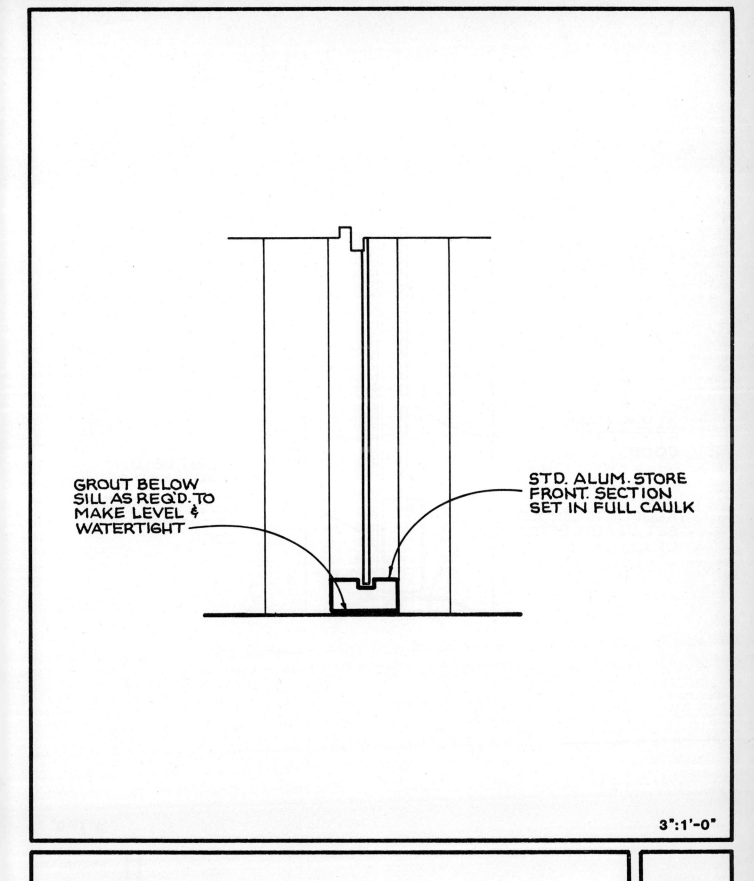

GROUT BELOW
SILL AS REQ'D. TO
MAKE LEVEL &
WATERTIGHT

STD. ALUM. STORE
FRONT. SECTION
SET IN FULL CAULK

3":1'-0"

STOREFRONT: GLASS SILL

DWI
11

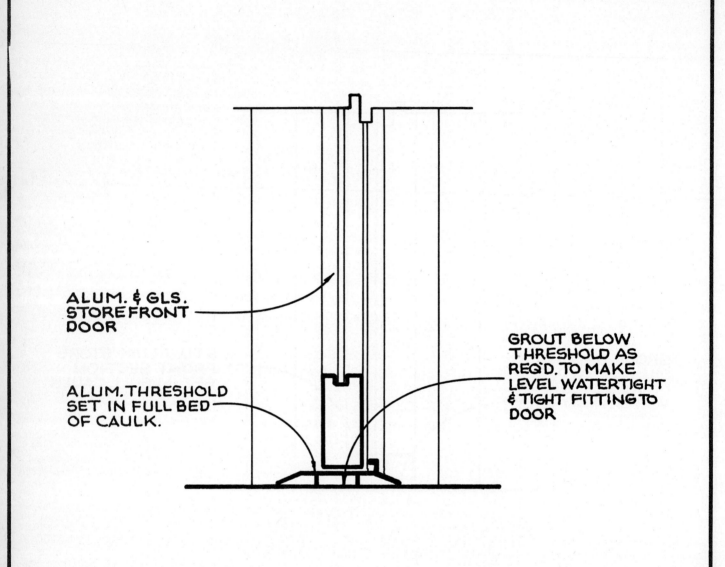

ALUM. & GLS.
STOREFRONT
DOOR

ALUM. THRESHOLD
SET IN FULL BED
OF CAULK.

GROUT BELOW
THRESHOLD AS
REQ'D. TO MAKE
LEVEL WATERTIGHT
& TIGHT FITTING TO
DOOR

3"1'-0"

STOREFRONT: DOOR THRESHOLD

DWI
12

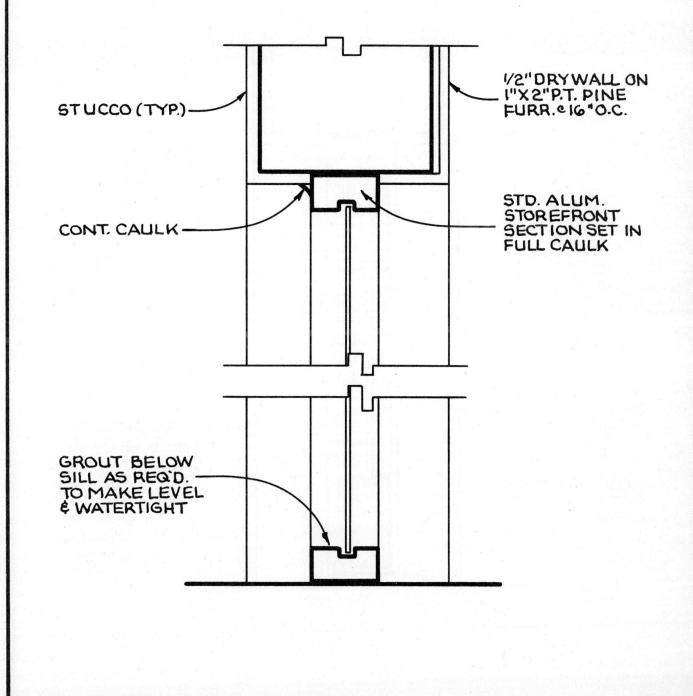

STUCCO (TYP.)

1/2" DRYWALL ON 1"X 2" P.T. PINE FURR. @ 16" O.C.

CONT. CAULK

STD. ALUM. STOREFRONT SECTION SET IN FULL CAULK

GROUT BELOW SILL AS REQ'D. TO MAKE LEVEL & WATERTIGHT

3":1'-0"

STOREFRONT: GLASS SECTION SILL TO HEAD

DWI 13

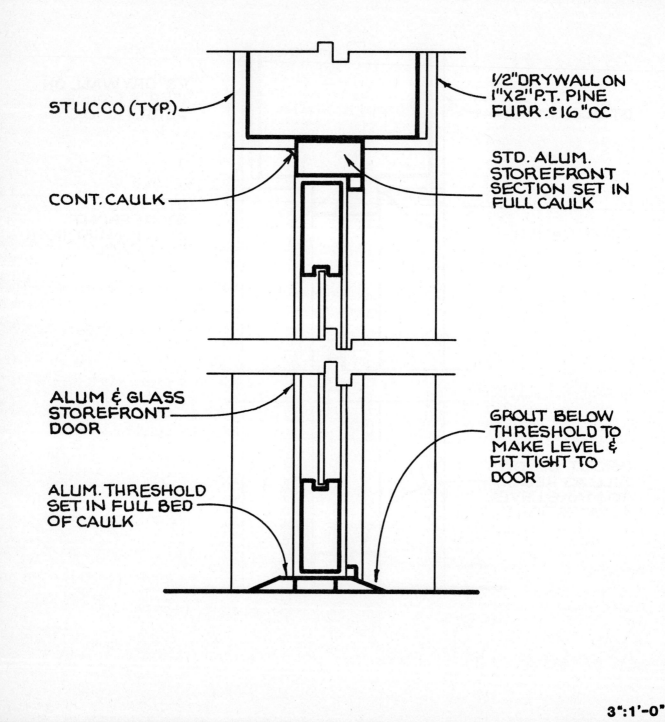

STUCCO (TYP.)

½"DRYWALL ON
1"X2" P.T. PINE
FURR. @ 16"OC

CONT. CAULK

STD. ALUM.
STOREFRONT
SECTION SET IN
FULL CAULK

ALUM & GLASS
STOREFRONT
DOOR

GROUT BELOW
THRESHOLD TO
MAKE LEVEL &
FIT TIGHT TO
DOOR

ALUM. THRESHOLD
SET IN FULL BED
OF CAULK

3":1'-0"

STOREFRONT:
DOOR SECTION THRESHOLD TO HEAD

DWI
14

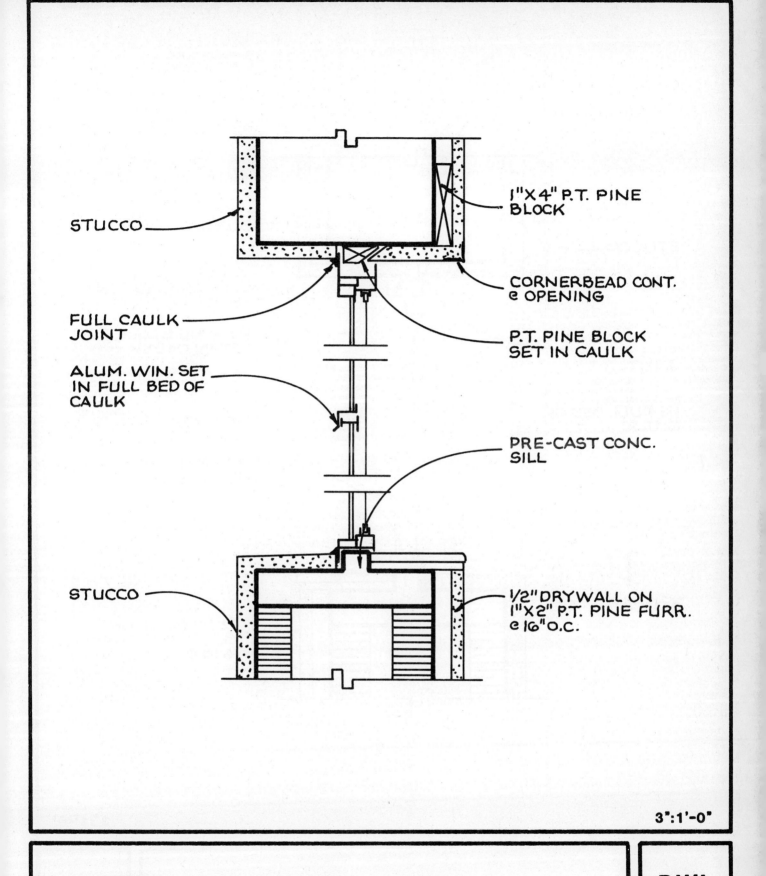

STUCCO

1"X4" P.T. PINE BLOCK

CORNERBEAD CONT. @ OPENING

FULL CAULK JOINT

P.T. PINE BLOCK SET IN CAULK

ALUM. WIN. SET IN FULL BED OF CAULK

PRE-CAST CONC. SILL

STUCCO

1/2" DRYWALL ON 1"X2" P.T. PINE FURR. @ 16" O.C.

3":1'-0"

ALUMINUM WINDOW: SILL TO HEAD

DWI
15

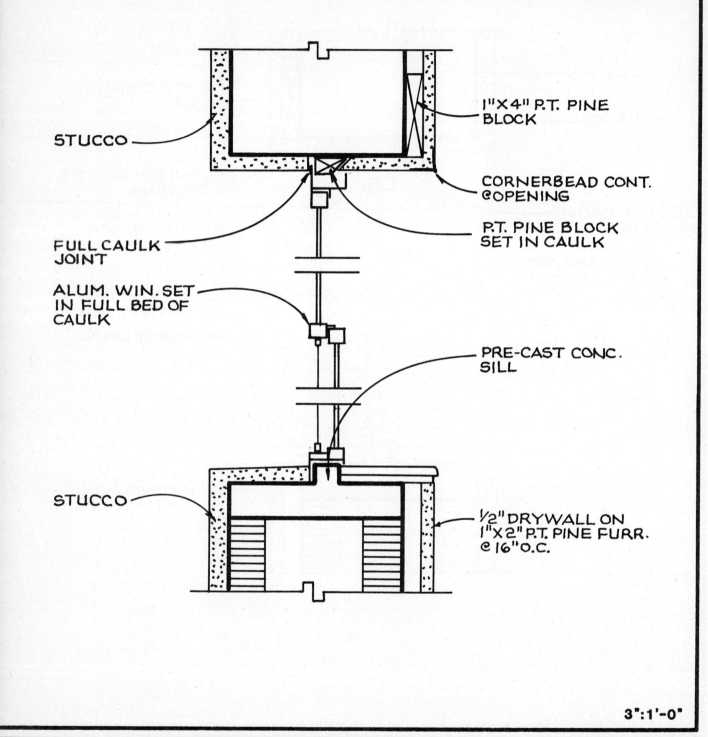

STUCCO

1"X4" P.T. PINE BLOCK

CORNERBEAD CONT. @ OPENING

FULL CAULK JOINT

P.T. PINE BLOCK SET IN CAULK

ALUM. WIN. SET IN FULL BED OF CAULK

PRE-CAST CONC. SILL

STUCCO

½" DRYWALL ON 1"X 2" P.T. PINE FURR. @ 16" O.C.

3":1'-0"

SINGLE HUNG WINDOW: SILL TO HEAD

DWI 16

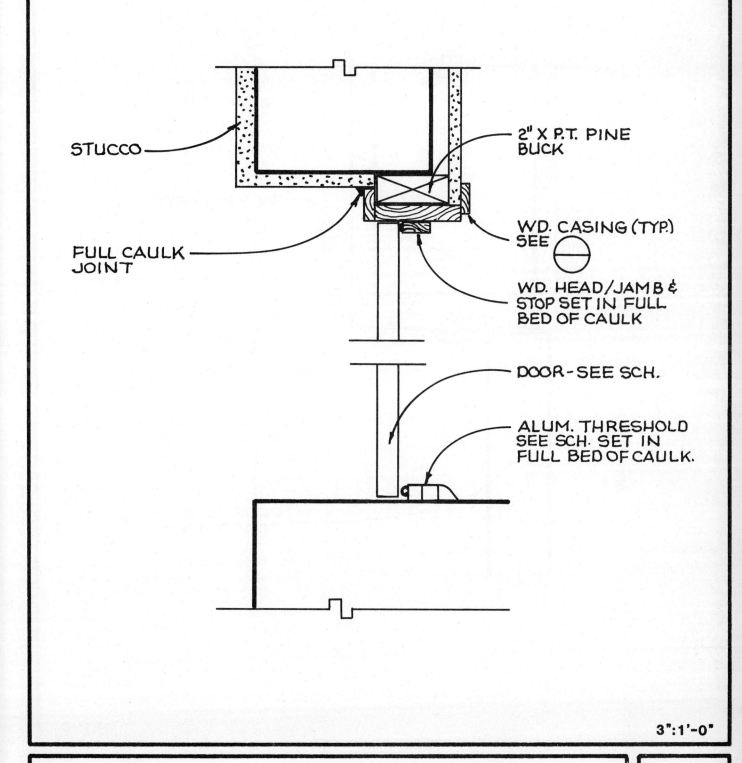

STUCCO

2" X P.T. PINE BUCK

FULL CAULK JOINT

WD. CASING (TYP.) SEE ⊖

WD. HEAD/JAMB & STOP SET IN FULL BED OF CAULK

DOOR-SEE SCH.

ALUM. THRESHOLD SEE SCH. SET IN FULL BED OF CAULK.

3":1'-0"

INTERIOR DOOR: THRESHOLD TO HEAD

DWI 17

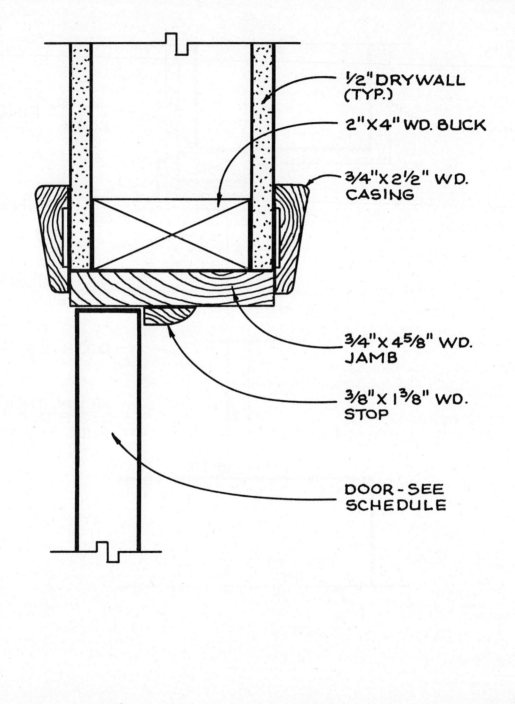

½" DRYWALL (TYP.)

2" X 4" WD. BUCK

¾" X 2½" WD. CASING

¾" X 4⅝" WD. JAMB

⅜" X 1⅜" WD. STOP

DOOR - SEE SCHEDULE

3":1'-0"

INTERIOR DOOR CASING

DWI 18

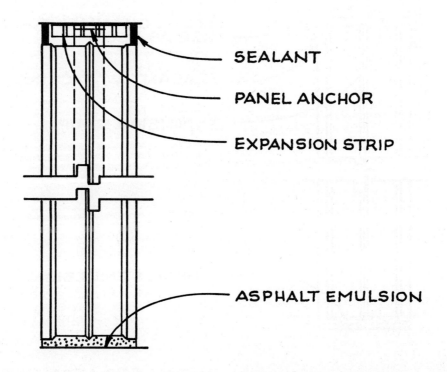

SEALANT

PANEL ANCHOR

EXPANSION STRIP

ASPHALT EMULSION

INSTALLATION SHALL BE
IN ACCORDANCE WITH ALL
MANUF. REQ. & RECOM.

3":1'-0"

**GLASS BLOCK WITH PANEL ANCHORS:
SILL TO HEAD**

DWI
19

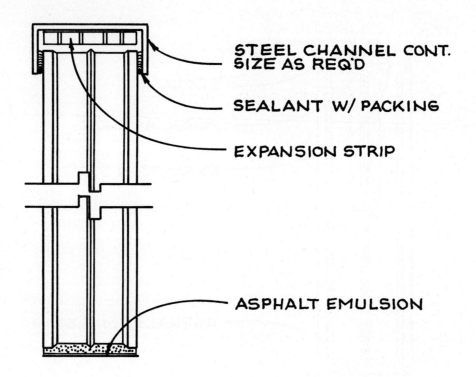

STEEL CHANNEL CONT.
SIZE AS REQ'D

SEALANT W/ PACKING

EXPANSION STRIP

ASPHALT EMULSION

INSTALLATION SHALL BE
IN ACCORDANCE WITH ALL
MANUF. REQ. & RECOM.

3":1'-0"

GLASS BLOCK W/ STEEL CHANNEL ANCHORS: SILL TO HEAD

DWI
20

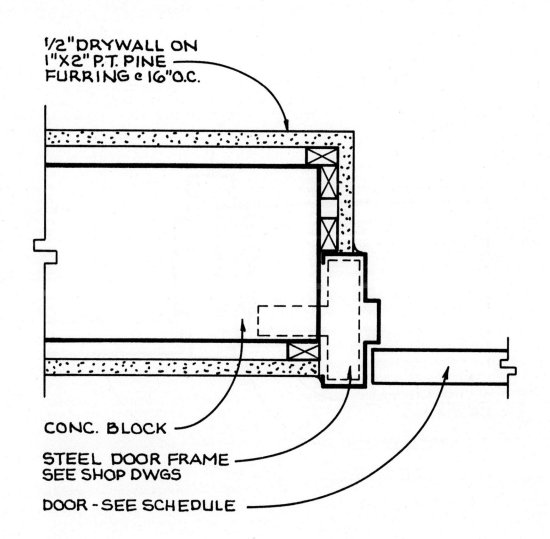

½"DRYWALL ON
1"x2" P.T. PINE
FURRING @ 16"O.C.

CONC. BLOCK

STEEL DOOR FRAME
SEE SHOP DWGS

DOOR - SEE SCHEDULE

3":1'-0"

STEEL DOOR FRAME AT CONCRETE BLOCK: END CONDITION

DWI
21

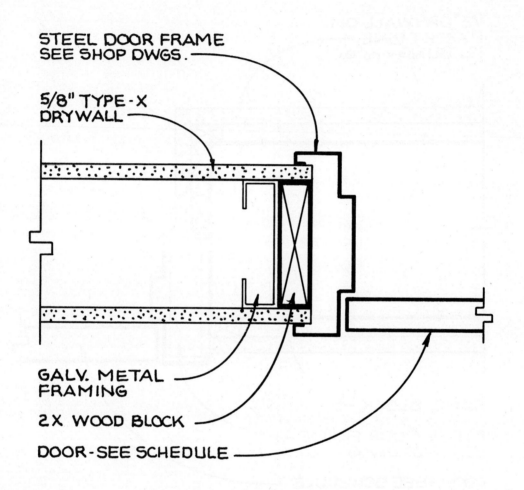

STEEL DOOR FRAME
SEE SHOP DWGS.

5/8" TYPE-X
DRYWALL

GALV. METAL
FRAMING

2X WOOD BLOCK

DOOR-SEE SCHEDULE

3":1'-0"

STEEL DOOR FRAME AT CONCRETE BLOCK: SIDE CONDITION

DWI 22

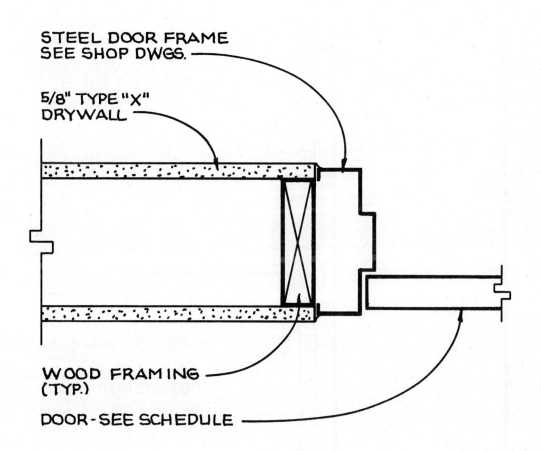

STEEL DOOR FRAME
SEE SHOP DWGS.

5/8" TYPE "X"
DRYWALL

WOOD FRAMING
(TYP.)

DOOR-SEE SCHEDULE

3"1'-0"

STEEL DOOR FRAME AT METAL FRAMING: END CONDITION

DWI
23

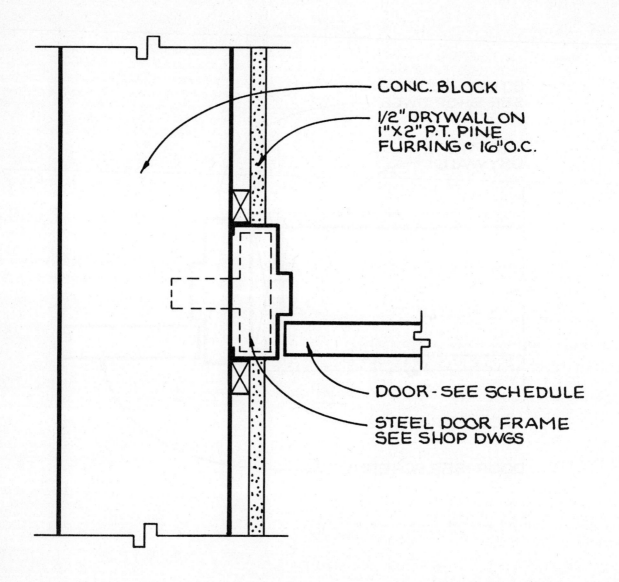

CONC. BLOCK

1/2" DRYWALL ON
1"X2" P.T. PINE
FURRING ⊂ 16"O.C.

DOOR - SEE SCHEDULE

STEEL DOOR FRAME
SEE SHOP DWGS

3":1'-0"

**STEEL DOOR FRAME AT METAL FRAMING:
SIDE CONDITION**

**DWI
24**

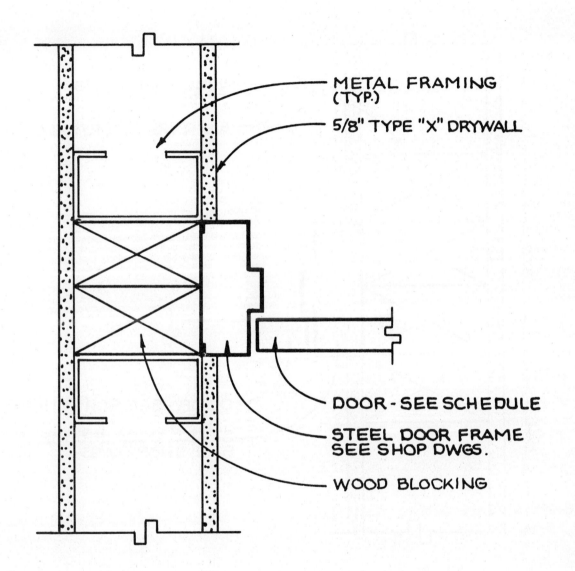

METAL FRAMING (TYP.)

5/8" TYPE "X" DRYWALL

DOOR - SEE SCHEDULE

STEEL DOOR FRAME SEE SHOP DWGS.

WOOD BLOCKING

3":1'-0"

STEEL DOOR FRAME AT WOOD FRAMING: END CONDITION

DWI 25

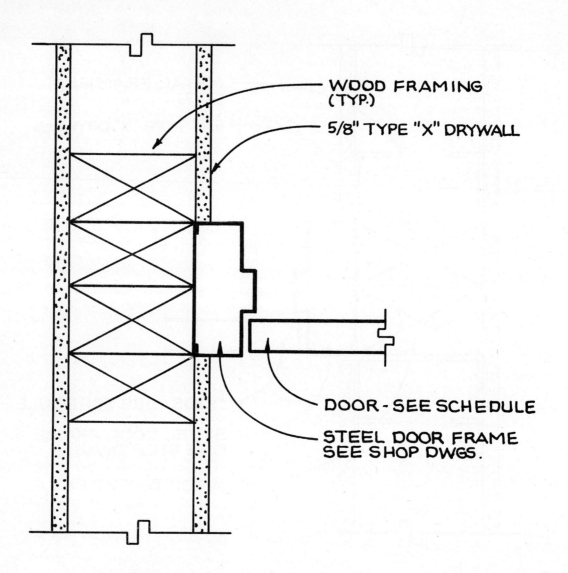

WOOD FRAMING (TYP.)

5/8" TYPE "X" DRYWALL

DOOR - SEE SCHEDULE

STEEL DOOR FRAME SEE SHOP DWGS.

3":1'-0"

STEEL DOOR FRAME AT WOOD FRAMING: SIDE CONDITION

DWI 26

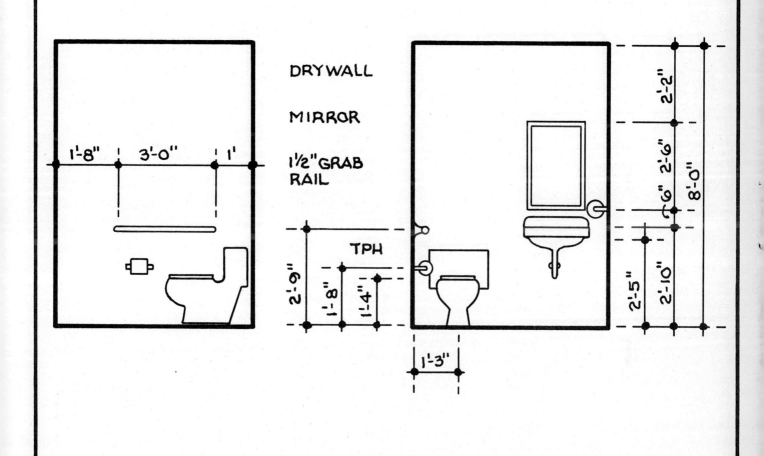

DRYWALL

MIRROR

1½" GRAB RAIL

1'-8" 3'-0" 1'

TPH

2'-9" 1'-8" 1'-4"

1'-3"

2'-2" 2'-6" 6" 8'-0"

2'-5" 2'-10"

3/8":1'-0"

SINGLE STATION BATHROOM: RIGHT HAND

DWI 27

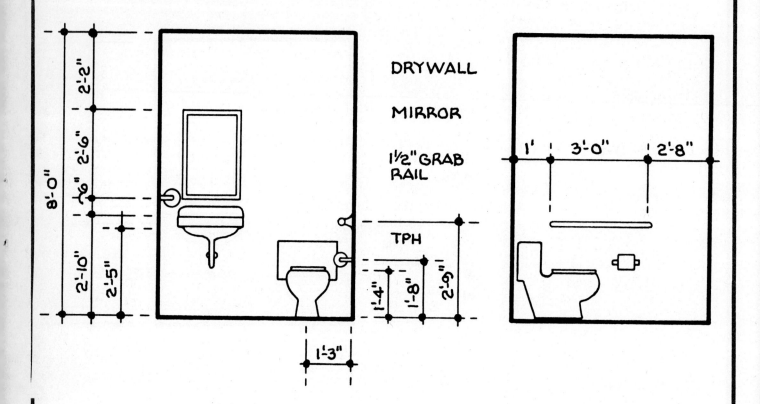

DRYWALL

MIRROR

1½" GRAB RAIL

TPH

8'-0"
2'-2"
2'-6"
6"
2'-10"
2'-5"

1'-4"
1'-8"
2'-9"

1'-3"

1'
3'-0"
2'-8"

3/8":1'-0"

SINGLE STATION BATHROOM: LEFT HAND

DWI 28

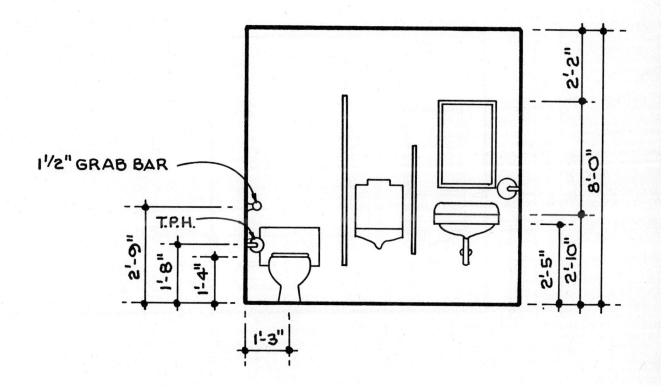

1½" GRAB BAR

T.P.H.

2'-9" 1'-8" 1'-4"

1'-3"

2'-2" 8'-0" 2'-5" 2'-10"

3/8":1'-0"

MULTI STATION BATHROOM: RIGHT HAND

DWI
29

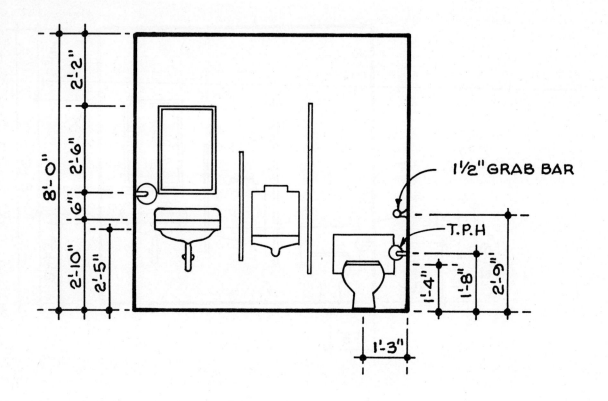

1½"GRAB BAR

T.P.H

8'-0"

2'-2"

2'-6"

6"

2'-10"

2'-5"

1'-4"

1'-8"

2'-9"

1'-3"

3/8":1'-0"

MULTI STATION BATHROOM: LEFT HAND

DWI
30

SECTION 23: MISCELLANEOUS

ARCHITECTURAL DETAILING
FOR
COMMERCIAL CONSTRUCTION

23

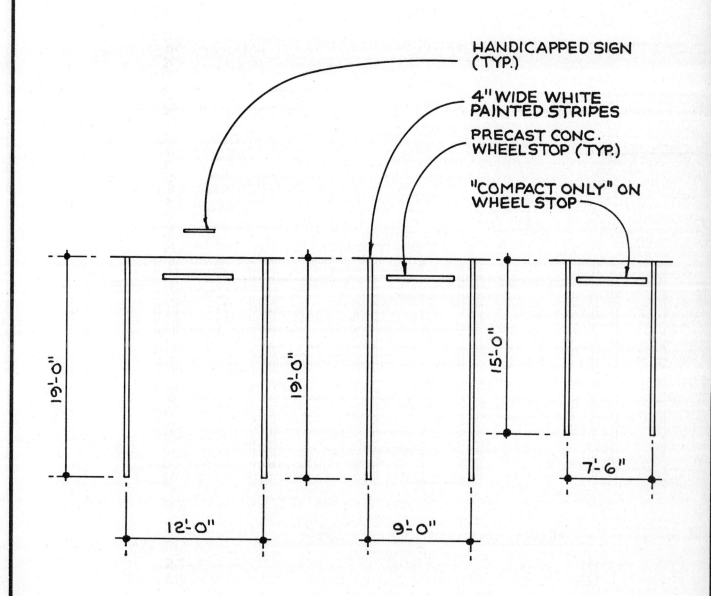

HANDICAPPED SIGN (TYP.)

4" WIDE WHITE PAINTED STRIPES

PRECAST CONC. WHEEL STOP (TYP.)

"COMPACT ONLY" ON WHEEL STOP

19'-0"

19'-0"

15'-0"

7'-6"

12'-0"

9'-0"

PARKING SPACES: SINGLE LINE

M 1

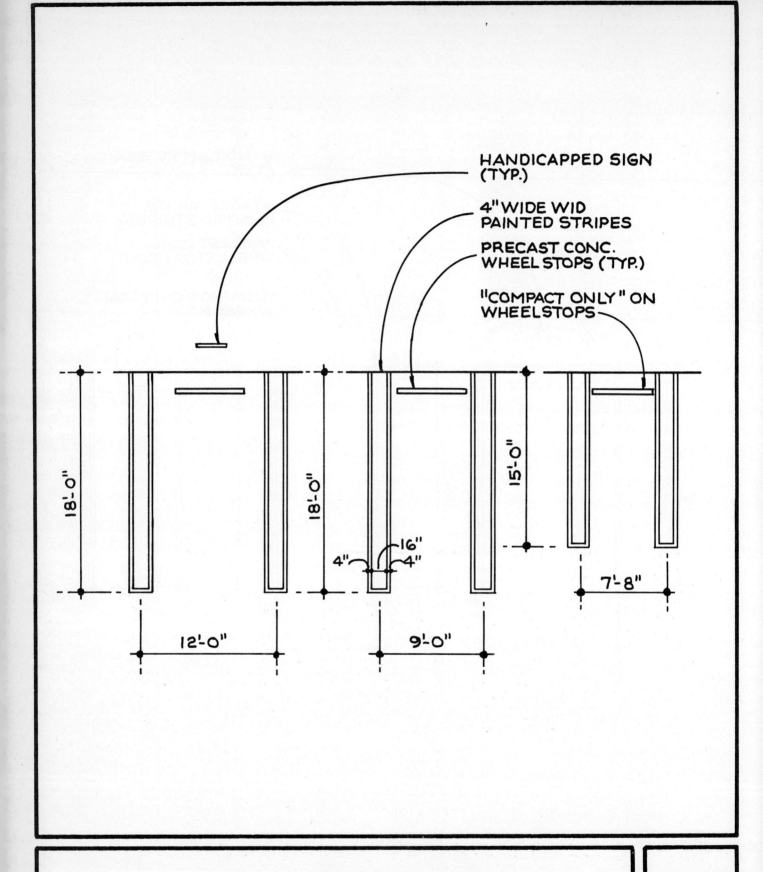

HANDICAPPED SIGN
(TYP.)

4" WIDE WID
PAINTED STRIPES

PRECAST CONC.
WHEEL STOPS (TYP.)

"COMPACT ONLY" ON
WHEELSTOPS

18'-0"

18'-0"

15'-0"

16"

4"   4"

12'-0"

9'-0"

7'-8"

PARKING SPACES: DOUBLE LINE

M 2

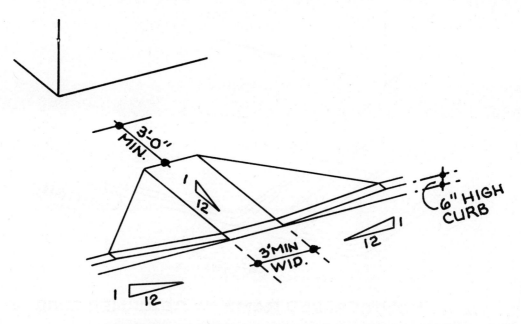

HANDICAPPED RAMP W/ FLARED SIDES

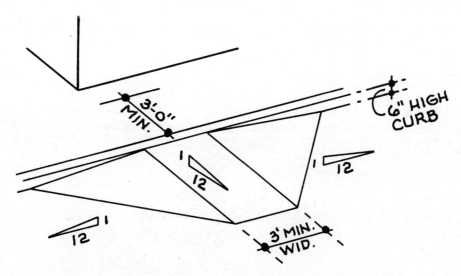

HANDICAPPED RAMP W/ BUILT UP CURB

NO SCALE

HANDICAP RAMPS

M 3

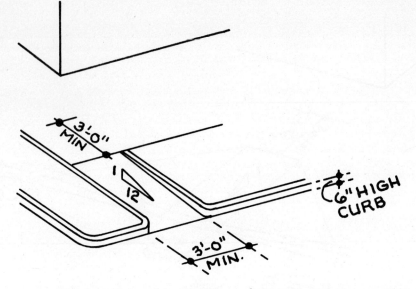

HANDICAPPED RAMP W/ RETURNED CURB

6" HIGH CURB

3'-0" MIN

3'-0" MIN.

1 / 12

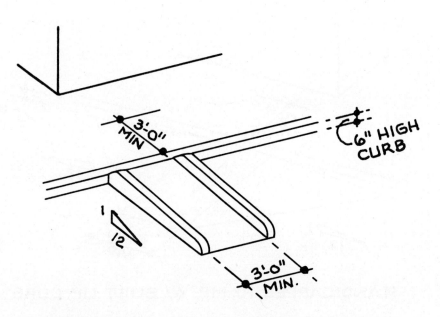

HANDICAPPED RAMP W/ BUILT-UP RAMP

6" HIGH CURB

3'-0" MIN

3'-0" MIN.

1 / 12

NO SCALE

HANDICAP RAMPS

M 4

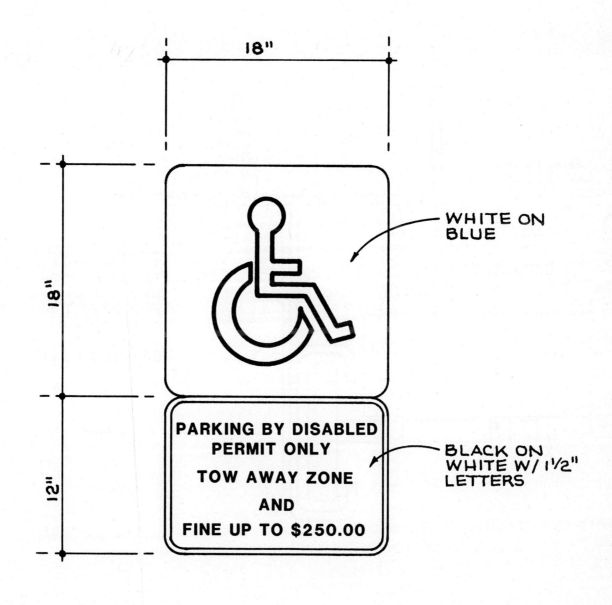

18"

18"

12"

WHITE ON
BLUE

PARKING BY DISABLED
PERMIT ONLY

TOW AWAY ZONE

AND

FINE UP TO $250.00

BLACK ON
WHITE W/ 1½"
LETTERS

NO SCALE

HANDICAP SIGN

M 5

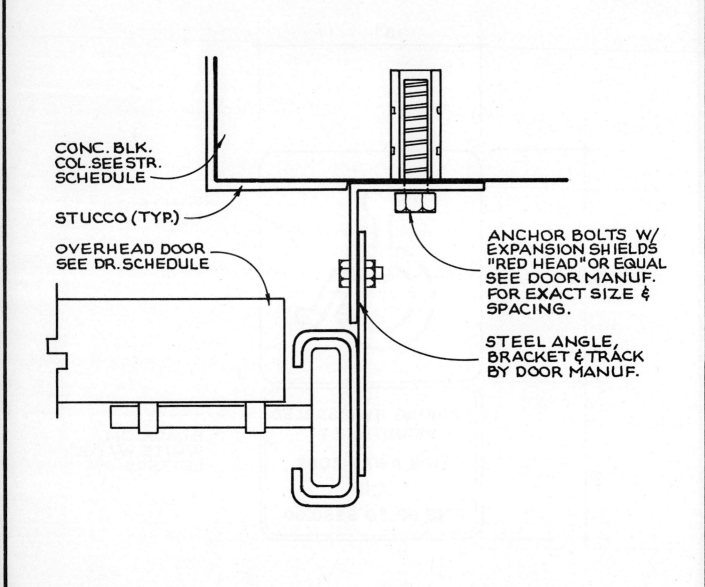

CONC. BLK.
COL. SEE STR.
SCHEDULE

STUCCO (TYP.)

OVERHEAD DOOR
SEE DR. SCHEDULE

ANCHOR BOLTS W/
EXPANSION SHIELDS
"RED HEAD" OR EQUAL
SEE DOOR MANUF.
FOR EXACT SIZE &
SPACING.

STEEL ANGLE,
BRACKET & TRACK
BY DOOR MANUF.

NO SCALE

OVERHEAD DOOR FRAME: CONCRETE BLOCK

M 6

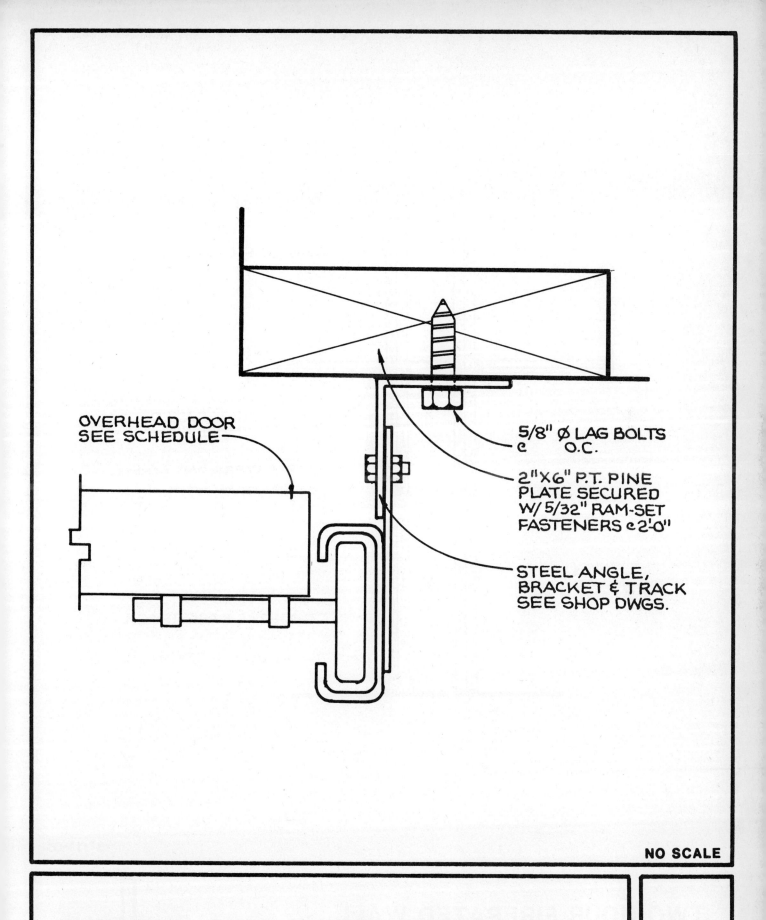

OVERHEAD DOOR
SEE SCHEDULE

5/8" ∅ LAG BOLTS
℮   O.C.

2"X6" P.T. PINE
PLATE SECURED
W/ 5/32" RAM-SET
FASTENERS ℮ 2'-0"

STEEL ANGLE,
BRACKET & TRACK
SEE SHOP DWGS.

NO SCALE

OVERHEAD DOOR FRAME: WOOD BLOCK

M 7

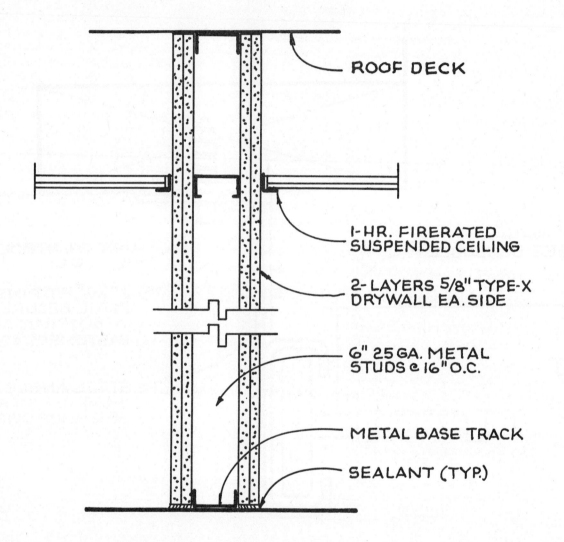

ROOF DECK

1-HR. FIRERATED
SUSPENDED CEILING

2-LAYERS 5/8" TYPE-X
DRYWALL EA. SIDE

6" 25 GA. METAL
STUDS @ 16" O.C.

METAL BASE TRACK

SEALANT (TYP.)

3":1'-0"

TWO HOUR FIRERATED WALL
TO UNDERSIDE OF ROOF DECK

M 8

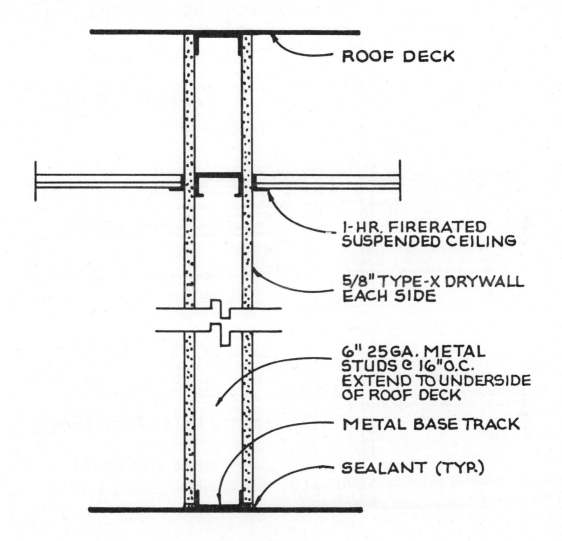

ROOF DECK

1-HR. FIRERATED
SUSPENDED CEILING

5/8" TYPE-X DRYWALL
EACH SIDE

6" 25 GA. METAL
STUDS @ 16" O.C.
EXTEND TO UNDERSIDE
OF ROOF DECK

METAL BASE TRACK

SEALANT (TYP.)

3":1'-0"

ONE HOUR FIRERATED WALL
TO UNDERSIDE OF ROOF DECK

M 9

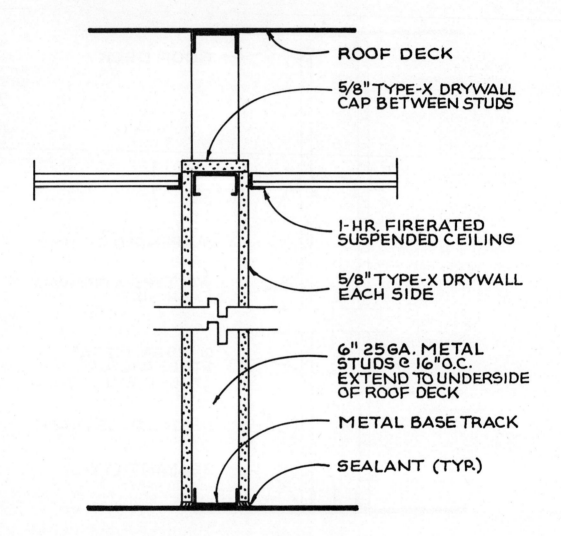

ROOF DECK

5/8" TYPE-X DRYWALL
CAP BETWEEN STUDS

1-HR. FIRERATED
SUSPENDED CEILING

5/8" TYPE-X DRYWALL
EACH SIDE

6" 25GA. METAL
STUDS @ 16"O.C.
EXTEND TO UNDERSIDE
OF ROOF DECK

METAL BASE TRACK

SEALANT (TYP.)

3":1'-0"

ONE HOUR FIRERATED WALL TO CEILING

M 10

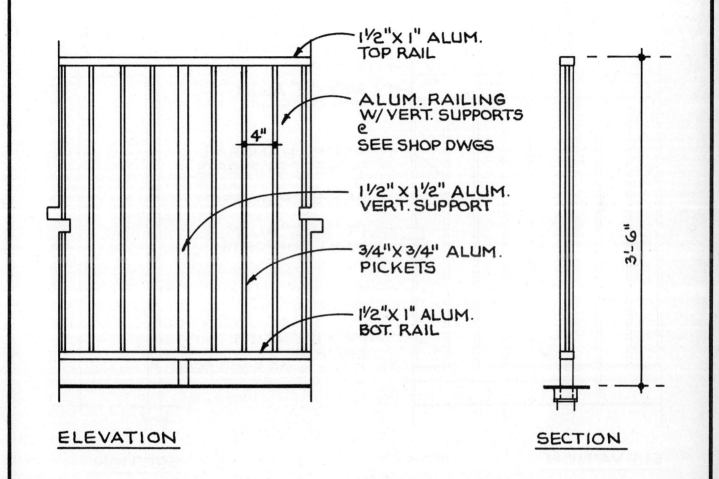

1½" x 1" ALUM.
TOP RAIL

ALUM. RAILING
W/ VERT. SUPPORTS
@
SEE SHOP DWGS

1½" x 1½" ALUM.
VERT. SUPPORT

3/4" x 3/4" ALUM.
PICKETS

1½" x 1" ALUM.
BOT. RAIL

4"

3'-6"

ELEVATION

SECTION

1":1'-0"

ALUMINUM HANDRAIL: ALUMINUM CAP

M 11

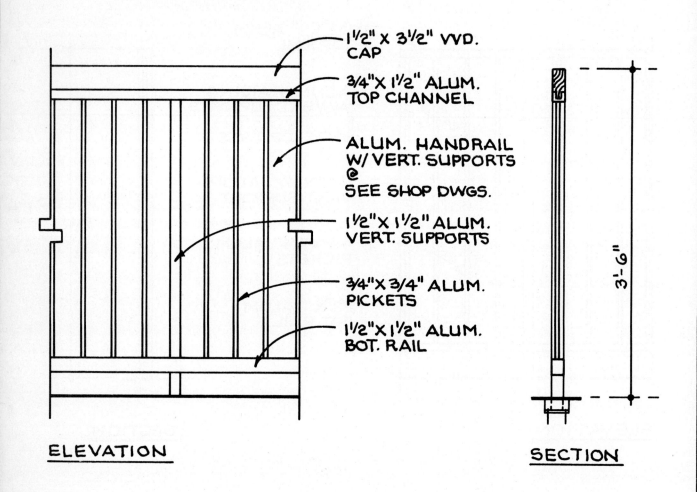

1½" x 3½" WD. CAP

3/4" x 1½" ALUM. TOP CHANNEL

ALUM. HANDRAIL W/ VERT. SUPPORTS @ SEE SHOP DWGS.

1½" x 1½" ALUM. VERT. SUPPORTS

3/4" x 3/4" ALUM. PICKETS

1½" x 1½" ALUM. BOT. RAIL

ELEVATION

SECTION

3'-6"

1":1'-0"

ALUMINUM HANDRAIL: WOOD CAP

M 12

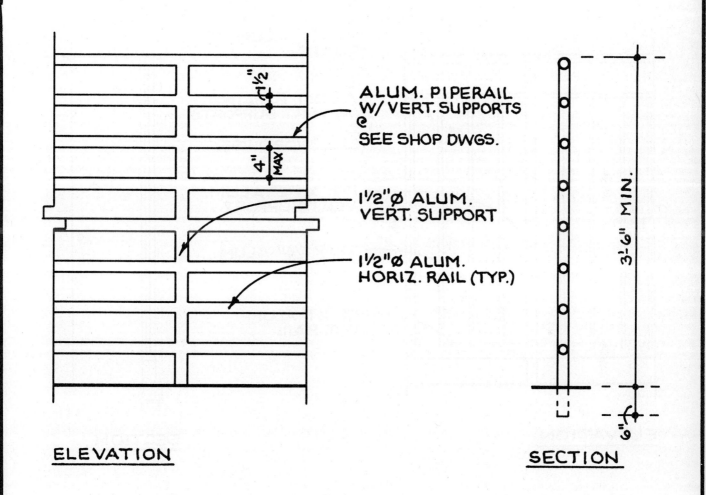

1½"

4" MAX

ALUM. PIPERAIL
W/ VERT. SUPPORTS
@
SEE SHOP DWGS.

1½"ø ALUM.
VERT. SUPPORT

1½"ø ALUM.
HORIZ. RAIL (TYP.)

3'-6" MIN.

6"

ELEVATION

SECTION

1":1'-0"

ALUMINUM PIPE RAIL

M 13

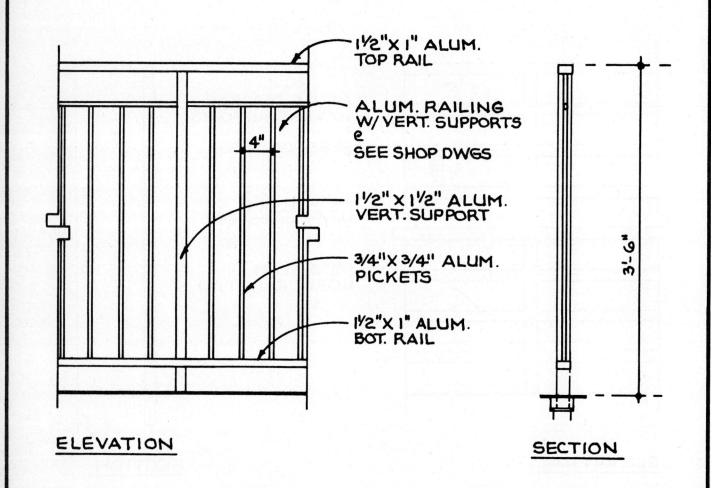

1½" X 1" ALUM.
TOP RAIL

ALUM. RAILING
W/ VERT. SUPPORTS
e
SEE SHOP DWGS

1½" X 1½" ALUM.
VERT. SUPPORT

3/4" X 3/4" ALUM.
PICKETS

1½" X 1" ALUM.
BOT. RAIL

4"

3'-6"

ELEVATION

SECTION

1":1'-0"

ALUMINUM CLEARVIEW HANDRAIL

M 14

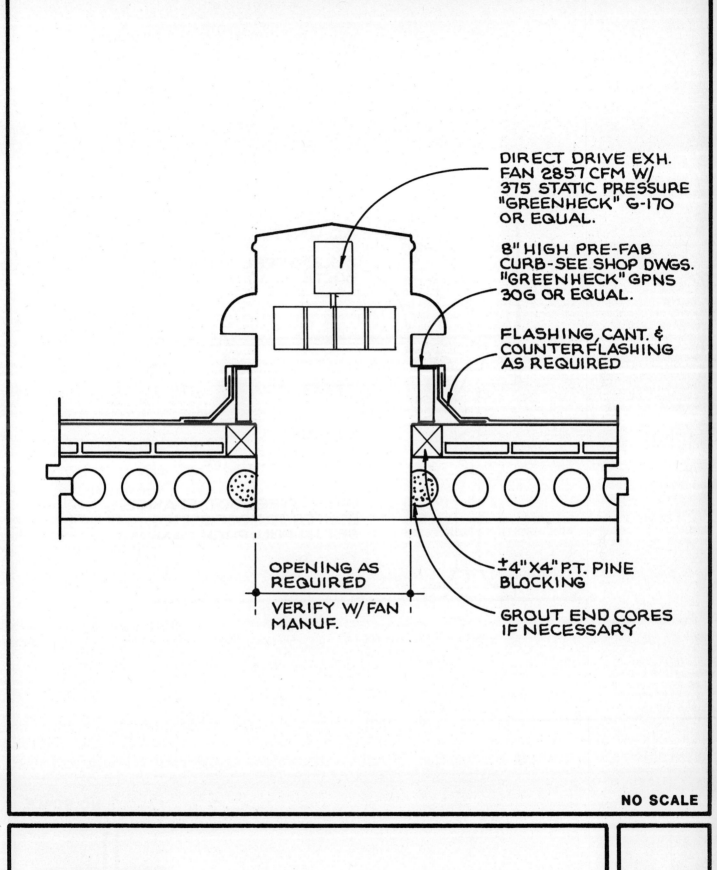

DIRECT DRIVE EXH.
FAN 2857 CFM W/
375 STATIC PRESSURE
"GREENHECK" G-170
OR EQUAL.

8" HIGH PRE-FAB
CURB-SEE SHOP DWGS.
"GREENHECK" GPNS
30G OR EQUAL.

FLASHING, CANT. &
COUNTERFLASHING
AS REQUIRED

OPENING AS
REQUIRED

VERIFY W/FAN
MANUF.

±4"X4" P.T. PINE
BLOCKING

GROUT END CORES
IF NECESSARY

NO SCALE

ROOF FAN

M 15

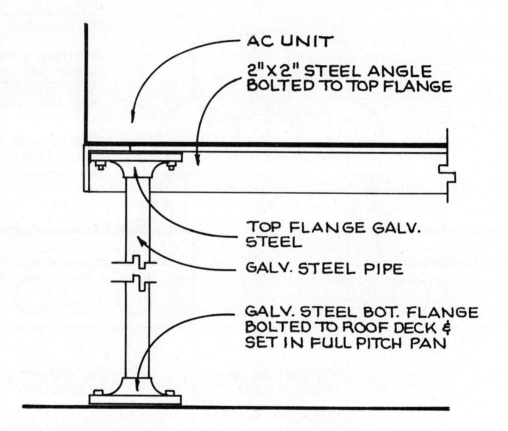

AC UNIT

2"X2" STEEL ANGLE
BOLTED TO TOP FLANGE

TOP FLANGE GALV.
STEEL

GALV. STEEL PIPE

GALV. STEEL BOT. FLANGE
BOLTED TO ROOF DECK &
SET IN FULL PITCH PAN

NO SCALE

AIR COMPRESSOR ROOF SUPPORT

M 16

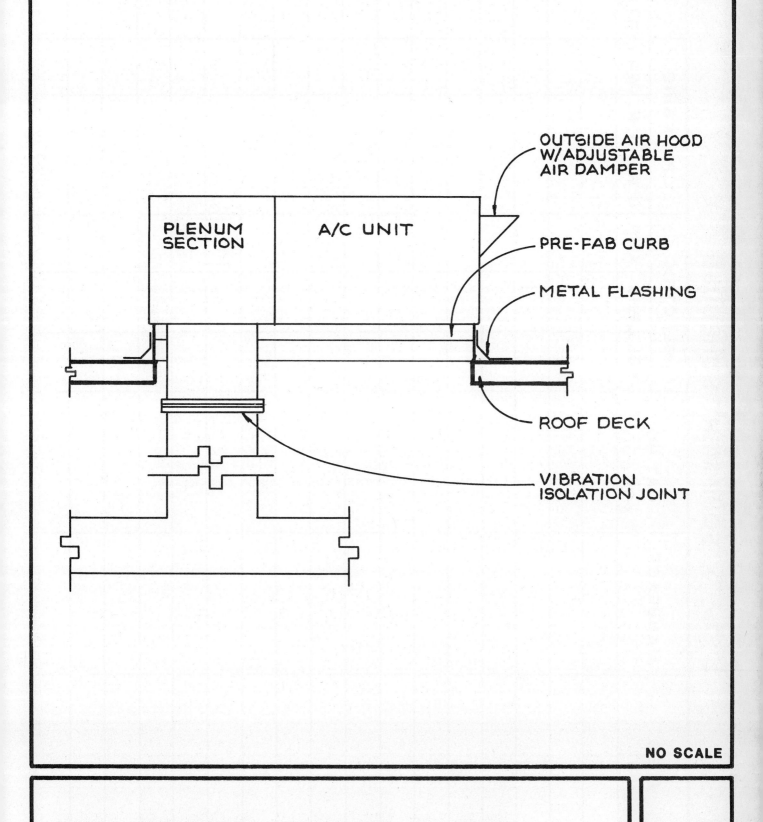

OUTSIDE AIR HOOD
W/ADJUSTABLE
AIR DAMPER

PLENUM
SECTION

A/C UNIT

PRE-FAB CURB

METAL FLASHING

ROOF DECK

VIBRATION
ISOLATION JOINT

NO SCALE

ROOF MOUNTED PACKAGE AC UNIT

M 17

EQUIPMENT SCHEDULE

NO.	ITEM	MANUFACT.	CAT.NO.	ELECTRIC			PLUMBING			GAS	
				VOL	PHS	AMP	C.W.	H.W.	WAS	BTU	DIA

EQUIPMENT SCHEDULE

NO.	ITEM	MANUFACT	CATALOG #	UTL.

M 19

HARDWARE SCHEDULE

ITEM	MANUFACTURER	CATALOG #	FINISH

SECTION 24: ELECTRICAL

ARCHITECTURAL DETAILING
FOR
COMMERCIAL CONSTRUCTION

24

ELECTRICAL SYMBOL LEGEND

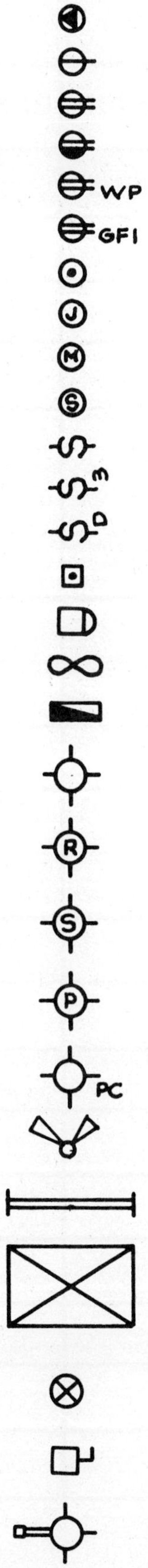

◑	220 V. SPECIAL PURPOSE RECEPTACLE
⊖	110 V. SPECIAL PURPOSE RECEPTACLE
⊜	110 V. DUPLEX RECEPTACLE
⊜	110 V. DUPLEX RECEPTACLE, ½ HOT
⊜ WP	110 V. DUPLEX WATERPROOF RECEP.
⊜ GFI	110 V. GROUND FAULT
⊙	110 V. FLOOR RECEPTACLE
Ⓙ	JUNCTION BOX
Ⓜ	MOTOR
Ⓢ	SMOKE DETECTOR
⌒S	TWO WAY SWITCH
⌒S₃	THREE WAY SWITCH
⌒S_D	DIMMER SWITCH
▣	PUSH BUTTON SWITCH
▭	ELECTRIC METER
∞	EXHAUST FAN
◣	ELECTRIC PANEL
⊕	INCAND. BRACKET LIGHT FIXTURE
⊕R	INCAND. RECESSED LIGHT FIXTURE
⊕S	INCAND. SURFACE MTD. LIGHT FIXTURE
⊕P	INCAND. PENDANT MTD. LIGHT FIXTURE
⊕ PC	PULL CHAIN OPERATED FIXTURE
⋎	EXTERIOR FLOOD LIGHT
⊢—⊣	EXPOSED BULB
⊠	COVERED BULB
⊗	EXIT LIGHT FIXTURE
�□┐	DISCONNECT SWITCH
⊶⊕	EXTERIOR POST LIGHT FIXTURE

PANEL SCHEDULE

LOAD	BRKR	WIRE	FUNCTION	#		#	FUNCTION	WIRE	BRKR	LOAD
				1		2				
				3		4				
				5		6				
				7		8				
				9		10				
				11		12				
				13		14				
				15		16				
				17		18				
				19		20				
				21		22				
				23		24				
				25		26				
				27		28				
				29		30				
				31		32				
				33		34				
				35		36				
				37		38				
				39		40				
				41		42				

PANEL SCHEDULE

LOAD	BRK	WIRE	FUNCTION	#		#	FUNCTION	WIRE	BRK	LOAD
				1		2				
				3		4				
				5		6				
				7		8				
				9		10				
				11		12				
				13		14				
				15		16				
				17		18				
				19		20				
				21		22				
				23		24				
				25		26				
				27		28				
				29		30				

PANEL SCHEDULE

LOAD	BRK	WIRE	FUNCTION	#		#	FUNCTION	WIRE	BRK	LOAD
				1		2				
				3		4				
				5		6				
				7		8				
				9		10				
				11		12				
				13		14				
				15		16				
				17		18				
				19		20				
				21		22				
				23		24				

PANEL SCHEDULE

LOAD	BRK	WIRE	FUNCTION	#		#	FUNCTION	WIRE	BRK	LOAD
				1		2				
				3		4				
				5		6				
				7		8				
				9		10				
				11		12				
				13		14				
				15		16				

LIGHT FIXTURE SCHEDULE

NO.	MANUFACT.	CATALOG #	MT	LAMPS

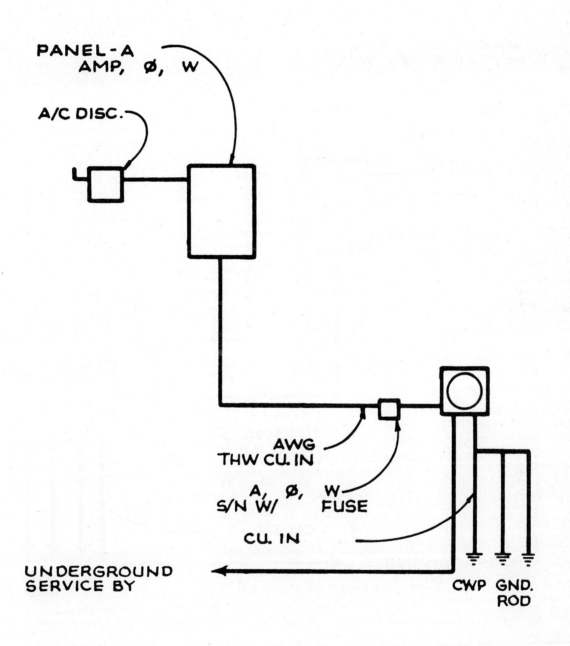

PANEL-A
AMP, Ø, W

A/C DISC.

AWG
THW CU. IN

A, Ø, W
S/N W/   FUSE

CU. IN

UNDERGROUND
SERVICE BY

CWP GND.
        ROD

NO SCALE

ELECTRICAL RISER DIAGRAM
UNDERGROUND SERVICE
1 PANEL & 1 DISCONNECT

E 7

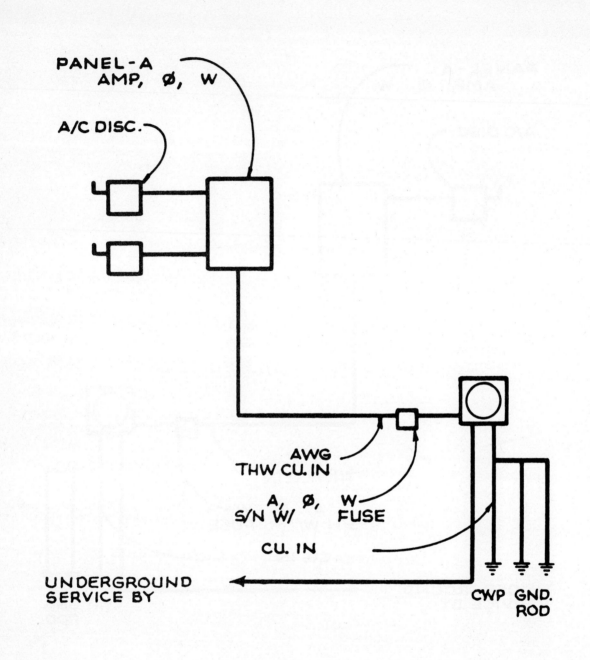

PANEL-A
AMP, Ø, W

A/C DISC.

AWG
THW CU. IN

A, Ø, W
S/N W/ FUSE

CU. IN

UNDERGROUND
SERVICE BY

CWP GND.
ROD

NO SCALE

ELECTRICAL RISER DIAGRAM
UNDERGROUND SERVICE
1 PANEL & 2 DISCONNECTS

E 8

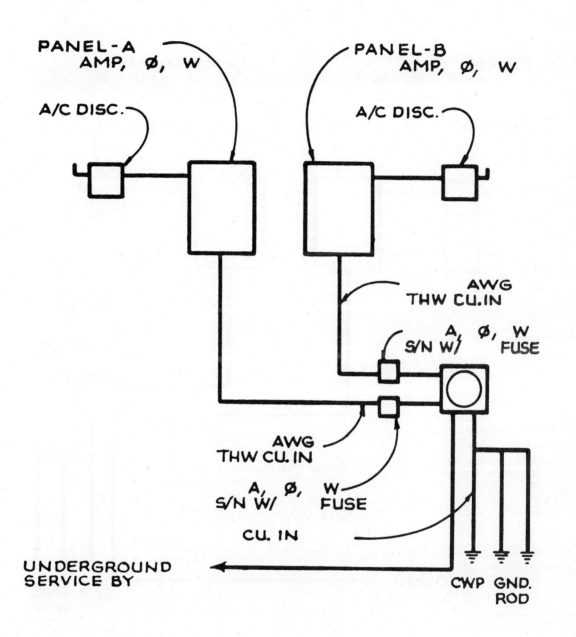

PANEL-A
AMP, Ø, W

A/C DISC.

PANEL-B
AMP, Ø, W

A/C DISC.

AWG
THW CU. IN

A, Ø, W
S/N W/ FUSE

AWG
THW CU. IN

A, Ø, W
S/N W/ FUSE

CU. IN

UNDERGROUND
SERVICE BY

CWP GND.
ROD

NO SCALE

ELECTRICAL RISER DIAGRAM
UNDERGROUND SERVICE
2 PANELS & 2 DISCONNECTS

E 9

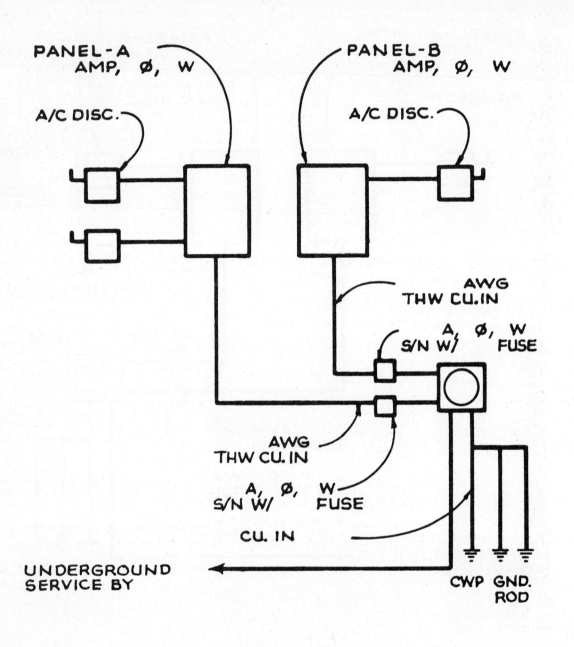

PANEL-A
AMP, Ø, W

A/C DISC.

PANEL-B
AMP, Ø, W

A/C DISC.

AWG
THW CU. IN

A, Ø, W
S/N W/ FUSE

AWG
THW CU. IN

A, Ø, W
S/N W/ FUSE

CU. IN

UNDERGROUND
SERVICE BY

CWP GND.
ROD

NO SCALE

ELECTRICAL RISER DIAGRAM
UNDERGROUND SERVICE
2 PANELS & 3 DISCONNECTS

E 10

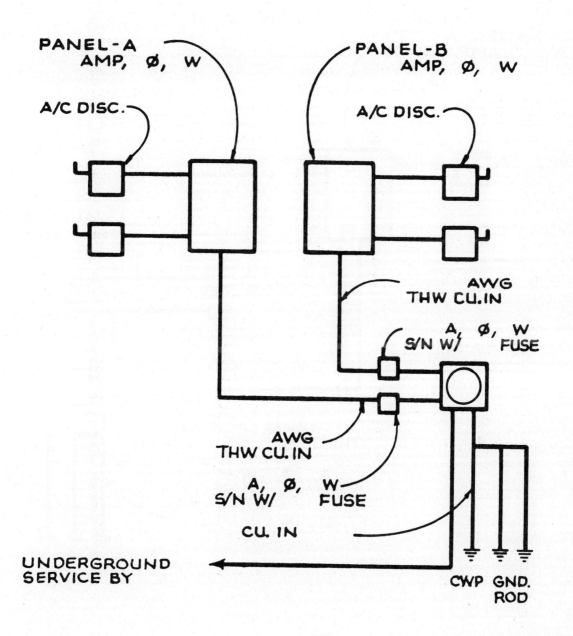

PANEL-A
AMP, Ø, W

A/C DISC.

PANEL-B
AMP, Ø, W

A/C DISC.

AWG
THW CU. IN

A, Ø, W
S/N W/ FUSE

AWG
THW CU. IN

A, Ø, W
S/N W/ FUSE

CU. IN

UNDERGROUND
SERVICE BY

CWP GND.
ROD

NO SCALE

**ELECTRICAL RISER DIAGRAM
UNDERGROUND SERVICE
2 PANELS & 4 DISCONNECTS**

E 11

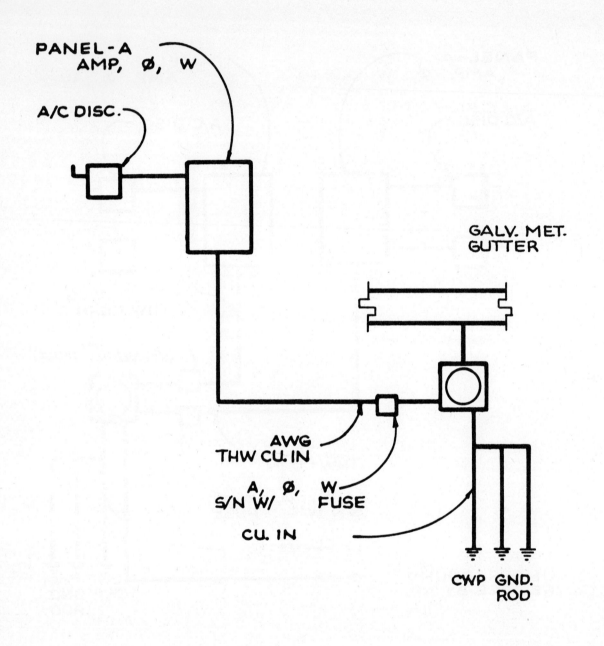

PANEL-A
AMP, Ø, W

A/C DISC.

GALV. MET.
GUTTER

AWG
THW CU. IN

A, Ø, W
S/N W/ FUSE

CU. IN

CWP GND.
ROD

NO SCALE

ELECTRICAL RISER DIAGRAM
GUTTER SERVICE
1 PANEL & 1 DISCONNECT

E 12

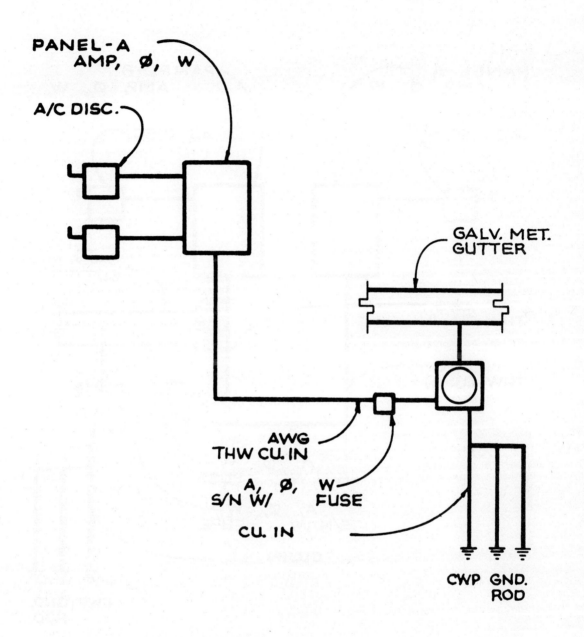

PANEL-A
AMP, Ø, W

A/C DISC.

GALV. MET.
GUTTER

AWG
THW CU. IN

A, Ø, W
S/N W/ FUSE

CU. IN

CWP GND.
ROD

NO SCALE

ELECTRICAL RISER DIAGRAM
GUTTER SERVICE
1 PANEL & 2 DISCONNECTS

E 13

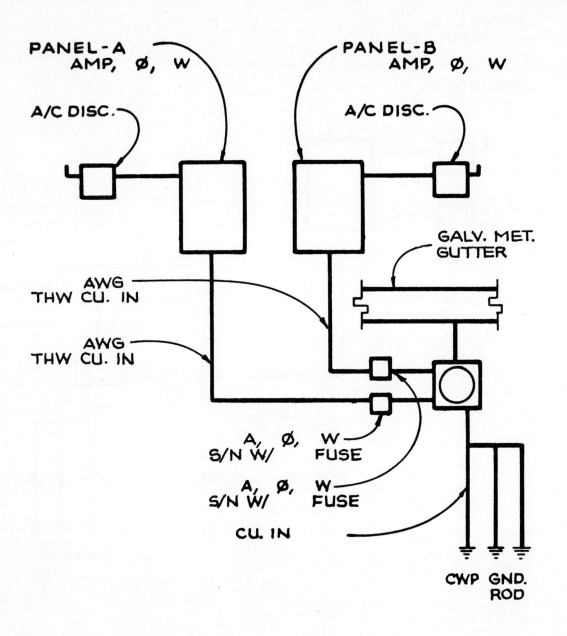

PANEL-A
AMP, Ø, W

PANEL-B
AMP, Ø, W

A/C DISC.

A/C DISC.

GALV. MET.
GUTTER

AWG
THW CU. IN

AWG
THW CU. IN

A, Ø, W
S/N W/ FUSE

A, Ø, W
S/N W/ FUSE

CU. IN

CWP GND.
ROD

NO SCALE

ELECTRICAL RISER DIAGRAM
GUTTER SERVICE
2 PANELS & 2 DISCONNECTS

E 14

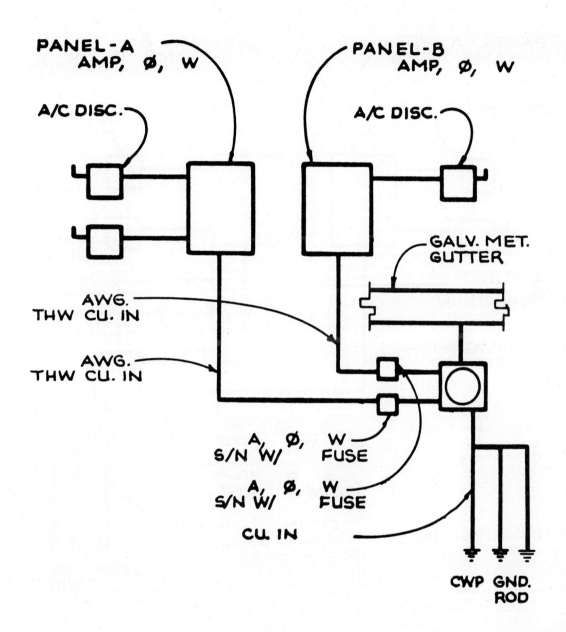

PANEL-A
AMP, Ø, W

A/C DISC.

PANEL-B
AMP, Ø, W

A/C DISC.

GALV. MET.
GUTTER

AWG.
THW CU. IN

AWG.
THW CU. IN

A, Ø, W
S/N W/ FUSE

A, Ø, W
S/N W/ FUSE

CU. IN

CWP GND.
ROD

NO SCALE

ELECTRICAL RISER DIAGRAM
GUTTER SERVICE
2 PANELS & 3 DISCONNECTS

E 15

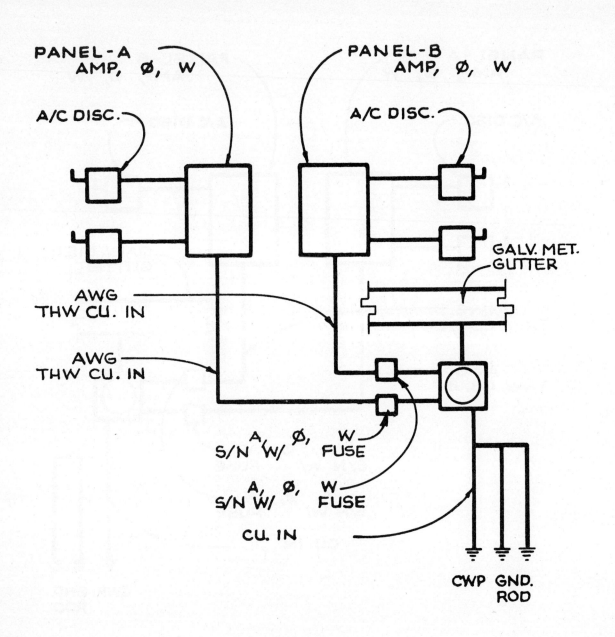

PANEL-A
AMP, Ø, W

A/C DISC.

PANEL-B
AMP, Ø, W

A/C DISC.

GALV. MET.
GUTTER

AWG
THW CU. IN

AWG
THW CU. IN

A, Ø, W
S/N W/ FUSE

A, Ø, W
S/N W/ FUSE

CU. IN

CWP GND.
ROD

NO SCALE

ELECTRICAL RISER DIAGRAM
GUTTER SERVICE

2 PANELS & 4 DISCONNECTS

E 16

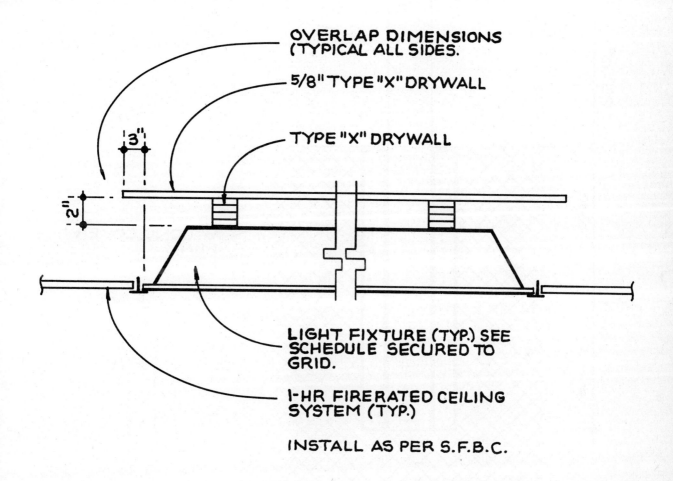

OVERLAP DIMENSIONS
(TYPICAL ALL SIDES.

5/8" TYPE "X" DRYWALL

TYPE "X" DRYWALL

3"

2"

LIGHT FIXTURE (TYP.) SEE
SCHEDULE SECURED TO
GRID.

I-HR FIRERATED CEILING
SYSTEM (TYP.)

INSTALL AS PER S.F.B.C.

NO SCALE

FIRERATED DROP-IN LIGHT FIXTURE

E 17

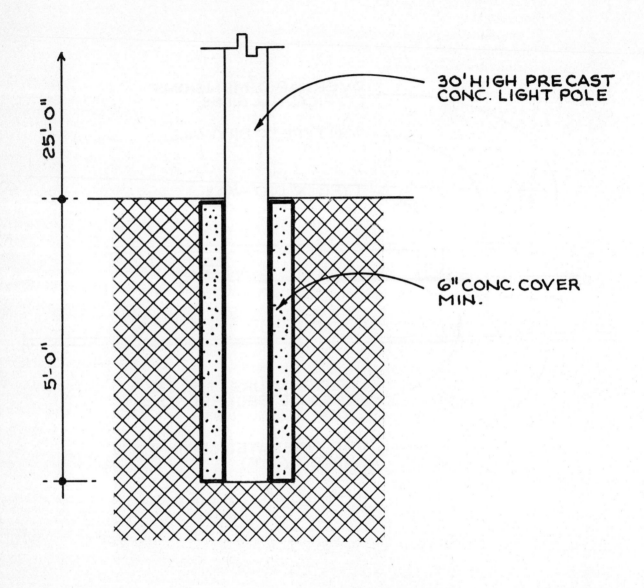

25'-0"

5'-0"

30' HIGH PRECAST CONC. LIGHT POLE

6" CONC. COVER MIN.

NO SCALE

LIGHT POLE FOUNDATION

E 18

SECTION 25: PLUMBING

SECTION 25: PLUMBING

ARCHITECTURAL DETAILING
FOR
COMMERCIAL CONSTRUCTION

25

PLUMBING FIXTURE SCHEDULE

ITEM	MANUFACTURER	CATALOG #	COLOR

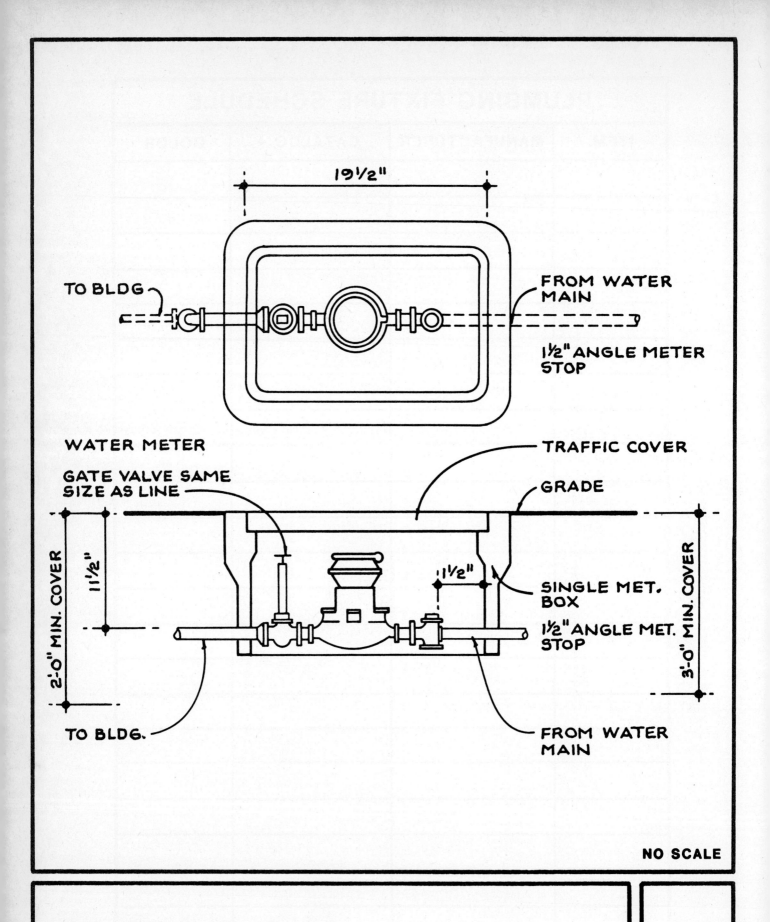

19½"

TO BLDG

FROM WATER MAIN

1½" ANGLE METER STOP

WATER METER

GATE VALVE SAME SIZE AS LINE

TRAFFIC COVER

GRADE

2'-0" MIN. COVER

11½"

1½"

SINGLE MET. BOX

1½" ANGLE MET. STOP

3'-0" MIN. COVER

TO BLDG.

FROM WATER MAIN

NO SCALE

WATER METER: INLINE

P 2

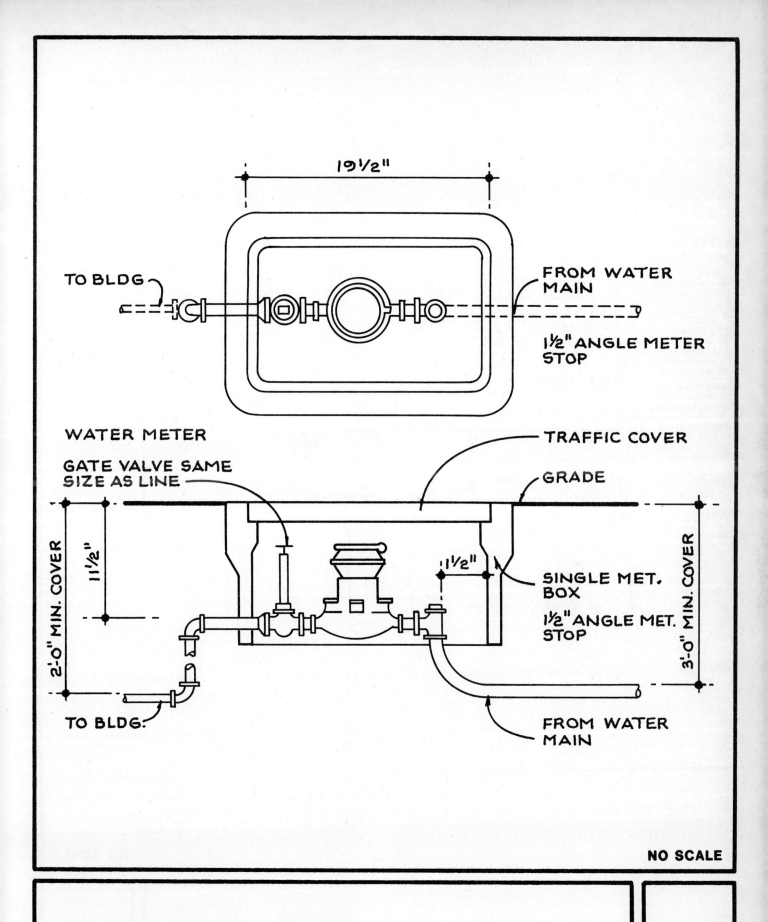

19½"

TO BLDG

FROM WATER MAIN

1½" ANGLE METER STOP

WATER METER

GATE VALVE SAME SIZE AS LINE

TRAFFIC COVER

GRADE

2'-0" MIN. COVER

11½"

1½"

SINGLE MET. BOX

1½" ANGLE MET. STOP

3'-0" MIN. COVER

TO BLDG.

FROM WATER MAIN

NO SCALE

WATER METER: ABOVE

P 3

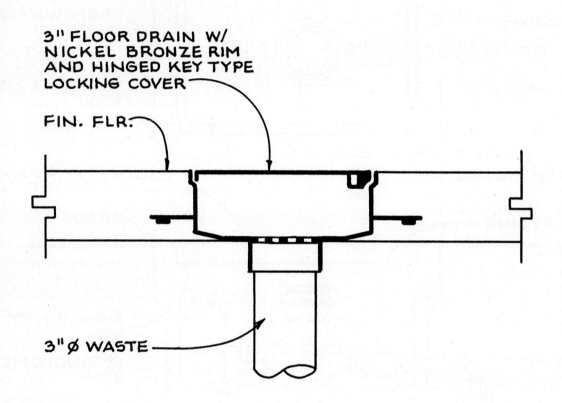

3" FLOOR DRAIN W/
NICKEL BRONZE RIM
AND HINGED KEY TYPE
LOCKING COVER

FIN. FLR.

3" Ø WASTE

NO SCALE

FLOOR DRAIN

P 4

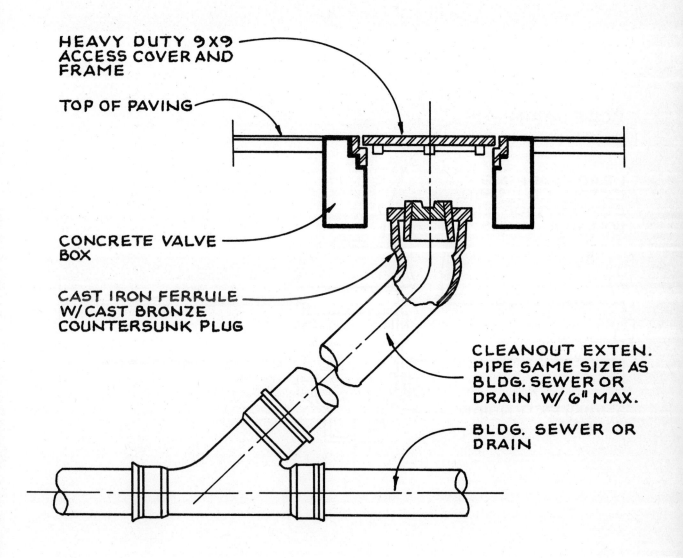

HEAVY DUTY 9X9
ACCESS COVER AND
FRAME

TOP OF PAVING

CONCRETE VALVE
BOX

CAST IRON FERRULE
W/ CAST BRONZE
COUNTERSUNK PLUG

CLEANOUT EXTEN.
PIPE SAME SIZE AS
BLDG. SEWER OR
DRAIN W/ 6" MAX.

BLDG. SEWER OR
DRAIN

NO SCALE

FLOOR MOUNTED CLEAN OUT

P 5

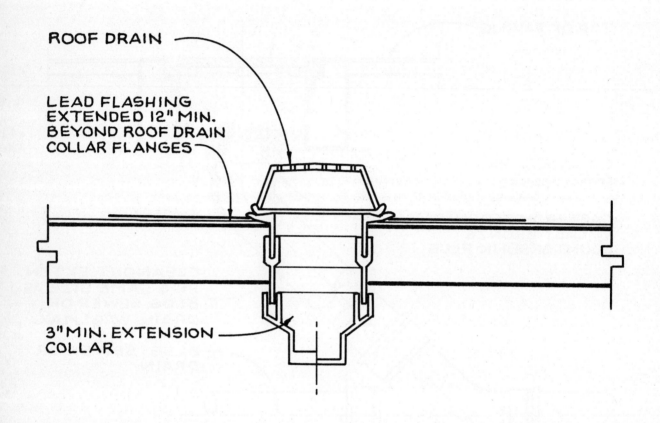

ROOF DRAIN

LEAD FLASHING
EXTENDED 12" MIN.
BEYOND ROOF DRAIN
COLLAR FLANGES

3" MIN. EXTENSION
COLLAR

NO SCALE

ROOF DRAIN

P 6

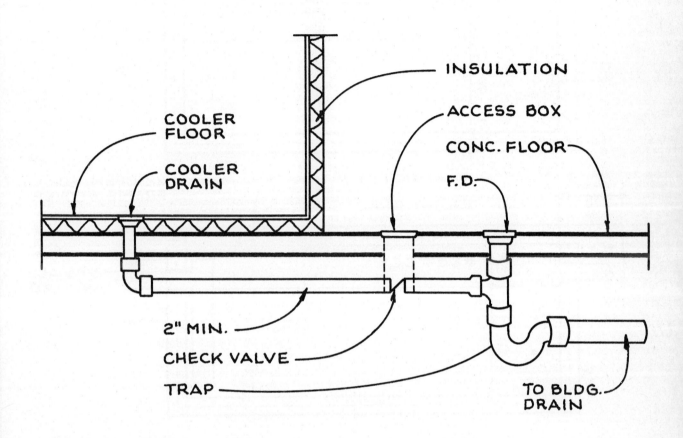

COOLER
FLOOR

COOLER
DRAIN

INSULATION

ACCESS BOX

CONC. FLOOR

F.D.

2" MIN.

CHECK VALVE

TRAP

TO BLDG.
DRAIN

NO SCALE

REFRIGERATED COOLER DRAIN

P 7

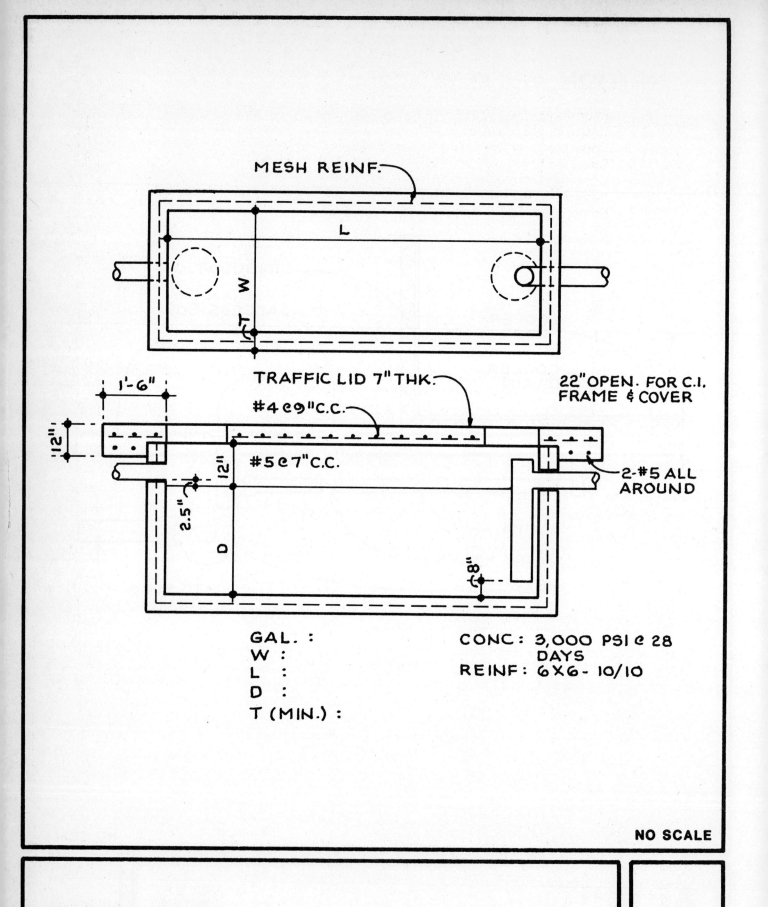

MESH REINF.

L

W

T

TRAFFIC LID 7" THK.

#4 @ 9" C.C.

22" OPEN. FOR C.I.
FRAME & COVER

1'-6"

12"

12"

#5 @ 7" C.C.

2.5"

D

8"

2-#5 ALL
AROUND

GAL. :
W :
L :
D :
T (MIN.) :

CONC : 3,000 PSI @ 28
DAYS
REINF : 6X6 - 10/10

NO SCALE

SEPTIC TANK

P 8

SECTION 26: MASTERS

ARCHITECTURAL DETAILING
FOR
COMMERCIAL CONSTRUCTION

26

MAS 1

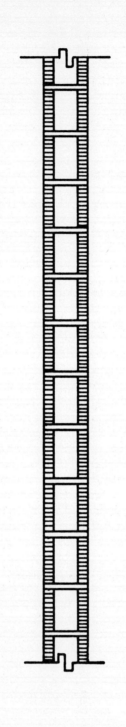

3/4":1'-0"

CONCRETE BLOCK WALL

MAS
2

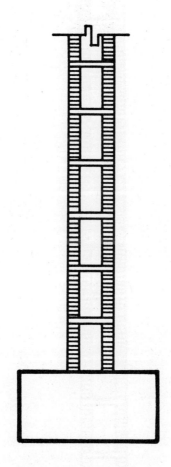

3/4":1'-0"

**CONCRETE BLOCK WALL
WITH SPREAD FOOTING**

**MAS
3**

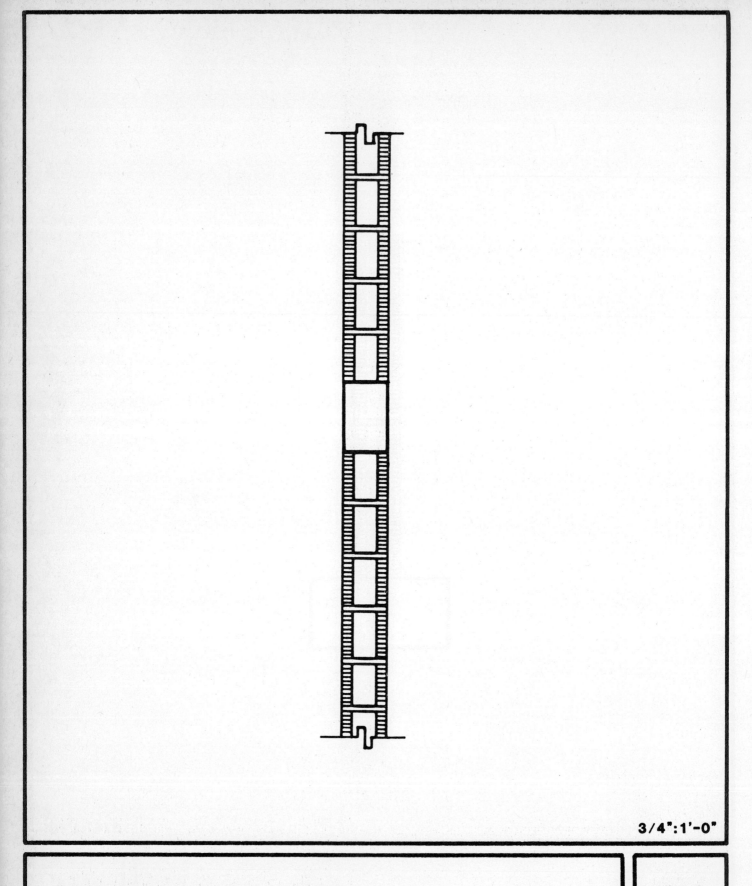

3/4":1'-0"

**CONCRETE BLOCK WALL
WITH INTERMED CONC TIE BEAM**

MAS
4

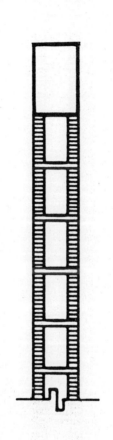

3/4":1'-0"

**CONCRETE BLOCK WALL
WITH CONCRETE TIE BEAM**

MAS
5

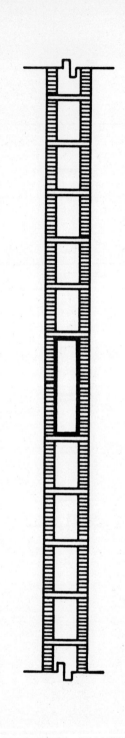

3/4":1'-0"

REINFORCED MASONRY WALL WITH INTERMEDIATE BLOCK BEAM

MAS
6

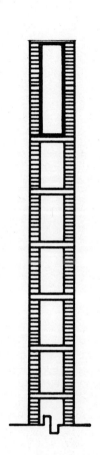

3/4":1'-0"

**REINFORCED MASONRY WALL
WITH BLOCK BEAM CAP**

**MAS
7**

About the Author

Gene Farmer is the president of Gene Farmer and Associates, an architecture and planning firm in Miami, Florida, specializing in residential, commercial, and light industrial structures. He is also Assistant Professor of Architecture in the College of Engineering and Design at Florida International University, where he teaches courses in architectural design, architectural and construction drawing, building codes and specifications, and legal aspects of construction and labor law.

Mr. Farmer obtained his B.A. in architecture at the University of Florida, and he received his M.A. in architecture from the University of Illinois. He served as a member of the Legislative Committee of the Builders' Association of South Florida, Dade County, and the South Miami-Kendall Chamber of Commerce.

In addition to receiving numerous awards for both residential and commercial projects, including a Certificate of Appreciation from the city of Miami, Mr. Farmer was the recipient of the prestigious 1990 Up-and-Comer Award for Architecture and Engineering, from Price Waterhouse. His work also has been featured in several architecture and construction publications.